Colorado

DAY BY DAY

Colorado
DAY BY DAY

Derek R. Everett

UNIVERSITY PRESS OF COLORADO
Louisville

HISTORY COLORADO
Denver

Copublished by University Press of Colorado and History Colorado

University Press of Colorado
245 Century Circle, Suite 202
Louisville, Colorado 80027

History Colorado
1200 Broadway
Denver, CO 80203
HistoryColorado.org

 The University Press of Colorado is a proud member of
the Association of University Presses.

The University Press of Colorado is a cooperative publishing enterprise supported, in part, by Adams State University, Colorado State University, Fort Lewis College, Metropolitan State University of Denver, Regis University, University of Colorado, University of Northern Colorado, University of Wyoming, Utah State University, and Western Colorado University.

∞ This paper meets the requirements of the ANSI/NISO Z39.48–1992 (Permanence of Paper)

ISBN: 978-1-64642-006-3 (paperback)
ISBN: 978-1-64642-007-0 (ebook)
https://doi.org/10.5876/9781646420070

Library of Congress Cataloging-in-Publication Data

Names: Everett, Derek R., author.
Title: Colorado day by day / Derek Everett.
Description: Louisville, Colorado : University Press of Colorado, [2020] | Includes bibliographical references and index.
Identifiers: LCCN 2019036776 (print) | LCCN 2019036777 (ebook) | ISBN 9781646420063 (paperback) | ISBN 9781646420070 (ebook)
Subjects: LCSH: Colorado—History—Chronology. | Colorado—Social life and customs.
Classification: LCC F776 .E84 2020 (print) | LCC F776 (ebook) | DDC 978.8—dc23
LC record available at https://lccn.loc.gov/2019036776
LC ebook record available at https://lccn.loc.gov/2019036777

This publication supported in part by the Josephine H. Miles Trust.

COVER PHOTO CREDITS. Denver Public Library, Western History Collection, call number X-33812 (top left); History Colorado, Stephen H. Hart Research Center, Denver, object I.D. 2001.149.9 (middle left); History Colorado, Stephen H. Hart Research Center, Denver, object I.D. 89.451.3383 (bottom right). All other photographs by Derek R. Everett.

For December 23 and April 4
(and mindful of June 25)

with love from September 15

Tomorrow, and tomorrow, and tomorrow,
Creeps in this petty pace from day to day
To the last syllable of recorded time,
And all our yesterdays have lighted fools
The way to dusty death.

—THE KING, FROM SHAKESPEARE'S
MACBETH, ACT V, SCENE 5

CONTENTS

ACKNOWLEDGMENTS

In the late 1990s, as a student in the humanities program at Arvada West High School, I started each day by copying the "This Day in History" column from the *Denver Post* on the whiteboard, inflicting a daily dose of the past on my peers. This book echoes my high school–era curiosity, and to that end I thank my teachers Teresa Neal and Monica Sparks for tolerating my youthful obsession, as well as the 1998 A-West Honors Humanities class, the finest of them all.

This book would not exist without the tireless efforts of Steve Grinstead at History Colorado and Charlotte Steinhardt at the University Press of Colorado, whose dedication, effort, and enthusiasm make it difficult for me to put into words the extent of my gratitude. For their help in securing images from the History Colorado collections for the book, I thank Aaron Marcus, Darren Eurich, and Jason Hanson. For their assistance in accumulating images, I am also indebted to Coi Drummond-Gehrig of the Denver Public Library Western History Collection, Francisco A. Gallegos of the Colorado Society of Hispanic Genealogy, Katalyn Lutkin of the City of Greeley Museum's Hazel E. Johnson Research Center, Rachel W. Smith of the Royal Gorge Regional Museum and History Center, and Leah Davis Witherow of the Colorado Springs Pioneers Museum. This book is the result of countless invaluable contributions by many folks at the University Press of Colorado including Laura Furney, Dan Pratt, Darrin Pratt, Beth Svinarich, copyeditor Cheryl Carnahan, and the two anonymous, thoughtful reviewers who backed my cause.

For fostering a love of history and affection for my native state, I am indebted to my parents, Dave and Sandy Everett, my grandparents, Don and Glenita Emarine and the late Claire Everett, and my aunt, Sue Everett. Similarly, the visitors' services staff and volunteers at the Colorado State Capitol, where I have given tours and conducted research since 1997, have encouraged and shared my enthusiasm, especially Edna Pelzmann, Theresa Holst, Simon Maghakyan, and Erika Österberg. My time as either a student or a professor at Western State College, Colorado State University, and Metropolitan State University of Denver has offered myriad opportunities to explore and impart my passion for Colorado history both in and out of the classroom. Finally, I owe special thanks to my wife, Heather, and my daughter, Louisa, who endured this all-consuming project with love and good humor. Louisa, you're the best research assistant a daddy could want, and I treasure the memories of our many weekend afternoons in the library and office.

Colorado
DAY BY DAY

COLORADO

INTRODUCTION

Here, where the great backbone of the Continent rears and rests itself; here, where nature sets the patterns of plain and mountain, of valley and hill, for all America; here, where spring the waters that wash two-thirds [of] the western Continent and feed both its oceans; here, where mountains are fat with gold and silver, and prairies glory in the glad certainty of future harvests of corn and wheat—here, indeed, is the center and the central life of America,—fountain of its wealth and health and beauty.

Samuel Bowles, a Massachusetts newspaperman, wrote these words after spending a summer holiday in Colorado Territory—which he called "the Switzerland of America"—in 1868. The opportunities he saw in the prairies, peaks, and plateaus of Colorado have inspired countless people over the centuries. Colorado offers fascinations, challenges, rewards, frustrations, catastrophes, and glories. This book explores many of Colorado's facets through distilled tales of the people, places, events, and trends that have shaped and continue to shape the region.

All too often, history can feel like little more than "one damn thing after another," a dismissive mind-set this book seeks to challenge in both blatant and subtle ways. Offered in a day-in-history format with a cross-referenced index and sources, *Colorado Day by Day* allows the reader to explore and comprehend the state's heritage as individual threads or as part of the greater tapestry. It was researched and written with academic rigor but intended to appeal to readers of diverse backgrounds, ranging from those whose ancestors have resided here for many generations to those who arrived yesterday. Sources at the end provide avenues to pursue more detailed information to supplement these daily entries. This book also hopes to combat other stereotypes about history generally and Colorado's past in particular. Far too often the state is viewed as the Rocky Mountains alone, with the Great Plains and western plateaus included as afterthoughts, or Denver and Colorado are considered synonymous, with places outside the metropolitan area overlooked or dismissed. In *Colorado Day by Day*, however, entries incorporate tales from each of the state's sixty-four counties, ensuring that all regions receive credit for contributing to the community's broader story. It is difficult to deny Denver's often overwhelming influence; nonetheless, the pages that follow seek to demonstrate how the Centennial State's past has unfolded from places

Detail of a mural in the US Department of the Interior headquarters in Washington, DC, depicting the diverse uses of public lands in Colorado

cosmopolitan and humble alike. Throughout, stories of infamy and sorrow are interspersed with ones of innovation and triumph, reflecting the spectrum of experiences in Colorado. The reader can expect to smile and laugh at times, to seethe and weep at others. But that's life, after all, and history is life.

Colorado Day by Day began as an intriguing half-idea that morphed into an obsessive quest, as my wife can attest. How many times did I tell Heather that I would only be a minute while I looked up something, and minutes turned into hours? From the late seventeenth century through the early twenty-first, this book traces Colorado's story through tales from every county in the state. When I started this project, I wondered if I might struggle to track down enough issues, events, and people to cover 366 days (counting Leap Day, of course). As the work progressed, however, the challenge evolved into paring down the myriad facets of Colorado history, casting aside far too many worthy stories to accommodate what I discovered were surprisingly limited options. There is in my possession a list of guilt and frustration, hidden safely from the light of day, including all the worthwhile tales that for one reason or another didn't make the cut. If this project hadn't nearly driven me mad more than a few times, I might have added a year or two to cover even more worthy adventures.

And now, it's time to begin another exciting year in the Centennial State.

Introduction

January

Legalizing a "Rocky Mountain High"

Colorado started the year on a "high" note on January 1, 2014, when it became the first US state to legalize the growth, sale, and consumption of recreational marijuana.

Cannabis came to Colorado during the boom times of the 1880s, along with other popular drugs of the era including opium, cocaine, and alcohol. It flourished in the early twentieth century, thanks to Latino immigrants recruited for beet sugar work who brought it with them for medicinal and recreational reasons. After the General Assembly outlawed marijuana in 1917, its illicit use emerged as both a legal issue and a source of ethnic tension. By the 1930s, law enforcement launched an anti-cannabis crusade, prompting a Denver-based federal judge to declare: "I consider marijuana the worst of all narcotics. Marijuana destroys life itself."

Attitudes shifted by mid-century, reflected in John Denver's 1972 song "Rocky Mountain High" and its thinly veiled references to marijuana. Yet attempts to permit the drug's use for medicinal purposes, authorized in a bill signed by Governor Richard Lamm in 1979, encountered federal resistance. Nonetheless, cannabis cultivation and use thrived even as authorities cracked down; estimates in 1986 identified it as Colorado's second most valuable crop, behind wheat.

In 2000, an initiative approved by voters permitted medicinal marijuana provided by regulated dispensaries. A dozen years later, nearly 55 percent of Coloradans joined residents of Washington state in permitting marijuana sales to anyone twenty-one years of age and older. Stores run by "ganjapreneurs" opened on New Year's Day in 2014, months before Washington's debuted. State officials struggled to manage a substance that remained banned by federal law, and cities and counties chose whether to permit marijuana shops in their communities. Legalized marijuana has been credited with a "green rush" of newcomers to the state, like the mining rushes of the late nineteenth century. It also led to lawsuits from neighboring states trying to halt the drug's influx. For many people in the early twenty-first century, cannabis and Colorado are synonymous.

The Legislature Comes to the Capitol

Colorado's capitol ranks as the most important symbolic place in the state. This significance comes not just from the structure's design or history but mostly because it houses the General Assembly. The boundaries of Colorado embrace diverse cultures and environments, and the democratically elected legislature brings these disparate groups together to debate their common needs, goals, and desires. When the General Assembly first convened at the statehouse on January 2, 1895, architectural form and political function blended together for the first time.

The building in which legislators met remained a work in progress—it had been under construction for nearly nine years, and six more would pass before it was considered finished. Officials including the governor, supreme court justices, treasurer, and auditor occupied their quarters in late 1894, but the Tenth General Assembly's arrival transformed the capitol into the symbolic center of the state. Its members in 1895 included James H. Brown, whose father, Henry, had donated the land on which the capitol stood (and built the Brown Palace Hotel), and the state's first African American legislator, Joseph H. Stuart. "Perpetual senator" Casimiro Barela—then halfway through his four decades of service—and three representatives from Conejos, Costilla, and Huerfano Counties lobbied on behalf of Latino issues in the building's marbled halls.

Three members of the Tenth General Assembly, elected in 1894 during Colorado's first campaign with equal suffrage regardless of sex, earned national attention. The first women elected to a legislative body in American history— Clara Cressingham, Carrie Holly, and Frances Klock—served in the House of Representatives. Their distinguished and effective service set a precedent for women serving in elected government in Colorado and across the country. In many ways, the 1895 General Assembly established the capitol's symbolic potential and created a lasting legacy. As a reporter commented in 1950: "You look at this fine old building and you think of all the tremendous work and pride that went into it. It is the heart of Colorado."

January 3, 1899

Colorado's Sweetest Industry

With the collapse of silver mining in the 1890s, Coloradans searched for an economic lifeline. Residents found hope in the form of a homely yet versatile root vegetable, the sugar beet. During the nineteenth century, European factories distilled beets into sugar, and Americans adopted the industry with factories in California, Nebraska, and Utah. Desperate for a new source of income, Colorado entrepreneurs gave the sweet beets a try. On January 3, 1899, investors including John F. Campion, Charles Boettcher, and James J. Brown (husband of the unsinkable Margaret) filed to incorporate the Colorado Sugar Manufacturing Company (CSMC).

After considering several agricultural regions, the CSMC chose Grand Junction as the site of Colorado's first beet sugar factory. Boettcher imported more than 37 tons of beet seed from his native Germany, where the industry had originated a century earlier. Grand Valley farmers planted the beets among their fruit orchards in the summer of 1899, while a brick and steel factory arose in Grand Junction—one that could produce as much as 45 tons of granulated sugar a week during the "campaign," the post-harvest sugar processing season.

Many challenges undermined Colorado's first attempt at beet sugar, including late spring downpours, summer droughts, and an insect infestation. Early frosts forced a premature harvest, and the beets rotted in piles outside the factory before it was ready to operate. As a Denver newspaper opined, "The rose-colored hopes that were as bright in the springtime as the sunset flush that rests on the Book Cliff range in summer, faded to an ashen gray when the harvest moon shed its silvery rays down the valley." Disappointing totals from the campaign inspired the CSMC to sell the factory to Grand Junction businessmen and invest elsewhere, although the refinery operated for local farmers until 1931. In 1950, the Cold War offered the facility a new purpose—processing western Colorado uranium for nuclear weapons. In the meantime, beet sugar shifted to more lucrative territory in the Arkansas and South Platte River valleys.

A Longmont-area farmer poses with his load of sugar beets bound for a Great Western Sugar Company factory in the early twentieth century.

January 4, 1941

Putting the Bang into World War II

A contract signed in Washington, DC, on January 4, 1941, authorized construction of one of the nation's largest armament factories, the Denver Ordnance Plant, on a cattle ranch in Jefferson County. The works contributed to Colorado's dramatic growth during World War II, as civilians and military personnel alike flocked to the Centennial State to assist the United States in building up its defenses against the international threats of fascism and totalitarianism.

Most Americans preferred to stay out of the conflict raging in Asia and Europe in the early 1940s. Nonetheless, President Franklin D. Roosevelt called for preparedness in case the United States got drawn into the fight. To that end, the US Department of War contracted with the Remington Arms Company to manufacture small arms and ammunition. The January 1941 contract, announced by US senator Edwin C. Johnson, authorized $122 million to purchase a site, erect a factory, and commence production. Surveyors selected the 2,100-acre Hayden Ranch southwest of Denver, and the first phase stood complete by October. When Japan attacked Pearl Harbor two months later, the Denver Ordnance Plant had already produced 14 million rounds. By 1943, it employed nearly 20,000 people and operated around the clock, producing millions of rounds a day. In addition, thousands more Coloradans and newcomers alike worked at Denver's Rocky Mountain Arsenal producing chemical weapons, at Pueblo's steel mill and munitions depot, and at many other facilities. Colorado's economy flourished as companies and the federal government erected facilities far from the reach of wartime enemies.

The Denver Ordnance Plant closed in 1944, but private manufacturers operated at the site until World War II ended. The government retained most of the property and during the Cold War turned it into the Denver Federal Center, the largest assemblage of national government offices outside of Washington, DC. Now surrounded by Lakewood, the federal center remains a major source of employment and reflects Colorado's long dependence on national largesse.

January 5, 1859

Finding Gold at Idaho Springs

George A. Jackson, looking for gold in present-day Clear Creek County, had a difficult start to 1859. On January 4 he wrote in his journal: "Mountain lion stole all my meat today in camp; no supper tonight; D—n him." But things looked better the next morning: "Up before day. Killed a fat sheep and wounded a Mt. lion before sunrise. Eat ribs for breakfast; drank last of my coffee." Once he finished his gustatory report, Jackson recorded even better news: "After breakfast moved up half mile to next creek on south side; made new camp under big fir tree. Good gravel here, looks like it carries gold." His entry on January 5 offered the first recorded evidence of gold on the upper reaches of Clear Creek, at what is now the town of Idaho Springs.

The placer flakes scooped out of streams by prospectors came from veins, or lodes, of gold upstream, worn away gradually by the erosion of wind and water. Placer deposits found along the eastern slope since the summer of 1858 hinted at substantial gold sources in the Rocky Mountains. Jackson joined Tom Golden— who founded the town named for him in Jefferson County—in searching up Clear Creek for color by the year's end. Two days after his find on January 5, Jackson sifted many flakes and a small nugget of gold, suggesting a vein nearby. Winter weather forced him out of the mountains by the month's end, but he returned that spring. Other miners joined him and laid out a camp named Idaho Springs near a source of thermal waters. Jackson prospected near present-day Leadville until early 1861, when he returned to his native Missouri to serve as a Confederate soldier. Following the Civil War, Jackson came back to Colorado, settled near Ouray, and promoted mining there until his death in 1897.

Idaho Springs remained a vibrant lode gold mining community for decades, although it lost the seat of Clear Creek County to Georgetown, a larger community upstream, in 1867. Commercial mining in the area dwindled long ago, but tourists still prospect for some color of their own at the Argo Gold Mine and Mill, hoping to emulate the luck of Jackson.

January 6, 1942

Founding Fort Carson

Starting in the late nineteenth century, Colorado Springs had enjoyed an international reputation as a vacation destination for the rich and powerful. But a new industry debuted in El Paso County on January 6, 1942, when the US Army announced plans for a training facility on donated land south of the city. The local newspaper described the news as "a belated Christmas present, twice welcome . . . that affords this region, primarily a resort, a place in the war economy and we think it affords the army a location not excelled anywhere for the training of men."

The army appropriated $25 million for the project and erected a headquarters building before the end of the month. It took the name Camp Carson in honor of renowned scout and officer Christopher "Kit" Carson. A crew of more than 11,000 workers erected barracks and other facilities within a matter of months, enough to serve more than 37,000 soldiers, officers, and nurses at a time—roughly the equivalent of the population of neighboring Colorado Springs. More than 100,000 service personnel passed through Camp Carson during World War II. It supported satellite posts including the mountain facility at Camp Hale on Tennessee Pass and housed 9,000 German and Italian prisoners of war who performed manual labor across the state.

Camp Carson faced decommissioning after World War II, but the Korean War offered the post a new purpose. It earned a promotion to fort status in 1954 and flourished as an armored combat facility, expanding to more than 200 square miles in El Paso, Fremont, and Pueblo Counties. In 1983 the army added the Piñon Canyon Maneuver Site, roughly 370 square miles in Las Animas County northeast of Trinidad, to provide more land for vehicular training. Fort Carson prepared soldiers for combat in Iraq and Afghanistan and remains an integral part of the national defense. It also heralded the military-dominated economy of El Paso County, which includes Peterson (1942) and Schriever (1983) US Air Force bases and the Cheyenne Mountain Complex. The legacy of World War II in Colorado resonates loudly in Colorado Springs.

January 7, 1865

Julesburg Suffers for Sand Creek

Six weeks after the murder and butchery of Cheyennes and Arapahos in the Sand Creek Massacre, enraged American Indians on the Great Plains struck back. Their target, the vital crossroads of Julesburg in Colorado Territory's northeastern corner, felt the wrath of native cultures eager to give Americans a taste of their own medicine on January 7, 1865.

Once the shock of Sand Creek wore off, American Indians went on the offensive. A band of seven Cheyenne led by Big Crow struck the first blow by firing on a stagecoach just east of Julesburg in the wee hours of January 7. Several hours later they killed a teamster driving supply wagons nearby. Then they taunted soldiers at Camp Rankin, a post west of Julesburg renamed Fort Sedgwick later that year. Falling for the ruse, Captain Nicholas O'Brien led thirty-seven soldiers in pursuit toward the sand hills beyond the South Platte River. Suddenly, more than sixty native warriors crested the hills and set upon the troops, killing fourteen. The rest retreated to their camp, evacuating the residents of Julesburg at the same time. A sympathetic officer later reflected on O'Brien's actions: "Whether or not this battle should have been fought is a question that may arise in the reader's mind; but, Captain O'Brien was full of fight and was devoted to duty, and the fight had to be." Considering the odds the troops faced, the battle near Julesburg could have gone far worse for the US Army. Cheyennes looted the unprotected town and destroyed telegraph poles to disrupt communications but did not destroy Julesburg. Reason dictated that if they left the town standing, it would be reoccupied and make a convenient target again.

Raids on nearby ranches continued throughout the month, as northeastern Colorado became a war zone. American Indians returned on February 2 to pillage Julesburg again, but this time they burned the town to the ground. By the end of 1865 a new Julesburg would rise from the ashes, and the nearby military post expanded as well. Yet the message was clear—Colorado would reap the high plains whirlwind it had sown with the Sand Creek Massacre.

January 8, 1976

Elvis versus the Fords in Vail

The King ran afoul of the first family in the winter mecca of Vail on January 8, 1976, when Elvis Presley spent his forty-first birthday celebrating with friends in Eagle County.

Presley sought a quiet, press-free vacation and rarely left the home where he and his entourage stayed. When he did, he wore a full winter face mask to conceal his identity while the King of rock 'n roll indulged in his favorite winter pastime: snowmobiling. He dashed through the forest far from the busy ski runs and particularly enjoyed riding the vehicle at night. When he did so on January 8, he raised the hackles of a nearby resident who complained to Vail authorities about the obnoxious noise made by someone violating the municipal code. The disgruntled caller happened to be Susan Ford, daughter of the president of the United States.

Although he was one of the most athletic presidents, comedians branded Gerald Ford a klutz for stumbling down the stairs of Air Force One. Ford had enjoyed skiing since his college days and kept up the pastime during his political career. During the winter of 1974–75, a few months after Richard Nixon's resignation and his ascension to the presidency, Ford spent enough time resting and recreating in Vail that a local newspaper declared its community the "Winter White House." Gerald and Betty Ford rang in 1976 in Vail, and during his visit the president gave replicas of Theodore Roosevelt's skis to a local museum, honoring both TR's Colorado connections and his status as the first president known to ski. A week later, after the first couple returned to Washington, DC, their college-age daughter, Susan, vacationed in Vail with friends. Her complaints about the noisy rocker drew the attention of the *National Enquirer* tabloid, which a month later published photographs ostensibly showing Presley snowmobiling by moonlight.

After his presidency, Gerald and Betty Ford returned to Vail each year to dedicate the town Christmas tree, and they kept a vacation home in nearby Beaver Creek. Tourists relax during the summer months in the Betty Ford Alpine Gardens, located in Gerald R. Ford Park.

January 9, 1974

From the Moon to the Mile High City

Governor John Vanderhoof accepted an out-of-this-world gift on behalf of the state on January 9, 1974. Astronaut Jack Lousma presented him with a plaque containing a Colorado flag that had traveled on the Apollo XVII mission in December 1972—the last manned visit to the moon—and a few small pieces of the lunar surface collected during the trip. Every state and most countries received a similar gift, but tracking their fate in later years proved quite a space case.

Born in Rocky Ford, Vanderhoof served as a pilot in World War II's Pacific theater and earned numerous commendations for bravery and injuries. He worked his way up through the state government, including well-regarded service in the General Assembly. In 1973, when "Johnny Van" held the post of lieutenant governor, Governor John Love announced his resignation after a decade in that position to take a federal job. Vanderhoof took over the executive branch but failed to win his own term in 1974. That year, Richard Lamm captured the governor's office for the Democrats for the first time in a dozen years, and Vanderhoof retired to the western slope. Among his souvenirs from many years of public service was the Apollo XVII plaque.

In 2010, a college student tried to track down the wayward moon rocks. Searches at History Colorado, the state archives, several science museums, and the state capitol ended in disappointment, but inquiries to Vanderhoof resolved the puzzle—the plaque hung on his home office wall in Grand Junction. The former chief executive had tried to donate it to a museum over the years, but none expressed interest. He chuckled to report that the rocks, valued at $5 million, had once served as his grandson's show-and-tell at school. Vanderhoof donated the plaque to a geology museum at the Colorado School of Mines. Governor Bill Ritter dedicated a new exhibit including the moon rocks in 2010, an appropriate tribute to Colorado's aeronautics and aerospace industries at the state's most scientifically oriented university.

Bidding Farewell to "Buffalo Bill"

A world-famous showman who presented a caricatured vision of the American West to global audiences died at his sister's house in Denver on January 10, 1917. William F. "Buffalo Bill" Cody's life reflected the saying that the truth should never interfere with a good story.

Born in Iowa in 1846, Cody first came to Colorado Territory in 1861 as a teamster on the road to Denver. His life led him across the West, although often not in such dramatic fashion as contemporary sources suggest. Cody made an early career—and earned the nickname "Buffalo Bill"—in the late 1860s when he hunted bison in western Kansas. In 1868, he signed on as a civilian scout with the US Army to track American Indians. Cody often patrolled from Fort Lyon on the Arkansas River and joined Pawnee allies of the federal government to pursue Cheyenne Dog Soldiers in the summer of 1869. A battle at Summit Springs in northeastern Colorado that July proved to be the last major conflict between soldiers and native cultures in eastern Colorado. Cody later reenacted a fanciful version of the fight in his Wild West extravaganza.

Buffalo Bill's Wild West debuted in 1883. Four years later, a Fort Collins newspaper illustrated nineteenth-century rivalries between Colorado towns when it editorialized a letter from a local man touring with the show: "'New York was bad enough, but London is as bad as Greeley.' London must be bad." Cody's show performed in Colorado numerous times, but by the 1910s he faced declining interest and ticket sales. A circus owned by the *Denver Post* bought the Wild West, and Cody's career ended in subservience. Nonetheless, his death in 1917 led to a frenzy of mourning. Cody's body lay in state at the capitol, and 18,000 people walked by the open coffin before his burial on Lookout Mountain in Jefferson County. To ensure that jealous interests in Wyoming and Nebraska could not disinter his remains, they lie under several feet of concrete and a massive stone marker in a park operated by the City and County of Denver. The grave and a nearby museum represent Cody's final stage, upon which he takes his eternal bow.

SUGGESTION FOR A STATUE TO BE ERECTED ON THE CAPITOL GROUNDS INCOM-
MEMORATION OF THE VISIT TO COLORADO OF THE VICE-PRESIDENT ELECT.

TEDDY THE LION KILLER.

Editorial cartoon proposing a memorial at the Colorado State Capitol to honor Theodore Roosevelt's 1901 mountain lion hunt in northwestern Colorado

January 11, 1901

A Bully Time in Meeker

Theodore Roosevelt, war hero and New York governor, won election as William McKinley's running mate in 1900. The outdoorsy vice president–elect made ready for his new job in a decidedly nontraditional way. To prepare for the rigors of high office, the politician decided on a hunting spree in northwestern Colorado. He came to the state by rail and rode the Colorado Midland Railway from Colorado Springs through the Rocky Mountains to Rifle. On the morning of January 11, 1901, Roosevelt left the comfortable life behind for an overland trek to the Keystone Ranch, northwest of Meeker, for several weeks of big game hunting.

With guide John Goff and fifteen hunting dogs as his only companions, Roosevelt spent more than a month in Rio Blanco and Moffat Counties. Despite their isolation, stories of derring-do appeared in the papers, which the politician minded less than articles that downplayed his bravado. "The governor is very indignant over the lies that have been published about his hunt," one correspondent declared. "He wishes the news to say that his being treed by wolves, chased by bears, and his killing deer to be absolutely false." Roosevelt and Goff targeted mountain lions specifically, seen as a threat to ranchers and wildlife. Several of Goff's dogs died in fights with lions, and Roosevelt dove into the scrum with his hunting knife on several occasions. When the pair returned to Meeker on February 15, Goff stated that they had killed lynx, badgers, and seventeen mountain lions, twelve of which Roosevelt bagged personally. Of those, the vice president–elect shot eight and stabbed four to death. The press reported: "Governor Roosevelt expresses himself as having had the most enjoyable time of his life." After processing at Meeker, the lion skins joined Roosevelt's hunting trophy collection in his New York home.

Just over two weeks later, Roosevelt took office as vice president in Washington, DC, but he returned to Colorado many times to hunt. Perhaps hand-to-hand combat with mountain lions is just the training politicians need to steel themselves for the hurly-burly of elected office.

January 12, 1981

Catfights at Altitude

The oil shale boom of the 1970s promised to invigorate Colorado's economy and expand its population, as had the nineteenth-century gold and silver rushes and the wartime boom of the 1940s. So heady seemed the times that broadcast network ABC deemed the Centennial State worthy of its own nighttime soap opera. To compete with the scandalous Ewing family on *Dallas*, which debuted on CBS in 1978, ABC premiered *Dynasty* on January 12, 1981.

Like *Dallas*, the premise of *Dynasty* centered on the travails of a wealthy oil brood. At the show's outset, "Denver-Carrington" tycoon Blake Carrington, played by John Forsythe, married his kindly secretary Krystle Jennings, portrayed by Linda Evans, much against his children's wishes. Disputes within the conniving family and feuds over ways to keep the profits high fueled the plot. In the second season, *Dynasty* introduced its most glamorous and notorious character, Joan Collins's Alexis Colby, Blake's ex-wife and scheming thorn in the side. The opening credits included a montage of Colorado landscapes, oil fields, and the Denver skyline, as well as a mansion representing the Carrington home—although that house actually stood in California, where exterior shots for the series were filmed.

Story lines grew more lavish and ludicrous over the years, even by soap opera standards. Beyond evil doppelgangers and terrorists riddling a wedding with bullets, the most memorable scene was a shrieking, hair-pulling, name-calling fight between Alexis and Krystle, whacking away at one another in a lily pond on the Carrington estate. The audience appreciated the over-the-top style—*Dynasty* ranked first in the Nielsen ratings in the 1984–85 season. The cast included Diahann Carroll, Rock Hudson, and Heather Locklear, while Henry Kissinger and part-time Colorado residents Gerald and Betty Ford guest-starred. For nine seasons, bigger was always better for *Dynasty*, from the plot and actors to the hairdos and shoulder pads.

January 13, 1900

A Shooting at the *Denver Post*

Attorney William W. Anderson met with Frederick G. Bonfils and Harry H. Tammen, owners of the *Denver Post*, in their office on Sixteenth Street in downtown Denver on January 13, 1900. What started as a conversation about securing the release of convicted cannibal Alfred Packer nearly transformed into a double homicide when an argument about legal tactics escalated and Anderson shot both owners. Bonfils and Tammen survived, but the episode reflected the chaotic and scandalous nature of the *Post*'s early years.

Newspapers flourished in the late 1800s as the most prolific and popular means of mass communication. The *Rocky Mountain News*, founded in 1859, dominated Denver as the oldest and most respected newspaper for decades, although it faced serious competition from several daily and weekly challengers. A newspaper called the *Post* debuted in 1892 but closed the following year as the Panic of 1893 led to a decline in advertisers and subscriptions. Two years later, Bonfils and Tammen— purveyors of tacky souvenirs and promoters of circuses and lotteries—bought the resurrected *Post* and published their first issue on October 28, 1895. The paper specialized in sensational local gossip; as Bonfils stated, "A dogfight on Sixteenth Street is a better story than a war in Timbuctu." The *Post* gained readership through its emphasis on scandal mixed with the occasional valid news story. Ownership of the paper passed to Helen G. Bonfils in 1930 upon her father's death; Tammen had died childless in 1924. The new owner nurtured the paper until her own death in 1972. She also used her fortune and status to promote cultural development in Denver, helping to establish the Denver Center for the Performing Arts.

The *Post* and the *News* survived the Great Depression as Denver's two remaining dailies, and they battled for readership. They merged operations in 2000 to save money. After the *News* closed in 2009, the *Post* survived as Denver's primary paper. It endures in a streamlined form while expanding its online presence, as print journalism clings to life in the internet age.

January 14, 1868

Naming the Colorado Central

Colorado's first railroad received its third name in as many years on January 14, 1868, one it kept for the next two decades: the Colorado Central Railroad. Chartered by the territorial legislature in 1865 to connect the competing capitals of Golden and Denver with the gold mining districts up Clear Creek, the Colorado Central proved essential to the region's growth.

Golden booster William A.H. Loveland hoped to breach the Continental Divide by rail and hired Edward L. Berthoud to survey a route, although Berthoud Pass proved unsuitable for a railroad. In the meantime, mining districts hoped that a railroad connection would boost flagging production and investment. Construction on the standard gauge line between Denver and Golden concluded on September 26, 1870, making it the third railroad with a Denver terminus that year. From Golden, the Colorado Central proceeded via narrow gauge up Clear Creek to Black Hawk, which it reached by December 1872. Extending a mile farther to Central City took nearly six years because of the Panic of 1873. By the time of that national economic collapse, another branch of the Colorado Central stretched north from the Denver-Golden line to Boulder and Longmont.

Once investors returned, the Colorado Central pushed beyond Longmont to Fort Collins, building a town named for Loveland along the way. It linked with the Union Pacific Railroad in Wyoming on November 7, 1877. Three months earlier, a branch of the narrow gauge route had reached Georgetown. An early 1880s effort to cross the Continental Divide at Loveland Pass—also named for the founder—failed, but it left Coloradans with an engineering marvel known as the Georgetown Loop. The Union Pacific bought and merged the Colorado Central, the Denver, South Park & Pacific, and several other lines in 1889.

Ten years later, they reorganized as the Colorado & Southern Railway, which operated independently until a buyout from the Burlington Route in 1908. Regardless of its myriad names, the Colorado Central encouraged mining and agricultural expansion in the late nineteenth century and created and served many communities.

January 15, 1859

A Boulder County Bonanza

A party of gold seekers, one of many exploring upstream from the nascent settlement of Boulder, made camp on a high tributary of Boulder Creek on January 15, 1859. Their choice proved a good one, as the community they established took the name Gold Hill, built along the bank of Gold Run, in honor of the ore discovered at the site by prospectors that spring.

Placer deposits found along the eastern slope of the Rocky Mountains in 1858 inspired fortune seekers to press into the mountains, searching for the lode gold sources from which the flakes had eroded. Prospectors established Boulder that October as a base of operations. Throughout the winter they probed the mountains, and early the next year their search bore fruit. Mining in the summer of 1859 brought great profit, especially after the introduction of stamp mills to process the ore. In the absence of law and order from distant Nebraska Territory, whose westernmost reaches then included Gold Hill, residents created their own extra-legal government. The following year, Mollie D. Sanford described the community: "The grandeur of these mountains is deeply impressive. They seem of endless extent. We could look down into the gulches and see where several mills are in operation, stamping and grinding the precious ores that are dug from the bowels of those hills. The shrill steam whistles would come reverberating and echoing over the hills, making it seem that there is some enterprise somewhere."

Gold Hill struggled after a fire in 1860 and the exhaustion of easy gold sources early in the decade. By the late 1860s, Nathaniel P. Hill's smelter at Black Hawk helped reinvigorate the Boulder County mining district. Gold Hill emerged as a social hub for the area's mining towns, aided by several pianos and organs hauled by wagon across the Great Plains and up into the high country. The *Rocky Mountain News* noted in 1873 that "those who visit Gold Hill may be certain of metropolitan accommodations almost at the summit of the Rocky Mountains." Mining peaked in the early 1870s, but the town has endured as a small but proud community.

Stanley Biber Dies

Dr. Stanley H. Biber, who died on January 16, 2006, might have been just one of many small-town doctors across the United States were it not for the fact that he was the reason the Las Animas County seat of Trinidad earned the nickname "the sex-change capital of the world."

Born in Iowa in 1923, Biber earned a medical degree from the University of Iowa in the late 1940s and served with the US Army during the Korean War, patching up wounded soldiers brought to his mobile hospital. Biber mustered out at Fort Carson, near Colorado Springs, and signed on at a clinic in Trinidad in 1954. There, he practiced out of an office in a historic bank building and performed surgeries at the Mount San Rafael Hospital in town. Fifteen years after his arrival, a social worker who appreciated his skill at repairing children's harelips asked him if he could perform surgery to replace her male genitalia with female ones to reflect her gender identity. Biber had performed reconstructive surgery on the battlefields of Korea and found the task straightforward, although he later cringed when thinking of the quality of his first effort.

From that 1969 surgery through the end of the century, Biber averaged three sex-change operations a week, more often than not replacing male genitalia with female ones. His patients included a wide range of transsexuals from around the world and all walks of life. Some residents of Trinidad resented the reputation their town earned, while others appreciated the economic boon to the community; his surgeries helped keep the town hospital afloat financially.

Old age forced Biber to retire in 2003. A colleague took over the practice and within a few years moved the office out of state. Biber died at a Pueblo hospital three years after he laid down his scalpel. Between 1969 and 2003 he performed over 4,000 sex reassignment surgeries, not bad for someone whose first such patient had to explain to him what "transsexual" meant.

Paving the Way for Better Roads

Members of the Colorado Highway Commission met for the first time at the state capitol on January 17, 1910, to create a plan for developing a patchwork of paths into a network of roads sufficient to handle the proliferation of a new technology: the automobile.

Steam-powered cars appeared in Denver in the 1890s, including one that gave rides at Manhattan Beach on Sloan's Lake. Cars eventually succeeded the era's other transportation fad, the bicycle, a vehicle one Denver visitor had declared "an abomination in the sight of the Lord." William B. Felker Jr. opened a "locomobile" dealership in Denver in 1900, the state's first, and the following year drove the first car to reach the summit of Pikes Peak, fourteen years before Spencer Penrose built a road to the top. In the summer of 1901, one enthusiast drove over the mountains to Leadville, while another paraded through Cañon City after law enforcement cleared the main street of horses spooked by the contraption. On January 14, 1902, Denver courts charged an automobile driver for the first time. The motorist claimed that his car drove 8 miles per hour through downtown, while police argued that he reached speeds of 40 mph; the court fined him twenty-five dollars. Felker demonstrated the technology's potential and danger alike—he won a relay from Denver to Colorado Springs in 1902 but died when his car crashed in a race in Denver in 1907.

Automobiles reinvented Colorado's landscape. Advocates sought better roads as both a safety and a tourism measure and lobbied to preserve scenic destinations like Rocky Mountain National Park. Early highways often followed pioneer pathways, including the Cherokee, Santa Fe, Smoky Hill, and Trapper's Trails. During the first half of the twentieth century, the automobile succeeded railroads as Colorado's primary mode of transportation. Many rail lines closed during the Great Depression, with their routes later reconstructed as highways. The shift from steam and electric to gasoline-powered vehicles also encouraged oil production in the state. For better or worse, modern Colorado's character owes much to the proliferation of automobiles.

January 18, 1881

From Silverthorn to Silverthorne

Marshall Silverthorn came to present-day Colorado in the spring of 1859 in search of gold and healthier air. He brought his wife and their three children from Pennsylvania a year later, and in 1861 they proceeded into the mountains, settling in Breckenridge. Nicknamed "the Judge" for presiding over informal hearings, Silverthorn operated a hotel, loaned money to build a fire house, and supported Samuel Adams's quixotic attempt to float from the Blue River to the Pacific Ocean in 1869. A contemporary described Silverthorn as "a diminutive man, almost dried to a crackling, and [he] has such a strange, weird look that you couldn't help wondering to what age or order of human beings he belongs," but the person praised his humor and generosity. On January 18, 1881, Silverthorn purchased 160 acres from the federal government down the Blue from Breckenridge, on which he failed to find gold and where the town of Silverthorne stands today.

Mining companies bought and sold the tract in the decades that followed, although it retained the name of its original owner—with an "e" added at the end in the 1930s in an attempt at gentrification. In the mid-1950s, a developer built subdivisions on the land to house workers who came to Summit County to build Dillon Reservoir. Designed as a trans-mountain diversion to sate Denver's thirst, the reservoir dammed the Blue River and inundated the town site of Dillon, which relocated a few miles from its original site. Silverthorne's growth continued after the reservoir's completion in 1963 with the construction of Interstate 70. The town stood at the base of the western ascent to the Eisenhower-Johnson Tunnel under the Continental Divide and emerged as a major destination along the new highway. Commercial development and year-round tourism followed, and today Silverthorne overflows with condominiums and outlet stores.

Depending on one's perspective, Silverthorne reflects either the prosperity and popularity of Colorado's high country or the modern sprawl that chokes the Rocky Mountains with traffic and pollution. Silverthorn would likely appreciate that his plot of land eventually made a profit.

January 19, 1948

A Fire Finishes off McPhee

Some people might consider using a reservoir's worth of water to put out a fire an overkill. On January 19, 1948, after nearly a quarter century of both economic prosperity and ethnic tension, a fire destroyed what had been the most productive lumber mill in Colorado. The mill site and the town that surrounded it now sit at the bottom of McPhee Reservoir.

The timber industry flourished in southwestern Colorado by the early twentieth century. After World War I, the Denver firm McPhee and McGinnity moved disused machinery from exhausted timber fields elsewhere to the San Juan National Forest in Dolores and Montezuma Counties. They opened a mill on the Dolores River in early 1924 and platted a town around it, named after company founder William McPhee. By that autumn, McPhee boasted a link to the Rio Grande Southern Railroad and shipped lumber to consumers as far away as New England. The mill produced tens of millions of board-feet a year by the late 1920s, sating demand for railroad ties, packing crates, and house construction. During the Great Depression, it provided lumber for federal make-work projects built by the Civilian Conservation Corps. It struggled through the 1930s but remained the largest employer in southwestern Colorado. McPhee developed as a segregated community, with 75 percent of the workforce—mostly Hispanos from northern New Mexico—living in humble accommodations while the rest, descended from northwestern Europeans, enjoyed more comfortable houses on the other side of the mill.

McPhee declined in the 1940s, with many of its workers leaving for military service or better-paying jobs during World War II. By the decade's end the company had changed hands several times, and the January 1948 blaze finished off the mill and the community. What was once the largest lumber operation in Colorado disappeared. By the early 1990s, construction of McPhee Reservoir on the Dolores River inundated the once bustling site.

January 20, 1872

Bison Hunting with a Royal Russian

The red carpet met frozen dirt streets when Colorado hosted its first royal visitor, Grand Duke Alexei Alexandrovich, the fifth child of Russia's Tsar Alexander II. On a tour through Europe, the Americas, and Japan, Alexei endured countless formal events and flirted with as many women as possible. But the American West offered the duke a unique opportunity: a bison hunt. He delighted in that adventure for the final time in Cheyenne County on January 20, 1872.

Bison numbers on the Great Plains declined steadily starting in the early 1700s, with horses and gunpowder weapons easing the hunt for American Indians and Euro-Americans alike. By 1872, although American Indian groups had been forced out of eastern Colorado, small herds of bison remained. Alexei hunted in Nebraska with army officers Philip H. Sheridan and George A. Custer before coming to Colorado. He arrived in Denver on the Denver Pacific Railway on January 17, escorted by territorial governor Edward M. McCook and John Evans. Over the next two days, the Russian attended a ball in Denver and a soiree in Golden and met with crews building the Colorado Central Railroad up Clear Creek toward the mining districts.

Alexei's train left Denver via the Kansas Pacific Railroad late on January 19, heading eastward toward Kansas. The following morning the train stopped at Kit Carson, where a cavalry escort guided the duke, Sheridan, and Custer on one last bison hunt. According to the *Rocky Mountain News*: "The buffalo were soon reached, when Alexei, in great excitement, plunged into the midst of them in advance of the whole party, and shot down the first buffalo—an enormous bull. He immediately dismounted, and General Custer was at his side instantly. The grand duke cheered, and in his great delight clasped his arms around General

Custer and kissed him." The party hunted in Cheyenne County for seven hours, with the duke killing five bison, Custer three, and Sheridan two, before proceeding eastward by rail. Alexei's visit reflected the West's late nineteenth-century status as a place of both romance and exploitation.

Alfred Packer's Birthday

Alfred Packer, born on January 21, 1842, in Pennsylvania, earned his infamy at age thirty-two when he joined a group of twenty-one prospectors in Provo, Utah, headed for the San Juan Mountains. They reached Ouray's home near present-day Montrose in late January 1874. The Tabeguache Ute peacemaker advised that they wait there until the weather cleared, but six men including Packer took their chances. On April 16, Packer arrived alone at the Los Piños Agency near Cochetopa Pass. He continued on to nearby Saguache, where he spent freely at Otto Mears's store. Other members of the Provo party doubted that the party of six would have split up and wondered how he came into so much money. When an artist discovered five bodies near what is now Lake City in Hinsdale County, bearing evidence of murder, the finger of suspicion pointed to Packer.

Packer escaped from the jail in Saguache but was found in Wyoming in 1883 and sent to Lake City for trial. He claimed that one of the party, Wilson Bell, had killed the others and that Packer killed Bell in self-defense but admitted to cannibalism. A jury found Packer guilty, but the state supreme court overturned his conviction because the crime had occurred during territorial days, and the state legislature had accidentally negated the earlier murder statute. In Gunnison in 1886, Packer went on trial again, this time for manslaughter. Declared guilty once more, the judge sentenced him to five sequential terms of eight years, one for each of his victims. After receiving petitions in favor of prisoner #1389, Governor Charles S. Thomas approved a parole before he left office in January 1901. Packer died six years later and was buried in Littleton.

Packer's legacy lives on in myriad, often tacky ways (usually with the common misspelling of "Alferd"). College campuses in Boulder and Gunnison operated cafeterias bearing his name. A play about his trial took place in the Hinsdale County Courthouse in the 1990s. Trey Parker and Matt Stone, creators of the *South Park* cartoon series, produced a gruesome musical called *Cannibal!* in 1993. A memorial to the murdered, eaten members of the party stands on Cannibal Plateau south of Lake City.

Roche Goes to the Treasury

The US Senate voted unanimously to confirm Josephine A. Roche as the assistant secretary of the treasury on January 22, 1935. The skill and drive Roche brought to Washington, DC, echoed her decades of similarly distinguished work in Colorado.

Originally from Nebraska, Roche attended Vassar College and Columbia University. A liberal education imbued Josephine with Progressive-era principles,

Josephine Roche, an industrialist, civil servant, and advocate of progressive social and political reforms during much of the twentieth century in Colorado

including a belief in government as a tool of social betterment. After the Roches moved to Denver in 1906, their daughter visited them during academic breaks. She returned for good in 1912 and won appointment as the state's first woman law enforcement officer, joining the Denver police. Roche advocated for the rights of children, immigrants, and labor unions, while Progressive icons like Benjamin B. Lindsey and Edward P. Costigan mentored her. Roche inherited her father's holdings in the Rocky Mountain Fuel Company (RMFC) upon his death in 1927, and her principles transformed the boardroom. A statewide coal miners' strike that same year led to bloodshed at the RMFC's Columbine Mine in Weld County, which left six miners dead. Roche responded with improvements in wages and working conditions and earned the loyalty of workers. When competitors like the Colorado Fuel & Iron Company tried to put her out of business, her employees ran "Buy from Josephine" ads.

Liberal Democrats opposed to Governor Edwin C. Johnson, a conservative Democrat who disdained President Franklin D. Roosevelt's policies, convinced Roche to challenge him in the 1934 primary. In response to critics who considered a woman unsuitable for the office, a Julesburg newspaper declared that "a wide-awake woman is more valuable than a drowsy man." Johnson prevailed in the bitter campaign and won reelection that November, but Roosevelt rewarded his stalwart with the treasury position. Roche spent two years in Washington, DC, before returning to the RMFC's helm, and she lobbied for workers' rights for the rest of her career. Always an exception to the rule, Roche fought her whole life for fairness and equality.

January 23, 1968

A Part of Pueblo in North Korea

"The *Pueblo* was deathly quiet. Stillness also enveloped the boat alongside. No orders came from it, no yells. The feeling was one of hearing a last breath followed by the silence of death. The *Pueblo* died at 2:30 p.m. on January 23, 1968, on the high seas off Wonsan." Thus wrote Lieutenant F. Carl Schumacher of the USS *Pueblo*, captured in the Sea of Japan by the Democratic People's Republic of Korea (DPRK), commonly known as North Korea.

Of all the vessels to bear names related to Colorado, none boasts a history as dramatic as the *Pueblo*, whose title refers to both the city and the county. Built as a supply ship during World War II, it served until 1954. A dozen years later, it was recommissioned ostensibly for environmental surveys, but its true purpose was espionage. Stocked with the latest surveillance and communications equipment, the *Pueblo* set out from Japan in early January 1968 under the command of Lieutenant Commander Lloyd M. Bucher. Its mission to shadow the Russian and North Korean coasts seemed dull until DPRK ships and airplanes opened fire on it on January 23. Bucher chose surrender over the death of his entire crew; one sailor received a mortal wound, and the other eighty-two Americans onboard attempted to destroy all classified equipment and documents before the DPRK took over. North Korean agents subjected the *Pueblo* survivors to months of mental and physical torture, while family members of the hostages organized a "Remember the Pueblo" campaign back home to lobby for their release. The federal government issued an apology to the DPRK for spying, and on December 23—333 days, exactly 11 months after their capture—the crew was bussed to the South Korean border and released.

The *Pueblo* was later moved to a river berth in the DPRK capital of Pyongyang, where supreme leader Kim Jong Un rededicated it as an anti-American museum on July 27, 2013, the sixtieth anniversary of the Korean War armistice. Still listed on the US Navy's active roster, the vessel represents a symbol of the nation and the state of Colorado, held hostage in North Korea.

January 24, 2008

Censuring the Man behind TABOR

An unrepentant legislator stood in the House of Representatives at the state capitol on January 24, 2008, facing the General Assembly's first-ever censure of one of its members. A vote of 62–1 added another element of notoriety to Douglas Bruce's already extensive résumé.

A transplanted Californian who dabbled in law and real estate, Bruce lived in Colorado Springs and emerged as a political activist in the late 1980s. He advocated strict limits on a government's right to tax its citizens, an issue Coloradans had rejected at the polls a half-dozen times since the 1960s, including measures for which Bruce had lobbied in 1988 and 1990. Two years later, his was the public face of a campaign for the "Taxpayer's Bill of Rights" (TABOR), which required voter approval of any tax increases and constrained government spending at the state and local levels. Voters added TABOR to the state constitution by over 53 percent in 1992, the same year they banned special protections for non-heterosexuals. The latter amendment fell before the US Supreme Court four years later, but TABOR endured. Its principal architect entered Colorado's political lexicon—measures put before voters to temporarily lift fiscal limits go by the nickname "de-Brucing." No other state has adopted such a constraint, in part because of Colorado's example. TABOR's fate remains uncertain as legal challenges mount, including a bipartisan effort claiming that by restricting the legislature's power to tax, it violates the US Constitution's guarantee to each member of the Union a republican form of government.

Bruce remains as controversial as his amendment. Appointed to the General Assembly in 2008 by El Paso County Republicans to fill a vacancy, he earned the body's first censure on his first day for kicking a *Rocky Mountain News* photographer. His colleagues demanded that Bruce "hereafter conduct himself in a manner that comports to the highest standards of legislative conduct." Denied nomination for his own run at the state House of Representatives in 2008, Bruce appears regularly in Colorado's courtrooms and headlines, a consequential and cantankerous individual.

January 25, 1998

A Super Day for the Broncos

In their fifth championship appearance, the Denver Broncos found triumph at last by defeating the Green Bay Packers in Super Bowl XXXII in San Diego, California, on January 25, 1998. As *Denver Post* columnist Woody Paige declared: "This is the 1. This 1's for Colorado; this 1's for the Rocky Mountains, this 1's for the Broncos; and, as owner Pat Bowlen said, 'This 1's for [quarterback] John [Elway].' John The Bronco is a winner."

The Broncos debuted in 1960 as one of eight teams in the new American Football League, intended to compete with the National Football League, organized forty years earlier. They played at the Denver Bears' baseball field across the South Platte River from downtown Denver, which was expanded over the years and renamed Mile High Stadium in 1968. The team struggled through embarrassingly poor performances in its early seasons, but a stalwart defense nicknamed the Orange Crush helped raise the team's stature in the mid-1970s. The Broncos reached the Super Bowl in 1978 for the first time, losing to the Dallas Cowboys. They enjoyed a solid fan base, exemplified by Tim "Barrelman" McKernan, who attended games for three decades in all weather wearing only a cowboy hat, cowboy boots, and a Bronco-decorated barrel.

The team strengthened under coach Dan Reeves, owner Bowlen, and quarterback Elway in the 1980s. They made it to the Super Bowl in 1987, 1988, and 1990 but fell to the New York Giants, Washington Redskins, and San Francisco 49ers, respectively. Coach Mike Shanahan, hired for the 1995 season, and Elway led the Broncos to their first Super Bowl win in 1998, a feat they repeated in 1999 against the Atlanta Falcons, then coached by Reeves. Residents of metropolitan Denver rewarded the Broncos by paying for a new stadium, with the field retaining the "Mile High" name. The Broncos reached the Super Bowl with quarterback Peyton Manning in 2014 and 2016, losing to the Seattle Seahawks and defeating the Carolina Panthers, respectively. Through their ups and downs, the Broncos remain Colorado's most devoutly followed team.

January 26, 1875

Range Wars Make National Headlines

"Neither sheep-owners nor stock-raisers, of whom there are so many in Colorado, will ever be able to determine who was originally in the wrong. The feud sprang up, grew, and was nourished by excesses at the hands of both factions. The shepherds were anything but passive and peaceful; the cow-herds were aggressive and sanguinary." Thus reported the *New York Times* on January 26, 1875, under the headline "War in Colorado."

Sheep rearing started in present-day Colorado in the mid-nineteenth century, as Hispano settlers in the San Luis Valley tended small flocks. Cattle herds appeared on the eastern plains after the gold rush at the end of the 1850s. Livestock represented an essential aspect of the territory's agriculture, but the interaction between cow and sheep interests often proved difficult to manage. Cattlemen railed against the impact of sheep on the landscape, including close-cropping of grass and water depletion. In turn, shepherds bemoaned arrogant cattle barons who claimed vast swaths of public land and resisted encroachment from flocks or farmers. Violence erupted by the 1870s. The New York newspaper reported incidents of cattlemen poisoning sheep or cutting their throats and intimidating ranchers who brought sheep into Colorado. The terrifying situation intensified as the years passed. Vigilantes wiped out a flock of nearly 4,000 sheep in Garfield County in 1894 by clubbing some to death and driving others over a cliff. Eight years later, a Mesa County commissioner was murdered and his 300 sheep were killed. In 1909, along the line between Mesa and Garfield Counties, attackers shot, clubbed, and disemboweled nearly 2,000 lambs and ewes. Some bled to death after their front legs were cut off.

The brutal interaction between cattle and sheep ranchers lingered into the Great Depression. In 1934, the Taylor Grazing Act established a land management system that promoted environmental protection and regulation of public tracts. Violence diminished, although both factions found a new target of resentment—federal land officials.

Jefferson Learns of Colorado's Silver

President Thomas Jefferson, who approved the Louisiana Purchase in 1803 and sent five expeditions into it to learn about what he had bought, received a tantalizing letter from one Anthony G. Bettay, written on January 27, 1808. Bettay told Jefferson about lucrative silver deposits along the upper Platte River in the central Rocky Mountains, in the heart of modern Colorado.

Bettay claimed to have spent three years in the Rockies and to have found "an immence bed of Rich Silver ore" on an upper tributary of the Platte River, 1,700 miles from St. Louis. He offered to lead a federal survey team there in exchange for 1 percent of its profits for seventy-five years. Bettay informed Jefferson of another discovery that appealed to the president who sought an easy route across North America: "I have likewise discovered an eligible passage across that chain of mountains dividing the waters of the atlantick from those of the Passifick by way of the River platte and Cashecatrango River, a learge navigable River of the Passifick." Bettay also promised to send a few seeds of "Silk nettle," a useful plant for manufacturing that he found along the mysterious Cashecatrango. In a response on February 18, Jefferson promised Bettay a share of the silver ore but cautioned that tensions with Spain would delay its extraction. Their interaction ended here—Bettay never wrote Jefferson back or mailed the seeds.

Whether Bettay ever actually traveled beyond his home in southwestern Pennsylvania or simply passed along rumors he heard from others remains unknown, as does his life in general. Was he a fraud? An opportunist? A genuine altruist who wanted only to see his country prosper? No one seems to know. It is certain that Spain worried about American interlopers searching the Rockies for precious minerals as early as 1796. The north and south branches of the Platte River both head in Colorado, in Jackson and Park Counties, respectively, but those headwaters stand far from "an eligible passage" of the Continental Divide. Bettay was right about one thing—by the century's end, silver proved to be Colorado's essential mineral.

The National Silver Convention

"It is appropriate that a city which owes its phenomenal growth to the development of the silver mining industry," the *Rocky Mountain News* declared about Denver on January 28, 1885, "should be chosen as the meeting place of a body of men representing the silver producers of the country." The press welcomed more than 1,500 delegates from across the West to the National Silver Convention, intent on protecting and promoting the profitable mineral.

Silver's use as a part of American currency fluctuated during the late nineteenth century. In 1873, President Ulysses S. Grant approved the Coinage Act, which barred the use of silver as part of the federal monetary system. Discoveries of the mineral in Colorado and elsewhere throughout the decade led to calls for its resumption, however. The Bland-Allison Act of 1878, adopted over President Rutherford B. Hayes's veto, permitted use of silver for coins worth less than one dollar and opened a reliable market for the ore extracted from the Rocky Mountains. Although federal officials adopted the gold standard for American currency the following year, basing the economy on that mineral, silver proved a useful addition to national commerce.

Advocates of bimetallism—using silver and gold in balanced measure to back American money—included miners and farmers nationwide, who opposed the constrained cash supply of a gold standard. Silver mining's boom days in the 1880s encouraged action. The 1885 convention, held in silver magnate Horace A.W. Tabor's theater, illustrated bimetallism's appeal. Delegates from across the state's political spectrum included Alva Adams, Benjamin H. Eaton, James B. Grant, Thomas M. Patterson, Henry M. Teller, and other Colorado icons of the age. They organized the National Bimetallic Association at the end of the three-day convention to continue the campaign. Another meeting, this one in St. Louis in 1889, inspired the Sherman Silver Purchase Act in 1890. The law, approved by President Benjamin Harrison, adopted bimetallism and provided a guaranteed market for Colorado's silver, then 60 percent of the national supply. The heady times lasted until the act's repeal three years later during the devastating Panic of 1893.

January 29, 1906

The First National Western Stock Show

After several years of disorganized attempts, a group of Colorado ranchers inaugurated a festival celebrating their industry on January 29, 1906. The event, which took place under a borrowed circus tent near stockyards northeast of Denver, evolved over the decades into an institution that celebrates Colorado history—the National Western Stock Show (NWSS).

To promote the quality of livestock raised in Colorado, ranchers banded together in professional organizations at the turn of the twentieth century. A group led by Douglas County stockman and politician Elias M. Ammons raised

Performers and competitors at the National Western Stock Show fill the arena at the new Denver Coliseum in the 1950s.

funds for the 1906 Western Live Stock Show, an exhibition that drew participants from across the Rocky Mountain and Great Plains states. The state agricultural college in Fort Collins showed the grand champion steer in the first show; now known as Colorado State University, the school retains close ties to the NWSS. Three years later, the event earned its current name and opened a brick and steel stadium that demonstrated the show's viability. Teller Ammons, the twelve-year-old son of founder Elias, won a prize for his steer in 1909. The Ammonses remain to date the only father-son governors in Colorado history, Elias from 1913 to 1915 and Teller from 1937 to 1939. Fellow chief executive and rancher Dan Thornton of Gunnison County served on the NWSS board in the 1940s. Organizers canceled the show in 1915 to prevent the spread of a livestock disease, the only year missed. During the Great Depression, the Public Works Administration built additional facilities for the popular event. The Coliseum opened in time for the stock show in 1952 to relieve pressure on the 1909 stadium, which survives as a historic, if cramped, facility at the sprawling show grounds.

The NWSS boasts an optimistic future with plans to expand the facility, in conjunction with proposals to redesign Interstate 70, which cuts through its center.

More visitors come to Colorado for the annual celebration than for any other event, a confluence of millionaires and manure. When the champion steer takes the place of honor in the Brown Palace Hotel's lobby, Coloradans are reminded of their state's rich (and occasionally pungent) ranching heritage.

January 30, 1956

Public Broadcasting Comes to the Rockies

Coloradans lucky enough to own a television set could tune into a new broadcast network at six on the dial on January 30, 1956. Still officially known by the call letters KRMA, most residents know the channel as Rocky Mountain PBS, the Public Broadcasting Service.

Produced in conjunction with Denver Public Schools, KRMA broadcast from a makeshift studio in the auto repair shop at the Emily Griffith Opportunity School in downtown Denver. Presaging the diverse educational entertainment provided by Colorado's first public television channel, the first two-hour block of programming ran the gamut of style and substance, with shows roughly fifteen minutes in length. Viewers who tuned in at 6:45 that night saw the humble premiere program starring teacher and puppeteer Earl Reum. His "Thimble Theatre" included magic tricks and a duo of puppets—Watahea, an American Indian boy, and a burro named Columbine—on a treasure hunt. The rest of the evening included two history programs, one detailing the story of Denver's Cheesman Park and another indelicately titled "Redman's America." KRMA also broadcast a film from the federal government praising the benefits of atomic power for electric generation, an exploration of world religions, and a discussion of pet care produced by the veterinary school at Colorado A&M University, now Colorado State University. Most of KRMA's early broadcasts originated live at the studio, as videotape and other recording systems remained in their infancy.

Since the 1960s, KRMA has developed award-winning programming beamed across the country. Building on the tradition set on its first day, Rocky Mountain PBS offers something for everyone. Colorado's only statewide television network, its five stations transmit news and business shows, documentaries, cultural performances, children's educational entertainment, British comedies and dramas, scientific and cooking programs, and much more. State residents have long depended on Rocky Mountain PBS for engaging, enlightening programming.

Beer and Books at the Tivoli

When the doors closed on January 31, 1992, at the old Tivoli-Union Brewery, a local landmark standing across Cherry Creek from downtown Denver for more than a century, a new era began as the edifice prepared for its reinvention as a college student center.

In 1866, German immigrant Moritz Sigi opened a brewery a block away from the Rocky Mountain Brewery, later renamed Zang's. Max Melsheimer purchased the property at Tenth and Larimer Streets in 1879. He rechristened it the Milwaukee Brewery after the Wisconsin town where he worked as a brewer after emigrating from Germany. The facility flourished in the 1880s and served as the heart of Denver's German community. By 1890, it boasted the tower-capped structure familiar today, funded by developer John Good, who took it over in 1900. Good reopened the works as the Tivoli—named for a Danish amusement park— and merged it with another beer maker to establish the Tivoli-Union Brewery. For seven decades it competed with Zang's and Coors, endured Prohibition by producing a near-beer product, and released the popular Denver Beer in 1965. After suffering damage from the South Platte River flood that year, and costly labor disputes, the Tivoli-Union closed its doors in 1969.

Along with several churches and houses, reinvented as the Ninth Street Historic Park, the brewery survived the demolition of most of the Auraria neighborhood in the early 1970s. The Auraria Higher Education Center, a complex of brick and glass buildings, opened near the Tivoli in 1976. The edifice languished, and development in the 1980s proved ineffective. Reinvented as a blended academic and commercial facility in the early 1990s, the Tivoli now serves as the campus center for Metropolitan State University of Denver, Community College of Denver, and the Denver branch of the University of Colorado. In 2015, Metro State introduced a program in brewing and marketing, which led to the production of Tivoli beer at the brewery once again.

February

Pike Camps on the Conejos River

Exhausted from hunger and wintry conditions and teetering on the brink of mutiny, the bedraggled members of Lieutenant Zebulon M. Pike's expedition into the Louisiana Purchase started construction on a small stockade on February 1, 1807. Built along the Conejos River in the San Luis Valley, it offered a temporary base from which to recuperate and explore the region.

Pike sought to locate the Red River, a key part of the US border with the Spanish empire. In late 1806, his band proceeded up the Arkansas River from a similar fortified camp at what is now Pueblo. They veered around the Royal Gorge into South Park, crossed Trout Creek Pass into the upper Arkansas River valley— which Pike mistook for the Red—and followed the eastern slope of the Sangre de Cristo Mountains as far south as modern Huerfano County. Crossing the range, they descended through the Great Sand Dunes to the Rio Grande—which Pike also mistook for the Red. He found himself in the prime hunting territory of the Ute culture, and word spread quickly to their Spanish allies in Santa Fe.

On February 26—less than four weeks after Pike's company started construction on the stockade—a Spanish force of 100 arrived to arrest the interlopers, whose astonished leader humbly lowered the American flag upon discovering his geographic misjudgment. Yet the Spanish treated his band more like refugees than invaders. They alternately interrogated and nursed Pike's command back to health and returned them to the United States via Texas by July. American scouts did not locate the source of the Red River, in the prairie canyons of the Texas panhandle, until the 1840s, long after its location ceased to matter as a diplomatic issue.

Although less well-known today than the Lewis and Clark expedition, Pike earned fame at the time when his journals appeared in print before those of the better-known expedition and were sold to fascinated audiences nationwide. The Colorado Historical Society built a replica of the stockade in Conejos County in the 1960s.

Mexico Surrenders Most of Colorado

The United States secured claim—but not control—over all of the modern state of Colorado on February 2, 1848, when American and Mexican officials signed the Treaty of Guadalupe Hidalgo near Mexico City, ending the brief but bloody Mexican-American War.

President James Polk asked Congress to declare war against Mexico in the spring of 1846, having failed in his efforts to buy California from the southern neighbor. That July, about 1,700 regular soldiers and volunteers commanded by Colonel Stephen W. Kearny traveled the Santa Fe Trail on their way to New Mexico. They stopped at Bent's Fort, the center of the Bent, St. Vrain & Company fur trade empire, which faced Mexico across the Arkansas River. Susan S. Magoffin wrote in her diary on July 30: "The Fort is crowded to overflowing. Col. Kearny has arrived and it seems the world is coming with him." William Bent fired a cannon salute to Kearny's troops and hosted the officers for mint juleps inside the fort. Kearny conferred with William and Charles Bent about Mexico's northern defenses and promised federal reimbursement for the supplies his soldiers took from the fort. Within weeks, Santa Fe fell to Kearny's troops without a shot fired, and his army proceeded to California.

In the short term, the war and the Treaty of Guadalupe Hidalgo made little impact in Colorado. It transferred the claim to roughly two-thirds of the present state from Mexico to the United States, but control of the region remained in the hands of American Indians. The real loser of the war, from Colorado's perspective, was Bent, St. Vrain & Company. It had dominated the eastern slope for a decade and a half, but the disruption of trade and the federal government's failure to pay for the supplies Kearny appropriated weakened the company. To make matters worse, Charles Bent, appointed by Kearny as governor of New Mexico in September 1846, died in Taos in an anti-American uprising four months later. Establishing American control over what is now the state of Colorado inspired as many problems as opportunities for the Americans living there.

February 3, 1920

History and Headlines in Deer Trail

Officials in the small Arapahoe County town of Deer Trail filed incorporation paperwork with the secretary of state's office on February 3, 1920, which enabled the community to organize a local government and exercise greater control over its own affairs. For a place the humble size of Deer Trail, it boasts a remarkable legacy and draws widespread attention.

A settlement had existed along East Bijou Creek for over half a century before Deer Trail incorporated. The town owes its existence to Texas cattle baron John Hittson, who brought a herd into Colorado Territory over Raton Pass on Richens L. Wootton's toll road in 1866. Hittson used the route, which became the Goodnight-Loving Trail, to import thousands of cattle and selected the area around present-day Deer Trail as open range grazing land. The Smoky Hill Trail, a popular route to the gold fields, provided access to the east and west. On Independence Day in 1869, the camp held a bronco-busting competition for local cowpunchers, described by later generations as the first-ever rodeo—a record contested by towns in Arizona, New Mexico, and Texas. A sign along Interstate 70 heralds the claim: "Home of the World's Oldest Rodeo."

A year after Hittson's cowboy challenge, the Kansas Pacific Railroad laid tracks into Deer Trail. Ranchers and farmers settled the area, which grew into a small but successful town. It hosted rodeos again by the 1910s, in part to reinforce its claim to history. Battered by the Great Depression like so many high plains towns and nearly wiped out by a flood in 1965, Deer Trail recovered sufficiently to celebrate the rodeo's centennial in fine style four years later.

Deer Trail made international headlines in 2013, when a few residents concerned about government surveillance sought to issue drone-hunting licenses. Advocates claimed that such actions were necessary to defend freedom but also viewed the scheme as a money-making proposition for the town. Many voters feared vigilantism in their community, and in April 2014 they rejected the measure by 73 percent. One thing is for sure—Deer Trail never fails to entertain.

February 4, 1954

"Billy" Adams Dies

William H. "Billy" Adams, the first Colorado governor elected to three consecutive terms, died at his home in Alamosa on February 4, 1954. A political force for decades, Adams offered an effective voice for conservative, rural Coloradans and a cool head in elected office.

Born in Wisconsin in 1861, Adams traveled to Colorado with his family a decade later to help a brother recover from tuberculosis. After that sibling died and his parents returned home, Billy remained in Colorado with his older brother, Alva. The two operated a hardware store in Pueblo and franchised in the San Luis Valley to profit off the San Juan Mountains mining boom. Alva turned to a career in politics, culminating in gubernatorial victories in 1886, 1896, and 1904. Billy settled in Alamosa as a rancher in 1878. He touted irrigation projects and dabbled in local politics, holding city offices and positions in Conejos County (Alamosa County did not exist until 1913). He won election to the General Assembly in 1886 and served as a legislator for four decades. Adams sponsored few measures during those years; he later recalled, "I spent more time killing bills than trying to pass 'em." He secured a teacher training school for Alamosa in 1921, known as Adams State College until promoted to university status in 2012.

Adams helped stymie the Ku Klux Klan's dominance of state government in the mid-1920s, and he won the governor's office in 1926. A staunch conservative Democrat, he authorized the use of deadly force against striking coal miners in Weld County in 1927 and crushed a riot at the state penitentiary in Cañon City two years later. Roy Best, the controversial warden Adams appointed to reform the prison, stood at Adams's deathbed in 1954. Adams won three consecutive terms—unlike his brother's staggered ones—by demanding fiscal restraint, especially during the Great Depression. He stepped aside for his friend and ally, Edwin C. Johnson, who succeeded Adams as governor in 1932. Adams remained a respected elder statesman, happily in the saddle on his San Luis Valley ranch, until his death at age ninety-two.

February 5, 1868

Utes at the White House

President Andrew Johnson escorted nearly a dozen prominent Utes on a tour of the executive mansion in Washington, DC, on February 5, 1868. Part of an East Coast tour for the Utes, such visits were intended to impress—or terrify—American Indians into agreeing to treaties ceding their land claims and autonomy to the vast, powerful United States.

Having resisted Spanish, Mexican, and American encroachment in the central Rocky Mountains for years, the Utes faced an unprecedented onslaught after the Pikes Peak gold rush. A treaty in 1863 surrendered their claims east of the Continental Divide, but it applied only to one Ute faction, and the Civil War prevented even that limited deal's enforcement. To keep the peace and promote the transformation of Utes into English-speaking farmers, federal officials negotiated a new deal in early 1868. Territorial governor Alexander Hunt accompanied the sojourn eastward, as did Indian agents Christopher "Kit" Carson and Lafayette Head and influential Utes including Ouray and Nicaagat. Ouray, who had traveled to the capital five years earlier on a similar mission, proved the most compromising Ute, and federal officials negotiated with him as the leader of all Utes, a status he did not possess and that caused resentment.

The 1868 treaty designated most of western Colorado as a common Ute reservation. Agencies would distribute food and supplies and serve as training centers for American-style agriculture. The first, called Los Piños and located near the summit of Cochetopa Pass in modern Saguache County, opened in 1869. The treaty also promoted American-style education for Ute children to hasten their transition away from native lifestyles. It pledged Ute domain over the reservation and forbade non-native people from living on or even passing through it.

Almost immediately, the treaty proved impossible to enforce. Trespassing prospectors sought riches on the forbidden land, and the federal government proved unwilling to favor American Indians over American citizens, setting the stage for new tensions and negotiations.

February 6, 1967

Watching the Skies from Underground

Brinksmanship and suspicion during the Cold War inspired the United States and the Soviet Union to build ever larger, more powerful nuclear arsenals, weapons that depended on the fear of mutual destruction to prevent their use. To ensure a functional American military in the event of such a catastrophe, in the 1960s the federal government carved out the granite heart of Cheyenne Mountain, looming

A US Air Force officer watches the skies for threats from the Cheyenne Mountain headquarters of the North American Aerospace Defense Command in the 1970s.

south of Colorado Springs, to house the nation's emergency command system. The engineering marvel hummed to life on February 6, 1967.

Best known for hosting the North American Aerospace Defense Command (NORAD), the Cheyenne Mountain Complex (CMC) has housed numerous organizations, most connected to the US Air Force. For three years, crews dug out rock from Cheyenne Mountain, reinforced the cavern with concrete, and shielded it with blast doors. Workers needed three more years to build fifteen three-story buildings on springs to cushion them from direct attacks. In early 1967, the CMC opened for business. Linked with Ent Air Force Base in nearby Colorado Springs, it coordinated satellites and radar for the United States and Canada. After the Cold War, its use dwindled and most operations moved to Peterson Air Force Base, which abutted and eventually absorbed Ent. Although its use varies, the CMC remains a valuable facility and an impressive feat of design and construction, perhaps the most famous of El Paso County's many military installations.

Aside from its essential role in national defense, NORAD draws attention every Christmas as it tracks Santa Claus's movements. In 1955, an advertisement for a Colorado Springs business accidentally listed the operations center's telephone number for children to call Kris Kringle. Colonel Harry Shoup gamely stepped into the role of "Santa Colonel," fielding calls all Christmas Eve. NORAD continues the tradition with the internet's *NORAD Tracks Santa* program. One wonders if it gets crucial intelligence from Santa's workshop at the nearby North Pole amusement park, just around the corner from CMC on the north flank of Pikes Peak.

February 7, 1937

Catching a Lift on Berthoud Pass

A Ford V-8 engine rumbled to life atop Berthoud Pass on February 7, 1937, operating an 878-foot-long rope tow that pulled skiers to the top of a nearby run, allowing enthusiasts to enjoy their favorite pastime with greater ease. The rope tow, paid for by Denver's May Company department store, helped establish Berthoud Pass as an early Colorado commercial ski area.

A gap in the Continental Divide between Clear Creek and Grand Counties, Berthoud Pass had offered trans-mountain access since time immemorial. The Rocky Mountains long represented something to avoid rather than approach during the winter months, but the construction of US Highway 40 over the pass and the nearby Moffat Tunnel allowed visitors to reach the area more easily by the 1920s. Skiing had been an informal, disorganized activity in Colorado for decades, but the 1937 innovation and access to eastern slope cities placed Berthoud Pass on the cutting edge of the industry, one that inspired ever more growth in the decades to come.

Berthoud Pass hosted tourists from far and wide, including a national slalom competition, during its first season. Sorrow befell the area as well—on the same day the rope tow started, two refugees from Nazi Germany died in an avalanche, although their bodies were not recovered until the spring thaw. Nonetheless, Berthoud Pass impressed all who visited it. Otto Schniebs, instructor for the United States Olympic ski team, schussed there in 1937 and called the region "a skier's and mountaineer's playground of world fame, because its mountains are so entirely new to skiers, so unspoiled." Schniebs raved: "The best scenery, the best slopes from a sporting standpoint, are these high in the Colorado Rockies. They are [as] beautiful as anything I have ever seen in Europe. As a matter of fact, I have never seen better snow conditions anywhere."

The ski area at Berthoud Pass operated until 2001, and almost all traces have disappeared into the Arapaho National Forest. Its legacy resonates, however, in the thousands of people who come to the Colorado high country every year to delight in the winter sports wonderland.

February 8, 1879

Making a Home for Mental Health

Governor Frederick W. Pitkin signed a bill to establish "the Colorado Insane Asylum, for the treatment and cure of such persons as may become insane from any cause" on February 8, 1879. Members of the General Assembly, opposed to the incarceration approach used for the mentally ill in many other states, argued that because "the insane of this state are now sent at great expense to remote places for treatment, we therefore believe that the cause of humanity and the greatest good to the whole people will be advanced by a speedy operation of this act."

Construction crews erected the asylum's first building in Pueblo on land donated by US senator George M. Chilcott, a resident of that city. The first inmates—eleven Coloradans who had lived at state expense at an Illinois institution—arrived in October 1879. But not everyone supported the legislature's call for therapeutic treatment of mental illness. A Pueblo newspaper, for example, seemed content with more traditional approaches. It ridiculed at length a morbidly obese woman from Denver named Lizzie Halpin, who needed several orderlies to help her get out of bed. The press proposed "that the county officers might purchase a tent upon her arrival, and meet a portion of the county expenses by a judiciously managed side-show exhibition."

Attitudes and regimens alike improved gradually over the years. The General Assembly changed the asylum's name to the Colorado State Hospital in 1917, to challenge its perception as a dumping ground for the mentally ill. The facility grew to seventy-five buildings on 300 acres plus a 120-acre dairy farm 2 miles west of the campus, operated by the hospital's residents. By the early 1960s, the institution had become unwieldy, with more than 6,000 patients. Modernization demanded by Governor Steve McNichols emphasized the use of medications to treat mental illness, enabling many residents to return to less constricted facilities in their home counties. Renamed the Colorado Mental Health Institute in 1991, it cares for several hundred residents and operates in conjunction with a similar facility at Fort Logan in southwest Denver.

February 9, 1878

John W. Iliff Dies

A small town in present-day Logan County bears the name Iliff, which it inherited from rancher John W. Iliff, who controlled grazing land throughout northeastern Colorado from that spot. Upon Iliff's death in Denver on February 9, 1878, a newspaper described him as "the Cattle King of Colorado." The family name remains prominent today, in large part thanks to the generosity and business acumen of his widow, Elizabeth, who outlived John by forty-two years.

Born in Ohio in 1831, John Iliff traveled to Denver in 1859 and found profit in "mining the miners" by selling supplies. Iliff bought land along the north bank of the South Platte River and imported cattle to graze there. He sold meat to crews building the Union Pacific, Denver Pacific, and Colorado Central Railroads in the late 1860s. Iliff bought thousands of Texas cattle each year and moved them north along the Goodnight-Loving Trail. He cultivated relationships with Cheyennes and Arapahos by inviting them to hunt from his herd and supplement their food supply, earning respect and appreciation from his native neighbors. By the time of his death, Iliff owned more than 15,000 acres and dominated as much as 650,000 acres that drained into his tracts along the river. The press attributed his passing at age forty-six to years of drinking water tainted with alkali and noted his status as perhaps the richest man in Colorado upon his death.

Elizabeth S.F. Iliff, who came to Colorado as a saleswoman for Singer sewing machines and married John in 1870, was described by one newspaper as "thoroughly capable of continuing the business on the same scale upon which it was conducted by her husband, and will probably do so." She proved an adept stockwoman and in 1883 married Henry W. Warren, Colorado's Methodist bishop.

The following year, Elizabeth donated $100,000 to fund a Methodist school in Denver named for her irreligious late husband. The Iliff School of Theology operates today in conjunction with the neighboring University of Denver. John and Elizabeth Iliff represent one of Colorado's most successful, benevolent couples, with a much admired legacy.

February 10, 1958

History in a Highway Median

The Colorado Historical Society (now History Colorado) took ownership of a small tract near Platteville in Weld County on February 10, 1958, the site of a once bustling fur trading post known as Fort Vasquez.

Trapper Louis Vasquez established several small commercial hubs in what is now the Denver metropolitan area in the late 1820s and early 1830s, including one at the confluence of Clear Creek and the South Platte River in modern Adams County. In 1836, he joined Andrew Sublette, from a prominent St. Louis merchant family, to erect a square adobe structure just north of the new Fort Lupton. Fort Vasquez, located along the well-traveled Trapper's Trail between New Mexico and the North Platte River, included a single entrance of cottonwood gates on the south side and a short tower on the northwest corner. Vasquez and Sublette traded metal and glass goods, tobacco, and other wares with Arapaho, Cheyenne, Hispano, and American trappers who provided beaver and bison pelts. One visitor in 1839 described Fort Vasquez as "quite a nice place . . . built of daubies, or Spanish bricks, made of clay baked in the sun." He wrote that "the men at the fort have been carousing, having got drunk on alcohol," but also that "nothing remarkable has happened" during his visit, which suggests that such behavior was commonplace.

The waning fur trade and competition from nearby Forts Lupton, Jackson, and St. Vrain led to Vasquez's abandonment in 1842, although gold seekers camped there in the late 1850s. The Works Progress Administration erected an adobe re-creation on the site in the 1930s, but it bore little resemblance to the original. The project and construction on US Highway 85—in whose median the site stands—destroyed most of the fort's remains. After the historical society acquired the spot in 1958, it sponsored several archaeological digs but found that little of value survived. The Great Depression–era reproduction remains the focal point of a museum operated by History Colorado, perched between lanes of the busy route between Denver and Greeley. Fort Vasquez reflects the challenge of restoring and interpreting the past for future generations.

Students and faculty gather outside the main building, later called "Old Main," at the Colorado Agricultural College in Fort Collins in 1887.

Colorado's Land Grant School

President Abraham Lincoln, eager to demonstrate that the Civil War had not over-shadowed other issues of national importance, signed legislation in the summer of 1862 to provide federal land to every state, which the states could sell to fund institutions of higher learning dedicated to agriculture and industry. Since then, every American state and territory has availed itself of the "land grant" system, including Colorado, which authorized the Colorado Agricultural College through a bill signed by Governor Edward M. McCook on February 11, 1870.

Nine years passed before a simple, dignified structure of brick and stone, later called Old Main, stood ready to receive students. The campus stood on the southern edge of Fort Collins, and the Colorado Central Railroad passed through it—a useful excuse for tardy students to this day. A Denver correspondent visited the school grounds a month after it opened and reported corn stalks growing an astonishing ten to eighteen ears apiece. "If our farmers could see and hear what we saw and heard, and initiate their boys into the grand mysteries of scientific farm-ing," the reporter declared, "we believe that hundreds who drift away from the noblest of all human industries and wreck themselves upon the rocks of a vicious and fictitious society, would be saved to honored lives." Classes focused on farm-ing, ranching, and industrial work to create valuable contributions to Colorado's economy. The college also established agricultural experiment stations across the state, furthering its goal of promoting innovation.

The college's name evolved as the school developed, from the Colorado State College of Agricultural and Mechanical Arts (Colorado A&M) in 1935 to Colorado State University in 1957. It houses a branch of the Centers for Disease Control, a renowned veterinary teaching school, and the National Center for Genetic Resources Preservation, a biological storehouse beyond compare. Founders Day festivities take place at CSU each February 11, as the university commemorates its past and rededicates itself to useful work for all Coloradans.

Kidnapping Charles Boettcher II

Verne Sankey lurked in the shadows at 777 Washington Street in Denver on February 12, 1933. When a car pulled into the driveway, Sankey and his partner, Gordon Alcorn, rushed it, blindfolded the driver, shoved him into a nearby vehicle, and handed the passenger a ransom note demanding $60,000. Sankey and Alcorn got into their car and drove away, bound for their hideout in South Dakota. Their unwilling fellow traveler was Charles Boettcher II.

Third in a line of Colorado tycoons, the kidnapped Boettcher bore the name of his grandfather, a German immigrant whose investments created a fortune and whose father, Claude, had nurtured it. During the 1930s, prominent kidnappings garnered headlines nationwide, and Boettcher's was no different. He spent two weeks imprisoned in a basement on a South Dakota ranch while Sankey coordinated the ransom. The kidnappers released Boettcher on March 1, dropping him at the Denver stockyards, but they demanded their money nonetheless. The family tossed a satchel from a bridge into a dry creek bed on US Highway 87 (present-day Interstate 25) north of Denver, and Sankey and Alcorn made off with the cash before law enforcement could catch them. They hid in a Greeley warehouse until they could escape to South Dakota.

An anonymous tip sent authorities to Sankey's ranch, but he and Alcorn fled to Chicago. The Federal Bureau of Investigation declared Sankey their first "Public Enemy #1," a criminal's badge of honor during the Great Depression. Agents captured him while he was getting a shave at a barber shop in Chicago on January 31, 1934, and took Alcorn the next day. They returned to South Dakota to stand trial. Sankey committed suicide on February 8, four days short of a year since the kidnapping. Alcorn pled guilty and received a life sentence, which he served at two federal penitentiaries—Alcatraz in San Francisco Bay and Leavenworth in Kansas. Paroled with Boettcher's support in 1949, Alcorn was deported to his native Canada. In response to the incident, Colorado's General Assembly made kidnapping for ransom a capital offense.

February 13, 1950

It's All Downhill in Aspen

Over 100 athletes from fourteen countries assembled in the Pitkin County seat of Aspen for a week-long competition hosted by the International Ski Federation. The races that started on February 13, 1950, inaugurated Colorado's first skiing competition with participants from around the world and reflected Aspen's emerging status as a winter resort community.

Founded as an offshoot of the booming Leadville mines in 1879, Aspen's pioneers sought gold and silver from the mountains overlooking the Roaring Fork River. Aspen was accessible seasonally over the Continental Divide at Independence Pass. Its early residents maintained control over who moved into the region, an exclusivity that echoes in the modern town, considered by many to be Colorado's most privileged. Mining's collapse in the Panic of 1893 weakened Aspen's economy, but the isolated settlement clung to life in the early twentieth century.

Aspen's renaissance commenced with a mock invasion during World War II. US Army trainees from nearby Camp Hale staged an attack on Aspen as they prepared for combat in the summer of 1943. One of the participants, an Austrian immigrant named Friedrich Pfeifer, marveled at Aspen's picturesque site and perfect skiing mountains. After the war, he returned to Colorado and teamed up with a Chicago businessman, Walter Paepcke, to develop Aspen as an upscale winter resort destination on European Alpine and Scandinavian models. They tapped into the budding interest in skiing that had percolated in Colorado since the turn of the twentieth century and developed Aspen as the state's first winter resort by the late 1940s.

The competition in February 1950 demonstrated Colorado's ability and desire to draw visitors year-round and, like the Olympics, offered a moment of camaraderie even as tensions simmered around the globe. Flouting the Cold War, Governor W. Lee Knous sipped vodka with Russian athletes before they and others crushed the American challengers. Aspen's success in 1950 fueled the winter sports industry and the town's own popularity in the years to come.

February 14, 1884

John W. Prowers Dies

John W. Prowers, one of the essential figures of southeastern Colorado in the mid-nineteenth century, died in his hometown of Kansas City, Missouri, on February 14, 1884, forty-six years after his birth in what was then the trailhead of Westport Landing on the Missouri River.

In 1856, at age of eighteen, Prowers set out on the Santa Fe Trail to seek a living. He went to work for William Bent at his trading post near present-day Lamar, in what eventually received the name Prowers County. Prowers fostered relationships with American Indian cultures in the area and married a Cheyenne woman named Amache in 1861. The following year, John and Amache traveled to Missouri to buy 100 head of cattle in the hope that he could raise livestock to sell to travelers and the US Army at Fort Lyon. The Prowers returned to the Arkansas River valley and let their herd meander and multiply. With few settlements in the area, John had little competition for grazing territory, and his cattle business flourished.

The Prowers' ties to native cultures caused Colonel John M. Chivington to detain John and his ranch hands to prevent them from warning the Arapaho and

Cheyenne about plans for the Sand Creek Massacre in 1864; Amache's father, Ochinee, was among its victims. Three years later, after Fort Lyon relocated to a new spot on the Arkansas River, the Prowers family moved to the Boggsville settlement south of modern Las Animas. Their house sheltered the first offices for Bent County, organized in 1870, and served as an ethnically diverse social hub for the river valley. John and Amache moved to Las Animas early in that decade and used his fortune and—as a member of the General Assembly—political connections to develop the town. By the 1880s, the Prowers dominated a 40-mile stretch of the Arkansas River and controlled 400,000 acres of open range. Upon his death in 1884, John's herd numbered around 10,000 head and his estate was valued at a princely $775,000. The couple's remains lie under a large monument in the Las Animas Cemetery near Boggsville, where Amache joined John after her death in 1905.

February 15, 1904

"Honest John" Shafroth Resigns

The public often belittles politicians as conniving and self-serving, regardless of any evidence to the contrary. A few officials buck the trend, such as John F. Shafroth, who resigned from the US House of Representatives on February 15, 1904, simply because it was the right thing to do. He earned the nickname "Honest John" for placing principle above his career.

A native of Missouri, Shafroth came to Colorado in 1879. He made his name in law and real estate and won the first of five elections to Congress as a Republican in 1894. Shafroth supported women's suffrage and conservation of natural resources. He worked with US senator Henry M. Teller to advocate bimetallism and oppose imperialism after the Spanish-American War, and the two men joined the pro-silver Democrats by the early twentieth century. Presented with evidence that his reelection in 1902 was fraudulent, Shafroth resigned in a speech that received bipartisan approbation from the house. A Golden press declared, "No one, of whatever political faith, can have any but good words for the Honorable John F. Shafroth, who has proved himself one of the best and most conscientious members Colorado ever had."

"Honest John" parleyed his reputation into a successful run for the governor's office in 1908. The model of a Progressive-era politician, Shafroth battled a hesitant General Assembly to pass reforms like initiative and referendum to give citizens control over laws, regulation of banks and railroads, encouragement for agricultural settlement, and public health and child labor measures. He won reelection in 1910, and the legislature sent him to the US Senate two years later. There, Shafroth allied with President Woodrow Wilson to extend Progressive principles nationwide. His reelection campaign in 1918 suffered from the influenza epidemic, which made speechifying impossible. Shafroth lost a scurrilous, media-driven contest to the deep pockets of Republican capitalist Lawrence C. Phipps and died in Denver four years later. Nonetheless, "Honest John" Shafroth remains perhaps the most respected politician in Colorado history.

February 16, 1865

Soule Speaks the Truth

Captain Silas S. Soule sat in front of a congressional panel meeting in Denver on the morning of February 16, 1865, with his former commander John M. Chivington perched nearby. Soule proceeded to describe in grisly detail the previous November's Sand Creek Massacre.

Born in Maine in 1838, Soule grew up in an abolitionist family. They moved to Kansas in 1854 and allied with John Brown, whom Soule tried in vain to save from execution five years later. Soule joined the Pikes Peak gold rush in 1860 and enlisted in the First Colorado cavalry. He fought at Glorieta Pass, guarded the Santa Fe Trail, and participated in peace talks with American Indians. Soule joined Colonel Chivington's march to Big Sandy Creek in November 1864 but, horrified at his commander's plans, refused to participate in the massacre. He later described it to his immediate superior, Major Edward W. Wynkoop:

> I tell you Ned it was hard to see little children on their knees have their brains beat out by men professing to be civilized . . . One squaw with her two children, were on their knees begging for their lives of a dozen soldiers, within ten feet of them all, firing—when one succeeded in hitting the squaw in the thigh, she took a knife and cut the throats of both children, and then killed herself . . . One woman was cut open and a child taken out of her, and scalped . . . Squaw's snatches were cut out for trophies. You would think it impossible for white men to butcher and mutilate human beings as they did there, but every word I have told you is the truth, which they do not deny.

Soule's testimony to the congressional hearing proved less graphic but just as damning. The commission found Chivington responsible of inexcusable atrocities but, as he had already resigned his commission, could not punish him. Governor John Evans had not ordered the massacre but fostered a hysteria that made it almost inevitable and lost his job in the summer of 1865. For testifying against Chivington, whom many Coloradans considered a hero, on April 23, 1865, Soule was murdered on the streets of Denver, a crime that remains unsolved.

Georgians Set out to Find Gold

A band of fortune seekers, organized by farmer and prospector William G. Russell, departed from their homes in northern Georgia on February 17, 1858, on an excursion to the eastern slope of the Rocky Mountains. The result of their trek was the Pikes Peak gold rush.

The Panic of 1857 had weakened the nation's economy and inspired Americans to find new ways to survive. The notion of money for the taking proved appealing. A small party of men, experienced in prospecting from the rushes in Georgia and California, led by Russell set out from the former state early the next year. The group included Russell's two brothers and their neighbor Lewis Ralston, who, on his way to California in 1850, had panned a few flakes in modern Jefferson County, Colorado's first recorded gold discovery. Russell's party paused in what is now Oklahoma, where several Cherokees related to the Georgians joined their trek. By the time they reached western Kansas Territory, the group had swelled to more than a hundred men filled with hope. Prospectors found scant color in Cherry, Clear, Fountain, and Ralston Creeks and the Arkansas and South Platte Rivers, however, and most of the party returned home. Russell and his brothers remained, along with ten others, not including the disillusioned Ralston.

In early July the remaining prospectors focused on the South Platte in modern Denver and Arapahoe Counties. They made their major strike where Dartmouth Avenue crosses the river at its junction with Little Dry Creek in present-day Englewood. Russell and his companions panned several hundred dollars' worth of gold there. Word spread via travelers on the Trapper's and Cherokee Trails that passed through the region, and thousands of people set their sights on the eastern slope of the Rocky Mountains. Late that summer, a party of Kansans organized a camp named Montana City just downstream from the Russells' discovery site, between today's Evans and Iliff Avenues on the east side of the South Platte. The rush was on, inspired by Russell and his band of prospectors searching for salvation in the creek beds of modern Colorado.

Peacemaking on the Eastern Plains

Leaders of the Arapaho and Southern Cheyenne cultures signed the Treaty of Fort Wise in what is now Bent County on February 18, 1861. The agreement reinforced peaceful relations between native and American populations in modern Colorado

Artist's depiction of a delegation of Cheyenne and Arapaho leaders visiting Denver for peace talks with territorial officials in 1863

in the wake of the Pikes Peak gold rush. It also presaged the end of American Indian authority east of the Rocky Mountains.

A decade earlier, the 1851 Treaty of Fort Laramie had recognized Arapaho and Cheyenne claims to land between the Arkansas and North Platte Rivers, from the Continental Divide extending eastward into present-day Kansas. In the late 1850s, tens of thousands of American gold seekers trespassed into the heart of this region. American Indian groups kept their distance, a rare yet fearful example of peace between native cultures and American interlopers.

William Bent had established a trading post along a wooded stretch of the Arkansas River known as Big Timbers in 1849, replacing the larger Bent's Fort about 50 miles upstream. The US Army bought the smaller Bent's New Fort in 1860 and used it as a storehouse for a post built nearby. It took the name Fort Wise for Virginia's governor, Henry A. Wise, but after he declared his state out of the Union in early 1861, the moniker seemed inappropriate. In 1862 the post was renamed Fort Lyon for General Nathaniel Lyon, the first Union Army commander killed in the Civil War. The post served as a negotiation center for the treaty, which sought to ensure that the calm situation east of the Rocky Mountains endured as eastern states squabbled.

The Fort Wise treaty shrank Arapaho and Cheyenne claims to a reservation bounded largely by the Arkansas, Purgatoire, and Huerfano Rivers and Big

Sandy Creek. It insisted that native cultures adapt to American agricultural methods, for which the federal government would provide logistical aid. The United States enforced only the land-grab aspects of the treaty over the next few years, even though the Arapaho and Cheyenne—hoping to maintain peace with a powerful challenger—kept their part of the bargain until the Sand Creek Massacre in 1864.

Preserving a Whitewater Playground

White-knuckle adventures in Colorado often include whitewater rafting, shooting the rapids while admiring spectacular scenery. The Arkansas River in Chaffee County, especially between Buena Vista and Salida, boasts some of the best rafting territory in the state, and the companies that offer trips along it take as much pride in the vistas as they do in their services.

Starting in the 1970s, advocates of the industry sought to preserve the area through which the Arkansas River flowed to prevent over-development. A group of concerned citizens and businesses organized the Friends of Browns Canyon in 2003 to lobby for federal protection. With bipartisan support from Colorado's congressional delegation, Representative Joel Hefley—a Colorado Springs Republican whose district included Chaffee County—introduced a bill to designate Browns Canyon as a wilderness area in 2005. Although Congress failed to act on the legislation, support for the idea built steadily. In 2014, Democratic senator Mark Udall sponsored a bill to set aside 21,000 acres as a national monument and wilderness area, but the legislation met with similar congressional lethargy. The idea remained popular nonetheless.

The Friends of Browns Canyon identified themselves as "a group of passionate outdoors recreationists, hikers, equestrians, whitewater enthusiasts and guides, anglers, mountain bikers, rock climbers, hunters, photographers, and more." Politicians and private citizens alike touted the natural beauty and biodiversity of the upper Arkansas River valley, as well as the economic benefits and agricultural protections federal designation would provide. To that end, on February 19, 2015, President Barack Obama used his authority under the Antiquities Act to authorize Browns Canyon National Monument. As a result, generations of screaming, laughing visitors who ride the rapids will enjoy a landscape that meets the needs of local residents while preserving the beauty of an adrenaline-fueled journey through Browns Canyon.

Allotment Comes to the Utes

Euro-Americans sought either to subjugate or obliterate American Indian populations from the earliest days of colonization. By the late nineteenth century, native
autonomy had all but disappeared in the United States, and an 1887 law called the
General Allotment (or Dawes) Act intended to finish the transition. It set up a
framework for subdividing reservations to force native cultures to adopt American
farming practices and abandon old lifestyles. Abolishing each reservation required
its own specific law, however. On February 20, 1895, President Grover Cleveland
signed the Hunter Act to do just that to Colorado's surviving Ute population.

Various treaties had reduced Ute territory in Colorado to a sliver of land in
the southwestern corner of the state, on which dwelled the remnants of three Ute
bands—the Caputa, Mouache, and Weenuchiu. Intent on reconstructing the Utes,
Congress passed the Hunter Act to allot reservation land as private farms and sell
any tracts left over to American settlers. Federal officials hoped the new neighbors
would inspire the Utes to embrace new lifestyles. The Caputa and Mouache bands
agreed to allotment, but the Weenuchiu refused to replace tribal holdings with
individual plots. The groups divided, and the Weenuchiu moved to the western
end of the reservation near the slopes of Sleeping Ute Mountain. Eventually the
tract split, with the westerly Ute Mountain Ute Reservation remaining intact and
the eastern half, the Southern Ute Reservation, balkanized into a patchwork of
land allotted to the Caputa and Mouache. American settlers moved in quickly to
buy valuable parcels left over in La Plata and Archuleta Counties. Disputes over
water in the region simmered between the groups until an agreement in 1988,
which included the Utes in a deal to create the Animas-La Plata storage project.

Allotment ended as a federal policy in 1934, but its legacy lingers as American
Indians nationwide struggle to survive and preserve their culture, made all the
more difficult as the country at large alternately calls for the abolition of or simply
ignores native groups.

Autobees Puts Down Roots

A day after Charles Autobees and a small party of settlers arrived near the junction of the Huerfano and Arkansas Rivers in present-day Pueblo County, they
set to work building a community. As they started digging ditches and planning

structures on February 21, 1853, the party laid the foundation for one of southeastern Colorado's most important early settlements.

Born in St. Louis in 1812, Autobees trapped as a teenager before working for a purveyor of foul whiskey in Taos, New Mexico. That job sent him to El Pueblo, Fort Lupton, and along the Santa Fe Trail, occasionally working with his stepbrother Tom Tobin. He speculated in Mexican land grants in New Mexico in the 1830s and 1840s and spread the word about an anti-American rebellion there in 1847. Five years later, Autobees accepted an offer from Ceran St. Vrain—a wealthy merchant and former co-owner of Bent's Fort—to establish a settlement on land St. Vrain claimed south of the Arkansas River and east of the Sangre de Cristo Mountains.

Autobees's party transformed the prairie into farm fields starting in February 1853. By the following October, another settlement arose nearby, founded by Richens L. Wootton. They produced crops and livestock to support themselves and to sell to trail travelers, towns in New Mexico, and American Indians. After the attack on El Pueblo in 1854, Autobees relocated his settlement up the Huerfano River while Wootton retreated to New Mexico. The town numbered about fifty residents during the Pikes Peak gold rush and served as the first seat of Huerfano County, which covered most of southeastern Colorado Territory upon its creation in 1861.

Autobees fought for control of his land starting in 1867, when the US Army authorized Fort Reynolds nearby. He also struggled to prove his claim to the land St. Vrain granted him in a series of court battles that lasted into the 1870s. Autobees eventually secured legal title to less than 700 acres and died at what was left of his once prosperous settlement in 1882.

February 22, 1819

Colorado as a Borderland

The Louisiana Purchase's vague boundaries—described simply as the western drainage of the Mississippi River—nearly led the United States and Spain to war over who claimed what on the Great Plains in the early nineteenth century. To calm the situation and allow Spain to focus on a rebellion in Mexico, Secretary of State John Q. Adams and Spanish envoy Luis de Onís signed an agreement in Washington, DC, on February 22, 1819. It transferred Florida to American control and drew a clear border across North America between the two countries.

In modern Colorado, the Adams-Onís boundary followed the Arkansas River from what is now the Kansas line up to the headwaters near Leadville. From there, the border extended due north through Middle and North Parks and into present-day Wyoming. No surveyors ever marked this divide and no soldiers ever patrolled it, but its theoretical existence was enough to reduce international tensions. As Susan S. Magoffin wrote in what is now Otero County in 1846: "I am now entirely out of 'The States,' into a new country. The crossing of the Arkansas was an event in my life I have never met with before: the separating me from my own dear native land."

Although the Adams-Onís line had little real impact on Colorado, the Arkansas River also served as a limit between the real authorities in the region—American Indian cultures. In the early 1800s, Arapahos and Cheyennes had migrated southward along the eastern slope of the Rocky Mountains and taken up residence in what is now eastern Colorado. These close allies competed with another influential pair, the Comanches and Kiowas, whose presence had forced the Apaches off the Great Plains in the late 1700s. All four cultures competed with the Utes, who would descend from the Rockies to hunt, but none could dominate the others. The Arkansas River, known locally as the Napestle, emerged as a divide between Arapahos and Cheyennes to the north and Comanches and Kiowas to the south. The natural barrier between distant countries thus served a far more important, contemporary role—to separate native powerhouses.

February 23, 1981

Alan Berg's Acerbic Airwaves

Denver radio station KOA, whose signal reached dozens of states and long represented the standard in Colorado broadcasting, rolled the dice on February 23, 1981. It debuted a new talk show, more combative in style than most on the state's airwaves, hosted by Alan Berg. A few years earlier, a poll had asked Coloradans for their best- and least-liked media figure. The ever-controversial Berg won both distinctions, reflecting his ability to both delight and disgust.

Born in Chicago in 1934, Berg attended the University of Colorado in the early 1950s. He married Denverite Judith Halpern after meeting her at a dance recital at Denver's East High School and sold men's shoes and clothes at stores in Denver. One of Berg's regular customers owned a small radio station in the suburb of Englewood and in 1971 offered him the chance to chat on the air. Berg's directness and passion excited the small audience. He returned regularly and eventually earned a show of his own. Berg floated from one station to another during the 1970s, often advocating liberal policies. He earned a reputation for honesty if not politeness, ridiculing people and groups with whom he disagreed, hanging up on callers, or interrupting them with questions on unrelated, controversial subjects like abortion and masturbation. Berg stated: "The beauty of talk radio is that you're paid to tell the truth. I can think of almost no other profession where that's true . . . The worst call is, 'I agree with everything you say.' They aren't thinking when they say that. I don't agree with myself all the time, so how can they?"

Berg earned the ire of radical groups like the Ku Klux Klan for his politics and Jewish faith. On June 18, 1984, white supremacists murdered him outside his townhouse in east Denver, a crime that inspired a nationwide crackdown on members of such groups. Berg's death remains an infamous moment in Colorado's criminal history, although his legacy of promoting controversial talk radio lives on. Although KOA now touts conservatism rather than Berg's liberalism, the media's shift toward punditry owes much to firebrands like Berg.

February 24, 1863

And Arizona Makes Four

President Abraham Lincoln signed an organic act for a new polity on February 24, 1863, identified as "all that part of the present Territory of New Mexico situate[d] west of a line running due south from the point where the southwest corner of the Territory of Colorado joins the northern boundary of the Territory of New Mexico," which earned the name Arizona Territory. Within this legalese lay the most famous boundary spot in the United States—Four Corners.

The only place where four states meet, Four Corners exists as the intersection of two geometric lines—the 37th parallel of north latitude and the 32nd meridian west of Washington. The former emerged as the divide between New Mexico and Utah in 1850, and the latter appeared with Colorado's Organic Act in 1861, separating it from Utah. Two years later, when New Mexico split roughly in half to make Arizona, Colorado's western line served as the starting point for the division. None of these boundaries recognized ethnic or geographic realities but served to demarcate authority quickly and clearly—the federal government's primary concern.

Four Corners existed only in theory until surveyor Chandler Robbins marked the spot in 1875. A rough-hewn stone pillar a few feet tall designated the intersection. Surveyors replaced the broken stone in 1899, and in 1931 a team constructed a concrete slab at the site. It expanded in 1962 with the names and seals of each state and has since grown into an accessible, well-designed complex, surrounded by Ute and Navajo craftspeople selling their wares.

Family photographs of awkward poses, with a limb in each state, became a necessity on road trips. Tourists with global positioning systems grumble that the monument does not stand on the 109th west Greenwich meridian, although it is not supposed to—Washington meridians, including the one used for the north-south boundary through Four Corners, stand a few miles west of the Greenwich measurements. Although each of Colorado's key boundary points has some form of monument, none boasts the prominence, accessibility, or fame of Four Corners.

February 25, 1896 and 1907

A Big Literary Birthday

Two of Colorado's icons of literature share the same birth date, February 25—poet Thomas Hornsby Ferril, born in 1896, and playwright Mary Coyle Chase, born in 1907.

Ferril hailed from Denver, where his father curated the state historical society in the capitol's basement. He lived in his family's home at 2123 Downing Street from 1900, when they moved in, until he died eighty-eight years later. Ferril graduated from Colorado College in Colorado Springs, served in the US Army during World War I, and worked at the *Rocky Mountain News* and as a press agent for the Great Western Sugar Company. Ferril's first published poetry—aside from a verse that appeared in a Denver newspaper when he was ten years old—in 1925 won great acclaim. His work graced the statehouse walls a dozen years later, when he collaborated with Allen T. True on a series of historical murals celebrating water in the West. The closing stanza—"Beyond the sundown is Tomorrow's Wisdom / Today is going to be long long ago"—ranks as one of the most prominent phrases penned in Colorado. Governor Richard Lamm named Ferril as the state's fifth poet laureate in 1979. Ferril died in 1988 at age ninety-two.

Chase, also a Denver native, attended the University of Colorado and the University of Denver and worked at the *Rocky Mountain News* as well. She found her niche in playwriting, and her first play debuted at a Broadway theatre in New York City in 1937. As World War II raged, Chase delighted home front audiences in 1944 with her most famous work, *Harvey*, the story of a genial inebriate named Elwood P. Dowd and his invisible rabbit friend for whom the play was named. The charming work has graced countless stages in the decades since its premiere and earned Chase the Pulitzer Prize. Adaptations brought it to television and movie theaters, most famously a 1952 version starring James Stewart. As her career flourished with many more plays, Chase retained her Colorado ties, helping to establish the Denver Center for the Performing Arts. The playwright died in her hometown in 1981 at age seventy-four.

US Army members and their families gather outside the adobe officers' quarters at Fort Garland in the late nineteenth century.

Fort Garland Gets Its Due

In northern Costilla County stands a cluster of adobe buildings, preserved today as a museum for one of the state's most significant military history sites. For a quarter century, Fort Garland kept the peace among American Indians, Hispanos, and Anglos in the San Luis Valley.

As Hispano settlement moved northward onto Mexican land grants in the early 1850s, Ute factions resisted the encroachment on their territory. The US Army established Fort Massachusetts at the base of Blanca Peak in 1852, but its location proved unhealthful and too distant from transportation routes. Six years later, soldiers erected a new post a few miles away, one named for Colonel John Garland, commander of troops in New Mexico Territory who had campaigned against the Mouache Utes in the region in the mid-1850s. The new Fort Garland separated natives and newcomers in the valley. During the Civil War, its troops fought at Glorieta Pass and coordinated the search for the Espinosa vigilantes, led by scout Tom Tobin. Christopher "Kit" Carson served as Fort Garland's commander after the war ended. He hosted an inconclusive peace conference there between Ute leaders including Ouray and General William T. Sherman, territorial governor Alexander Cummings, and agent and local rancher Lafayette Head. The Utes surrendered the valley in a treaty signed in 1868, and a decade later the Denver & Rio Grande Railroad built over La Veta Pass to the post. Having evolved from a frontier outpost to just another stop on the track, Fort Garland lost its reason for being.

When the army finally abandoned Fort Garland in 1883, a newspaper observed that "its site is cold, and disease among the men frequent and fatal. It should have been deserted years ago." Its soldiers removed to Fort Lewis in La Plata County. The adobe buildings found use as homes and commercial structures until 1958, when the state historical society acquired the site and developed it into a museum, now operated by History Colorado. In recognition of Fort Garland's significance, it joined the National Register of Historic Places on February 26, 1970.

February 27, 1893

A Trial for Little Anton

Anton Woode, accused of murdering a man on his family's farm, appeared before Judge David V. Burns at the Arapahoe County Courthouse on February 27, 1893. A fascinated public followed the case, in large part because the defendant was only eleven years old.

Near Brighton on November 2, 1892, Woode shot rabbit hunter Joseph Smith to take his watch and rifle. Officers arrested the boy and his parents, whom the press derided as morally bankrupt degenerates. The trial, which included testimony about Woode's ability to comprehend his actions, resulted in a hung jury. A second jury found him guilty on March 24, 1893, and most sources expected a term of two years in the county jail, the maximum for someone his age; state law prohibited hanging someone that young. Burns shocked the state on April 5 when he sentenced Woode to twenty-five years at the penitentiary in Cañon City. A Boulder newspaper remarked, "With commutation for good behavior, he may be out long before thirty, and yet there can be little hope that a man reared in a penitentiary can ever become a serviceable member of society."

Woode ultimately served twelve years in Cañon City. In January 1900, at age eighteen, he joined three other prisoners in escaping after killing a guard, although a jury later found Woode blameless for that death. He was recaptured a few days later near Cripple Creek. Woode sounded the alarm when prisoners attempted another escape in 1903. In September 1905, state officials paroled Woode, by then age twenty-three, a decision supported by Burns and the penitentiary warden. The ex-convict moved to an artisan colony in New York, married the daughter of a New York judge, and changed his name to Charles H. Howard. Governor Jesse F. McDonald pardoned Woode in October 1907, by which time he and his wife, Mabel, lived in New York City, where they taught violin and drawing. They later moved to Wisconsin to live near his mother, and he died in Minnesota in 1950. Woode's situation encouraged reformers to adopt a juvenile court system to prevent other young offenders from joining the general prison population.

February 28, 1861

Colorado Appears on the Map

Historians credit President James Buchanan with little more than fiddling while the country burned in the descent toward civil war. Coloradans, however, owe him a great deal—after all, it was his signature on February 28, 1861 that created a place called Colorado.

The influx of Americans fueled by the gold rush of the late 1850s inspired a demand for law and order. With the mining areas divided between Kansas and Nebraska Territories and neither able to control their western reaches, residents of the Pikes Peak region fashioned their own laws. They established land claim districts for miners and farmers, operated courts, and even declared their own government known as Jefferson Territory. Since none of these actions were legal, the desire for territorial status—wherein federal officials would organize institutions with an eye toward eventual statehood—grew more intense with each passing day.

Eager to keep the lucrative region loyal to the Union as the Civil War loomed, Congress debated an Organic Act to make the mining area a territory in early 1861. Reflecting the need for alacrity and clarity, lawmakers designated four geometric boundaries—the 37th and 41st parallels of north latitude to the south and north and the 25th and 32nd meridians west of Washington to the east and west—that survive as Colorado's present bounds. Although those lines proved contentious for ethnic, economic, political, and practical reasons in the years to come, they sufficed to organize the territory as quickly as possible.

Congress exhaustively debated the new territory's name. Options included Arapahoe, Cibola, Colona, Columbus, Franklin, Lafayette, Lula, Nemara, Osage, Platte, Tahosa, Tampa, and Weappollao. Some officials advocated Idaho or

Montana, popular names for western states that eventually found homes elsewhere. But with the mighty Colorado River believed to head in the Rocky Mountains at the heart of the new territory, that name won the contest. With boundaries, a name, and Buchanan's signature on the Organic Act, Colorado came to be.

February 29, 1824

Robidoux Runs for the Border

What better day than Leap Day to take a chance? Antoine Robidoux reached for the stars when he acquired a passport to seek his fortune in Mexico on February 29, 1824.

The Santa Fe Trail, only a few years old when St. Louis resident Robidoux first traveled it, linked the United States and Mexico economically. He hoped to cash in on the fur trade but needed a new way to profit from the established industry. After his arrival in Santa Fe, Robidoux joined an expedition up the Old Spanish Trail into present-day western Colorado. There he found Utes eager to trade beaver pelts for manufactured goods. He spent four years in Santa Fe building his name and reputation. Emerging as a leading merchant, Robidoux won election to the city council, married local resident Carmel Benevides, and secured dual citizenship.

Governor Manuel Armijo, hoping to check interloping Americans by strengthening the Mexican presence, granted Robidoux a trade monopoly in 1828. Robidoux established Fort Uncompahgre near the junction of the Gunnison and Uncompahgre Rivers, where Delta stands today. Business thrived, with Utes providing pelts from the Rocky Mountains in exchange for globally produced goods shipped north from Mexico, west from the United States over the Santa Fe Trail, and east from the Pacific Ocean over the Old Spanish Trail. Robidoux opened two more trading posts in modern Utah, and he dominated the region into the 1840s.

As fashions changed from beaver hats to silk, however, Robidoux's profits declined. Utes resented this change, as well as settlers pushing north from New Mexico. In 1844 they blocked the Old Spanish Trail, raided the trading posts, and killed Mexican employees. As quickly as it had emerged, Robidoux's commercial empire disappeared. Two years later he helped the US Army conquer New Mexico and California during the Mexican-American War and retired to St. Joseph, Missouri, where he died in 1860. Volunteers erected a reconstruction of Fort Uncompahgre at Delta in 1990, a memorial to the fur trade kingpin of western Colorado.

March

Tabor Ties the Knot (Again)

A ceremony in Washington, DC, on March 1, 1883, attended by the rich and powerful—including President Chester A. Arthur—united in matrimony Colorado's newest senator, Horace A.W. Tabor, and his second wife, the vivacious Elizabeth "Baby Doe" McCourt. The event and his recently acquired position of influence reflected Tabor's unpredictable, ostentatious life.

Born in Vermont in 1830, Tabor moved to Kansas Territory in 1855. He married fellow New Englander Augusta Pierce, and they joined the Pikes Peak gold rush in 1859. Wandering from one strike to another, the Tabors tarried at Oro City on the Arkansas River headwaters but settled in the more stable South Park community of Buckskin Joe. The Tabors returned to Oro City in 1868 and dominated the mercantile business in that tiny town. Silver strikes nearby led to Leadville's founding in 1877, and the Tabors emerged as leading citizens of the boomtown.

In the spring of 1878, Tabor grubstaked prospectors who discovered the Little Pittsburg vein, making its co-owner a millionaire. An overnight sensation, the Republican Tabor won election to the lieutenant governor's office in 1878 and 1880. Along with partners Jerome B. Chaffee and David H. Moffat, he dabbled in mining, real estate, and other ventures—erecting buildings in Leadville, Denver, and elsewhere. His extravagance spilled over into his personal life when he divorced Augusta in 1882 and took up with the younger, gayer, beautiful McCourt.

That year, Arthur nominated Colorado's senator Henry M. Teller to serve as interior secretary, and a sordid struggle erupted to determine Teller's successor. The General Assembly, in a graft-fueled farce, split the office—Tabor would hold it for a month, and Thomas M. Bowen of Del Norte would serve the rest of the term. After Tabor's brief tenure and fancy nuptials, Teller declared: "Tabor has gone home. I thank God he was not elected for six years; thirty days nearly killed us." The flush times ended for Tabor with the Panic of 1893, and he died penniless in Denver six years later. In 1935, neighbors found "Baby Doe" frozen to death in the Matchless Mine, their last remaining Leadville property, a sorrowful end to the Tabors' salacious tale.

Colorado's Midnight Reserves

President Theodore Roosevelt never liked to be told what he could or could not do. His "wisest use" policy of managing natural resources angered western politicians, who wanted to harvest timber, minerals, and water as they saw fit. They especially resented his use of the 1891 Forest Reserve Act, which allowed presidents to designate national forests unilaterally. To prevent further regulation, Congress repealed the act in early 1907. On March 2, only days before the president signed the bill and lost the right to set aside forests unilaterally, he announced the protection of 16 million acres in addition to the approximately 60 million acres of preexisting timber reservations. Upon discovering TR's unexpected, last-minute victory—known as the "midnight reserves"—his political opponents fumed but could do little to retaliate.

Roosevelt wanted to use "natural resources of the country for the benefit of the present generation, also to use them in such manner as to keep them unimpaired for the benefit of the children now growing up to inherit the land." He sought to slow the loss of American forests to avaricious lumber and paper companies. Through the midnight reserves, Roosevelt added an additional 3 million acres to Colorado's existing 12.7 million forest acres, nearly a quarter of its total land. The local press generally opposed his move. The *Rocky Mountain News* wailed that "one-fourth of the state is withdrawn from local control and turned over to the fostering care of a Washington bureaucracy." A Montezuma County newspaper quipped that "soon we will have no place to bury folks except on the forest reserve . . . On the reserve please bury me not, for I never would be free; for the forest ranger would dig me up in order to collect his fee."

National forests boast a better reputation today, as places of regulated timber and year-round recreation. In Colorado, the United States Forest Service manages over 14.5 million acres in eleven forests and two grasslands, down slightly from the 1907 total after various land trades and sales. One of those tracts earned the name Roosevelt National Forest in TR's honor in 1932.

Minoru Yasui Day

Governor Richard Lamm and Denver mayor Federico Peña issued joint proclamations declaring March 3, 1984, as "Minoru Yasui Day," in commemoration of a Denver lawyer whose life and career emphasized the protection and promotion of human rights.

March

Born in Oregon to Japanese immigrant parents in 1916, Yasui earned a law degree from the University of Oregon in 1939 but struggled to find employment because of his ethnicity. He opened a law office in Portland after the Pearl Harbor attack two years later, intent on helping Japanese Americans protect themselves against racism. Yasui and others faced internment in a local livestock pen and eventually an Idaho concentration camp. He resisted by defying curfew. Although a judge dismissed that charge, he ruled that Yasui had forfeited his American birthright citizenship by working for the Japanese consulate before Pearl Harbor. After his release from the Idaho camp, he moved to Denver and refreshed his legal knowledge at the University of Denver. Admitted to the Colorado bar in 1946, Yasui lobbied on behalf of civil rights for Japanese Americans, Latinos, handicapped persons, the poor, and many other groups. He fought for years for many disadvantaged people, seeking protections that had been denied to him.

Through the efforts of Yasui and others, in the 1980s the federal government apologized for its illegal, immoral internment of Japanese American citizens during World War II. He received numerous honors over the years, including the plaudits of Colorado and Denver leaders authorized by Lamm and Peña in 1984. Yasui died in Denver two years later, and his remains were returned to his native Oregon for burial. Statues of Yasui stand in Sakura Square, the heart of Denver's Japanese American community, and in a city government office building named for him across Colfax Avenue from Civic Center. In honor of Yasui's life of hard-earned dignity, President Barack Obama issued him a posthumous Presidential Medal of Freedom in 2015.

March 4, 1847

Casimiro Barela's Birthday

The Barela family sought refuge in the village of Embudo in northern New Mexico to escape the violence of an anti-American rebellion sweeping the region after the US Army's invasion in the summer of 1846. A new child, Casimiro, arrived in the family on March 4, 1847. By the century's end, he ranked as the most prominent, powerful Hispano in Colorado.

Barela studied for the priesthood until the early 1860s, when he developed a flair for business. At age twenty he moved to Trinidad, below Raton Pass on the Santa Fe Trail in Colorado Territory. Casimiro and his wife, Josefa, raised nine children before her death in 1883. He remarried the following year and with his second wife, Damiana, adopted nine more children. Barela emerged as a powerful figure, operating newspapers and businesses in Trinidad and El Moro. He

Casimiro Barela, entrepreneur and politician during Colorado's territorial and early statehood days, in his private office in Barela in the early twentieth century

invested in railroad and land companies, eventually owning properties as far away as Mexico and Brazil, all managed from a ranch east of Trinidad that developed into a town called Barela. Elected assessor, sheriff, and treasurer of Las Animas County, Barela also won a seat in the territorial legislature. During the 1872 session he lobbied for printing laws in Spanish to benefit southern territorial residents. As a member of Colorado's constitutional convention four years later, Barela worked to protect minority rights in the state's foundational document.

Las Animas County voters elected Barela to the Colorado Senate in 1876, in which he served for almost four decades, earning the nickname the "Perpetual Senator." Barela promoted issues including bilingual public education, statehood for New Mexico and Arizona, and enforcement of Mexican land grants. He also served as the Denver-based consul for the governments of Mexico and Costa Rica. Barela switched from the Democratic to the Republican Party in 1904 and continued winning elections until 1914. He died six years later, two decades after state officials had placed a stained glass portrait of him in the capitol. Its visage gazed down upon its honoree for a decade and a half as Barela toiled in the state-house on behalf of all Coloradans.

March 5, 1935

Colorado Claims the Cheeseburger

Ask any miner—if you are going to strike it rich, you have to stake your claim. Louis Ballast owned the Humpty-Dumpty Barrel Drive-In in northwest Denver, one of the state's first businesses that catered to motorists. On March 5, 1935, Ballast pursued his claim by filing paperwork to trademark a sandwich he purportedly invented at his restaurant: the cheeseburger.

The Humpty-Dumpty stood on Speer Boulevard a few blocks east of North High School and enjoyed a brisk business from students and adults alike. To liven up the hamburgers, Ballast experimented with various toppings including peanut butter and chocolate bars, to no avail. But he struck gold with cheese, an addition other restauranteurs around the country had already employed. Eager to secure rights to the innovation, Ballast filed to trademark it but never finished the process, and the cheeseburger entered the public domain. Louis met his wife, Dorothy, at Elitch Gardens the following year. They married in 1937, and their five children operated the Humpty-Dumpty for decades. In addition to burgers, they introduced deep-fried chicken sandwiches to Denverites. Louis died in 1975 and Dorothy passed away in 2011. Their son David, reflecting on the failed trademark, quipped, "That's why I'm not a millionaire."

Other Colorado ideas include the "Denver boot" that immobilizes automobiles; Crocs, the plastic shoes reviled by fashionistas but praised for their comfort; aluminum cans, introduced by the Coors Brewing Company; restaurant chains Chipotle, Quiznos, and Smashburger; candy companies including Hammond's and Jolly Rancher; and the root beer float, shredded wheat, and Celestial Seasonings tea. Entrepreneur "Papa" Jack A. Weil, inventor of the snap shirt and bolo tie, dressed generations of westerners from Denver's Rockmount Ranch Wear before his death in 2008 at age 107. Although Ballast's efforts on behalf of the cheeseburger fell short of legal recognition, a small granite marker placed in 1987 where the Humpty-Dumpty once stood reminds passers-by of the culinary concoction he cooked up on that spot long ago.

A Banquet for Clara Brown

Frances W. Jacobs and other prominent women hosted a banquet at Denver's city hall on Larimer Street on March 6, 1884, to support one of their own. As the *Rocky Mountain News* reported, "The object of the entertainment was to raise a fund for the relief of Aunt Clara Brown, the old colored lady who played so important a part in the early settlement of the country."

Few details of Brown's early, enslaved life—including her birth date or location and her husband's name—are known today. While she was in Kentucky in 1835, her owner died, and the estate sold Brown, her husband, and three surviving children—none of whom expected to see the others again, the fate of many slaves. In 1856, upon the death of her second owner whose surname she took, Brown purchased her freedom and left Kentucky. She found work as a laundress in Missouri and in 1859 joined a party of miners bound for the Pikes Peak country. After a brief sojourn in Denver, Brown traveled to Central City, at the heart of the first lode gold boom in what is now Colorado, where she found modest prosperity washing clothes for the otherwise-occupied miners. Brown parleyed her earnings into real estate, renting several cabins in town. She also proved active in organizing Protestant churches in present-day Gilpin County.

Brown dreamed of finding her children after the Civil War end, and while searching for traces of them, she encouraged freed African Americans to come to Colorado Territory looking for a fresh start. In 1882 Brown located one of her daughters, Eliza Jane, living in Council Bluffs, Iowa. With financial help from her neighbors, Brown affected a tearful reunion. By then she lived in a small cottage in Denver loaned to her for life, as her search and generosity alike had left Brown destitute. The fundraising banquet in 1884 demonstrated the affection many Coloradans felt for a woman whose quest they had long followed. Brown died in Denver in October 1885, and a stained glass window bearing her portrait stands in the state capitol.

Englewood Tries on Its Glass Slipper

Thousands of shoppers came to Englewood on March 7, 1968, to dedicate Cinderella City, the largest shopping mall in the western United States. The temple of commerce reflected the country's mid-twentieth-century suburbanization and Denver's seemingly incessant sprawl.

After World War II, automobile ownership emerged as a vital part of American identity, and the landscape transformed around it. Multilane, controlled-access highways obliterated old neighborhoods and replaced mass transit systems like Denver's streetcars. Drive-in theatres, fast food restaurants, houses with attached garages, and more reflected an architectural transition dependent on the car. Shopping malls supplanted downtown commerce, and Denver's once bustling Sixteenth Street department stores grew shabby and neglected. Fast-growing suburbs swallowed up decades-old farms and ranches around the capital city, and their residents turned increasingly to all-in-one destinations to spend the money burning holes in their pockets.

Architect Temple H. Buell pioneered the shopping mall in Colorado. A prolific designer with statewide commissions, Buell designed the Cherry Creek Shopping Center, Colorado's first commercial destination with stores that faced inward and were surrounded by parking lots. It opened in 1950 and spawned many look-alikes, some of which served as the hubs of new communities like Northglenn and Southglenn. Yet none compared to Cinderella City. Embracing 1.6 million square feet with more than 200 storefronts on three floors, the complex centered on the grand Blue Room and its towering fountain. Architect Gerri von Frellick—responsible for Lakewood's Villa Italia as well—joined Governor John A. Love to dedicate the shopping center in 1968.

Changing tastes by the century's end led to the demolition of many malls, often replaced by a mix of indoor and outdoor retail venues. Both Cinderella City and Villa Italia evolved into hubs for their core-less suburbs. Bypassing congested highways, light rail trains now link Englewood's hub to downtown Denver, yet another reminder that everything old is new again.

March 8, 1897

Lafayette Head Dies

Lafayette Head, a rancher from the San Luis Valley who died in Denver on March 8, 1897, boasted one of the most colorful careers of any nineteenth-century Coloradan.

Mystery shrouds much of Head's life, including his birthplace, placed by some sources in Ohio and others in Missouri. In his early twenties, Head joined the American invasion up the Santa Fe Trail to New Mexico in 1846. He immersed himself in Hispano culture, learning Spanish and marrying into a prominent family, steps toward cooperation few other Americans cared to make. For his flexibility, Head emerged as an influential figure in business and government. He settled north of Santa Fe and held positions as a US marshal, sheriff, and other county jobs. Head won election to New Mexico's territorial legislature in 1853 and the following year joined a group of settlers on the upper Rio Grande. They established several communities on the Conejos Grant, designated by Mexican officials in 1842. Head helped organize one on the Conejos River, in the modern Colorado county of the same name, which he also served in the New Mexican assembly. In 1855 he joined Ceran St. Vrain's campaign against Utes resisting the encroaching Hispanos.

With the help of his friend Christopher "Kit" Carson, Head won appointment as an agent for Apaches and Utes in the San Luis Valley in 1859, two years before Colorado Territory claimed his homesite. He hosted Governor John Evans at a peace conference in 1863 and made two trips to Washington, DC, with Ute delegations. Head joined three Hispano politicians, including the influential Casimiro Barela, as southern delegates to Colorado's constitutional convention in 1876. That year, he won election as a Republican as the state's first lieutenant governor, leading one newspaper to declare that "by an upright and industrious life [he] has won the esteem and friendship of all who know him." After a single term, Head retired to Conejos. His remarkable career came to an end during a visit with family in Denver in 1897.

March 9, 2002

The First Frozen Dead Guy Days

Colorado boasts more than its fair share of the bizarre, but little compares to an annual festival in Nederland, high in the mountains of Boulder County, known as Frozen Dead Guy Days. The morbid, tongue-in-cheek event took place for the first time on March 9, 2002.

In 1989, a Norwegian civil servant named Bredo Morstøl died of heart disease at age eighty-nine, and his family sent his body to a cryogenic company in California to freeze him in hopes that he might be revived and cured in the future. Morstøl's grandson, Trygve Bauge, lived in Boulder and earned a rebellious, eccentric reputation. He helped inaugurate the annual Polar Bear Plunge of jumping into the frigid water of Boulder Reservoir on New Year's Day in 1982. Bauge brought his grandfather's body to Nederland in 1993, but federal immigration officials deported Bauge back to Norway the next year, his visa long since expired. Soon after, his mother (and Morstøl's daughter), Aud, was evicted from an unorthodox house they were building near Nederland. The city thus found itself in unexpected possession of Morstøl's frozen remains.

The controversy transformed into a celebration in 2002, when the community inaugurated a unique winter event inspired by its most famous, frigid resident. Activities included tours of Morstøl's shed, cardboard coffin races, a dance, Morstøl look-alike contests, and an icy dip into a pond akin to the Polar Bear Plunge. The town's newspaper exhausted its supply of puns, observing that "the competition should be stiff. Lots of folks have been dying to try their hand at racing a coffin down Nederland's streets." It told readers of numerous calls "from the curious about how they too can chill out in Nederland" and stated that the event "should ice our proper place in history." A local baker, according to the paper, scoffed at the rigmarole: "I don't understand all the fuss about Norwegians on ice when I have a dozen Danish baking in my oven."

Frozen Dead Guy Days, voted one of the top cultural festivals in the country, has grown into a phenomenon. If only Morstøl had any clue of the fuss outside his chilly tomb.

March 10, 1884

Looping the Loop across Devil's Gate

Crews for the Colorado Central Railroad (CC) laid tracks into the mining town of Silver Plume, in Clear Creek County, on March 10, 1884. Their work completed an engineering marvel known as the Georgetown Loop, a quixotic attempt to cross the Continental Divide.

In the 1870s, William A.H. Loveland's CC attempted what several other lines had tried and failed—to reach the Pacific Ocean watershed by rail. The line proceeded up Clear Creek from its home base in Golden but ran short of funds because of the Panic of 1873. The Union Pacific Railroad (UP) bought and operated Loveland's company as a subsidiary, and it continued westward by the decade's end. The CC reached Idaho Springs and Georgetown by 1877, but to continue to Silver Plume—just over 2 miles upstream—the line needed to climb 638 feet in a canyon too narrow for switchbacks and too steep to approach directly. UP engineer Robert Blickensderfer offered a solution—a looping track that would spiral trains the needed elevation between Georgetown and Silver Plume. Two hundred laborers worked for three years on the track, small bridges, and a spidery iron span over Devil's Gate, completed in early 1884.

The sensational Georgetown Loop became a popular excursion trip. It never achieved the goal of crossing Loveland Pass, named for the CC's founder, however, and the line dead-ended 4 miles above Silver Plume. Operated by several firms, including four decades as part of the Colorado & Southern Railway (C&S), tour-

Painting of three trains—one on the High Bridge, one under it along Clear Creek, and one in the distance—on the Georgetown Loop by William Henry Jackson in 1896

ists gradually lost interest as automobile jaunts grew more popular. Passenger and freight traffic dwindled during the Great Depression, and in 1939 the C&S closed the line, dismantled the track and the Devil's Gate Bridge, and scrapped them.

The loop's centennial inspired its restoration, and in 1984 the reconstructed track and Devil's Gate Bridge opened. Now owned by History Colorado, it celebrates Colorado's rich railroad history. Interstate 70, which parallels the line, pierced the Continental Divide in the 1970s with the Eisenhower-Johnson Tunnel, a century after Loveland's failed attempt.

March 11, 1945

Japan Balloon-Bombs Western Colorado

The federal government poured money into Colorado during World War II, establishing military bases and munitions plants. It considered the state protected against invasion and therefore a safe place to locate valuable war-related institutions. Nonetheless, Colorado came under attack on March 11, 1945, when a Japanese balloon bomb crashed on the western slope.

As the Allies encircled Japan's home islands in late 1944, the military dictatorship grew desperate. They had experimented with explosives attached to balloons a decade earlier and returned to the concept in an attempt to spread panic in the United States. Sending aerial bombs into the jet stream and across the Pacific Ocean might set forest fires or damage infrastructure, but its real value lay in the potential to terrify Japan's enemy. More than 9,000 balloons made of paper, filled with hydrogen, and equipped with various explosive devices launched from Japan between November 1944 and April 1945. It took them fifty to sixty hours to reach North America. United States authorities accounted for 285 bombs in nineteen states (as far east as Michigan), Canada, and Mexico, as well as wreckage in the ocean. Agreements with and occasional intimidation of the press kept news of the bombs away from the public until the deaths of six people in Oregon.

The federal government confirmed three bomb-related sites in Colorado in 1945. The first, located on March 11, was discovered near Delta along the Delta-Montrose County line. Not realizing its threat, hikers collected shards of the unexploded bomb and handed them over to law enforcement. Eight days later, an explosion on the Swets farm near Timnath, in Larimer County, made a crater 4 feet deep. A bomb from the balloon detonated underground, and the vacuum it created consumed the family's tractor. Parts of a third balloon were found near Collbran in Mesa County that June. Additional fragments undoubtedly lie hidden across the state. The balloon bomb campaign failed to incite fear, primarily because of government censorship, but it reminded seemingly isolated Coloradans that they were not immune to danger.

March 12, 1895

Walsenburg's Italian Massacre

A party of masked men stopped a wagon southwest of Walsenburg, in Huerfano County, on the evening of March 12, 1895. Inside the wagon rode a party of Italian immigrants, accused of fatally beating a saloon owner in the nearby mining town of Rouse two days earlier. Rather than wait for the courts, the disguised group decided to mete out their own brand of justice.

Immigration from southern and eastern Europe increased dramatically at the end of the nineteenth century, and Italians and others found opportunities in Colorado's coal mines. Established residents of Colorado resented the ethnic competition, and the barkeep's beating death offered a chance for retribution. Returning from a coroner's inquest at Rouse, the wagon halted when several armed men blocked its crossing of a bridge. Rifle shots rang out from nearby bushes. One of the accused, Stanislao Vittone, and wagon driver Joe Welby fell dead, while another Italian was wounded and two others escaped. The wounded man, Francesco Ronchietto, was taken back to Walsenburg, where he and another prisoner, Lorenzo Andinino, were murdered later that same night when a mob broke into the jail.

The lynchings incited international tension when the Italian government demanded an investigation. Ethnic animosity was reflected in newspaper coverage, as when a Leadville press informed readers that Governor Albert McIntire was "inquiring into the status of the dead dagos." McIntire insisted, wrongly, that the men were American citizens and dismissed Italy's interference. Over the objections of prominent Walsenburg residents, a grand jury met in Huerfano County eleven months later. It conducted a brief, halfhearted investigation. Ignoring testimony from another occupant of the jail and one of the escapees, the jury concluded that it could not discover the vigilantes' identities. To restore goodwill with Italy, the federal government paid $10,000 to the families of the dead. Italians continued to come to the coal fields, but suspicion remained high between newcomers and established Coloradans.

March 13, 1997

Commemorating a Fossil Find

The South Platte River emerges from the Rocky Mountains and flows northeastward, as it has since time immemorial. Thousands of years ago, a natural spring near that outlet drew diverse creatures and those who hunted them, including both animal and human predators. Located in modern Douglas County and known today as the Lamb Spring Archaeological Preserve, the site protects some of the oldest evidence of the human presence in Colorado.

Rancher Charles Lamb sought to turn the spring into a pond in 1960 and started excavating the sodden ground. He turned up massive bones and called geologists to investigate. They found fossils belonging to prehistoric *megafauna*, massive mammals living in the Western Hemisphere at the time the earliest human cultures spread through the Americas, including specimens of mammoths, bison, camels, and horses. Digs in subsequent years turned up more evidence of mammoths that died at the watering hole, including work organized by the Smithsonian Institution in the early 1980s. Those digs found the remains of thirty mammoths and evidence of butchering tools that suggested they had died at the hands of human hunters around 12,000 BC, pushing the date for the human presence in Colorado and much of the region back much farther than previously assumed. A nearby site, discovered in 2010, offered more mammoth remains, exposed by prairie dogs kicking flecks of ivory out of their burrows.

Development threatened Lamb Spring in the 1990s, until a nonprofit group purchased 35 acres to prevent it from succumbing to Denver's suburbanization. On March 13, 1997, the site joined the ranks of other important locales in the United States with a listing in the National Register of Historic Places. Archaeologists consider Lamb Springs one of the most important in the nation for studying ancient humans in the Americas. It ranks with essential sites in the state like Lindenmeier in Larimer County and Tenderfoot and Curecanti in Gunnison County, among many others that offer tantalizing details about the earliest Coloradans.

March 14, 1915

A Farming Refuge on the Western Slope

In the wake of the Panic of 1893, many Coloradans turned to agriculture in the hope that it might prove a more stable economic foundation than mining. A group of unemployed Denver residents founded the Colorado Cooperative Company to establish a farming colony in western Colorado. For $100, scrounged from whatever sources they could find, subscribers joined a communal effort planned for the San Miguel River valley in Montrose County.

The first settlers crossed the Continental Divide in 1894 and scouted about 20,000 acres of farmland. With the aid of a local rancher they started construction on an irrigation system the following year, although disputes between colonists and the company's headquarters in Denver slowed progress. Nonetheless, by 1896 the residents constructed a town named Pinon along the San Miguel River. The small but successful colony flourished from agriculture and timber, making boxes for fruit farmers in western Colorado to ship their produce across the country. At times they traded wood for food and supplies in Montrose. By the early twentieth century, Pinon boasted a library, school, dining hall, and stores. It operated as a cooperative, eschewing private land claims and sharing profits from the farm and lumber industries equally.

Colonists finally finished the canal in 1904, and Pinon dwellers moved to more appealing irrigated land about 10 miles to the west. Their new town site stood on a rocky ledge above the river, as they could not waste arable land on such an unproductive use. Fruit and vegetable farms flourished, as did cattle and sheep herds. Residents named the new town Nucla, expecting it to serve as the nucleus of communal societies across the West. Although they gradually abandoned communalism for private ownership, the town prospered. When Nucla filed with state officials to incorporate on March 14, 1915, it reflected the triumph of early settlers, desperate to escape economic ruin in Denver, who found their salvation in Montrose County.

March 15, 1877

The State Seals the Deal

Colorado's first state legislature met in Denver in the spring of 1877, affirming decisions made during territorial days and creating new laws appropriate for a full-fledged member of the Union. The General Assembly and Governor John L. Routt hammered out legislation on myriad issues, some fundamental and some symbolic. Among the latter, no statute trumped the one signed by Routt on March 15, designating an emblem known as the state seal.

The icon debuted in 1861 as the territorial seal, designed by Governor William Gilpin and Secretary Lewis L. Weld, whose namesake counties remain on Colorado's map. It included a shield with mining tools and a mountain scene, a fasces from Roman iconography, the all-seeing eye of God, and a Latin motto, "Nil Sine Numine," meaning "Nothing without Providence." The 1877 act added the words "State of Colorado" and the year of admission to the Union. Until the early twentieth century, the state flag consisted of the seal on a blue field. The secretary of state once affixed the image to all signed legislation, and it appears in the state capitol from embossed doorknobs to a woven one hanging in the governor's reception room.

Colorado's roster of symbols and emblems includes the flower (Rocky Mountain columbine, adopted 1899), flag (1911), songs ("Where the Columbines Grow" and "Rocky Mountain High," 1915 and 2007, respectively), bird (lark bunting, 1931), tree (blue spruce, 1939), animal (Rocky Mountain bighorn sheep, 1961), gemstone (aquamarine, 1971), fossil (stegosaurus, 1982), grass (blue grama, 1987), folk dance (square dance, 1992), fish (greenback cutthroat trout, 1994), insect (Colorado hairstreak butterfly, 1996), tartan (1997), mineral (rhodochrosite, 2002), rock (Yule Creek marble, 2004), reptile (western painted turtle, 2007), winter sports (skiing and snowboarding, 2008), summer heritage sport (pack burro racing, 2012), amphibian (western tiger salamander, 2012), pets (rescue dogs and cats, 2013), and cactus (claret cup cactus, 2014).

Fighting for the Governor's Office

The election of 1904, in which corruption of unprecedented proportions saturated the state, led to the most embarrassing farce in Colorado's political history. On March 16, 1905, partisanship and personalities collided to place three men in the governor's office in twenty-four hours.

In the early twentieth century, both the Republican and Democratic Parties won elections through chicanery, considering themselves above statutory or moral law. Democrats ruled over Denver through an alliance between the public utility companies and Mayor Robert Speer, while Republicans used corporate partners—such as the Colorado Fuel & Iron Company in Huerfano and Las Animas Counties—to bully workers to either support them or lose their jobs. The incumbent Republican governor, James H. Peabody, used the Colorado National Guard to protect corporate interests after his election in 1902. Two years later, Peabody faced Democratic former governor Alva Adams. Both parties stopped at nothing to gain an advantage, from stuffing boxes with fraudulent ballots to bribing or intimidating officials. Of the roughly 236,000 ballots counted, Adams won about 10,000 more than Peabody, enabling his return as chief executive.

Controversy dogged the 1904 contest. Republicans dominated the state supreme court and manipulated their way to majorities in the General Assembly. Democrats sought to strike a compromise, but soon after Adams's inauguration the other branches of government turned against him. A legislative investigation returned three reports—one favoring Peabody, another preferring Adams, and a last railing against the "brazen, shameless, and far-reaching frauds" that obscured a justifiable winner. The scale of corruption demanded a speedy resolution. On March 16, the General Assembly ousted Adams and declared Peabody governor, on the condition that he serve only one day and do no official business. The following day Peabody resigned, and Lieutenant Governor Jesse F. McDonald took over for the rest of the term, until January 1907. All three governors' political careers ended in the chaos of March 1905. In the wake of such nonsense, Coloradans found the motivation to force political reforms by the decade's end.

Nicholas Williams and his grandfather, Robert Kenney, return from a sand-sledding adventure on the Great Sand Dunes in 2007.

Setting Aside the Great Sand Dunes

In January 1807, as his expedition approached the point of mutiny, Lieutenant Zebulon M. Pike led his men through the San Luis Valley and scaled a towering sand dune to scout the Rio Grande. Pike described the landscape of dunes on which he perched: "Their appearance was exactly that of the sea in a storm, (except as to color) not the least sign of vegetation existing thereon."

Erosion and wind pushed earth from the valley floor against the mountains, and the dunes piled up over the eons, obscuring water sources flowing down from the Sangre de Cristos. The dunes witnessed a parade of humanity, as Hispanos and Anglos intruded into the valley long traversed by American Indian cultures. Nineteenth-century settlement threatened the picturesque region, as firms sought to extract gold from the sand or use it to manufacture concrete. Residents of Alamosa and Saguache Counties, whose boundary passes through the site, sought to protect a treasured part of their own backyard and a potential tourist attraction. They received state support in the spring of 1931, when the

General Assembly memorialized Congress "to set apart and dedicate all of the territory now occupied by The Sand Dunes . . . as a National Park, monument, or playground, in order that this monument of unsurpassed scenic attraction may be preserved for the future enjoyment of the people of this State and the people of the Nation."

President Herbert Hoover signed a bill to designate Great Sand Dunes National Monument on March 17, 1932. In 2000, President Bill Clinton promoted the site when he signed a bill authorizing the Great Sand Dunes National Park and Preserve. The park's core of more than 44,000 acres, dominated by the dunes, now boasts nearly as much land surrounding it—particularly in the Sangres—as a preserve. An additional 97,000 acres to the north, a former Mexican land grant known as the Baca Ranch, was purchased by the Nature Conservancy in 2002. The efforts of many groups to preserve the Great Sand Dunes reflect the dramatic contrast they provide, nestled between a fertile valley and imposing mountains.

March 18, 1998

Honoring the Most Honorable

Four men who grew up in Pueblo returned there on March 18, 1998, to receive the congratulations and cheers of their hometown. No ordinary folk, each member of the quartet had received the nation's highest military commendation: the Medal of Honor. William Crawford, then living in El Paso County, earned it during World War II. Carl Sitter and Jerry Murphy, residents of Virginia and New Mexico, respectively, received theirs during the Korean War. Drew Dix, who divided his time between homes in Pueblo and Alaska, earned his in the Vietnam War. President Dwight D. Eisenhower, upon awarding Murphy in 1953, quipped: "What is it . . . something in the water out there in Pueblo? All you guys turn out to be heroes!"

In 1993, Congressman Scott McInnis, a Glenwood Springs Republican, told the US House of Representatives that Pueblo then held the distinction of claiming more living Medal of Honor recipients than any other American town. Puebloans had recognized this fact over the years by naming a park after Dix and streets after the other three honorees. McInnis's remarks inspired city residents to nickname their community "the Home of Heroes." About 200 people braved a spring snowstorm to attend the 1998 ceremony at the Pueblo Convention Center. Reproduction uniforms and medals for each honoree, accompanied by audio biographies, graced display cases in the lobby. The four recipients were rendered speechless as they viewed the exhibit and expressed heartfelt gratitude at their hometown's affection.

Puebloans expanded the tribute in 2000 to include bronze statues of the men standing on granite bases describing their battlefield heroics. The memorial—created by Colorado artists David Dirrim and William Yates—included the statues in an arc around a flagpole rising from a pool of water, a reference to Eisenhower's off-the-cuff remark. Stone plaques bearing the name of all Medal of Honor recipients stand nearby. Pueblo's tribute to its hometown heroes reflects the pride Coloradans and Americans in general have in their armed forces.

March 19, 1855

A Scuffle in Saguache County

Residents of southeastern Colorado faced slaughter from a renegade faction of Mouache Utes led by Tierra Blanca in late 1854. On Christmas Eve, his band attacked El Pueblo on the Arkansas River and killed any outsiders they could find well into the next year. On March 19, 1855, the US Army and volunteers from New Mexico struck back near present-day Saguache.

Ute resentment escalated in the mid-1840s as the fur trade declined and their access to trade goods weakened. Hispano settlement in the San Luis Valley caused further aggravation. Tierra Blanca embodied the Utes' anger more strongly than anyone, and his assault on El Pueblo terrified the region. Colonel John Garland, responsible for keeping the peace in what is today New Mexico and Colorado, organized a party "to carry the war into the Utah country and force upon them the necessity of looking after their own security and that of their women and children" in early 1855. Five companies of American and Hispano volunteers, led by merchant Ceran St. Vrain, joined the soldiers on a campaign led by Colonel Thomas T. Fauntleroy. Christopher "Kit" Carson joined as a scout, and Fort Massachusetts—founded three years earlier in present-day Costilla County—served as the military's base of operations.

An advance party stumbled upon Tierra Blanca's band near what is now Saguache on March 19, and a battle ensued. An American physician there complained, "My horse seemed determined to bring me into uncomfortably close quarters with a young warrior, who constantly turned and saluted me with his arrows." The Ute attack ended when reinforcements bolstered their opponents, and Tierra Blanca's party dispersed. In April, St. Vrain led parties east of the Sangre de Cristo Mountains while Fauntleroy scoured the upper Arkansas River. Battles in modern Chaffee and Saguache Counties sapped Tierra Blanca's strength, and he sued for peace that summer. New Mexico's governor, David Meriwether, reported to federal authorities: "I can now have the pleasure of informing you that peace has once more been restored to this territory."

March 20, 1914

Striking a Blow against Segregation

A newspaper in the San Luis Valley town of Alamosa informed its readers of a court decision on March 20, 1914, ending a debate that had roiled the community. Judge Charles C. Holbrook, presiding over a state district court in Alamosa County, had issued one of the country's first rulings against public school segregation, in this case affecting Hispano children.

Colorado's constitution forbade racial discrimination in education, but that did not stop the Alamosa school board from filtering out students with Spanish-sounding last names. A Spanish-language school opened in the town in 1909, in which ten-year-old Miguel Maestas was enrolled four years later. His father, Francisco, resented the segregation of his son, who spoke English fluently and could perform perfectly well in the town's Anglo school. The Maestas and several other local Hispano families joined with Latino immigrants to the community, pulled their children out of the segregated school in protest, and sued the Alamosa school district for violating the state constitution. Although intimidated by the proceedings, Miguel Maestas testified; he surprised onlookers by answering questions in English before a translator provided by the court could finish phrasing them in Spanish. In the spring of 1914, Holbrook ruled that racially motivated Alamosa officials had acted illegally. Rejecting the town's separate schools, he declared that "the only way to destroy this feeling of discontent and bitterness which has recently grown up, is to allow all children so prepared, to attend the school nearest them."

Holbrook's decision proved a hollow victory. Although often viewed as the problem of southern states, segregation pervaded the United States in the twentieth century, as established Americans singled out whatever ethnic group they most suspected or resented. In Colorado, many communities segregated people of Spanish descent at schools, movie theaters, swimming pools, and other public facilities. Ethnic divisions, including those defined by law and those unspoken alike, pervaded and polluted many Colorado towns, and their bitter legacies linger.

Colorado's First Shot at Statehood

President Abraham Lincoln signed an enabling act on March 21, 1864, to permit residents of Colorado Territory to write a state constitution and apply for membership in the Union. His action reflected Lincoln's desire to emphasize the country's future even as the Civil War raged. It also reflected the partisan nature of statehood—as a Republican-dominated territory, Lincoln hoped Colorado might offer him much-needed electoral votes to hold the presidency that year.

Congress approved enabling acts for Colorado, Nebraska, and Nevada Territories in 1864. Nebraskans ultimately passed on the chance, while Nevadans won their promotion. Colorado voters rejected a proposed constitution when Republican support divided. Small-towners like Henry M. Teller and William A.H. Loveland resented Denver's domination through figures including John Evans, John M. Chivington, and Jerome B. Chaffee. Another constitution in 1865 won voter approval overall but not from Democratic-leaning Hispano areas—95 percent of the Costilla County electorate opposed it, while only 1 of 466 voters in Conejos County backed the document. A proposal to ban African Americans from voting passed overwhelmingly in the same election, however. Disputes over the 1865 constitution's legitimacy and concerns about Colorado's maturity after the Sand Creek Massacre led to its rejection by Congress.

President Andrew Johnson vetoed enabling acts passed in 1866 and 1867, claiming that Colorado lacked a sufficiently large and enthusiastic population for statehood. In the meantime, feuds between local residents and territorial officials—appointed by the federal government but often lacking in tact or capability—soured many Coloradans to politics. Partisanship surrounded another enabling act approved in 1875, but that time the conflict remained a Washington, DC, issue. A relatively tame convention met in Denver the following spring to draw up a constitution, approved by voters on July 1, 1876. A month later, a dozen years after the abortive first attempt, President Ulysses S. Grant approved adding Colorado's star to the national banner.

A Ship for a Landlocked State

Ruth N. Melville, daughter of US senator Samuel D. Nicholson, smashed a bottle of mineral water from Manitou Springs in El Paso County on the US Navy's newest battleship, the USS *Colorado*, at a New Jersey shipyard on March 22, 1921. The

March

christening brought the Centennial State, perched far above the high seas, a bit closer to the brine.

The vessel launched into the Delaware River in 1921 bore the same name as two previous navy ships. In 1856, the first *Colorado* launched, named for the river, as neither the territory nor the state existed at the time. It coordinated the federal blockade of Confederate ports during the Civil War and helped crush a rebellion against foreign influence in Korea in the 1870s. The navy sold it for scrap in 1885. A new *Colorado* launched in 1903 as part of President Theodore Roosevelt's state-of-the-art "Great White Fleet" to showcase American military might. Rechristened the USS *Pueblo* in 1916 to make way for the third battleship, it remained in service until 1930. A second USS *Pueblo*, captured by North Korea in 1968, remains anchored there as a museum, an eerie coincidence considering the first *Colorado*'s history in Korea.

The third *Colorado* boasted a design drawn from the lessons of World War I, described by one press as "a big ship all right, but none too big to carry the name Colorado." Designated BB-45, the vessel stretched more than 600 feet long and weighed more than 32,000 tons. Two years of tests for its systems and crew passed before its commissioning on August 30, 1923. A refit on the West Coast prevented the *Colorado* from coming under attack at Pearl Harbor in 1941, but it served throughout the Pacific theater during World War II. Struck twice by kamikaze attacks, it survived to float in Tokyo Bay during Japan's surrender in September 1945. Decommissioned two years later, the navy sold it for scrap in 1959. A fourth USS *Colorado*, a nuclear submarine, was announced in 2012 and built in Connecticut. Designated SSN-788 and launched in 2016, it carries the Centennial State's naval tradition into the twenty-first century.

March 23, 1843

Frances Jacobs's Birthday

At the end of the nineteenth century, commissioners charged with erecting and decorating the Colorado State Capitol selected sixteen pioneers to honor in stained glass high in the rotunda. Among the politicians and entrepreneurs who have gazed down from that lofty perch ever since stands only one woman, Frances W. Jacobs, Denver's beloved "Mother of Charities."

Born Frances Wisebart in Kentucky on March 23, 1843, she grew up in the bustling city of Cincinnati, Ohio. A family friend named Abram Jacobs joined the Pikes Peak gold rush in the late 1850s, where he "mined the miners" by operating a clothing store in Central City. His tailor shop also served as the hub of the Jewish

Frances Wisebart Jacobs, philanthropist in Denver during the late nineteenth century, depicted in stained glass at the Colorado State Capitol, as photographed in 2019

community there. Jacobs opened another store in Denver and emerged as a business leader in that fledgling community as well. He returned to Cincinnati in 1863, where Abram and Frances married before returning to Colorado Territory.

Frances put her husband's money to work when she established a Jewish benevolent organization in 1872. Two years later she joined Elizabeth Byers and Margaret Evans—the wives of *Rocky Mountain News* founder William N. Byers and former governor John Evans, respectively—to found the Ladies' Relief Society to aid distressed Coloradans regardless of their faith. Jacobs spent most of her time tending to the legions of tuberculosis victims who came to Colorado in search of relief. She ensured that patients received medical care and hygiene while raising funds for a free kindergarten in Denver. In 1892, a sanatorium bearing her name opened in the capital city. The building was later renamed National Jewish Hospital, and a statue of Jacobs stands in the lobby.

Although fires in Central City destroyed much of the family's wealth and property, Jacobs never surrendered her charitable work, even as her family grew impoverished themselves. Upon Jacobs's death, shortly after the hospital opened, the *News* observed that "the poor have lost an earnest and sympathetic friend. The city loses one of its most generous workers in the cause of charity, one who knew no creed nor denomination when the cry of distress was heard."

A Grand Idea: The Colorado River

Governor Oliver H. Shoup signed a bill on March 24, 1921, one approved unanimously by the General Assembly. It asked the federal government to rename a western waterway, a request that stemmed from a long-standing dispute: Where exactly was the Colorado River?

Debate swirled for decades about whether the Green or Grand River was the primary source of the American Southwest's vital Colorado River. The Grand flowed through western Colorado and joined the Green in eastern Utah. John Wesley Powell, on his 1869 Colorado River Exploring Expedition, confirmed the general consensus that the longer Green was the primary upper branch. Whether the Green or the Grand carried more water, however, depended on the year. As the seven states that drew on the Colorado River's water planned to divvy up the precious resource in the early 1920s, some scientists and geographers suggested renaming the Green the Colorado to acknowledge its status. The notion infuriated many Coloradans, who demanded that the Grand River claim the distinction and, most important, the name as the source of the Colorado River. Some people claimed that Congress had intended the connection between polity and river when it bestowed the name "Colorado" on their territory in 1861 and that the federal government should reinforce the link by renaming the Grand.

Members of Congress considered the proposal in the spring of 1921. Utah politicians expressed support, and the notion proved popular on both sides of the state line. A committee encouraged the name change that May. It considered the Grand the larger of the two flows and argued "that the State of Colorado is expressing a commendable sentiment, and has a patriotic right to have that river bear the name of 'Colorado' from its mouth in the Gulf of California to its source in the Rocky Mountain National Park in the central portion of northern Colorado." In the summer of 1921, Congress renamed the Grand River the Colorado, although the former name survives in Grand County, Grand Mesa, Grand Junction, the Grand Valley, and more.

New Hope for an Iconic Rail Line

Train service to Durango commenced with the Denver & Rio Grande Railroad (D&RG) in 1880. It lasted until 1969 when its successor, the Denver & Rio Grande Western Railroad (D&RGW), tore up the tracks leading into town from the south. The famous route in the Animas River canyon, popular with tourists and filmmakers, remained in operation, but the D&RGW struggled to keep it going. On March 25, 1981, Florida businessman Charles E. Bradshaw purchased the line, intent on maintaining its charm while making it a must-ride experience.

When the D&RG built into the Animas River valley in 1880, it employed brutish tactics that had worked in Colorado Springs, Pueblo, and Trinidad. It demanded concessions from local communities before providing them with rail service and denied it to them if they refused. When residents of Animas City protested, the D&RG erected its own town, named Durango, a few miles away, leading to the abandonment of the first community. Two years later the tracks reached Silverton, high in the San Juan Mountains, and hauled rich silver ore to a smelter in Durango for processing. The route proved popular with vacationers, as a Leadville newspaper explained: "Here is the traveler's, the artist's, the poet's paradise. There are few canyons as attractive as this; there are several grander and greater ones in Colorado, but none more weird or possessing so many features to delight the eye and thrill the senses." By the mid-twentieth century, directors of western films employed the scenery and the railroad in their productions.

Bradshaw and residents of La Plata and San Juan Counties invested time, money, and energy to revitalize the line after its purchase in 1981. Renamed the Durango & Silverton Narrow Gauge Railroad (D&SNG), it offers excursion trains between the two towns and lures railroad aficionados from around the world to southwestern Colorado. The D&SNG represents the gold standard of the many excellent historic rail lines operating in the state.

March 26, 1931

Snow and Sorrow in Kiowa County

Some of the worst winter storms in Colorado take place after the official end of winter, as spring moisture combines with cool air to produce heavy snowfall and bitter temperatures. Often, these storms offer little more than one last chance to gripe about the departing season, but sometimes they come at a much higher cost. Residents of the high plains discovered exactly that on March 26, 1931, when an intense burst of wintry weather proved deadly.

The worst weather of the 1930–31 winter hit eastern Colorado that day, making roads and railroads impassable. The southeastern counties—battered in recent years by the Dust Bowl and the Great Depression—endured particularly harsh conditions. The two teachers at the Pleasant Hill Schoolhouse in Kiowa County decided that the forecast warranted closing the school early. Bus driver Carl Miller set out with twenty-two students as the snow and wind set in. Less than 3 miles from the school, the bus skidded off the road into a ditch, breaking windows that let in the wintry blast. Children huddled together to keep warm, but the weather proved merciless. A 10-foot snowdrift built up behind the bus, and the students—many of whom lacked warm clothing—grew cold and frightened. The next morning, Miller set out to find help. Rescuers found the bus 33 hours after it left the school, by which time five students—Bobbie Brown (age 9), Kenneth Johnson (7), Mary Miller (8, daughter of driver Carl), Louise Stonebreaker (14), and Orville Unteidt (7)—had died. Carl Miller's body was found less than 4 miles from the bus.

Airplanes carried the seventeen survivors to a hospital in Lamar. The press praised 13-year-old Bryan Unteidt, who lost one of his three siblings in the ordeal, for keeping the rest alive, with the five bodies lying nearby as a terrifying inspiration. Five days after the accident, thousands of people attended a mass funeral in Holly, 20 miles south of the crash site, to honor the six people lost during the Pleasant Hill bus accident. Its victims rest today under matching stones in the Holly cemetery, with a memorial monument at the center of the communal plot.

March 27, 1877

Lakes Finds Fossils near Morrison

Professor Arthur Lakes, clambering on sedimentary rocks north of Morrison in Jefferson County, searched an ancient swamp site for fossilized plant life on March 27, 1877. What looked like a tree branch "was too smooth a cast to be left by any tree and further on one end were little patches of a purplish hue which I at once recognized as fragments of bone." Lakes's discovery represented one of the first scientific finds of dinosaur remains in Colorado.

In the mid-nineteenth century, teams from preeminent museums harvested fossils—and destroyed digs run by their competitors—in what became known as the Great Dinosaur Wars. Lakes represented one of the few responsible scholars at work at the time, although he collaborated with the more swashbuckling figures at fossil quarry sites in Morrison and Cañon City in Fremont County. He came to Colorado Territory in 1869 and taught at an Episcopal school in Golden, which became the Colorado School of Mines (CSM) in 1874. After his 1877 discoveries near Red Rocks, Lakes joined digs in Colorado and Wyoming Territory. He retired from CSM in 1893 and produced scholarship on the state's geology, cementing his reputation as one of Colorado's leading scientists. Lakes expanded the minds of his fellow Coloradans through public lectures detailing "the early inhabitants of this neighborhood, the pioneers of the country in that grand and mysterious geological past." He encouraged state residents "to step out and look with the eye of science and faith upon things lying but a few feet below the foundation of your own houses right here in Colorado." Today, CSM's library bears Lakes's name.

In addition to the plant and dinosaur fossils Colorado offers to the world, the state boasts two impressive sets of preserved footprints. Road builders found several hundred on the hogback near Lakes's Morrison quarry in 1937, preserved and visited by thousands of people annually at Dinosaur Ridge park. Over a thousand footprints—one of the largest concentrations ever discovered—stands in the Comanche National Grasslands in Las Animas County.

March 28, 1862

Colorado Troops Save the Day

The most consequential western Civil War battle—later nicknamed "the Gettysburg of the West"—took place along the Santa Fe Trail at Glorieta Pass, just east of Santa Fe, New Mexico Territory, on March 28, 1862. The Union victory prevented a Confederate invasion of the gold fields to the north, primarily because of the efforts of soldiers from Colorado Territory.

Desperate for cash to purchase supplies they lacked, Confederates looked longingly to the gold in Colorado's hills. In response, Governor William Gilpin authorized a regiment to defend the territory in the summer of 1861. Commanded by Colonel John P. Slough, the volunteers trained at Camp Weld southwest of Denver. As rebel troops moved up the Rio Grande from Texas in early 1862, Colorado's forces departed from Camp Weld and Fort Lyon on the Arkansas River to join New Mexico's defenders. To prevent the Confederates from capturing supply-rich Fort Union, Slough ordered a forced march that covered nearly 100 miles from Raton Pass to the post in two days. After recuperating, Slough decided to attack the Confederates rather than wait for them to besiege Fort Union. Both sides set out along the trail and unexpectedly clashed below the summit of Glorieta Pass on March 26, a prelude to the major battle two days later.

Union and Confederate forces slugged away near the pass on March 28, with neither side achieving a solid victory. Slough retreated toward a camp, but before the Confederates could pursue, they learned of a shocking development. While the battle had raged along the trail, nearly 500 Coloradans led by Major John M. Chivington slipped through the forest and burned their supply wagons. Lacking the materiel they needed to take Fort Union, let alone Colorado, the Confederates retreated. Slough's volunteers returned home in triumph, but Gilpin lost his job over the expense of equipping, training, and dispatching the volunteers. The governor's actions proved essential nonetheless; as a Texan declared, "they were regular demons, upon whom iron and lead had no effect, in the shape of Pikes Peakers, from the Denver City gold mines."

March 29, 1883

Sorting out the Querida War

The *Sierra Journal*, published in the Custer County town of Rosita, attempted on March 29, 1883, to make sense of the region's chaotic week, which it described as the Querida War.

Edmund C. and Rebecca Bassick came to the Wet Mountains in 1875, and two years later their prospecting paid off with the discovery of a rich source of gold and silver. The Bassicks' lucrative strike, 2 miles north of Rosita, rescued a faltering region. In 1880 the Bassick Mining Company platted a town named Querida to house hundreds of mining families. Three years later the corporation employed Superintendent C. C. Perkins, whose authoritarian rule inspired a committee of Querida residents to send a letter to the corporate officers in New York City on March 6, asking for his replacement. The company rejected the appeal. Instead,

The mining town of Querida in Custer County, dominated by the hillside Bassick Mine, as viewed in the 1880s at the time of the "Querida War"

it signed Perkins to a new contract with a higher salary, primarily because of his successful efforts to track down workers who had stolen ore from the mine. In response, the committee met on March 26 to affirm its loyalty to the firm and dismiss fears that they might retaliate by damaging property. Nonetheless, several armed miners appeared at the Bassick Mine to intimidate guards and managers. Most malcontents left Querida the next day, and the citizens' group demanded that any lingering sympathizers depart immediately. A party searched Querida and Rosita on March 28 and exiled six men from the county. The *Sierra Journal* declared, "We do not uphold mob law, but to the will of the substantial citizens of a community, all must render respect."

The Bassick Mine closed in 1885, reopened in 1898, and shuttered for good in the 1920s. Its earliest years helped fuel dramatic growth in Custer County, with nearby Silver Cliff—founded after a rich strike in 1878—ranking as the third-largest town in Colorado by 1880, behind Denver and Leadville. A lack of quality smelters and the Panic of 1893 shattered the mining industry in Custer County. In later years, cattle ranching proved a more stable economic foundation for the communities on the eastern slope of the Sangre de Cristo Mountains.

March 30, 1923

Western State on the Western Slope

The Colorado State Normal School at Gunnison, established on the east side of town in 1901, trained teachers for the western slope. On March 30, 1923, Governor William E. Sweet signed a bill renaming the school Western State College to reflect its broadening curriculum.

As early as 1885, Gunnison sought to host the state teacher's college and benefit from the appropriations and notoriety such a school would inspire. Greeley captured the honor in 1889, but a dozen years later the General Assembly authorized a branch in Gunnison to serve western Colorado. The school did not open until 1911, with free tuition for Colorado residents and out-of-state students paying five dollars per year. It closed during the influenza epidemic in 1919 and boasted a new president, Samuel Quigley, when it reopened. Quigley oversaw the transition to Western State College in March 1923, and five weeks later the school marked the change in grand style. On May 2, all 135 faculty and students helped mark a giant "W" on Tenderfoot Mountain south of campus, with freshmen carrying 100-pound sacks of lime to the construction site. Whitewash splashed over rocks shaped the "W," with legs 16 feet wide stretching 420 feet from side to side and 320 feet top to bottom. It remains the world's largest collegiate emblem.

Western State College buildings boast the names of many prominent Colorodans including Wayne N. Aspinall, Chipeta, Silvestre Vélez de Escalante, Otto Mears, David H. Moffat, Ouray, Antoine Robidoux, and Edward T. Taylor. It has lured diverse entertainment to the Gunnison valley, from singer John Denver to the Harlem Globetrotters. In the 1970s, Western inherited an Apatosaurus skeleton that students named Morris the Saurus. The school received a promotion in 2012 and is now Western Colorado University. Nonetheless, it remains a quirky, isolated, charming institution. As its first president declared in 1914, "We are somewhat removed from the busy whirl of life and are in what may come to be truly an academic retreat."

March 31, 1933

A More Modern Mode of Execution

Governor Edwin C. Johnson signed legislation on March 31, 1933, that changed the way Colorado carried out the death penalty for inmates sentenced to capital punishment. Since territorial days, the prison in Cañon City had executed prisoners by hanging, but that spring the General Assembly updated the practice to conform to other states that used a gas chamber. The law called for "a suitable and efficient room or place, enclosed from public view, within the walls of the penitentiary, and therein construct, and at all time have in preparation all necessary appliances requisite for carrying into execution a death penalty by means of the administration of lethal gas" until and unless "the death penalty be abolished and prohibited in this State."

Capital punishment in the region predates the creation of Colorado Territory. On April 9, 1859, an extra-legal court sentenced John Stoefel to hang for the murder of his brother-in-law in Denver. Four more executions followed in 1860, and the first territorial legislature formally approved the death penalty the following year. Between 1861 and 1896, courts ordered thirty-two hangings. Governor Alva Adams signed a bill repealing the practice in 1897, a decision hailed by some people and ridiculed by others. A relieved Glenwood Springs newspaper called it "a long stride in the right direction." By contrast, a Leadville press declared that "sentimental senators think the way to prevent crime is to coddle criminals," while another in Silverton feared the law would "prove an oasis on the desert of justice to the murdering fraternity of the state."

The General Assembly reinstated capital punishment in 1901 after several individuals died at the hands of vigilante mobs—politicians viewed state-sponsored death as more tolerable than lynchings. Colorado had executed ninety-seven people by 1967 but only 1 after that, by lethal injection in 1997. In 2011, Governor Bill Ritter issued a posthumous pardon to a mentally handicapped man executed on flimsy evidence in 1939. His successor, John Hickenlooper, paused executions temporarily in 2013, and the future of capital punishment remains uncertain.

April

A Place to Teach the Teachers

Governor Job A. Cooper chose the perfect day, April 1—best known for foolishness—to approve legislation to make the Centennial State smarter. On that date in 1889, he signed a bill establishing the Colorado State Normal School in Greeley to train public school teachers.

One of the state's most successful farming communities, Greeley flourished after its founding in 1870. Residents sought to reinforce that reputation with an institution of higher education. Colorado's university, agricultural college, and mining school had gone to Boulder, Fort Collins, and Golden, respectively, and several private universities operated elsewhere. Greeley's last chance was for the normal school, for which it lobbied hard in the spring of 1889. The bill Cooper signed authorized a facility to provide "instruction in the science and art of teaching" that April, which would make Colorado's education system self-reliant rather than dependent on faculty prepared in other states. Within a month, Greeley officials bought land southwest of town, and construction started soon after. A Fort Morgan newspaper reported on the prosperity: "Greeley is taking on quite a real estate boom, following the establishment of the Normal school, water works, and the vacuum pump works. Greeley has ever been a pleasant home place and may yet make a real lively town." Classes convened in the fall of 1890, a remarkable pace considering that most Colorado colleges took years to open their doors.

By the early twentieth century, the normal school enjoyed a strong nationwide reputation. As the years passed its offerings grew more diverse, a transition that eventually demanded a change of title to the University of Northern Colorado (UNC), approved by the General Assembly in 1970. Two years later it named a new library in honor of a professor who taught there in the late 1930s, James A. Michener, a prolific American novelist. When UNC celebrated its centennial in 1989, it boasted an impressive record—the school had trained the fifth-most teachers of any institution in the country, and it remains a university of renown and respect.

Tancredo Tries for the Presidency

US representative Tom Tancredo, representing a metropolitan Denver district, announced his candidacy for the Republican presidential nomination in interviews on Iowa radio stations on April 2, 2007. He focused his attention on a signature issue—immigration.

Born in Denver in 1945, Tancredo attended the University of Northern Colorado in Greeley. He taught history at public schools in Jefferson County and in 1976 won election to the Colorado House of Representatives. Tancredo served in the General Assembly until President Ronald Reagan appointed him to a federal education post in 1981, where he remained under President George H.W. Bush until 1992. Six years later, Tancredo won a seat in Congress from a district encompassing Denver's southwestern suburbs. For a decade in Washington, DC, he built a national reputation as a firebrand on immigration policy. Tancredo even criticized fellow partisans like President George W. Bush for what he deemed permissive attitudes toward migrants, legal and illegal alike. He suggested preemptive strikes against Muslim holy sites and warned about the supposedly murderous intent of Mexicans, Muslims, and other cultures. Tancredo's nativist attitudes earned him wide fame and, in some cases, infamy.

Tancredo made immigration the focus of his long-shot presidential bid, which ended in December 2007 when he withdrew before any primaries or caucuses for the 2008 contest. He remained active in state and national politics nonetheless. Dissatisfied with businessman Dan Maes as the Republican nominee for governor in 2010, Tancredo allied with the American Constitution Party to combat Democratic candidate John W. Hickenlooper, Denver's mayor. Hickenlooper outpolled Maes and Tancredo combined, and the latter rejoined the Republican Party. He sought the 2014 Republican nomination for governor unsuccessfully but refrained from launching another third-party bid. The grandson of Italian immigrants remains a prominent, often incendiary voice in debates over immigration policy and enforcement.

The Boys from Joes Make the Big Time

When five boys from Joes, a farm town in Yuma County, dashed out onto a Chicago basketball court on April 3, 1929, their remarkable tale blossomed into legend.

Joes earned its name in 1914 from the large number of people named "Joe" living on area farms. Its school lacked sufficient numbers to field a baseball or football team, but it could make up a basketball squad. Players practiced on an outside gravel court, as their small school lacked a gymnasium. They passed more than they dribbled because of the rough surface and gusts of wind that made controlling the ball difficult. Basketball grew into an obsession in Joes within a few years, as exemplified by the astonishing 1929 season. The team crushed Denver's East High School 30–11, a score that reflected the era's emphasis on defense over offense in basketball. The Joes team traveled to Greeley in mid-March and swept the state championships held at the teachers college, defeating squads from Julesburg, Gunnison, Fort Lupton, and Fort Collins.

As state champions, the boys from Joes earned an invitation to the national high school contest in Chicago. Donations poured in to help them make the trip, especially after the team routed players from the University of Colorado. They bested a squad from Delaware on April 3 and defeated teams from South Dakota and Michigan. Exhaustion caused by Chicago's humidity led to their loss to an Oklahoma school, however. They returned home heroes all the same. A Steamboat Springs newspaper praised the "well trained country boys [who] waded thru all the Colorado crack teams and placed third in the national tournament. Colorado is proud of her Joes." The boys from Joes won the state title again in 1930, but disputes at the national level precluded another trip to Chicago. Joes's girls' basketball team earned triumph as well, winning the state championship in 1933. The community survives, small but proud, and fond memories linger of the days when Joes offered rural Coloradans a ray of hope during the Great Depression.

April 4, 1870

Hallett Returns to the Bench

When President Ulysses S. Grant nominated Moses Hallett for another term as chief justice of Colorado's supreme court on April 4, 1870, he recognized the effectiveness of one of the Centennial State's most influential legal minds and set the stage for a "watershed" ruling.

Most territorial officials won their positions through political connections in Washington, DC, appointed as a favor or reward rather than for their ability. Few actually understood the reality of their assigned polities, but the experienced and insightful Hallett bucked the trend. Hailing from Grant's hometown of Galena, Illinois, Hallett headed westward to seek his fortune in 1860. Like most prospectors, he found scant treasure. Hallett then returned to his profession, partnering with lawyer and territorial delegate Hiram P. Bennet. The Illinois transplant earned renown for his work ethic and legal successes. In 1866, the legislature asked the federal government to appoint Hallett as its chief justice, and President Andrew Johnson complied.

Hallett served on the bench from 1866 until Colorado achieved statehood a decade later. His legal precedents promoted settlers' rights and industrial development, and courts across the West adopted them. Hallett affirmed extra-legal practices regarding mining claims on which the territory's economy depended and recognized the right of farmers and ranchers to irrigate their acreage. In a landmark 1872 decision he wrote, "In a dry and thirsty land, it is necessary to divert the waters of streams from their natural channels, in order to obtain fruits of the soil, and this necessity is so universal and imperious that it claims recognition of the law." Hallett thus invented a new legal right to water that granted primary claim to the first settler on a particular source and a place in line for each subsequent settler—the doctrine of prior appropriation. It has inspired a thicket of legal tussles over water rights yet remains a cornerstone of Colorado law.

Hallett secured appointment as a federal judge overseeing Colorado cases in 1876 and served as such for thirty years. The pioneering jurist died in Denver in 1913 at age seventy-eight.

April 5, 1851

Founding San Luis de la Culebra

A party of Hispano settlers, intent on staking their claim to land gifted by the Mexican government years earlier, started work on Culebra Creek in modern Costilla County on April 5, 1851. Their labors laid the foundation for what is now Colorado's oldest permanent settlement, San Luis de la Culebra, a small but thriving community since the mid-nineteenth century.

To promote settlement on the northern fringe of New Mexico, the Mexican government allowed land grants to individuals who would bring farmers and ranchers to the country's frontier. Carlos Beaubien acquired the claim to a million acres in the San Luis Valley east of the Rio Grande, named the Sangre de Cristo Grant after the mountains that served as its eastern limit. The plan ran afoul of the Utes, however, who depended on the valley as a hunting ground. Utes forced a band of Hispano settlers out of the region in 1850, but ten men returned the following spring to try again. Several died in a Ute raid in the autumn of 1851, and the remainder returned to New Mexico for the winter but made their way back to San Luis in 1852. They dug an irrigation ditch to water agricultural fields, the first manipulation of Colorado's most precious resource since the Ancestral Puebloans had departed from the area centuries earlier.

Sheep and cattle rancher Francisco Gallegos pauses his horseback ride for a photograph in San Luis in 1885, with the Costilla County courthouse in the background.

Within a few years, numerous Hispano towns sprouted on land grants in the San Luis Valley, while Utes remained in control of its northern end. San Luis emerged as a center for the Penitente brotherhood, a devout group for whom self-inflicted pain connected them to the roots of Christianity. Generally made up of Catholics, the Penitentes and the church have long conflicted over ideology and practice. The Shrine of the Stations of the Cross stands on a bluff overlooking San Luis and reflects the vital role of religion in the town and the region.

Old by Colorado standards yet young to the rest of the world, San Luis celebrated its 150th anniversary in 2001 with a parade of schoolchildren and veterans. When asked how the modern community compared with its origins, the mayor quipped, "Well, it hasn't grown."

April 6, 1897

"Bat" Masterson Fights Election Fraud

William B. "Bat" Masterson fired his gun in the line of duty for the last time on April 6, 1897. While serving as a deputy sheriff in Denver during a disputed election, Masterson faced down corrupt poll officials, and when he felt threatened he shot at them, injuring one in the wrist. The episode reflected Colorado's often fraudulent politics, as well as Masterson's hair trigger.

As a lawman in Dodge City, Kansas, in the 1870s, Masterson often tracked criminals into nearby southeastern Colorado. In 1879, the Atchison, Topeka & Santa Fe Railroad asked for his help to battle the Denver & Rio Grande Railroad over the route to Leadville during the Royal Gorge War, where he coordinated a firefight at the Pueblo roundhouse. The following year he came to Leadville to scout gambling prospects, dismissing the Gunnison area as too cold and snowy. Masterson meandered through mining camps in the Rocky Mountains, making a living by dealing cards. In 1882 he served as Trinidad's city marshal and used his influence to prevent John H. "Doc" Holliday's extradition to Arizona Territory to face murder charges. Masterson spent much of the 1880s and 1890s working in gaming houses, promoting boxing matches, and enforcing laws in Denver. He also dealt faro in Creede and moonlighted as a lawman in Buena Vista and Silverton, where his reputation often proved enough to calm tense situations.

Masterson's affection for Colorado soured in the 1890s. He opposed women's suffrage and clashed with other boxing promoters. When he applied to serve as a sergeant-at-arms for the General Assembly, the legislature's women members opposed the checkered character serving at the capitol. In 1902, Masterson left Denver—which he once described as "a beautiful city"—after stating, "I hope nobody thinks I have been living in this rotten place because I loved it or because I was making money here or because I had no other place to go." He later told a reporter, "Denver can go to hell." The city undoubtedly felt the same way about Masterson, a man unable to move with the times and more than welcome to ply his various trades elsewhere.

April 7, 1903

Dry and Wet in Glenwood Springs

Motivated by a fiery determination to eradicate alcohol from American life, pro-hibitionist Carrie Nation came to the tourist town of Glenwood Springs on April 7, 1903. Unfortunately, she arrived on an election day, which meant that the town's saloons were closed. The undaunted Nation nonetheless railed against spirits to an interested crowd from the rear of her train during its hour-long stop. The *Glenwood Post* covered her visit with a sarcastic tone: "This lovely, sunshiney weather is wonderfully conducive to spring fever. It is to be hoped that under the circumstances, Carrie Nation will not forbid the moderate use of sarsaparilla and sassafras teas."

The community Nation visited already boasted a long history. Generations of Utes had enjoyed its thermal waters, bubbling up at the confluence of the Colorado and Roaring Fork Rivers. One spring produces 3.5 million gallons of water per day at 122°F, tempered for comfort by cooler river water. Prospectors led by Richard Sopris soaked there in 1860, and the expulsion of Utes from northwestern Colorado two decades later led to American settlement. A small cluster of cabins took the name Glenwood Springs, which served as the seat of the new Garfield County by 1883. It flourished through coal mining and coke (refined coal) production.

Tourism flourished by the late 1880s, enabled by the Denver & Rio Grande Railroad and Colorado Midland Railway. By the early 1890s a massive stone bath complex and the Hotel Colorado stood ready to receive the swelling numbers of visitors, whose ranks have included presidents Theodore Roosevelt and William H. Taft. In 1893, a local newspaper praised the "famous and unrivaled waters, with hotel comforts and amusements provided to induce the summer tourist to go there and spend his money." During World War II, the hotel served as a US Navy hospital; future governor John Vanderhoof convalesced there and later moved to the town. The completion of Interstate 70 through Glenwood Canyon in 1992 provided another access to the ever-popular mountain resort, which balances its historic and natural charm with the bustle of modern life.

April 8, 1852

Charles Boettcher's Birthday

Born in what is now Germany on April 8, 1852, Charles Boettcher came to the United States seventeen years later to find an older brother who had changed his mind about returning home. After finding his prosperous brother in Wyoming Territory, Boettcher chose to stay as well.

The opportunity and novelty of the United States appealed to Boettcher, who worked in his brother's hardware store in Cheyenne. In 1870 they opened a branch in the new colony town of Greeley, Colorado Territory. As the decade progressed, Boettcher set up shops in Evans, Fort Collins, and Boulder. When the silver boom hit Leadville in the late 1870s, Boettcher and his wife, Fannie, moved their family there. In addition to hardware, Boettcher invested in mines, banking, and other industries and flourished in the heady 1880s. He dabbled in ranching as well, homesteading land in North Park in 1882 that eventually grew to 180 square miles.

The Boettchers moved into a Denver mansion in 1890. Having weathered the Panic of 1893 better than most, Boettcher pondered retirement. While passing a sleepless night on a train in Europe, however, the workaholic made a decision: "I determined then and there that I should get back home to America and get to work." Boettcher recalled the farms of his birthplace when seeking an economic lifeline for Colorado. He worked with investors like John F. Campion and John J. Brown to introduce sugar beets in Grand Junction in 1899 and in Loveland in 1901. In the latter town, Boettcher helped found the lucrative Great Western Sugar Company. He also established the cement industry in Colorado, shepherded the Moffat Tunnel to completion, and managed the Denver Tramway Company, whose streetcars he rode to work to boost its profits.

The Boettcher Foundation, established in 1937, allows the family fortune to enrich the community, bestowing college scholarships and providing funds for hospitals and culture. The name also endures through the Boettcher Mansion in Jefferson County and the Boettcher Concert Hall, part of the Denver Center for the Performing Arts. Boettcher died in 1948 at age ninety-six.

April 9, 1993

The Rockies Come Home

Second baseman Eric Young, facing a full count in the bottom of the first inning— not to mention batting first for the Colorado Rockies in their home opening game on April 9, 1993—blasted a home run that brought a crowd of 80,227 people at Denver's Mile High Stadium nearly to hysterics. As Young stated after the 11–4 defeat of the Montreal Expos, "That was a game every ballplayer has dreamed about." Major league baseball had arrived in the Centennial State.

Colorado hosted several minor league baseball teams, including the Denver Bears, who played sporadically from the 1880s through the 1980s. Mile High Stadium, known originally as Bears Stadium, opened in 1948 and expanded over the years to house baseball and football games, among other events. In 1955, a new incarnation of the Bears arrived as a relocated team from Kansas City. They took the name Denver Zephyrs in 1985, after a mid-twentieth-century railroad line. When Major League Baseball approved Denver as the home for an expansion team in 1991, the Zephyrs moved to New Orleans. The Colorado Rockies struggled in their debut games against the New York Mets in April 1993, four days before their home opener, but their performance in Denver on April 9 earned the team a place in the hearts of local sports fans.

The Rockies moved to Coors Field in 1995 as part of the revitalization of Denver's Lower Downtown neighborhood. A quartet of sluggers earned the nickname "Blake Street Bombers" for the frequency of their home runs at the stadium located at Blake and 20th Streets. The benefit of playing at altitude faded in 2002 with the introduction of a humidor to store baseballs, however. The team recaptured the inaugural season's magic in the fall of 2007, when a winning streak—nicknamed "Rocktober"—carried it to the World Series, although the Boston Red Sox won in a sweep. Like Denver's former hockey team of the same name, the Rockies have struggled to build a winning reputation. Nonetheless, Coloradans retain affection and optimism for their baseball team and flock to Coors Field to root, root, root for the Rockies.

A Voice for the Western Slope

Depending on one's perspective, the Continental Divide either splits or links together the state of Colorado. For some, it represents the spine of North America, unifying the continent. For others, especially those in western Colorado, it offers a barrier between themselves and the eastern slope, to which they are attached by the state's geometric boundaries. The tumultuous relationship between Colorado's halves has even inspired talk of secession on the western side. Political and economic interests searching for a more constructive solution came together in Ouray on April 10, 1954, to organize a western Colorado lobbying group named Club 20.

The immediate inspiration for Club 20 was an inequality of roads. By the early 1950s, although nearly half of Colorado's designated highways stood on the western side of the divide, the state had paved only one of them. In 1953, a Grand Junction newspaperman named Preston Walker started a conversation among politicians and businesspeople about presenting a common voice for western Colorado in state affairs. When Walker and others met in Ouray the following spring, they created a framework for their organization, named Club 20 for Colorado's twenty counties primarily or entirely west of the divide. A month later, another session in Ouray elected Walker as the group's president. Western Colorado's press praised his efforts and compared Club 20 to the Continental Congress, building a voice to speak for ignored people dominated by a distant colonial rule. The new group won an early victory when, in 1955, the General Assembly more than doubled the amount of highway construction funds for the western slope.

Club 20 remains an advocate for western Colorado and a major political force in the state. Dozens of governments and businesses belong to it, and through economic and environmental policies, Club 20's members seek "to formulate, through careful analysis, plans, and progress for the development, improvement, and general welfare of the Western Colorado community."

Serial Murder in Central Colorado

A hotelier in Fairplay wrote a letter to Denver's *Rocky Mountain News* on April 11, 1863, expressing "sorrowful news . . . of the condition of the people in this neighborhood," the mining camps of South Park. His report helped awaken territorial residents—and the officials charged with protecting them—about Colorado's most prolific mass murderers.

Mysterious executions took place in Fremont and El Paso Counties in the early spring of 1863, followed by others on Kenosha and Red Hill Passes in Park County. A few days after the hotelier's letter, the First Colorado volunteers marched into South Park to investigate and prevent a feared depopulation inspired by terrorism. Swept up in the hysteria, the troops lynched a man suspected of the crimes only days before learning the true culprits' identities.

Felipe and Vivián Espinosa, whose family moved onto a Mexican land grant in what is now Conejos County in 1858, set out on a murderous rampage five years later. Their motives remain up for debate and range from avenging a molested family member to following the orders of a splinter group of Catholics known as the Penitentes to expressing the resentment of Hispanos about Anglo intrusion into the San Luis Valley. Charged with horse stealing in early 1863, the Espinosa brothers killed a Hispano soldier sent to arrest them. From that moment on, they dedicated themselves to spreading death and fear across Colorado Territory.

In early May, a posse killed Vivián Espinosa north of Cañon City, but his brother, Felipe, escaped and recruited his nephew, José, to carry on the bloody work. Murders continued through the summer of 1863. Some estimates list the number of victims at thirty-two, including Anglos and supposedly collaborationist Hispanos. The US Army, based at Fort Garland in the San Luis Valley, hired scout Tom Tobin to track down the Espinosas in October 1863. Three days of searching led them to a campsite in the Sangre de Cristo Mountains near La Veta Pass, where shots fired by Tobin and the soldiers put an end to the Espinosas' murderous rampage.

"Corky" Gonzales Dies

Rodolfo "Corky" Gonzales, who died in Denver on April 12, 2005, described himself as "an agitator and a troublemaker. That's my reputation, and that's what I'm going to be." One of Colorado's most influential social and political activists,

Rodolfo "Corky" Gonzales rallies other Chicano activists on the west front of the Colorado State Capitol during Mexican Independence Day celebrations on September 16, 1980.

Gonzales helped to unify Latinos during the tumultuous 1960s and spoke out for those at the bottom of the American economic ladder.

Born in Denver in 1928, Gonzales lived there with his family during the cooler months and spent summers working in Weld County sugar beet fields. He discovered a passion for boxing as a teenager and won numerous competitions from the late 1940s to the mid-1950s. While Gonzales pursued diverse occupations in Denver to help his family make ends meet, he dabbled in Democratic politics, rallying voters to support John F. Kennedy for president in 1960. Gonzales worked for the city government until 1966, when he was accused of discriminatory hiring practices by favoring Latinos over whites and African Americans. The previous year, he had published a poem titled *Yo Soy Joaquín* in praise of Mexican American (or "Chicano") identity. After his dismissal, Gonzales organized a Chicano group called the Crusade for Justice to fight poverty, segregation, and discrimination in law enforcement. He also spoke at civil rights rallies and worked to improve educational opportunities for Latinos.

Gonzales advocated Chicano nationalism through "El Plan Espiritual de Aztlán," which called for ethnic unity throughout the American Southwest. He also helped organize a national political party, La Raza Unida. In the early 1970s, clashes with law enforcement undermined the Chicano movement, and Gonzales feuded with other prominent Latinos for leadership of the effort. He made few public appearances after an automobile accident in 1978, but his influence endured, demonstrated in part by the election of Federico Peña—a Texas-born lawyer who came to Colorado after the peak of Gonzales's career—as Denver's mayor in 1983. Whether in the ring or in front of a microphone, "Corky" Gonzales never ran from a fight.

April 13, 1877

Secession Rumbles in the San Juans

Less than a year after Colorado joined the Union, silver miners in the booming San Juan Mountains felt ignored. Far removed from the political and economic power of the eastern slope, residents bemoaned the lack of representation their region had received in the first state election. State legislator Alva Adams, speaking to his constituents in Del Norte, gave voice to these frustrations on April 13, 1877. He suggested to an enthusiastic crowd that if they seceded from Colorado to make their own state—consisting of the San Juans, San Luis Valley, and portions of northern New Mexico—they would find the respect and influence they desired.

Statewide reaction to this proposed state of San Juan ranged from enthusiastic to sarcastic. By the summer, secessionism spread eastward to Pueblo, which saw the chatter as a way to free itself from Denver's domination. The movement culminated at the Independence Day festivities in Pueblo, which included a farcical ceremony to declare independence from Colorado. Local politician Eugene K. Stimson appointed himself San Juan's governor and gave an inaugural address. Other Puebloans portrayed ambassadors from Russia named "Pulldownyourvestsky" and "Wipeyourchinoff," a Prussian band leader called "Grasshoppersufferer," and an emissary from Denver who came to wish the new state well.

Secession talk waned after the Fourth of July farce, largely because advocates in the San Juans resented Pueblo's interference. In addition, voters elected Stimson as Colorado's auditor in 1878, and Ouray resident Frederick W. Pitkin won the race for governor, giving southwestern Colorado a greater political voice. Adams later served three terms as governor, and Adams County is named in his honor. Political divorce had devolved into a joke, but the idea lingered. In the words of Stimson on Independence Day, "As we leave this place, how many of us are there but that will wish . . . that the separation had really been made?" From time to time, disaffected Coloradans have made similar rebellious overtures and found just as little success.

Black Sunday in Southeastern Colorado

Insult piled upon injury on April 14, 1935, when, after enduring years of the Great Depression, one of the worst dust storms ever recorded beset the already hard-hit Great Plains.

The fundamental cause of the Dust Bowl was, oddly, prosperity. An agricultural boom in the early twentieth century had fueled settlement on the plains, as homesteaders broke up the native grasses and soils for irrigated and dry farms. But a price collapse after World War I made it almost impossible for many farmers to make a living. Hoping to turn a profit, many farmers grew as much as they could, but that only swamped the shaky market and made a bad situation worse. In addition, by the 1930s a drought turned already marginal lands into parched, dusty moonscapes. The farming boom that inspired so much settlement also broke up the natural root system of native grasses that held the soil in place during dry times. With nothing to hold down the earth, it sailed through the air whenever the wind blew. Dust storms carried dirt across the continent, depositing grit as far away as the decks of ships on the Atlantic Ocean. The storms that raged through the early 1930s inspired many plains denizens to sell or abandon their land.

A cold wind churned up the soil on April 14, 1935, which prairie residents declared Black Sunday for its misery and its color. It struck Baca County particularly hard and extended into Kansas, Nebraska, Oklahoma, and Texas. The storm produced dirt drifts 9 feet high in places, grounded airplanes, and halted automobiles and trains. Its intensity built up electric charges in the air, which reportedly electrocuted livestock and wildlife that touched barbed wire fences. The filth extended to Denver as well, where the *Rocky Mountain News* reported that "immaculate interiors of houses and apartments, recently scoured and scrubbed by housewives in the throes of spring cleaning, became murky with finely-sifted dust." Federal officials sent 20,000 Civilian Conservation Corps members to aid in repairs, but full recovery on the plains required decades of work and, in some cases, replacing agriculture with more natural landscapes.

Brown Proves Herself Unsinkable

Few Coloradans have had their story told with less accuracy than Margaret T. Brown, whom the world knows as the unsinkable Molly Brown, a nickname that originated in the wee hours of April 15, 1912, when she survived the loss of the RMS *Titanic*.

In 1886, at age eighteen, Maggie Tobin left her Missouri birthplace for the mining town of Leadville, where she worked in a department store and kept house for her brother Daniel. Late that spring she met James J. Brown, a manager for mines owned by banker David H. Moffat, and they married in September. They raised two children in Leadville, where James's career flourished and Margaret supported the women's suffrage movement. James provided hope to the forlorn city in 1893—beset by the collapse of silver—with the discovery of gold ore in the Little Johnny Mine that October. Bucking the Panic of 1893, the Browns emerged as wealthy investors and benefactors, as James parleyed his success into various business ventures.

The Browns moved to a house at 1340 Pennsylvania Street in Denver in 1894—now the Molly Brown House Museum—and rubbed elbows with high society. Margaret lobbied for women's and children's rights, including Benjamin B. Lindsey's juvenile court. She allied with John K. Mullen to raise funds for a Catholic cathedral in Denver, considered running for the US Senate, and traveled the world. After the *Titanic* sank, she collected contributions for its survivors and rescuers but criticized the accident, calling it "a tragedy that was as unnecessary as running the Brown Palace Hotel into Pikes Peak." Margaret's activism continued, even as her marriage disintegrated and family bonds strained, until her death in New York City in 1932.

Pseudo-histories by Gene Fowler and Caroline Bancroft, as well as Meredith Willson's stage and screen musical *The Unsinkable Molly Brown*, obscured much of Margaret Brown's legacy, not to mention her name. Yet even those who never let the truth stand in the way of a good story must admit that the real tale of Brown's life is as indomitable as the fabricated one.

April 16, 1880

An Advocate for American Indians

The *Solid Muldoon*, a newspaper published in Ouray, enjoyed nationwide attention. On April 16, 1880, editor David F. Day declared yet again his support for Ute removal from western Colorado. At the same time, he needled Helen H. Jackson—one of the nation's most prominent advocates for native cultures—by warning: "Select your Utes, Helen; time's most up."

Born in Massachusetts in 1830, widow Helen Hunt came to Colorado Springs in 1873 in the hope that altitude and thin air might strengthen her constitution. Intending only to spend a winter there, Hunt fell in love with the landscape. She married banker William S. Jackson in 1875, and they rebuilt his grand house to face west so she could draw inspiration from the Rocky Mountains. A writer, Helen Jackson produced essays, poems, short stories, children's books, and novels—fifteen books in all—extolling the glories of Colorado and drew on locales including Colorado Springs, nearby Cheyenne Mountain, and the mining town of Rosita in Custer County.

Jackson came to Colorado ignorant of its brutal treatment of American Indians. Shocked by stories of the Sand Creek Massacre and other atrocities, Jackson used her pen to challenge the portrayal of native cultures. Her efforts culminated in a massive 1881 tome titled *A Century of Dishonor*, which excoriated the nation's many crimes committed against American Indians: "The robbery, the cruelty which was done under the cloak of this hundred years of treaty-making and treaty-breaking, are greater than can be told. Neither mountains nor deserts stayed them; it took two seas to set their bounds." Jackson shamed the entire country: "Colorado is as greedy and unjust in 1880 as was Georgia in 1830, and Ohio in 1795; and the United States government breaks promises now as deftly as then, and with an added ingenuity from long practice."

A Century of Dishonor did little to change policies, but it opened the nation's eyes. Even the *Solid Muldoon* softened its tone toward Jackson, copying a praiseful obituary from a national newspaper upon her death in San Francisco in 1885. She lies buried in Colorado Springs.

April 17, 1882

Teller from Senator to Secretary

Henry M. Teller, one of Colorado's first two voices in the US Senate, resigned his post on April 17, 1882, to join President Chester A. Arthur's cabinet as the secretary of the interior. The first Coloradan to serve in the cabinet, Teller enjoyed a long and prominent public career.

A native of New York, Teller came to Colorado Territory in 1861 and established a law office in Central City. He invested in mining and railroads and erected the Teller House hotel in 1872. Teller also grew active in politics as a member of the dominant Republican Party. He opposed statehood, an idea backed primarily by Denver politicians, fearing a tyranny of that city. When Colorado joined the Union in 1876, Teller won appointment to the US Senate, along with Denver banker Jerome B. Chaffee, to provide an urban-rural balance in political representation. The two men collaborated on state and national issues, although Teller clashed with Chaffee's successor, smelter magnate Nathaniel P. Hill. In the Senate, Teller sought to crush American Indian identity. He advocated for boarding schools to expunge native identities and cultures and lobbied to remove Utes from western Colorado after the Meeker Massacre in 1879.

As secretary of the interior, Teller promoted homesteading and mining and aided Arthur's efforts to professionalize the federal civil service. He returned to the Senate in 1885 and lobbied in favor of bimetallism, the use of silver and gold to support the federal currency. When Republicans backed the gold standard in 1896, Teller and other "Silver Republicans" broke with the party. He supported pro-silver politician William Jennings Bryan and eventually drifted into the Democratic Party, remaining in the Senate all the while until his retirement in 1909.

Colorado's longest-serving senator died in 1914 at age eighty-three, survived by his wife, Harriet, and their three children. The curmudgeonly Teller credited his longevity to a few maxims: "Never drink. Whiskey is the nation's curse. Don't smoke. It is costly for the health and the pocketbook. Marry early if you can but late if not early. Bachelors are an abomination."

April 18, 1936

"Big Ed" Johnson and the Blockade

Railing against immigrants is as much an American political tradition as shaking hands and kissing babies. More than a few Colorado officials have employed nativism, but none more dramatically than Governor Edwin C. "Big Ed" Johnson, who on April 18, 1936, declared martial law along Colorado's southern boundary to protect Colorado jobs for Colorado workers.

With the nation mired in the Great Depression, any economic development seemed welcome. Johnson, a conservative Democrat, found a convenient target in Hispanic laborers, both American citizens and migrants from Mexico, who came to Colorado seasonally to work in sugar beet fields and other industries. He deployed the Colorado National Guard to highways and railroad lines coming in from New Mexico and ordered them to turn back anyone they considered financially incapable of supporting themselves. Although the blockade halted several hundred people, it proved controversial and nearly impossible to enforce. Farmers and agricultural industries, desperate for trusted labor they had long employed, encouraged trucks full of blockade runners to slip across unguarded dirt roads or open prairie or to go around the blockade and enter through Kansas. Some laborers decided to wait it out in camps just south of the state line, which Johnson infiltrated with Spanish-speaking guard members dressed as farm workers to gather intelligence. When New Mexico governor Clyde Tingley learned of the espionage, he threatened his own blockade of Colorado workers and goods heading south.

April

The farce culminated on April 28, when state officials reported that only 10 percent of unemployed Coloradans had agreed to work in the beet fields. The rest preferred to remain on welfare rather than deign to attempt the arduous stoop labor. With Coloradans rejecting the jobs he sought to protect for them, a chastened Johnson canceled the blockade the following day, and the decades-old system of migrant labor resumed once more. As a Denver resident wrote to the governor, "It takes more than a line of national guardsmen to bring prosperity to a state."

April 19, 1889

Reform and Rivals in Chaffee County

Colorado boasts a progressive tradition when it comes to young offenders in the criminal justice system, most famously the pioneering juvenile court of Benjamin B. Lindsey. Another example took shape on April 19, 1889, when Governor Job A. Cooper signed legislation creating the Colorado State Reformatory, a place to provide criminal youth with a second chance.

State officials intended the reformatory to offer an alternative to the state penitentiary in Cañon City and the insane asylum in Pueblo, a place where offenders between sixteen and thirty years of age could serve their sentences in less oppressive conditions and learn skills that might allow them to live a productive life outside the institution's walls. The law called for the state's "youthful, well behaved, and most promising convicts" to transfer to the facility, banned alcohol from the premises, prohibited brutal discipline including beatings and cold showers, and provided each inmate with religious texts in addition to schooling in manual labor.

The law establishing the reformatory located it in Chaffee County, and the two largest towns in that county competed for the prize. Longtime rivals Buena Vista, then the county seat, and the smelter town of Salida both sought the facility. Buena Vista donated 480 acres, including a stone quarry for construction and irrigated farmland, as well as a water right to support the site, while Salida depended on its commercial reputation. Newspapers in both towns exchanged bitter, sarcastic words about each other's claims until a meeting in Denver on May 20, when state officials awarded the facility to Buena Vista. An Aspen newspaper quipped: "Buena Vista has succeeded in getting the State Reformatory institution. A person who could not reform in that town should be taken thence to Cañon City or Pueblo without further ado." In the 1970s the General Assembly decentralized juvenile detention facilities, and the Buena Vista facility became a medium-security prison. As a consolation for Salida, it won the Chaffee County seat in a 1928 election, earning its own bragging rights in one of the state's longest-lasting rivalries.

The Ludlow Massacre

Shots rang out at a tent colony of striking coal miners in Las Animas County on April 20, 1914, instigating the Ludlow Massacre, the deadliest incident yet in a months-old labor dispute.

Coal fueled smelters, locomotives, power plants, and more at the turn of the twentieth century. Vast, high-quality deposits lay on both sides of the Rocky Mountains, the geological legacy of Colorado's ancient tropical past. No coal firm grew richer or more powerful than the Colorado Fuel & Iron Company (CF&I), which operated a steel mill in Pueblo and ran company towns in Las Animas and Huerfano Counties, among others. Its president, John C. Osgood, developed a model company town named Redstone along the Crystal River in Pitkin County, dominated by his palatial manse. CF&I ruled much of Colorado with an iron fist.

Members of the United Mine Workers (UMW), opposed to CF&I's policies, struck in southern Colorado in September 1913. Turned out of their company-owned homes, thousands of Italians, Hispanos, Greeks, Britons, and other ethnic and immigrant groups clustered in tent colonies to wait out the dispute. CF&I guards intimidated the camps with floodlights and a steel-plated car with a machine gun nicknamed the "Death Special," prompting many to dig cellars under their tents. Governor Elias Ammons sent the Colorado National Guard

A man overlooks the ruins of the burned Ludlow tent colony in the aftermath of the Ludlow Massacre in the spring of 1914.

April

(CNG) to keep the peace but faced bankrupting the state treasury to keep the troops posted indefinitely. The company assumed the guard's bills and in the process turned Colorado's troops into CF&I's private army.

Deadly skirmishes among strikers, the CNG, and CF&I's guards climaxed on April 20, 1914, when the 1,200-person Ludlow colony north of Trinidad came under attack. More than 30 people died there, including 2 women and 11 children who cooked to death in a cellar when an inferno destroyed the camp. Killings ebbed after President Woodrow Wilson sent the US Army to restore order. The UMW did not concede defeat until December, after as many as 100 fatalities during the fifteen-month strike. A memorial and a concrete-lined bunker where the 13 people died underground stand at Ludlow today, in memory of the nation's bloodiest labor war.

April 21, 1879

The High Court in the Royal Gorge

Most Americans consider the US Supreme Court the country's ultimate arbiter. The decision it reached on April 21, 1879, regarding a dispute between railroads over the Royal Gorge in Fremont County and the fracas that followed the ruling proved otherwise.

In the late 1870s, the vast riches of Leadville lured thousands of fortune hunters, and railroads sought to tap this prosperous, remote market. One line, the Denver & Rio Grande Railroad (D&RG), considered itself the obvious candidate—its main line paralleled the eastern slope of the Rocky Mountains, and spurs probed the high country. But the D&RG depleted its capital building toward Raton Pass and over La Veta Pass into the San Luis Valley in the late 1870s. Its competition, the Atchison, Topeka & Santa Fe Railroad (AT&SF), worked up the Santa Fe Trail to Pueblo in 1876 and wanted to secure Leadville's traffic for itself.

Competition between the lines focused initially on Raton Pass. In February 1878, the AT&SF beat the D&RG by mere hours to buy Richens L. Wootton's toll road for a rail path. The D&RG resolved to fight for the Royal Gorge, through which the Arkansas River flows along the natural route between Pueblo and Leadville. In April 1878, both attempted to build upstream from Cañon City. Workers sabotaged one another's tools and built stone fortifications to defend their respective company's interests with bullets. Meanwhile, company lawyers fought for the gorge in court, culminating in the April 1879 decision that both the D&RG and AT&SF could use the canyon but that they must share the route when it grew narrow enough to permit only one rail line.

The Supreme Court ruling resolved little. Armed men battled at Pueblo's depot and roundhouse in June 1879, killing one man, and other mercenaries remained in place at the gorge. A meeting in February 1880 resolved the dispute at last, granting the canyon to the D&RG but forbidding it from challenging the AT&SF for the primary cities of New Mexico. As the "Royal Gorge War" ended, the D&RG claimed its prize with service to Leadville by late July 1880.

April 22, 1896

Making Money in Denver

For $60,000, federal officials purchased a site on Colfax Avenue in Denver on April 22, 1896, to erect a facility to produce coin money. The structure built there remains in operation, along with similar works in San Francisco and Philadelphia, as a branch of the US Mint.

In the early 1860s, a private bank—Clark, Gruber & Company—processed gold mined during the Pikes Peak rush into coins of standard weights as decreed by law. The bank sold its machinery to the federal government in 1863, but as mining slumped the following year, support for producing coinage in Denver dissipated. Until 1905, federal assayers collected gold, silver, and other ores extracted from the Rocky Mountains at a stout yet humble structure located at the intersection of Sixteenth and Market Streets and shipped ingots to the mint at Philadelphia. To better serve the government's needs, it purchased land for an expanded building in 1896.

After a decade of construction, the new mint made of Colorado stone opened on February 1, 1906. It boasted $30 million in gold to coin and received shipments of $2 million in bullion each month, including from the prosperous Cripple Creek district. Several hundred spectators crowded the catwalks over the machinery to watch the facility churn out half dollars of gold and silver. Entrepreneur Charles Boettcher purchased the former mint building and demolished it to make room for new building projects. Prospectors carried dirt out from the basement to pan in the South Platte River in hopes of finding gold that had fallen through the floors over the years.

Having expanded several times to fill a city block, Denver's US Mint represents the largest American gold depository outside of Fort Knox, Kentucky. As such, it has drawn nefarious attention over the years. In December 1922, a gang attacked a Federal Reserve Bank truck parked outside the building and stole $200,000 in $5 bills after a gun battle that left one guard dead. In the early twenty-first century, the mint remains a coin producer and tourist draw. Every coin stamped with the letter "D" links American consumers to the Denver mint.

The *Rocky Mountain News* Debuts

William N. Byers beat out the competition by twenty minutes. On the morning of April 23, 1859, copies of his newspaper, the *Rocky Mountain News*, hit the streets of Denver just barely before the *Cherry Creek Pioneer*, which quickly conceded to its speedier rival. The first paper printed in what is now Colorado remained an institution for the next century and a half.

Byers arrived from Omaha, Nebraska, on April 21 and set to work. He represented one of the countless entrepreneurs who sought to "mine the miners" by making his fortune through goods and services rather than seeking gold. The twenty-eight-year-old Byers and three assistants put their weekly four-page sheet together in an attic above a general store and saloon owned by Richens L. Wootton. Byers, who boosted the region for the rest of his life, proclaimed with ethnocentric flair in the first edition: "We make our debut in the far west, where the snowy mountains look down upon us in the hottest summer day as well as in the winter's cold; here where a few months ago the wild beasts and wilder Indians held undisturbed possession—where now surges the advancing wave of Anglo Saxon enterprise and civilization, where soon we fondly hope will be erected a great and powerful state, another empire in the sisterhood of empires."

The *Rocky Mountain News* faced competition from man and nature alike. The Cherry Creek flood in May 1864 destroyed the office, but Byers bought a competitor, the *Weekly Commonwealth*, and resumed printing a month later. The *News* survived other challengers in the capital and locked horns with the *Denver Post* starting in 1895. One of the nation's great newspaper wars raged until 2000 when the two papers merged operations, retaining separate editorial boards but cooperating on logistics. By 2009, the *News*'s owner deemed it unprofitable, and it printed a final edition on February 27, two months shy of its 150th anniversary, with a farewell message superimposed on Byers's first front page from 1859. Colorado's inaugural newspaper survives on microfilm, in online archives, and in countless hearts and memories.

The First "Denver Series" Earthquake

In the category of natural disasters, Colorado fares comparatively well when it comes to earthquakes. Far from the edges of a tectonic plate, it registers little seismic activity. But a succession of earthquakes known as the "Denver series" commenced in the spring of 1962.

During World War II and the Cold War, the Rocky Mountain Arsenal in Adams County produced chemical weapons for military storehouses. It also offered space for corporations to test toxic manufacturing techniques. The arsenal's work created a great deal of hazardous waste, difficult to store or dispose of. In 1961, crews dug a 12,000-foot-deep well at the arsenal and the following spring commenced injecting toxic waste fluids deep under the Denver metropolitan area. This secret disposal project led to unexpected consequences—lubricating geologic fractures under the eastern slope of the Rocky Mountains and triggering earthquakes.

Early on April 24, 1962, a seismometer in Jefferson County recorded a tremor registering 1.5 on the Richter scale, too gentle for people to feel. But that quake proved a prologue to five years of shaking. Scientists registered approximately 1,500 earthquakes in eastern Colorado between then and the late summer of 1967. Temblors in 1965 caused damage in Commerce City, near the arsenal. Late that year, the arsenal ceased underground dumping to prevent further problems, but geology took several years to right itself. On April 10, 1967, a magnitude 5.0 quake caused widespread damage—schools in Boulder adjourned when cracks appeared on walls, and legislators fled their chambers at the state capitol as massive chandeliers above them swayed. A magnitude 5.3 shock hit on August 9, with 5 more major quakes that November.

To reverse the seismic damage, the US Army started to remove waste sludge from the arsenal well in 1968. The cleanup process inspired numerous additional tremors, but by the decade's end the "Denver series" of earthquakes dissipated, a reminder of the balance between human activity and the environment and of the consequences of seemingly obvious bad choices.

April 25, 1967

Love Liberalizes Abortion Law

With a name like John A. Love, who better to be governor of Colorado in the flower-power days of the late 1960s? His reelection campaign in 1966 even included the slogan "Luv the Guv." But the executive waded into uncertain waters on April 25, 1967, when he signed the most liberal abortion law in the country, placing Colorado at the forefront of a national debate.

Defeating incumbent governor Steve McNichols in 1962 to win his first elected office, Love proved a popular politician. The Colorado Springs lawyer was a progressive Republican, and two elections as governor reflected his statewide appeal. Early in Love's second term, state representative Richard Lamm, a Denver Democrat, introduced a bill in the General Assembly to reform Colorado's abortion law, which dated from territorial days. At the time, an abortion was legal only if the mother's life was endangered. Like most other prohibition measures, the bill did not stop the practice of abortion; it only made the procedure illicit, unregulated, and dangerous.

Lamm's bill extended the right to abort a pregnancy that resulted from incest or rape or if a child was likely to have a physical or mental deformity. It also approved "justified medical termination" of a pregnancy to protect a mother's mental as well as physical health. Thousands of protestors and supporters of the measure alike picketed the capitol, while large bipartisan majorities in both chambers approved the legislation. Upon signing the controversial legislation, the governor told reporters: "I have taken these communications into consideration and given the matter a thorough soul-searching. The fear that some have that Colorado will become an 'abortion mecca' if this bill becomes law does not seem to me well founded."

The controversy did not affect Love's political fortunes. In 1970 he won a third term, the fourth Colorado governor to date to reach that milestone. Love resigned in 1973 for a job in the Richard Nixon administration but soon returned to Colorado to avoid getting caught up in the Watergate scandal. The much-loved Love died in 2002, forty years after his first political victory.

April 26, 1951

Enriching the Relics of Hovenweep

President Harry S Truman, using his authority under the Antiquities Act, assigned two small tracts of federal land in southwestern Colorado to Hovenweep National Monument on April 26, 1951. His action added the Hackberry and Goodman Point ruins to a reserve that protected "structures of the finest prehistoric masonry to be found in the United States."

Hunter-gatherers lived in the Four Corners region for millennia, but permanent settlement did not start until about AD 900. In subsequent centuries, Ancestral Puebloans constructed stone dwellings, storehouses, and ceremonial buildings including towers and subterranean kivas. Residents of Hovenweep interacted with other prominent ancient Colorado settlements including Yucca House and Mesa Verde. Irrigated agriculture of terraces and dams allowed Hovenweep's population to flourish, growing to approximately 2,500 by the late 1200s. Yet drought and competition for resources forced abandonment of the region by the early 1300s. The survivors relocated to modern New Mexico and Arizona and developed the Puebloan and other cultures.

American exploration of Hovenweep's astonishing ruins commenced with a Mormon survey in 1854. Photographed by William H. Jackson and studied by archaeologists with the Smithsonian Institution, support built for the site's protection. President Warren G. Harding designated four structures along the Colorado-Utah boundary as Hovenweep National Monument in 1923, and Truman extended its scope to embrace two additional impressive ruins in 1951.

Nearly half a century later, President Bill Clinton bestowed similar protection over a vast swath of Montezuma and Dolores Counties surrounding Hovenweep, named Canyons of the Ancients National Monument. His declaration in 2000 embraced thousands of archaeological sites on 275 square miles, managed by the Bureau of Land Management. Both monuments reflect southwestern Colorado's vital role in the study of North America's earliest inhabitants.

April 27, 1917

Colorado's Worst Industrial Disaster

A couple of miles up Del Agua Arroyo from the Ludlow Massacre site and just over three years after that catastrophe, sorrow returned to the coal miners of Las Animas County. The ignition of a buildup of methane in the Hastings Mine caused an explosion that killed 121 miners on April 27, 1917, earning the site the dubious distinction of Colorado's worst industrial disaster.

Mining has long been a dangerous profession, the combustible quarry of fuel mining in particular. Hundreds of workers have perished in accidents big and small since the late nineteenth century, mostly in the bustling coal mines of Las Animas and Garfield Counties. In the twenty years before 1917, 181 people had died at the Hastings Mine alone. On April 27, 1917, as Frank Millatto piloted coal carts into the mine, an alarm stopped his tram. He saw smoke and rushed out to sound the general alarm, which made Millatto the sole survivor of the workers at Hastings that snowy spring day. Deep underground, a methane explosion killed many of the 121 victims while others suffocated in the collapsed works. In the weeks that followed, rescuers removed bodies of the victims while the United Mine Workers handled funeral arrangements and provided relief to the families of the men lost, including 62 widows and 141 children.

Officials investigated the explosion in the shadow of World War I, which the United States had entered only three weeks earlier. Some people suspected tension between immigrant miners, although Governor Julius C. Gunter dismissed the notion: "Does it seem reasonable that 33 Austrians might have blown themselves into eternity to carry out a plot against 15 Italians or 12 Americans? I think not, and my opinion is that this disaster is just one of the inevitable happenings of those who mine the coal of the world." An inquest later determined that an illegal use of matches to light a lamp by a mine inspector had caused the blast. Work resumed at the dangerous yet profitable Hastings Mine later that year, but it closed in 1923. A small granite memorial and ruins of coking ovens stand at the site as reminders of the Hastings disaster.

April 28, 1873

Grant's Stroll on a Silver Sidewalk

News broke in late April 1873 that President Ulysses S. Grant would make an unexpected visit to Colorado Territory. A Pueblo newspaper wrote, "He will be the first President of the United States to stand on Colorado soil . . . and the first to cross the great sea of the plains, and to look upon and perhaps ascend the cloud-capped and snow-crowned Rocky Mountains."

As Grant's train traveled over the Kansas Pacific Railroad, excitement grew to a fever pitch. Some people hoped the visiting president would open the Ute reservation to mining and legalize prospectors who had already trespassed into the San Juan Mountains. Grant's train arrived in Denver to great fanfare on April 26. The president, his wife, Julia, and their daughter, Nellie, lodged with John Evans during the visit, while prominent men including Governor Samuel H. Elbert, Edward M. McCook, and Jerome B. Chaffee escorted the party to various functions.

On April 28 the entourage rode the Colorado Central Railroad through Golden and up to Black Hawk. A reporter averred, "The presidential party were loud in their exclamations of wonderment upon the grand scenery of the cañon." From there they took carriages to Central City for a banquet at the Teller House. A Boulder County mine had sent $13,000 in silver bricks to pave the path to the hotel door, much to Grant's astonishment. After dinner they proceeded to Idaho Springs and then down Clear Creek to the tracks, where their train waited to return them to a reception in Denver. There, Grant greeted hundreds of guests, including a party of Utes who lobbied for their reservation's integrity. On April 29, his train departed on the Denver Pacific Railway, pausing for crowds in Evans and Greeley, and then turned eastward at Cheyenne, Wyoming.

The silver bricks at the Teller House hinted at a political controversy—bimetallism, the use of silver and gold to support federal currency, which Colorado miners advocated. Neither Grant nor his successor, Rutherford B. Hayes, embraced such a policy, although the Bland-Allison Act, which approved limited silver coinage, passed Congress over Hayes's veto in 1878.

A Denver & Rio Grande Western Railroad train emerges from the east portal of the Moffat Tunnel in May 1964.

April 29, 1922

A Deal to Dig the Moffat Tunnel

A special session of the General Assembly adjourned on April 29, 1922, after approving one of the state's greatest legislative compromises. In exchange for flood control appropriations for the Arkansas River valley, needed in the wake of Pueblo's inundation the previous summer, southern Colorado politicians agreed to support a long-debated tunnel under the Continental Divide to enable rail transportation west from Denver into the Rocky Mountains.

Banker David H. Moffat founded the Denver, Northwestern & Pacific Railroad in 1902 to fulfill Denver's decades-long dream of a westward railroad outlet, rejecting countless surveys that warned of steep grades and bad weather. The "Moffat Road" crested the Continental Divide at Rollins Pass and built toward lucrative coal deposits in northwestern Colorado. Moffat died in 1911, and his line's new owners renamed it the Denver & Salt Lake Railroad (D&SL). It ran out of money in Moffat's namesake county and dead-ended at Craig in 1913. Investors dismissed the plan to build into Utah, and the Moffat Road struggled to turn a profit. Northern Colorado politicians lobbied for state aid to build a tunnel to make year-round travel feasible but made little headway against southern Colorado's entrenched railroad interests. The Pueblo flood in 1921 opened the door for a deal. As Governor Oliver H. Shoup declared following the adoption of a tunnel and flood control package the next year, "No measures passed by any other legislative session mean as much, directly and indirectly, to the state as do these two bills."

Construction on the Moffat Tunnel—a joint railroad and water diversion project, the first time eastern Colorado pumped water from the western slope to sate its thirst—ended in 1928. In 1934, the D&SL linked with the Denver & Rio Grande Western Railroad via the Dotsero Cutoff, finally connecting Denver to points westward through the tunnel. The lines merged in 1947, and the Union Pacific Railroad later acquired the route. Passenger travel continues today via Amtrak and the Ski Train to Winter Park, and coal drags still traverse the tunnel to eastern markets.

April 30, 1898

Soldiers for a Splendid Little War

Governor Alva Adams appeared at a camp erected northeast of Denver's City Park and named in his honor on April 30, 1898. He reviewed 3,000 members of the Colorado National Guard mustered there in preparation for service in the Spanish-American War.

Eager to demonstrate American military might and feeling left behind in the age of imperialism, the United States found a convenient target in the ramshackle Spanish empire. An explosion destroyed an American naval vessel off Cuba in February 1898, and inaccurate reports blamed the Spanish for the loss. On April 25, Congress declared war, and President William McKinley ordered each state to provide fighting men proportionate to its population. The Colorado National Guard could provide nearly all of the state's allotment of 1,324 soldiers. Although most jingoistic press attention focused on Cuba, where an independence movement against Spanish rule had simmered for years, the federal government ordered most troops from western states to seize Spain's largest holding in the Pacific Ocean: the Philippine Islands.

Colonel Irving Hale led the First Colorado Regiment, which trained at San Francisco before crossing the Pacific Ocean. With the harbor of Manila held by the US Navy, Colorado soldiers and others seized the city on August 13. The US Army wanted them to suppress an insurrection against American control, which the Filipinos resented as much as Spain's. Adams protested the unexpected request, but not until July 1899 did the Coloradans head homeward.

Colorado lost 35 soldiers in the Philippines, a third in battle and the rest to disease, while another 35 survived their wounds. Approximately a tenth—135 men—remained in the South Pacific to make their fortunes. On September 17, 1899, Colorado's soldiers presented their tattered flags to Governor Charles S. Thomas at the capitol. Later that year, Coloradans who had served in the Philippines met in the statehouse basement to form an association that flourished nationally in the years to come, known today as the Veterans of Foreign Wars.

Elitch Gardens Opens Its Gates

Several amusement parks in northwest Denver have entertained Coloradans since the late nineteenth century. Manhattan Beach offered fun on the shore of Sloan's Lake from 1881 to 1914, and Lakeside has delighted guests drawn to its illuminated stucco tower since 1908. But only one merited the boastful slogan "Not to See Elitch's Is Not to See Denver."

In the 1880s, John and Mary Elitch bought a farm at 38th Avenue and Tennyson Street to support their Denver restaurant. They transformed the property into a picnic ground and zoo—Denver's first—with animals donated by P. T. Barnum. Mayor Wolfe Londoner helped dedicate the gardens with a speech in the "theatorium" on May 1, 1890. In addition to lions, camels, and wolves on display, bears in a pit would beg for treats from the crowd, "holding forth their paws supplicatingly and working their huge jaws mechanically, reminding one, as a gentleman said, of Romeo making a speech to Juliet in the balcony scene." John Elitch died in 1891, and Mary operated the gardens for a quarter century; she lived on-site for most of the rest of her life.

Elitch's evolved into an amusement park with a Ferris wheel, carousel, roller coasters, haunted house, and child-themed area called Kiddieland. By the 1920s, the park boasted two iconic attractions—the Trocadero ballroom and the Elitch Theatre. The best bands appeared at the Troc, including those of Les Brown, Tommy Dorsey, Benny Goodman, Dick Jurgens, Guy Lombardo, Freddy Martin, Frankie Masters, and Lawrence Welk. The summer stock theatre hosted stage and screen stars including Raymond Burr, Spring Byington, Douglas Fairbanks, Grace Kelly, Harold Lloyd, Frederic March, Antoinette Perry, and Edward G. Robinson.

Surrounded by neighborhoods that inhibited expansion, Elitch's moved to a new site along the South Platte River in downtown Denver in 1994. Stores and townhouses replaced the original park, but the theater and carousel shell survive. The relocated park's valuable real estate makes Elitch's future uncertain, but innumerable treasured memories made at both sites live on.

The Oil Shale Bubble Bursts

The news that broke on May 2, 1982, effected a body blow to northwestern Colorado and the state as a whole, leading many residents to declare it "Black Sunday." After promises of billions of dollars of investment and claims that the region's population would flourish, oil conglomerate Exxon announced the abrupt abandonment of its ambitious Colony Project.

Oil shale—porous rock saturated with hard-to-extract fossil fuels—exists in Garfield and Rio Blanco Counties in greater quantities than perhaps anywhere else on Earth. Utes long knew of the special stone, but American settlers discovered it the hard way. Mike Callahan, an early resident of Parachute, built a fireplace out of local stone in 1882 and then fled from his cabin when the hearth caught on fire the first time he used it. Interest in oil shale has fluctuated ever since, peaking at times of high oil demand like the 1970s international embargo. The estimated 500 billion barrels of trapped oil in northwestern Colorado proved irresistible. Exxon announced the Colony Project in 1980, centered on Parachute. It promised to bring hundreds of thousands of people to existing towns and to build a new community on nearby Battlement Mesa. Skyscrapers rose in Denver to accommodate offices for oil and gas firms, lawmakers planned to manage the growth, and television captured the spirit with the soap opera *Dynasty* set in Colorado.

Seemingly without warning, the heady days disappeared in 1982. Then-governor Richard Lamm reflected years later on the era's tenuous greed, noting "a new breed of non-Coloradoan was seen upon the land, with polyester suits and dollar signs in their eyes." The state's economy reeled for years to come. Many transplanted workers found themselves cast aside without a thought, and office towers in Denver stood practically empty. Battlement Mesa reinvented itself as a retirement community, while towns like Parachute learned a bitter lesson in trust. Interest in oil shale still percolates from time to time, but "Black Sunday" reminds Coloradans to tread carefully when someone makes promises seemingly too good to be true.

May 3, 1987

"Monkey Business" Sinks Senator Hart

A front-page story in the *Miami Herald*, printed on May 3, 1987, halted the presidential aspirations of Colorado's US senator Gary Hart by exposing his extramarital affair. In the process, it changed the relationship between politics and journalism in the United States.

Hart, a Kansas native, earned law degrees from several prestigious universities before coming to Colorado in the 1960s. A prominent member of the increasingly liberal Democratic Party in the state, Hart won election to the US Senate in 1974 and secured a second term six years later. He posed a strong challenge to former vice president Walter Mondale for the party's presidential nomination in 1984.

THE TOWN OF
DEARFIELD
WELD COUNTY

DEARFIELD LODGE

A Valley Resort

DEARFIELD LUNCH ROOM

NOW that we have the best of accommodations here, the next thing is "Where shall we go for a little recreation and a good country lunch or dinner?"

FILLING STATION

DEARFIELD IS THE PLACE!

LOCATED about 70 miles east of Denver on the Lincoln Highway 38, paved road all the way, this beautiful little town is an ideal spot for a summer outing. A beautiful 2-hour drive from Denver through many interesting towns and the finest farming section of Colorado. ¶ You can order your dinner in advance by phoning Weldona 68-R-5, and it will be ready when you arrive. After a splendid dinner you can——

 FISH

DANCE
at the
BARN PAVILLION
GOOD MUSIC

 GAME

BARN PAVILLION

GAS, OIL and AUTO SERVICE

IF you care to fish or hunt in season, you will find this territory well adapted to these sports. If you care for a swim, there are many lakes and canals close at hand. If you are on your vacation you can find no better place to stop. FREE camp grounds, camp cottages for rent; and everything to make your outing enjoyable. Fine drives on every hand — through beautiful farming communities and the famous Eastern Colorado Oil Fields.

Soft Drinks
Sandwiches
Ice Cream

DENVER BRANCH SERVICE STATION, 728 E. 26th AVE.

Cigars
Cigarettes
Candy

DEARFIELD is just and old-fashioned country visiting place of interest in Colorado. Don't miss a trip to Dearfield. You'll find a true western welcome awaiting you here!

O. T. JACKSON and MINERVA J. JACKSON, Proprietors
Postoffice Address: Dearfield, Masters, Colorado   Phone Weldona 68-R-5

Poster from 1931 advertising the benefits of life in the African American farming colony of Dearfield in Weld County hard times. My daddy had to work in Denver. Some of the time momma and all us children had to sit out there on that lonely hill all by ourselves." A drought compounded the problem, and the Great Depression finished off the colony. Jackson failed to sell the town site before his death in 1948, and it faded into history. A few decaying wooden ruins endured on the south side of US Highway 34 as Dearfield faded into the prairie grasses. However, Weld County permitted home construction on the site in 2019, endangering the last traces of a pivotal community.

May 6, 1859

Gold Discovered in Gregory Gulch

Gold fever spread rapidly on the eastern slope of the Rocky Mountains in the late 1850s, as thousands of Americans sought to blunt the Panic of 1857 by digging money out of the ground. Many achieved modest success in placer mining, sifting gold by panning in streams. The real profit lay in the lodes, however, the sources of gold in the mountains that erosion of wind and water filtered downstream to be panned out. On May 6, 1859, in what is now Gilpin County, John H. Gregory found the first lode gold source in present-day Colorado.

Like many early Colorado miners, Gregory hailed from Georgia, where a gold rush had taken place in the 1830s. He came to the Pikes Peak country via Fort Laramie on the North Platte River and panned his way down the eastern slope. After a spring snowstorm cleared in early May 1859, Gregory joined a dozen people in a prospecting party headed up Clear Creek. On May 6, Gregory dug into the side of a ravine—later named Gregory Gulch—and shoveled out a dollar's worth of gold ore. Each shovelful proved just as profitable, and Gregory and his compatriots organized an extra-legal body called a claim club to recognize each other's digging spots in the absence of a more formal land claim authority. The money kept flowing—in one three-day span, Gregory scooped out nearly $1,000 worth of gold ore. Once the word got out, miners flocked to "the richest square mile on Earth." Within a month, 2,000 people lived in Central City, the town built in Gregory Gulch, and by 1860 its population reached 5,000. Its ranks included luminaries like Jerome B. Chaffee, William G. Russell, and Henry M. Teller.

Historian Frank Hall, who had mined in the area, later credited Gregory's discovery with anchoring the mining communities that provided the foundation for Colorado. "It is the beginning of all things fixed and permanent which exist here today," Hall wrote in the late 1880s. "It established and fortified the institutions since created. It gave a substantial basis for the population then on the ground, and for hundreds of thousands who followed."

First Breach at Castlewood Dam

Castlewood Dam, on Cherry Creek east of Castle Rock, had long unnerved people downstream from its massive stone slope. Seven years after its completion, on May 7, 1897, a 100-foot wide breach threatened to inundate communities below it, including Denver, a danger reminiscent of a flood eight years earlier that had killed a thousand people in Pennsylvania. Although the 1897 crisis proved limited, it presaged the fatal future of Castlewood Dam.

Built of cemented stone and rubble, the dam stood 70 feet tall and 600 feet across. Its reservoir promised to control Cherry Creek, which had flooded communities for a quarter century. The dam guaranteed access to water for farmers in Douglas and Arapahoe Counties, and its presence encouraged settlement along the creek below the reservoir, seemingly protected from disaster. From the beginning, however, leaks cascading down the dam suggested serious problems. An 1891 investigation noted its weak sandstone foundation, and the reservoir's pressure made a worrisome situation worse. The dam's designer and builders, whose reputation was on the line, insisted on its safety, and its survival in 1897 allayed some of these fears.

By the early twentieth century, settlement increased below the dam at prosperous farms and towns including Franktown, Parker, and Denver. Local vacationers flocked to the reservoir every summer for boating, fishing, camping, and swimming. But happy times disappeared on August 3, 1933, when heavy rains exacerbated the dam's precarious condition and the structure crumbled. A wall of water rushed northward, causing extensive damage. Concrete barriers built in 1908 limited Cherry Creek's torrent through Denver, but the waters covered most of Lower Downtown, inundating Union Station and the rail yards. Only two people died, thanks to early warnings from telephone operators. The dam's ruins remain in Castlewood Canyon State Park, a haunting reminder of the need for vigilance over vital infrastructure.

Arson Claims CSU's Old Main

Colorado State University (CSU) marked its centennial in 1970 and planned to turn its oldest building, pictured on page 48, into a museum as a part of the commemoration. Instead, on May 8, the campus community watched as fire destroyed the structure that long represented the heart of the school.

Richard Nixon pledged to end the Vietnam War during his campaign for the presidency in 1968, but in the spring of 1970 his decision to bomb Cambodia and Laos inspired anger, especially at American colleges. Deadly clashes between students and troops at universities in Ohio and Mississippi intensified the situation. Students went on strike at Colorado universities while faculty staged "teach-ins," canceling classes in lieu of conversations about the war. CSU witnessed a protest rally of 2,000 on campus and a late night peace concert on May 8. During the concert, a police officer spotted smoke rising from Old Main and sounded the alarm. Flames also rose from the Reserve Officers Training Corps rifle range a few blocks away. The ROTC fire was extinguished easily, but firefighters struggled against an inadequate water line to quell the blaze at Old Main. When the sun rose the next morning, charred and crumbling brick walls were all that remained of the distinguished old Victorian structure that once housed an entire school.

Old Main, the first structure of the Colorado Agricultural College, had opened its doors to five students on September 1, 1879, nine years after the territorial legislature authorized the institution. The building and the campus expanded dramatically over the next century, and the structure's loss humbled the community. President A. R. Chamberlain called it "the work of a sick person," while another official declared: "Old Main has been a pillar of strength to CSU for many, many years. I feel badly that one of the truly great landmarks is gone." Although the vandals escaped prosecution, pieces of the lost edifice survive on campus. Old Main's bell found a new home in the football stadium, its cornerstone was incorporated into an expansion of the library, and stone and brick from its walls became a bridge honoring Vietnam War veterans.

May 9, 1916

Speer Wins One Last Time

Robert W. Speer won vindication and the Denver mayor's office on May 9, 1916. He had served from 1904 to 1912 until voters, fed up with corruption and his autocratic rule, ousted him and approved a new governmental structure for the city and county. When Speer returned to power in 1916, he relished the triumph and recognition of his success, however controversial.

Like so many people, Speer came to Colorado seeking relief from tuberculosis. The Pennsylvania native settled in 1878 and by the 1890s had worked his way into Democratic city politics. He allied with gamblers, prostitutes, and the powerful heads of public utilities that provided Denver with water, electricity, and streetcar service. Voters approved a city and county charter in 1902, to take effect in two years, and Speer finagled his way into the mayor's office.

Speer espoused the "City Beautiful" movement, which argued that parks and impressive public buildings would inspire civic pride and productivity in the Progressive era. He envisioned Denver as a "Paris on the Platte" and advocated projects including the City Auditorium (now the Ellie Caulkins Opera House), Cheesman Park and monument, flood control and reclamation along Cherry Creek (which allowed for a boulevard alongside that took Speer's name), and the Denver Mountain Parks system, wherein the city purchased land in the mountains to ensure that residents had access to high country refuges such as Red Rocks, Lookout Mountain, and Mount Evans. He cleared out houses and businesses in the heart of the capital to make Civic Center park, a hub of government buildings. Speer also provided trees to Denver homeowners to beautify the city.

Speer transformed Denver into a grand city, although his administration reeked of disrepute. He often clashed with Progressive politicians like fellow Democrat John Shafroth, and reforms instituted between 1912 and 1916 limited Speer's influence upon his reelection. Nonetheless, when he died in office on May 14, 1918, few could deny that he had reinvented the city. Although Denver has seen many powerful mayors, none can compete with Speer's legacy.

May 10, 2012

Mining Molybdenum Once Again

Trucks hauled more than 10 tons of molybdenum ore out of the Climax Mine at Fremont Pass, along the Continental Divide between Lake and Summit Counties, on May 10, 2012. The shipment marked the rebirth of one of Colorado's most successful and storied mines.

Prospectors in the Leadville area scouted Bartlett Mountain for gold and silver but found only a gray, greasy ore. It drew little attention until 1895, when geologists at the Colorado School of Mines determined the substance to be molybdenum, used to produce more durable steel. The market for molybdenum remained limited until European militarization in the 1910s. By the end of the decade, the Climax Molybdenum Company had bought out many overlapping claims to the Bartlett Mountain region and churned out the mineral during World War I.

Climax prospered after the war, providing "moly" for automobiles, locomotives, and other uses. It remained one of Colorado's few successful industrial works during the Great Depression and flourished during World War II. President Franklin D. Roosevelt made a personal appeal to the company not to provide

The Climax Molybdenum Company's mine beneath Bartlett Mountain on Fremont Pass during the boom times of World War II

molybdenum to Germany, Japan, and the Soviet Union. The entry of the United States into the war in 1941 more than made up for the loss of those markets. At that time, the federal government declared Climax the nation's first priority in mining. A Steamboat Springs newspaper reported in 1944, "The Allied nations are fortunate in having the great Climax molybdenum mine in Colorado supplying immense tonnages of this premier alloy metal to the manufacturers of planes, tanks, and munitions of war."

The molybdenum mine endured through the Cold War and remained a key element to the local economy after other mines shut down. As steelmaking moved out of the United States, however, domestic demand for the mineral dropped. Layoffs commenced in 1982, coinciding with the collapse of Colorado's oil shale industry. Climax clung to existence until the early 2010s, when rumors and promises of a mining renaissance proved accurate at long last.

May 11, 1891

Harrison Whistle-Stops across the State

President Benjamin Harrison, known as the "Human Iceberg" for his chilly personality, defied expectations during a whirlwind visit through Colorado in the spring of 1891. He arrived by train from Utah on May 10 and spent a day touring and speechifying in Glenwood Springs, accompanied by Governor John L. Routt and former US senator Horace A.W. Tabor.

The busiest day of Harrison's visit was May 11, which started in Leadville with a speech shortly after dawn. He quipped about the thin air, praised the hardworking silver miners, and drew cheers with the line "We stand here on this mountain-top and see what I think is the highest evidence of American pluck to be found in the United States." From Leadville, he proceeded down the Arkansas River valley to Buena Vista and Salida, delivering brief remarks from the train's rear platform at both towns. The presidential party continued through the Royal Gorge, pausing to marvel at the Hanging Bridge, and emerged at Cañon City. Observing blossoms in the town, Harrison joked that they had "a spring more genial here than it seemed at Leadville this morning." He touted the nascent oil industry in Fremont County at a short speech in Florence and arrived in Pueblo in the mid-afternoon. After an address at the courthouse, Harrison visited the Mineral Palace construction site, admiring the edifice that celebrated Colorado's mining industry. In the evening his entourage reached Colorado Springs, where he reviewed a parade of Civil War veterans and made one last speech—his seventh of the day.

Harrison's visit culminated on May 12 with a parade through Denver and a speech at the corner of Broadway and Colfax Avenue. Late that evening he made a final stop in Colorado, delivering brief remarks in Akron on his way to Nebraska. The president summed up his impressions best in Buena Vista, touting the prosperity of mining and agriculture: "I am glad to have an opportunity that I have not previously had in seeing the State of Colorado, great in her present condition and having a greater future development than perhaps you yourselves realize."

May 12, 1882

A Jewish Revolt in Fremont County

Residents of a nascent Jewish colony along the upper Arkansas River threatened to kill those responsible for settling them there on May 12, 1882. Far from the paradise described by boosters, the soil at Cotopaxi in Fremont County seemed suited for growing rocks and little else.

Russia commenced state-sponsored persecution against Jews in the early 1880s, and evacuees—bearing little more than the clothes on their backs—crossed the Atlantic Ocean in search of a safe haven. Many Americans affirmed the sentiment of this Leadville newspaper in 1882: "The probability is that an enormous immigration of Russian Jews will take place this year. They are welcome. No class of people have done more to build up and enrich this country." Emmanuel H. Saltiel, a former Confederate soldier who volunteered to join Union troops in the West after his capture, founded Cotopaxi as a mining center. He saw an opportunity to help fellow Jews fleeing eastern Europe and worked with immigrant groups in New York City to organize a colony at his town. The sixty-three settlers who arrived in early May 1882 ranged from farmers to craftspeople, but they all doubted the region's ability to support them. When they turned on an immigration company agent on May 12, an armed Saltiel faced them down.

The Jewish settlers at Cotopaxi scratched out an existence in the summer of 1882. They dug a 3-mile-long canal through rock to water their fields, but meandering livestock ate the crops and proved a danger to the nearby Denver & Rio Grande Railroad. All the while, the colonists retained their faith, using a small cabin in the town as a cozy synagogue. But the limits of the land proved their downfall. When a party of Jews from Denver investigated Cotopaxi, they found the settlers hungry, freezing, and desperate; some scavenged for coal that fell from passing trains. Most colonists moved elsewhere in Colorado or across the West after the first winter, and the entire Jewish colony was abandoned by 1884. The discredited Saltiel disappeared from the historical scene shortly thereafter, mirroring his ill-fated idea.

May 13, 1970

Colorado and the Winter Olympics

Headlines trumpeted Colorado's big news on May 13, 1970—the International Olympic Committee (IOC) had awarded the 1976 winter games to Denver. That excitement stood in marked contrast to the state's repudiation of the Olympics two years later.

Politicians and business leaders, including Governor John A. Love, sought the Olympics as a way to show off Colorado's winter sports industry. But opposition soon developed, especially in Jefferson County, where the Denver Olympic Committee (DOC) planned to build many outdoor facilities. Some Coloradans feared growth inspired by the games, feeling that the state's population had expanded more than enough since World War II. Cost estimates ranged wildly while potential profits remained uncertain, and many people objected to a proposal to cut social programs to pay for the bid. Scientists also warned of a lack of natural snowfall on the eastern slope in February, when it would be needed for the 1976 games. The DOC proved its own greatest obstacle—it belittled critics and pressed on with self-righteousness, even as opposition built to a crescendo. Lieutenant Governor John Vanderhoof gave naysayers ammunition when he said the DOC members "were pressed for time, so they lied a bit."

In the fall of 1971, an opposition group named Citizens for Colorado's Future unified objectors, and state representative Richard Lamm proved its most persuasive member. An initiative in 1972 placed a question on that November's ballot to ask Coloradans if they wanted to host the games, and 60 percent responded in the negative. Without public support, the stunned DOC informed the IOC that Denver would renege on its bid, a situation unique in Olympic history; the games took place in Austria instead. Lamm parleyed the campaign into a successful run for the governor's office in 1974 and stayed there for the next dozen years. Repudiating the Olympics reflected uncertainty over population growth, environmental degradation, and sketchy finances but mostly the arrogant ineptitude of those who led the ill-conceived charge for the 1976 games. That suspicion and doubt linger—in 2019, Denver voters approved a measure requiring a public vote before any future attempts to bring the Olympics to the Mile High City.

May 14, 2013

The Colorado Water Plan

"Whiskey's for drinking and water's for fighting" goes a well-worn western quip. To prepare for a future of increasing scarcity and promote cooperation over the region's most high-stakes resource, Governor John W. Hickenlooper issued an executive proclamation on May 14, 2013, to order a document known as the Colorado Water Plan.

Since the early twentieth century, Colorado has struggled with neighboring states, often in court, to parcel out scarce water sources. Yet competition begins at home, and the first duty of state officials has always been to provide for their own constituents. In 1937, Governor Teller Ammons approved legislation to create the Colorado Water Conservation Board (CWCB), an early recognition of the need to manage in-state water. Over the decades, the CWCB has negotiated between countless parties within and between headwaters basins across Colorado. By the early twenty-first century, ever-increasing demand from farms and cities alike inspired Hickenlooper to request a foundational plan for water usage to shape long-term policy.

After meetings with thousands of stakeholders, in November 2015 the CWCB approved the Colorado Water Plan, "a roadmap that leads to a productive economy, vibrant and sustainable cities, productive agriculture, a strong environment, and a robust recreational industry." The plan aims to preserve Colorado's doctrine of prior appropriation through a blend of conservation and water storage. It recognizes interstate water obligations while focusing on local needs, including the ever-contentious issue of diversions under the Continental Divide. Emphasizing cooperation to place Colorado's needs at the center of policy, the plan notes that "our water challenges necessitate that we pull together as one, innovate, and become more agile."

The Colorado Water Plan offers an optimistic, thoughtful vision for managing natural resources. Future generations will judge its efficacy, but few can doubt the sincerity and faith of officials who sought to create a structure to provide water to Coloradans for decades to come.

May 15, 2012

Calming the Waters in Grand County

Competition in Colorado has simmered for generations between the heavily populated eastern slope and the more sparsely settled western slope, especially over the distribution of water between the two sides. Since the early twentieth century, diversion projects to relocate water under the Continental Divide have proved essential to the east and infuriating to the west. Hoping to make the process less acrimonious, on May 15, 2012, representatives from eighteen state and local governments, water providers, and farming and recreation groups signed the Colorado River Cooperative Agreement in the Grand County seat of Hot Sulphur Springs.

An attempt to move beyond decades of bitterness, the agreement established a framework for more fairly dividing up Colorado's water—taking into account the state's inherent geographic challenges—to meet the needs of communities and environments on both sides of the divide. The manager of the Denver Water Department, seen by many on the western slope as a highwayman rather than the head of a government agency, won applause for declaring that his organization had obligations to the state as a whole, not only to its 1.3 million customers in the metropolitan area. Governor John W. Hickenlooper, who helped start the conversation five years earlier during his tenure as Denver's mayor, praised all parties involved in seeking a new way forward.

The agreement fueled optimism for water law reform and strengthened intrastate relationships. Denver Water earned further support on the western slope by enacting aspects of the water-sharing agreement before it took full effect in the fall of 2013. Commissioners in Grand County breathed a sigh of relief: "This example of cooperation and communication is what was envisioned when Grand County entered into the Colorado River Cooperative Agreement." Suspicions linger on both sides of the divide, but the promise of constructive discourse rather than dismissive accusations appeals to all involved in the high-stakes process.

A New Airport for Denver

Voters in Denver approved a $2.3 billion proposal to erect a massive new airport for the city on May 16, 1989. The proposed Denver International Airport (DIA) promised to be the world's largest, twice the size of Manhattan and seven times larger than the facility it would replace.

Opened in 1929, Denver's existing airport sat on the east side of the city and eventually took the name Stapleton International, in honor of longtime mayor Benjamin F. Stapleton. But by the 1980s, the city had grown up around Stapleton, and neighbors complained about the noise and traffic. Its small size posed problems as well—Denver's airport ranked as the nation's fifth busiest, but aviation bottlenecks caused by its limited space affected passengers and freight across the country. A vast new facility promised to increase Colorado's commercial and tourism potential, boosting an economy that remained in the doldrums after the oil shale collapse of the early 1980s. Mayor Federico Peña lobbied for the project, and it received bipartisan support at the state and local levels. Voters in Adams County ceded 45 square miles to Denver for the site in 1988, and the election in May 1989 sealed the deal.

Construction on DIA continued until 1995, two years after its scheduled opening date. Delays included technical glitches, such as a high-tech baggage system that never worked right and fossil discoveries that required pauses for scientists to remove the artifacts. Overnight on February 27–28, 1995—known as Push Night—crews moved 100 airplanes, 13,000 airport vehicles, and 6,000 rental cars from Stapleton to DIA on Peña Boulevard, named in honor of the mayor who had advocated the project. The new airport, best known for its tent-like main terminal evoking American Indian plains dwellings and the snow-capped Rocky Mountains, operates as a functional work of art. Most of the Stapleton site was redeveloped into a bustling neighborhood, but a few buildings, including the control tower, survive as community icons.

The Last Peaceful Nuclear Explosion

"A sneeze in Denver would have been louder" than three simultaneous underground nuclear blasts set off in Rio Blanco County on May 17, 1973, according to a local resident.

From 1957 through 1973, the Atomic Energy Commission conducted twenty-seven nuclear detonations and planned many more in Project Plowshare, intended to transform weapons into tools of progress through "peaceful nuclear explosions." Most of the tests, conducted in Nevada, experimented with the human impact of such activity, while others had more specific goals. Two bombings under western Colorado intended to promote oil development by fracturing shale saturated with natural fuel to enable its extraction. The project enjoyed influential support from Congressman Wayne Aspinall, whose district encompassed much of western Colorado, while other politicos, including Governor John A. Love, expressed hesitancy about the scheme.

The first detonation in Colorado took place at Rulison in Garfield County on September 10, 1969, near lucrative shale deposits at Parachute. A bomb much smaller than those used against Japan during World War II fractured an area 400 feet in diameter, but the oil and natural gas extracted proved too contaminated by radiation to use. The second Colorado explosion—and the last of Project Plowshare—went off in Rio Blanco County, south of the seat at Meeker, on May 17, 1973. Three bombs, each twice as powerful as the one dropped on Hiroshima in 1945, went off at the same time, but they also proved unsuccessful in releasing clean liquid fuel.

Unlike tests in Nevada and New Mexico, Colorado's peaceful nuclear explosions proved anything but, as protestors railed against potential consequences. Democrats divided over the issue between conservatives like Aspinall and liberals including US senator Floyd Haskell and US representative Patricia Schroeder. Coloradans amended their constitution in 1974 to ban nuclear detonations in the state without voter approval. National support for Project Plowshare fizzled in the face of environmental fears. In its place, the oil industry turned to hydraulic fracturing, or "fracking," in the early twenty-first century, which often proved just as controversial.

May 18, 1868

Abandoning Fort Morgan

Soldiers mustered one last time on the parade ground at Fort Morgan, located where the town of the same name now stands in Morgan County, on May 18, 1868. After lowering the American flag, they marched away with a hundred wagons filled with supplies and government property, bound for the Union Pacific Railroad line at Cheyenne, Wyoming Territory.

Fort Morgan operated for less than three years. Its first soldiers arrived in the summer of 1865 and consisted primarily of "galvanized Yankees," captured Confederates who preferred service in the West to a prison camp. Although violence erupted across the plains after the Sand Creek Massacre the previous fall, the new post remained quiet. Aside from a few skirmishes, its troops guarded overland emigrants, mail service, and the telegraph line in the South Platte River valley. Even in a time of conflict, an average of 140 wagons per day passed Fort Morgan, which earned its formal name in 1866 in honor of an officer who was asphyxiated in St. Louis when his gas stove malfunctioned. Traffic along the South Platte slowed to a trickle by the spring of 1868, as most Colorado-bound travelers took the railroad to Cheyenne and proceeded southward. The *Rocky Mountain News* observed Fort Morgan's closure and the transcontinental rails as linked phenomena: "Thus do the railroads push the insignia of power westward, ever westward."

After Fort Morgan's abandonment, cattle and sheep ranchers moved into the river valley. Farmers took over by the early 1880s, building irrigation ditches and a town site on the bluffs where the fort once stood. Railroad connections and excellent soil ensured success by the middle of the decade. In the early 1900s, Fort Morgan hit its stride, with new canals opening more farmland, a refinery built by the Great Western Sugar Company, and impressive commercial and residential architecture. It remains a prosperous community and boasts Colorado's sole surviving sugar factory. Nothing remains of the short-lived post, although a historic marker near the town's tennis courts overlooking Interstate 76 reminds passers-by of the martial past.

May 19, 1864

Denver's First Flood

Residents of Denver awoke in the wee hours of May 19, 1864, to a roaring, fearsome sound, described by one newspaper as "the water engine of death dragging its destroying train of maddened waves, that defied the eye to number them," a terrifying portrayal of Cherry Creek.

Built at the confluence of the South Platte River and Cherry Creek, Denver endured a century of flooding, with a dozen major deluges between 1864 and 1965. The first, which struck a town less than six years old, set the standard for destruction. At least eight people died as the water swept away Denver's city hall and jail and the *Rocky Mountain News* building, among many other structures that stood precariously close to the creek bed. Five of the newspaper's employees escaped by jumping out a second-story window and fighting the current to swim to shore. West Denver (formerly Auraria) fared worst, as it stood lower in elevation than Denver on the rise east of Cherry Creek. Members of the First Colorado Volunteers, organized during the Civil War and based out of nearby Camp Weld, rescued and sheltered countless people affected by the crisis. For days, the only communication

Panorama of Denver looking west toward the Rocky Mountains across the overflowing Cherry Creek during the May 1864 flood

across the creek involved notes tied to rocks and hurled across by the strongest arms on either side. Recovery came slowly. The *Rocky Mountain News* resumed publication a month after the flood after buying a competitor's printing press.

In the twentieth century, Denver officials attempted to rein in nature's fury. Mayor Robert W. Speer sought to beautify the muddy, trash-littered banks of Cherry Creek and contain it in concrete barriers in 1908. The boulevard built atop reclaimed land on either side bears his name. The completion of Cherry Creek Reservoir in 1950 finally tamed that waterway. Fifteen years later, the South Platte River swamped Denver again. It killed twenty-one people and wreaked havoc on the city's infrastructure. The 1965 flood inspired construction of Chatfield Reservoir to control the South Platte. Since then, although nature unleashes torrents from time to time, the capital city has avoided watery catastrophes like those seen by previous generations.

May 20, 1996

The Supreme Court versus the "Hate State"

In a 6 to 3 ruling, the US Supreme Court issued a decision in the case *Romer v. Evans* on May 20, 1996, one that invalidated an amendment to the Colorado State Constitution. That provision had inspired the nickname "Hate State" for its attitude toward gender minorities.

Colorado voters leaned conservative in 1992, adopting the Taxpayer's Bill of Rights—which restricted the state government's power to tax—and Amendment 2, which forbade local governments from adopting special protections for people with "homosexual, lesbian, or bisexual orientation, conduct, practices, or relationships." The electorate adopted Amendment 2 by a 53 percent to 47 percent majority, negating ordinances already approved in Denver, Boulder, and Aspen and forbidding future measures that might grant non-heterosexual Coloradans distinct rights. Advocates portrayed Amendment 2 as a way to ensure equality by refusing special treatment for gay Coloradans. Opponents noted uncontested legal protections for ethnic minorities and accused supporters of thinly veiled prejudice. A legal challenge emerged quickly, rising to the highest court in the land three years after the measure's adoption. Democratic governor Roy Romer found himself forced to defend a voter-approved measure that he opposed personally.

The state attorney general, Republican Gale Norton, defended the voters' decision before the court on October 10, 1995. The justices ruled the following May that Amendment 2 violated the US Constitution's equal protection clause. Justice Anthony Kennedy noted that, rather than promoting equality, the measure singled out a minority group to disallow it protections available to others. He wrote: "Amendment 2 classifies homosexuals not to further a proper legislative end but to make them unequal to everyone else. This Colorado cannot do. A State cannot so deem a class of persons a stranger to its laws." *Romer v. Evans* proved a significant step toward greater acceptance of diverse genders. In 2018, voters elected as governor Jared Polis, the first openly gay man to hold the office, a choice that reflected how far the once "hate state" had come.

May 21, 1863

A Plea for the Singing Wire

"The telegraph has become an institution of the country. It has run the [Pony] Express and stage coach off the track. No one waits for the mail or reads it when it comes. No matter how contradictory and provokingly unsatisfactory the dispatches, they are universally considered the Alpha and Omega of all that is necessary to know." Thus stated the *Weekly Commonwealth* of Denver on May 21, 1863, imploring investors to link Colorado Territory to the wider world.

Few technologies transformed humanity as dramatically as the telegraph. With an iron or copper wire and devices at either end to send and receive electronic pulses, people could for the first time reliably transmit complicated messages at speeds faster than a person could travel. In the spring of 1861, the first transcontinental telegraph line reached Julesburg, from which personal notes and news traveled by coach up the South Platte River to the mining districts. Volunteers bound for the Civil War marveled at the technology: "At Julesburg we struck the telegraph, and many of our boys who had been for four years delving in the bowels of the Rocky Mountains, did not repress a shout at the sight of this evidence that the confines of civilization had been approaching them." The line extended to Denver and Central City by November 1863. From then on—except during interruptions from weather, prairie fires, and sabotage—dispatches from across the country appeared in Colorado papers a day or so after the event.

The telegraph drew together formerly isolated regions and put the "united" in the United States. The press and the public grew accustomed, if not addicted, to instantaneous information, sometimes leading to disastrous results. Immediately dependent on the technology, Coloradans grew hysterical during interruptions to service in 1864. Panic about the territory's disconnection helped inspire the Sand Creek Massacre that November. Much like modern technology that follows in its footsteps, most notably the internet, the telegraph affected society in immeasurable ways, drawing the world together and making easier communication a necessity of life.

May 22, 1861

Berthoud Makes Camp in Middle Park

A party led by surveyor Edward L. Berthoud made camp near the Grand (Colorado) River in Middle Park on May 22, 1861, while on an expedition to find a railroad route across the Continental Divide. The pass they had recently traversed still bears their commander's name.

A native of Switzerland, Berthoud trained as a surveyor and engineer in New York and New Jersey. He worked on railroad and land projects in Panama, Kentucky, Indiana, and Kansas during the 1850s, earning a reputation for hard work and thoroughness. In the spring of 1860, Berthoud and his wife, Helen S. Ferrell, joined her family in Golden, a booming supply town at the base of the Rocky Mountains. Rumors circulated of a passable breach in the divide near the headwaters of Clear Creek, which flows through Golden, and town boosters like Berthoud saw a way to ensure their community's future. In May 1861, half a dozen men joined him to survey the region. They crested what they named Berthoud Pass on May 12, and ten days later they rested along the banks of the Grand River before returning to Golden on May 28.

Berthoud hoped to demonstrate his namesake pass's utility as a transcontinental railroad route. He accomplished a survey from it to the Mormon settlements in Utah Territory later that same year. Berthoud volunteered for service during the Civil War, spending most of his time along the Santa Fe Trail and at posts including Camp Weld and Forts Lyon and Sedgwick. In Golden after the war, Berthoud served in the territorial legislature. He proved invaluable as a surveyor and manager of the Golden-based Colorado Central Railroad (CC), although he failed to find a feasible crossing over Berthoud or Loveland Passes. He also promoted the Colorado School of Mines, which named a building on its campus after him. Berthoud's name survives in a Larimer County town along the CC's eastern slope route, and travelers on US Highway 40 follow in his path every time they cross between Clear Creek and Grand Counties.

May 23, 1868

"Kit" Carson Dies

One of the American West's most iconic characters, the trapper, scout, and soldier Christopher "Kit" Carson died at Fort Lyon in present-day Bent County on May 23, 1868.

For decades, Carson participated in essential events of Colorado and western history. Born in Kentucky in 1809, he grew up in Missouri and set out across the Santa Fe Trail in 1826. By the decade's end, Carson ranged across western North America as a fur trapper. He hunted on the upper reaches of the North Platte, Laramie, and South Platte Rivers in the early 1830s, harvesting beaver pelts in North and South Parks while wintering on the Arkansas River near modern Pueblo. By the decade's end, Carson trapped in western Colorado, supplying furs to the ramshackle Fort Davy Crockett on the Green River and Antoine Robidoux's vast trading empire.

The well-traveled Carson used Taos, New Mexico, as his base of operations. After his first two wives—an Arapaho and a Southern Cheyenne—died, Carson married Taoseña Josepha Jaramillo in 1843. By that time, William Bent had hired him as a hunter for Bent's Fort, the economic hub of the high plains. He also accompanied Lieutenant John C. Frémont on several expeditions across the West in the 1840s. In 1855, Carson joined his former boss Ceran St. Vrain on a campaign against Mouache Utes in what is now southern Colorado. When the Civil War commenced, he volunteered in New Mexico and fought at Glorieta Pass in 1862. After the war, Carson commanded Fort Garland in the San Luis Valley before retiring to Boggsville near present-day Las Animas. After escorting a Ute treaty-making delegation to Washington, DC, in early 1868, he moved to the new Fort Lyon, relocated from its flood-prone original location about 20 miles downstream the year before. That May, Carson's hectic pace caught up with him.

Carson's legacy endures through numerous Colorado place names, including Kit Carson County, a town in Cheyenne County, and a fourteener in the Sangre de Cristo Mountains of Saguache County. A stained glass window bearing his likeness also hangs in the state capitol.

May 24, 1911

Creating Colorado National Monument

President William H. Taft used the Antiquities Act to declare a vast tract of stone formations and canyons in Mesa County as Colorado National Monument on May 24, 1911.

The monument owes its existence to John Otto. Some people considered the Missouri native an eccentric, while others viewed him as dangerous. Denver authorities arrested him at the state capitol in 1903 after he sent Governor James. H. Peabody a threatening letter. Upon his release, Otto worked as a laborer in Fruita. In 1907, he relocated to the escarpment south of the Colorado River, where Otto built trails, lit bonfires to celebrate Independence Day and other holidays, and lobbied civic and business leaders in Grand Junction to advocate for the site.

The federal government removed the area from homesteading in 1907, and Taft raised the site to monument status four years later. Its name proved contentious—some people wanted to honor a prominent person, but no one could agree on the honoree. A Grand Junction newspaper proposed "Smith National Monument Park" to boost tourism: "The hills would be covered with [Smiths] and the broad mesas and plains would be carpeted with Smiths from the four quarters of the globe." In the end, the innocuous Colorado National Monument won the honor.

With the support of Congressman Edward T. Taylor, Otto won appointment as the park's superintendent and worked to preserve the natural landscape while continuing to build trails. He also advocated wildlife protection and introduced a bison herd in the mid-1920s. After one too many clashes with Grand Junction and Fruita officials, Otto lost his position in 1927. The peculiar promoter moved to California, where he had once served time in an insane asylum. During the Great Depression, the Civilian Conservation Corps built a meandering road called Rim

Rock Drive to enable automobile tourism. Proposals appear from time to time to promote the monument to a national park but have often failed as a result of congressional lethargy or the perennial debate over a proper name for the remarkable landscape on the western slope.

Bloodshed at Bull Hill

Tension among mine workers, owners, and law enforcement came to a head in western El Paso (now Teller) County on May 25, 1894, when shots rang out near Victor, a stronghold for striking laborers. The crisis represented Colorado's first—but far from last—labor war.

A labor dispute at Leadville in 1880 included a show of arms by strikers, local residents, and the Colorado National Guard (CNG), but cooler heads prevailed. Fourteen years later, the booming Cripple Creek district had no such luck. As the silver industry collapsed during the Panic of 1893, gold mining in the shadow of Pikes Peak offered a ray of economic hope. But early the next year, members of the Western Federation of Miners (WFM) protested new policies that required miners to work either longer shifts without a pay increase or the usual eight hours but at reduced pay. Protests fell on deaf ears, and the WFM called for a strike in early February.

In mid-March, mine owners imported workers to restart production, and strikers fought back. They occupied Victor and turned it into a union camp, while El Paso County sheriff M. F. Bowers appealed to Governor Davis Waite for help. The Populist executive, who sympathized with the workers, sent CNG units to investigate, but they reported calm. In response, Bowers created a volunteer army of 1,200 men paid by the mine owners to restore control. The strikers fortified Bull Hill near Victor, confiscated a mine operated by replacement laborers, and dynamited the offending works. Early on May 25, a party of 300 struck out to attack Bowers's force encamped nearby in preparation for their own assault on Bull Hill. One man on each side died in the battle and both groups took prisoners, which they exchanged the following day.

Waite headed for the Cripple Creek district on May 27. He disbanded Bowers's extra-legal force and called in the CNG as peacekeepers, although skirmishes continued into early June. At Colorado Springs and Denver, the governor negotiated a settlement that restored the status quo, one of the few episodes of labor conflict in Colorado history where the workers actually won.

The Zephyr Dashes from Denver

In the words of the *Denver Post*, "Write down 5:04:40 a.m., Saturday, May 26, 1934, as a moment in railroad history." With the snap of a tape stretched across the tracks at Denver's Union Station, which stopped a ceremonial clock at that exact time, a technological marvel set out to transform rail travel with a record-breaking sprint across the Great Plains.

The Chicago, Burlington & Quincy Railroad, commonly known as the Burlington Route, built across the prairies to Denver in the early 1880s. In the 1930s it experimented with high-speed travel between several major American cities and produced a stainless steel train known as the Zephyr. The first Zephyr made its trial "dawn-to-dusk" run from Denver to Chicago in May 1934. Blasting through Fort Morgan, Brush, Akron, Yuma, and Wray, it left Colorado just over two hours after departing from Denver. Law enforcement kept cheering, wind-whipped crowds at a safe distance all along the route. Spectators old enough to remember wagon travel across the plains marveled at the "Silver Streak" as it reached speeds of 112 miles per hour in eastern Colorado. Only one passenger seemed disturbed by the experience—Zeph, a burro accustomed to life on Berthoud Pass, who rode the Zephyr to reflect the changing nature of transportation. The nonstop train, traveling an average of 78 miles per hour, arrived in Chicago a few minutes past thirteen hours after it had left Denver, just over a thousand miles away.

The Burlington Route eventually ran more than a dozen Zephyrs, including ones linking Denver with Chicago and Houston and the luxurious California Zephyr that traversed the Colorado Rockies. The decline of passenger rail service as a result of air and automobile travel sealed the Zephyrs' fate, however, and their service ended in the 1970s. In 1985, Denver's minor league baseball team changed its name from the Bears to the Zephyrs to honor the historic line, and the team retained the moniker after moving to New Orleans in 1992. Chicago's Museum of Science and Industry displays the locomotive that made the record-shattering 1934 run.

Colorado Territory Gets a Governor

William Gilpin arrived in Denver to cheers, artillery salutes, and a gala reception on May 27, 1861, as Colorado Territory residents welcomed their newly appointed first governor.

William Gilpin, soldier and politician who served as Colorado's first territorial governor and a state entrepreneur and advocate through the late nineteenth century

Gilpin's career immersed him in western American affairs. Born in Delaware in 1815, he joined the US Army at age twenty and served in Florida before settling in Missouri. Gilpin joined Lieutenant John C. Frémont's western survey in 1842, which scouted much of what would become eastern Colorado. He advocated American expansion to the Pacific Ocean and volunteered for military service during the war with Mexico. Gilpin joined the invasion of New Mexico via the Santa Fe Trail in 1846 and guarded the route for the rest of the decade. During the 1850s, he promoted development in Missouri and the West generally. According to legend, Frank Blair, a prominent Missouri Republican, encouraged President Abraham Lincoln to name Gilpin as Colorado's first territorial governor in the spring of 1861: "Billy Gilpin has done more for that section of the country than any man now living. Why, Mr. President, Billy Gilpin built Pikes Peak." When Lincoln asked Blair how he knew, he responded "I saw him do it."

The new governor praised Colorado as a "commonwealth of the primeval mountains." He maintained peaceful relationships with American Indian cultures, organized the territorial government (which named a county for him), and rallied Coloradans against a Confederate invasion in the spring of 1862. His unauthorized defense spending cost Gilpin his job, however; word of his dismissal arrived in Denver the same day Colorado's volunteers won at Glorieta Pass. Gilpin remained active in local politics and economic development for the rest of his life. He purchased part of the Sangre de Cristo Grant in the San Luis Valley and fostered agricultural settlement there. Building relationships with Hispano residents, he even referred to himself as "Guillermo Guilpin." When Gilpin died in Denver in 1894, thousands of people attended his grand funeral, celebrating a visionary who never spoke of Colorado without smiling.

May 28, 2008

DU on the International Stage

A ceremony at the University of Denver (DU) on May 28, 2008, bestowed a new name on the college's international relations program. Rechristened that day as the Josef Korbel School of International Studies, it ranks as a preeminent center of study for global affairs. Two women with special connections to Korbel and DU emerged as leading American policymakers at the turn of the twenty-first century: secretaries of state Madeleine Albright and Condoleezza Rice.

Korbel, a Czechoslovakian diplomat, fled the country with his family in 1939 as it fell to Nazi Germany. He worked with his exiled government in Great Britain during World War II and returned home when the fighting ceased in 1945. Three years later, after a Soviet-backed government hijacked Czechoslovakia, the Korbels left one last time, finding refuge in the United States. The father obtained a teaching position at DU, and the family flourished in Denver. In 1964, Korbel organized a graduate program in international relations and served as its first dean. He trained students in the nuances of diplomacy at DU until his death in 1977.

The Korbels' daughter, Madeleine, inherited her father's fascination with global politics. While interning at the *Denver Post* during college, she met and married newspaperman Joseph Albright; they had three children before divorcing in 1982.

By then, Madeleine Albright was advising Democratic Party officials and candidates on world affairs. President Bill Clinton nominated her as ambassador to the United Nations in 1993, and four years later she won confirmation as secretary of state, the highest-ranking woman in American government to date. Meanwhile, her father's star pupil at DU, Rice, climbed the Republican Party ranks. She became national security adviser under President George W. Bush in 2001. Four years later, she was promoted as the second woman to serve as secretary of state, where she coordinated an interventionist policy. Although Albright and Rice espoused dramatically different visions of foreign affairs, the lessons they learned from Korbel in Colorado helped them shape the post–Cold War world.

May 29, 1998

A Cop's Murder Rocks Cortez

Near a bridge over McElmo Creek on the south side of Cortez, the seat of Montezuma County in Colorado's southwestern corner, Officer Dale D. Claxton pulled over a stolen water tank truck on May 29, 1998. Before he left his cruiser, a man jumped from the cab and riddled Claxton with bullets from a modified automatic rifle. The policeman's murder instigated the West's largest manhunt to date, as law enforcement descended on the Four Corners region.

Many questions linger about the intentions of the three men—Robert M. Mason, Jason W. McVean, and Alan L. Pilon—driving the stolen vehicle that day. All three expressed hatred toward authority, including government and law enforcement. McVean and his friend Mason, both of Durango, allied with Pilon, from the Dolores County seat of Dove Creek, over their mutual resentments. Why they stole the truck from a construction site near Ignacio, headquarters of the Southern Ute Reservation in La Plata County, is but the first of many uncertainties.

After Claxton's murder, the three fled westward into the desert straddling the Colorado-Utah line. Local, state, and federal officers pursued them, three of whom suffered gunshot wounds during the search. Rangers and tourists at Hovenweep National Monument hid in a ravine near the visitors' center to avoid the fugitives, who received aid from people who shared their views in the isolated region. Governor Roy Romer dispatched the Colorado National Guard to assist in the search, coordinated from Cahone in Dolores County. Romer permitted the guard to pursue leads into Utah, inspiring complaints of overreaching from the neighboring state.

Within a week, law enforcement found Mason's body on Navajo land in Utah. Hunters found Pilon's remains in the desert in 1999, but eight years passed before a cowboy stumbled on McVean's bones a few miles away. How and when each man died remain topics of debate, as do their plans for the stolen truck. A sign at the McElmo Creek bridge honors Claxton, as do the names of the police headquarters and a federal building in Cortez and Durango, respectively.

| May 30, 1881 |

Allen True's Birthday

Allen T. True, born in Colorado Springs on May 30, 1881, earned a reputation as one of the Centennial State's most popular and prolific artists through a number of prominent commissions in Colorado and across the country over the course of his decades-long career.

True spent his youth in the western United States and Mexico, imbued with the richness of a continent in transformation and a deep affection for its landscape and cultures. In the late 1890s his family settled in Denver. True graduated from Manual High School and discovered a love of art while studying at the University of Denver. He pursued his work with illustrators along the East Coast. True's first show took place in Denver in 1908, and he moved back to his native state to make it his professional base. He produced murals for homes, libraries, and movie theaters in the 1910s. True won his first major commission in 1917 to paint murals for the Wyoming State Capitol and a few years later won a similar contract for the Missouri statehouse.

In the 1920s, True provided art for several Denver projects, including the temples in Civic Center, the Colorado National Bank, and the Mountain States Telephone and Telegraph Company. Work slowed during the Great Depression, but he restored art in the Teller House and opera house in Central City, painted murals honoring transportation for the Brown Palace Hotel, and commemorated the role of water in the West through a series of murals installed at the Colorado State Capitol. Wyoming officials also hired True to design the bucking bronco logo still used on state license plates. True's last works, historically evocative like almost all of his paintings, found homes in Denver's City and County Building and the University of Colorado. True died in Denver in 1955 after suffering several strokes and was buried in Colorado Springs.

Some of True's works have been painted over, sold to collectors, or lost in demolished buildings, but many survive intact and in place. Their vibrancy and popularity endure decades after their installation, reflecting the appeal of True's subjects and his artistic style.

Elbert County Picks up the Pieces

Colorado endures more than its share of flooding, from gradually swelling waterways after days of rainfall to flash floods caused by cloudbursts. In late May 1935, after several weeks of spring rain, one more storm proved one too many. Flooding caused damage and cost lives across the eastern slope, but residents of Elbert County bore the brunt of the storm.

Kiowa Creek, a tributary of the South Platte River, heads in the Black Forest of El Paso County. Steady rains caused it to rise early on May 30, flowing into the towns of Elbert and Kiowa. The danger seemed to pass, but as residents assessed the damage, a new crisis brewed. A sudden storm around noon dropped 8 inches of rain, and Kiowa Creek's depth increased by 8 feet that afternoon. When darkness fell on May 30, the people of Elbert County knew they had been hard hit by nature's fury, but until the next morning they did not know how badly.

As the waters receded on May 31, Elbert County reeled. Half of the town of Elbert no longer existed. The flood inundated basements, and buildings collapsed as if imploded. Kiowa, the county seat, fared nearly as badly, although a railroad grade helped protect the community. The *Rocky Mountain News* reported "scenes of destruction as if a giant had strode thru the towns, smashing houses and business buildings with unbelievable force." The Colorado National Guard patrolled to keep out scavengers, while the Civilian Conservation Corps helped with repairs.

Farther downstream, water swept through Bennett in Adams County and washed out bridges leading into Wiggins in Morgan County, isolating the town. Floodwater saturated Brush's business district and its Great Western Sugar Company factory. As water moved down the Platte and Republican Rivers, flooding extended into Nebraska and Kansas. In Elbert County, damage to the Colorado & Southern Railway proved so severe that it abandoned the line, adding to the region's woes. Six of nearly twenty fatalities from the flood across eastern Colorado came from Elbert County, which considers the 1935 flood the most daunting crisis in its history.

June

Tesla Turns on the Lights

Scientist and inventor Nikola Tesla commenced a journal of cutting-edge experiments in electricity on June 1, 1899, a months-long project that he conducted in Colorado Springs.

Colorado boasted scientific fame before Tesla's arrival. In 1891, Lucien L. Nunn inaugurated a power-generating facility near Ophir in San Miguel County and offered electricity to mines and mills near Telluride. Nunn's facility—which remains in operation—demonstrated the benefits of alternating current (AC), in contrast to direct current (DC). It used techniques developed by Tesla, who came to the United States from southeastern Europe in 1884. By the late nineteenth century, Tesla's laboratory on Long Island proved insufficient—and dangerously close to New York City—for his experiments. A friend pointed Tesla toward Colorado Springs, and he secured a site on Knob Hill east of town for his laboratory. Upon his arrival in May 1899, Tesla attended a reception with Governor Charles S. Thomas and reporters. Tesla told them he hoped to send wireless messages from Pikes Peak to Paris using universal electrical conduits.

Tesla ensconced himself in his city-powered laboratory from June 1899 to January 1900. He raved about Colorado's high elevation and thin air, which encouraged electrical conductivity, allowed sound to travel vast distances, aided in the treatment of tuberculosis patients, and dried out his skin and hair. Tesla disdained the prairie landscape but marveled at the colorful sunrises and sunsets. "Despite the beautiful spectacle offered by the parting sun," he observed, "one feels sad when its disk sinks behind the mountains and one is thoroughly glad to see it rise again."

Tesla made his presence known in Colorado Springs. One experiment blew out the city's power generators and produced a thunder clap loud enough to be heard in Cripple Creek. In the process, though, Tesla demonstrated that he could reproduce the natural phenomenon of lightning. The experiments Tesla conducted over seven months in El Paso County aided his work for the rest of his life, one increasingly celebrated in the early twenty-first century.

Colorado Squared

President Abraham Lincoln signed a bill on June 2, 1862, to establish a federal land office in Colorado Territory. This agency, working with surveyors, divided up much of the territory within Colorado into easily defined and distributed units, encouraging American settlement.

From the air, much of the United States looks like a checkerboard, a vast series of squares. Some squares have circles inside, thanks to Strasburg resident Frank Zybach and the center-pivot irrigation sprinklers he patented in 1952. The geometric land division predates even the US Constitution. In 1785, the Confederation government—created during the American Revolution to bring the thirteen states together—adopted the Land Ordinance. It authorized a simple, practical way to define tracts west of the Appalachian Mountains, carving up land into square miles or fractions thereof. Its uniformity ignored regional conditions, treating swamps, deserts, forests, grasslands, and mountain peaks equally. For seven decades, Coloradans bought or homesteaded over 22 million acres, approximately a third of the state. The rest remained in federal hands for forests, parks, grazing, or military use; devolved to the state to sell for public education; or survived as American Indian reservations. One of the essential measurements used to carve up Colorado—40° north latitude—endures in Boulder County as Baseline Road. Many of Colorado's primary city streets stand a mile apart, another legacy of the Land Ordinance.

Since the mid-nineteenth century, advocates for local control of federal land have argued that those tracts in Colorado should belong to the people of Colorado, to use as they see fit without interference from Washington, DC. They forget that on behalf of the entire nation, the federal government bought that land from France, conquered it from Mexico, made oftentimes nefarious deals with American Indian cultures to extinguish their claims, and established Colorado Territory, which eventually achieved statehood. Colorado therefore owes its existence to the federal government, a reality some modern Americans would rather not acknowledge.

The Arkansas River Flood

According to newspaper reports, "Friday, June 3, was a dark day in the history of Pueblo, Colorado's second city. Flood waters . . . devastated the business and lower residence sections of the town, sweeping away hundreds of houses and causing

The swollen Arkansas River inundates Pueblo's downtown business district during the flood of early July 1921.

great loss of life." The Arkansas River flood of 1921 remains one of Colorado's deadliest and most destructive natural disasters.

Subject to floods since its founding in the mid-nineteenth century, Pueblo faced a wall of water in 1894 that inspired officials to re-channel the formerly meandering river and erect 18-foot-high levees to protect the city. Steady, heavy rains in early June 1921, however, proved too much for the system to bear. The Arkansas and its tributaries Fountain and Dry Creeks swelled by June 2, and the following day the water rose to 24 feet, overtopping and in places breaching the levees, which allowed water to pour into the city even as the level dropped. Water mains and electric lines severed, and sparks started fires that burned unchecked until they ran out of fuel. Devastation extended downstream, inundating farms and communities in Pueblo, Crowley, Otero, Bent, and Prowers Counties, turning an agrarian paradise into a wasteland.

The flood's cost in human and financial terms remains uncertain. Local governments claimed nearly $20 million in damage. Official records list seventy-eight bodies recovered in the Arkansas valley, but the death toll likely stands in the hundreds. Farmers found human bones in their fields as far away as the Kansas boundary for years afterward. As the flood receded, it left behind a mangled city, one the state and nation rushed to help. While crews rebuilt railroad tracks and bridges, the companies that owned them sent relief trains. Congress approved federal aid, while President Warren G. Harding encouraged food and clothing donations to the American Red Cross. In 1922, state legislators appropriated money for flood control projects along the Arkansas River. Within three years, concrete embankments held the river in place, just in time to contain another flood, but Pueblo's physical and emotional scars took far longer to repair.

June 4, 1869

Powell Crosses into Colorado

A ten-member mapping expedition entered Colorado Territory by boat via the Green River on June 4, 1869. Led by John W. Powell, a US Army surveyor who lost his right arm during the Civil War, the team arrived in a broad valley known as Browns Hole, named for a British fur trapper who had lived there four decades before, in present-day Moffat County.

Powell arrived at the Green River on the Union Pacific Railroad in Wyoming Territory. Four small boats filled with scientific instruments, journals, and supplies set out on May 24 for the Colorado River Exploring Expedition. After traveling through narrow defiles for a week and a half, Powell and his men marveled at the broad, lush valley with abundant wildlife and great agricultural potential. The party tarried at what Powell renamed Browns Park for three days before floating down the Green into a canyon through the Gates of Lodore on June 8, into what is now Dinosaur National Monument. Powell's description of ancient reptile fossils in the area was the first ever recorded. For nine days they struggled through rapids (including one particularly rough stretch they called Disaster Falls), portages, and an uncontrolled campfire that nearly destroyed their supplies and instruments. The company arrived at the confluence of the Green and Yampa Rivers on June 17, in a small widening of the canyon Powell named Echo Park for its auditory qualities. Writing at that spot, he waxed rhapsodic about the turbulent, noisy Green: "The roar of its waters was heard unceasingly from the hour we entered it until we landed here. No quiet in all that time. But its walls and cliffs, its peaks and crags, its amphitheatres and alcoves tell a story of beauty and grandeur that I hear yet— and shall hear."

The expedition continued downstream through the Grand Canyon and encountered Mormon settlers in northwestern Arizona Territory by the end of August. Powell returned east in triumph by year's end, having accomplished a daring and scientifically compelling journey.

Battling Wyoming over Water

The US Supreme Court decided *Wyoming v. Colorado* on June 5, 1922, which—for the moment—resolved one decades-old battle over the West's most precious resource: water.

Agricultural settlement in dry parts of the West depends on irrigation to supplement scarce rainfall. In territorial days, Colorado adopted the doctrine of prior appropriation to allot water rights on a first-come, first-served basis, a policy copied by Wyoming and other states. By the turn of the twentieth century, competition for water often led states to fight one another in court, starting with *Kansas v. Colorado* in 1902 and 1907, which challenged Colorado's practice of divvying up the Arkansas River so much that it ceased to flow at the state line. The high court ruled that in natural courses, some water must flow from one state to another regardless of law and practice. The dispute with Wyoming focused on the Laramie River, which starts in Larimer County and flows north. Thirsty farmers in northeastern Colorado wanted to divert water to the nearby Cache la Poudre River, which caused little argument within the state since few settlers lived along the isolated Laramie south of the boundary. Wyomingites, however, objected to the loss of a resource on which they depended and asked the high court to intervene in 1911.

More than a decade passed before the Supreme Court issued its ruling in *Wyoming v. Colorado*. The justices affirmed prior appropriation as a valid policy and rejected the notion that rivers crossing state boundaries trumped the right of upstream diversions. However, to ensure fair use of the Laramie River, the court shaped a byzantine formula to provide equitable distribution of the water. Colorado, Wyoming, and Nebraska all ended up in court over the Laramie and North Platte Rivers in later years to sort out controversies that developed as a result.

To avoid legal costs and extended court battles exemplified by *Wyoming v. Colorado*, many western states pursued water compacts as a way to divide the resource, most famously the seven-state Colorado River Compact adopted less than six months after that 1922 decision.

Fireworks at the Independence Station

"The most dastardly crime ever committed in the annals of the West," according to a newspaper correspondent, took place in Teller County on June 6, 1904. A bitter strike climaxed when members of the Western Federation of Miners (WFM) dynamited the Independence depot, killing more than a dozen workers brought in to replace them during a labor dispute.

The WFM organized many workers in the state's most lucrative industry at the turn of the twentieth century. A national organization, it won its first victory at Cripple Creek in 1894. The WFM convinced Colorado voters to adopt the eight-hour day for industrial workers in 1902. In the same election, Republican James H. Peabody won the governor's office. He intended to promote economic growth in Colorado by restricting union activities. In 1903, several strikes broke out as workers attempted to force their employers to abide by the eight-hour day. An anti-union mob chased striking WFM members in Idaho Springs out of Clear Creek County. Peabody ordered the Colorado National Guard (CNG) to protect mines in San Miguel County against WFM militancy and to defend ore-processing mills in Colorado City, on the western edge of Colorado Springs. In solidarity with the mill workers who processed ore from the gold mining districts in Teller County, WFM members there went on strike in September.

As they had in 1894, union members hunkered in Victor while the CNG took over Cripple Creek. Violent incidents punctuated the strike, none more gruesome than at Independence on June 6, 1904. In response, the CNG rounded up more than 1,500 people suspected of militancy and evicted 238 of them from the state, shipping them by rail to the Kansas and New Mexico lines and forcing them from train cars. The strike fizzled afterward, as did the WFM. Employers resisted the eight-hour industrial day for years until Governor John F. Shafroth, a Progressive Democrat, and the General Assembly enforced it by the decade's end. The Independence depot attack offers an excellent example of the high stakes and brutal tactics of Colorado's labor wars.

June 7, 1964

POWs in Peacetime at Trinidad

The federal government sent thousands of German and Italian prisoners of war to Colorado during World War II. While officers remained in the camps, enlisted men served as manual labor across the state. Large facilities at Camp Carson, Greeley, and Trinidad provided depots from which to send workers out to forty-five satellite camps. The prisoners harvested peaches, peas, and sugar beets and helped maintain Camp Hale on Tennessee Pass. They refused work in coal mines, however, arguing that it might aid the American war effort. Internees lived on subsistence diets, often supplemented by their employers, and planned escape attempts. A handful of Germans, aided by a sympathetic American soldier, escaped from Camp Hale in 1944 and made it to Mexico before federal authorities caught up with them. Many others considered their time in Colorado preferable to combat, so much so that on June 7, 1964, a group of former German prisoners of war returned to the camp at Trinidad for a reunion.

Around 600 of the 4,300 Germans held at Trinidad organized a club after they returned to Europe. In 1964, city officials invited the club to visit the place where officers had studied medicine, law, and engineering, which gave them a foundation for their future careers. Eleven men arrived in Denver on June 6—the twentieth anniversary of D-Day—and proceeded south to Las Animas County. The next day their reunion commenced with formal meals at a country club and visits to Trinidad's historic mansions. Over the course of four days they honored American forces with a wreath-laying ceremony at the county courthouse and visited the camp's ruins. The former prisoners pointed out a 150-foot-long tunnel that had allowed three Germans to escape, reaching the Texas panhandle before their recapture. One of the escapees attended the reunion.

Germans and Americans alike praised the 1964 reunion as an affirmation of friendship during the Cold War. Alfred Kraft, a paratrooper during World War II and a chemical engineer after it, quipped, "It's going to take me three weeks to recover from all this hospitality."

June 8, 2002

Colorado's Largest Fire

A spark struck at a campsite by a US Forest Service employee on June 8, 2002, ignited the largest recorded fire ever to beset Colorado. Over the span of six weeks that dry summer, the Hayman fire scorched about 215 square miles in Douglas, Jefferson, Park, and Teller Counties.

According to a confession made by Terry L. Barton, she accidentally set off the inferno deep in the Pike National Forest when she burned letters from her estranged husband, although many details of Barton's story remain in dispute. The fire spread rapidly through a tinder-dry forest, a situation complicated by squabbles between local fire departments over responsibility and strategy. The blaze claimed 133 houses and led to the deaths of six people, including a Florissant woman who succumbed to a smoke-induced asthma attack and five firefighters from Oregon whose van rolled on Interstate 70 in Garfield County while heading to fight it. Governor Bill Owens earned headlines—and the enmity of the state's tourism industry—with his awed, off-the-cuff remark: "It looks as if all of Colorado is burning." Hayman died out in late July 2002 after claiming more than 137,000 acres, roughly the size of nearby Fort Carson.

Although Hayman retains the record of Colorado's largest recorded forest fire by size, subsequent blazes surpassed its destructive power. A decade later, the High Park fire in Larimer County's Roosevelt National Forest claimed one life and nearly 250 houses and smothered Fort Collins in smoke and ash as it singed about 132 square miles in June 2012. High Park held the record of Colorado's most destructive inferno only briefly until the Waldo Canyon fire, burning at the same time in El Paso and Teller Counties, surpassed it. Although it covered less than 29 square miles by its containment in mid-July, Waldo Canyon destroyed 346 houses, including many on the western edge of Colorado Springs. A year later, the Black Forest fire broke the record yet again, taking more than 500 houses over 22 square miles in June 2013. Each inferno reminded Coloradans the hard way of the dangers of life among the splendor of scenic forests.

June 9, 1864

Washing away Camp Collins

The Cache la Poudre River, already swollen with mountain snowmelt, overflowed its banks after a summer rainstorm on June 9, 1864. The flood in Larimer County took no lives, but it destroyed a small military installation near present-day Laporte, known as Camp Collins.

In the summer of 1864, Coloradans feared the prospect of American Indians attacking across the northern plains into their territory. To provide a measure of defense for the mining regions and protect travelers on the Cherokee Trail that paralleled the Rocky Mountains' eastern slope between the Santa Fe and Oregon Trails, the US Army authorized a military base on the Cache la Poudre River in the spring of 1864. Colonel William O. Collins, operating from Fort Laramie on the North Platte River, authorized the post, and the soldiers who established it named it Camp Collins in his honor. Weeks after troops set up tents along the river, it swept away their camp. Collins sought a less exposed site and chose a low bluff 6 miles downstream, "having superior advantages in the way of wood, water, and grass without danger of overflow and where sufficient territory could be obtained without interfering with the claims of any citizens."

As soldiers built a new post in October 1864—soon promoted to Fort Collins— paranoia intensified. Nervous settlers moved closer to the base, although Collins thought "much of the alarm unnecessary and hope[d] the panic will soon subside." Fort Collins remained on the outskirts of conflict after the Sand Creek Massacre, and its troops continued to watch the trails. Most of its compliment consisted of "Galvanized Yankees," former Confederate volunteers who served in the West to avoid waiting out the Civil War in a prison camp. Danger passed by the spring of 1867, and the army abandoned the post. In the 1870s it served as the nucleus of a colony that took the name Fort Collins, a city best known today as the home of craft breweries and Colorado State University. Nothing remains of either post, although downtown Fort Collins stands on the rise above the Cache la Poudre River where soldiers erected the replacement fort in late 1864.

First News of the Lindenmeier Site

The Coffin family sent a letter to Jesse L. Nusbaum, a Greeley native and the National Park Service's first archaeologist, on June 10, 1931. Their missive informed Nusbaum and the scholarly world about evidence of prehistoric activity they had found in Larimer County near the Wyoming boundary. The location—known to modern scholars as the Lindenmeier Site—has contributed essential and diverse information about the earliest inhabitants of Colorado.

Named for William Lindenmeier Jr., who owned the property in the early twentieth century, the Lindenmeier Site includes a camp and hunting zone used by some of the first humans in the American West. Academics refer to its inhabitants

View of the Soapstone Prairie Natural Area in Larimer County, with the Lindenmeier archaeological site in the foreground arroyos, as viewed in 2009

as Folsom people, after a New Mexico town near the first discovery of their stone tools; many items collected there reside in the Denver Museum of Nature & Science. Evidence of tool making and daily life suggests that dozens of Folsom people occupied Lindenmeier annually and likely seasonally more than 12,000 years ago when ancestors of American Indian cultures spread across the Western Hemisphere at the end of the last ice age. Lindenmeier suggests that Colorado's high plains offered plentiful game for hunter-gatherers and that generations of people gathered there to hunt antelope, bison, and deer. They fashioned stone points for spears and processed their kills, cleaning hides and shaping bones for needles and perhaps even to play games. For the earliest Coloradans, Lindenmeier was the hub of a large community, a gathering point beyond compare.

Members of the Coffin family—who studied at the Colorado School of Mines and Colorado A&M College (now Colorado State University)—located the site in 1924 and conducted careful amateur digs for seven years before informing Nusbaum and other scholars about it. Teams from the Smithsonian Institution and elsewhere organized digs in the 1930s, although much of Lindenmeier awaits future study. Fort Collins owns the site today, and visitors can ponder their predecessors from an overlook at the Soapstone Prairie Natural Area.

June 11, 1864

The Hungate Massacre

Relations between American Indians and gold seekers proved peaceful during the Pikes Peak gold rush, although a harsh winter forced some native groups to raid for food in early 1864. The calm evaporated with the murder of the Hungate family—Nathan, Ellen, and their daughters Florence (age 4) and Laura (age 2½)—on June 11, 1864, in present-day Elbert County.

A Sioux rebellion in Minnesota in 1862 inspired other native cultures to reclaim their sovereignty by force, especially with the federal government distracted by the Civil War. Like ripples in a pond, the riotous mood spread across the Great Plains. Americans considered the Southern Cheyennes and Arapahos in eastern Colorado Territory amicable neighbors, but the potential for violence—and the view of American Indians as a monolithic, dangerous group—overwhelmed reason in the summer of 1864. The attack on the Hungates fueled the fire.

Nathan and a hired hand went looking for stray cattle on June 11 when they saw smoke rising from the homestead. The father rushed toward his family while the employee sought help. Rescuers found all four Hungates dead and mutilated and brought the bodies back to Denver to display in a shed behind the city hall on Larimer Street, incensing the populace. The *Weekly Commonwealth* declared, "Talking at the corners of the streets does less good than meeting together for drill, and being ready at a moment's warning to put after the murdering thieves."

Although investigations failed to determine the party responsible for the Hungate murders, all American Indians fell under suspicion. Panic built throughout the summer of 1864, fostered by Governor John Evans. On August 11, he issued a proclamation "authorizing all citizens of Colorado, either individually or in such parties as they may organize . . . to kill and destroy as enemies of the country wherever they may be found, all such hostile Indians." This vigilantism culminated in the Sand Creek Massacre that November against Cheyennes and Arapahos unconnected to the Hungate murders but seen as a convenient target all the same.

June 12, 1996

An Avalanche in Downtown Denver

A parade through downtown Denver, culminating in a rally at Civic Center park, allowed an estimated 450,000 people to celebrate the state's first championship in a professional sport when the Colorado Avalanche hockey team brought home the Stanley Cup on June 12, 1996.

The National Hockey League (NHL) came to the Centennial State for the first time in 1976 with the Colorado Rockies, not to be confused with the baseball team that shares the same name. The Rockies played at McNichols Arena in Denver for six seasons but ranked repeatedly at the bottom of the league and moved to New Jersey in 1982. Several non-NHL teams skated through Colorado after that, including the International Hockey League's Denver Grizzlies, who won their championship in 1995 during their first and only season before heading to Utah. That year, the NHL's Quebec Nordiques relocated to Denver and took the name Colorado Avalanche.

After a stellar inaugural year, the Avs swept the Florida Panthers to win the Stanley Cup in early June 1996, including a fourth game that remained scoreless until the third overtime. The *Denver Post* reported on statewide celebrations, with parties at homes and in bars and restaurants from Steamboat Springs to Grand Junction to Durango. A Colorado Springs resident gushed: "Everybody in the state feels great. The state finally got a champion." The parade and rally on June 12 reflected Colorado's euphoria. The Denver crowd bested the audience that had gathered for Pope John Paul II's mass in Cherry Creek State Park three years earlier by 75,000 people.

The Avalanche defeated the New Jersey Devils—formerly the Colorado Rockies—to win the Stanley Cup again in 2001. Several members of the first season's team returned to the organization, including team captain Joe Sakic as general manager and goaltender Patrick Roy as head coach. Their 1996 victory helped convince officials to approve replacing McNichols Arena with a more modern structure, the Pepsi Center, which opened three years later. The Avs remain a beloved part of Colorado's sports landscape, remembered as the state's first champions.

Devils Head Joins the National Register

Along the Rocky Mountains' eastern front looms Devils Head, a granite outcropping that supposedly resembles Beelzebub in profile, one of the highest points in Douglas County at 9,748 feet. Perched atop the mountain stands a small wooden building with a peaked roof, one of the last manned fire watches in Colorado. The Devils Head lookout, a historical structure and a hiking destination, joined the National Register of Historic Places on June 13, 2003.

As the federal government designated national forests in the early twentieth century, the US Forest Service authorized watch towers to spot and report fires. The agency planned seven for the eastern slope from New Mexico to Wyoming but only built four, including Devils Head, which commenced operations in 1912. Views extend from Pikes Peak—seemingly within touching distance to the south— toward Longs Peak and beyond to the north, deep into the Rockies to the west, and far out over the Great Plains to the east. Originally boasting views of perhaps a hundred miles in every direction, air pollution from urban growth along the eastern slope has limited the vista and made the fire watcher's job more complicated.

Originally, a ranger clung to a precarious table atop the mountain to watch for fires, with a tiny log building nearby as a refuge during storms. The forest service added a cabin for the ranger below the summit of Devils Head in 1914. Five years later, Helen Dowe accepted a job as the fire watcher, the first woman to hold such a position in the United States. The Denver native kept watch over the Pike National Forest and the surrounding countryside for two years before taking a job as a topographer. Stories about Dowe appeared across the country, inspiring other young women to pursue their own adventurous careers in the national forests.

Crews replaced the well-worn lookout and cabin in 1951 and substituted metal stairs for the rickety wooden climb to the summit. A beautiful destination located close to Colorado's largest cities, Devils Head still offers a breathtaking experience—in more ways than one.

The Savior of Colorado Mining

A thirty-two-year-old chemistry professor stepped off a stagecoach in Denver on June 14, 1864, where former territorial governor William Gilpin greeted him. Nathaniel P. Hill had traveled to Colorado Territory to scout mineral resources on a San Luis Valley ranch recently purchased by Gilpin and to explore opportunities of his own around Black Hawk and Central City. Denver's *Weekly Commonwealth* reported that "his visit cannot fail to have a most favorable bearing upon our future development." No one could have imagined how true that statement was.

The year 1864 proved a daunting one for Colorado. It failed in its first attempt to secure statehood, relations between settlers and American Indians disintegrated, and the gold rush had fizzled. Stamp mills, which crushed ore to powder in an attempt to separate gold and other minerals from less valuable rock, proved insufficient to process the mines' output. Investors turned from Colorado to more profitable, promising regions like Idaho and Montana Territories. Hill's reputation as a scientist who could solve thorny problems gave Coloradans hope. He purchased cheap property in Gilpin County to provide ore for testing. Hill traveled to England in early 1866 to confer with colleagues about a new process called smelting, which heated ore to separate its component metals. Hill secured investors and built the Boston & Colorado Smelting Company in Black Hawk in 1867, surrounded by abandoned mines with which to experiment.

The smelter proved a rousing success and led to a renaissance in mining. By the early 1870s, Hill shipped ore from across Boulder, Clear Creek, and Gilpin Counties to his Black Hawk works and opened another smelter in Alma to process the mines in South Park. His first plant relocated to Denver and opened as the Argo Smelter in 1879. Hill invested his fortune in other industries, including the oil fields of Fremont County. His economic triumph led to a political career—after service in the territorial legislature, Hill won election to the US Senate in 1879. A stained glass portrait of Colorado's smelter king stands today in the state capitol.

Dedicating the Red Rocks Amphitheatre

According to a *New York Times* critic who attended Red Rocks amphitheatre's inaugural concert on June 15, 1941, "Nothing in the US could equal the beauty and scenery of the outdoor theatre." Decades of audiences and performers echo the praise of Colorado's most famous stage.

The New York Philharmonic performs at the Red Rocks amphitheatre near Morrison on August 13, 1960.

Iconic names of history and entertainment alike are tied to Red Rocks. In the 1860s, Mouache Utes led by Colorow camped there while George and Isabella Morrison homesteaded nearby; the Jefferson County town of Morrison bears their name. A decade later, Arthur Lakes of the Colorado School of Mines excavated dinosaur fossils in the region. In 1880, developer John B. Walker recognized the commercial value of the perfect natural acoustics between two massive sandstone blocks and promoted the "Garden of the Titans" as an amusement park. He sold the site to Denver for its mountain parks system in 1927. The Civilian Conservation Corps (CCC) cleared the site for architect Burnham Hoyt's tiered seating and stage arrangement.

Early concerts at Red Rocks featured classical music at the insistence of parks director George Cranmer, who also approved the first annual Easter sunrise service in 1947. Audiences clamored for new and old music alike, however, and the park's roster runs the gamut—Johnny Cash, Ray Charles, Nat King Cole, Judy Collins, Bob Dylan, Fleetwood Mac, the Grateful Dead, Jimi Hendrix, the Kingston Trio, Led Zeppelin, the Mormon Tabernacle Choir, Willie Nelson, Phish, Bruce Springsteen, U2, and many more. Local artists—including Big Head Todd and the Monsters, John Denver, and the Nitty Gritty Dirt Band—proved especially popular. The Beatles coasted through a performance in 1964, exerting themselves little since their screaming audience could hardly hear anything

June

anyway. After a Jethro Tull concert in 1971 devolved into a riot, officials restricted events to artists they thought would draw responsible crowds.

A visitors' center celebrating Red Rocks' role in music history opened in 2003. It also displays a statue of a CCC worker, recognizing those who built the incomparable concert venue.

June 16, 1934

A Shortcut in Eagle County

A ceremony along the Colorado River in Eagle County on June 16, 1934, dedicated the Dotsero Cutoff, a thirty-eight-mile-long connection between two railroad lines. It provided Denver with a western rail outlet to the rest of the country, one sought by city leaders for seven decades. Yet the cutoff's dedication proved as complicated as had the route's planning and construction.

Attempts to breach the forbidding Rocky Mountains west of Denver failed until banker David H. Moffat conquered the Continental Divide at the dawn of the twentieth century. His Denver, Northwestern & Pacific Railroad—better known as the Moffat Road—crossed the barrier at Rollins Pass and proceeded into northwestern Colorado. Unfortunately, it dead-ended at Craig, the seat of Moffat County, named in the financier's honor after his death in 1911.

From 1903 on, efforts to connect the Moffat Road and the Denver & Rio Grande Western Railroad (D&RGW) percolated. Separated by an easy route down the Colorado River, the battle over how to build the connection and who would own and operate it delayed work until 1932. The D&RGW extended a spur from Dotsero, at the junction of the Colorado and Eagle Rivers, but feuds between executives delayed its link with the Moffat Road at a switch named Orestod (Dotsero spelled backward). When Moffat Road workers laid the final 200 yards of track without D&RGW permission in May 1934, the latter firm blockaded the line with chained logs.

The dedication a month later echoed the struggle to complete the Dotsero Cutoff. It took place at Bond, a town near Orestod, in a valley wide enough for a party. The Moffat Road's president refused to leave his railcar for the event, however, while the D&RGW's president and Governor Edwin C. Johnson failed to reach the ceremony in time. The lackluster festivities also reflected broader problems during the Great Depression as railroads faced increasing challenges from automobiles, undermining the cutoff's value. The Dotsero line nonetheless remains in operation as part of the Union Pacific Railroad system and still carries passengers via Amtrak.

Griffith Strikes Gold at Georgetown

George F. Griffith came to the Pikes Peak region in 1859 in search of gold, like so many others. He traveled up Clear Creek that summer, an area prospected earlier in the year with limited success. After the lode strike at Gregory Gulch to the north in May, interest in Clear Creek faded, leaving Griffith nearly alone in his pursuit. On June 17 he found color in a broad valley, and other prospectors soon joined him in a camp named Georgetown after its founder.

A native Kentuckian, Griffith mined in California in the early 1850s before joining his family on the Missouri River in Iowa. With rumors of gold in the central Rocky Mountains trickling across the Great Plains in late 1858, Griffith joined a party of gold seekers bound for the Pikes Peak country. His placer strike in the summer of 1859 proved as limited as the one at nearby Idaho Springs earlier in the year, and the lode from which the loose gold eroded also offered little profit. For several years the Georgetown camp struggled to survive, but the discovery of profitable lode sources in the spring of 1861 promised a second chance. Griffith and his brothers—who proved better bureaucrats than miners—wrote up a code of laws for the community, constructed a road from Central City, and imported a stamp mill to process ore. Colorado Territory's mining boom faltered in early 1864 as investors grew concerned about high expenses and low returns, and Georgetown suffered along with many other communities.

Following the temporary collapse of gold mining, the Griffiths and many other Georgetown residents left for greener pastures. The discovery of silver later that year, though, offered a lifeline. Silver had been found elsewhere in the territory, but never in such quality and quantity. Georgetown became Colorado's first silver boomtown and presaged the transition from gold to silver that fueled prosperity for the next three decades. As one miner recalled about Georgetown's renaissance, "It was the maddest, merriest time that Colorado ever saw."

Colorado Campaigning and Competing

Coloradans witnessed a confluence of politics and sports on June 18, 1960, when state Democrats assembled in Durango while the US Open golf tournament culminated in Denver.

The state's annual Democratic Party meeting drew only one contender for that year's presidential nomination: Senator John F. Kennedy of Massachusetts, who spoke to an audience of 2,500 people at Fort Lewis College in Durango. Kennedy touted his support for water diversion projects and pledged to nominate a western secretary of the interior, hinting at popular Governor Steve McNichols. Kennedy secured more than half of Colorado's delegates, thanks in large part to his staunch advocate Byron "Whizzer" White, a lawyer and former University of Colorado football player. The meeting also heralded a political shift in Colorado. Conservatives had dominated the party for decades, led by three-time governor and US senator Edwin C. Johnson. But his fellow Democrats refused to send Johnson to the national convention as a Colorado delegate, as he opposed the liberal Kennedy and supported Senator Lyndon B. Johnson of Texas instead. The rejection shocked a man who had not been defeated for any position he had sought since the 1920s and foreshadowed an increasing liberalization of Colorado Democrats.

Meanwhile, at Cherry Hills Country Club in Denver, a little-known golfer named Arnold Palmer made history of his own. Golf had long held a reputation as an elite pastime, and by the mid-twentieth century Colorado boasted numerous courses catering to the upper crust. Palmer, from a humble Pennsylvania family, challenged that notion with a come-from-behind triumph at the US Open in 1960. On the third day of competition, he trailed a dozen players and stood eight shots behind the leader, but a slew of birdies erased the deficit and inspired cheers from the usually sedate onlookers. Palmer's subsequent career encouraged the masses to hit the course for themselves, a life on the links that found its first great triumph in Denver. Both Kennedy and Palmer offered Coloradans their unique brands of charm and skill in the summer of 1960.

June 19, 1885

Last Camp on Beaver Creek

By the 1880s, Utes had lost all but a small sliver of land on the southwestern edge of Colorado. Federal agents, facing a dearth of supplies on the reservation, permitted them to cross onto open land to hunt, which often led to the killing of cattle as well as deer and other wildlife. Local ranchers railed against this perceived intrusion and demanded that Utes remain on the reservation regardless of its scarcity. This tension boiled over in June 1885 on the banks of a small tributary of the Dolores River in Dolores County known as Beaver Creek.

For many years, Utes of various bands had camped in an aspen grove at a crossing along Beaver Creek, about 30 miles north of the reservation. Ranchers blamed the native hunters for livestock depredations, stealing horses and other property, and attacking and killing residents of southwestern Colorado. The last group of Utes to occupy the site came into camp on June 19. The following morning, in response to the mounting woes and hoping to scare the Utes into remaining on the reservation, a group of ranchers and cowboys hid behind rocks and bushes on a bluff near the campsite. They attacked the party of eight people, and five men and one woman (indelicately identified as "five bucks and a squaw" in the local press) died in the ambush. The survivors fled southward and, joined by other Utes, set fire to a ranch near Cortez in retaliation. In the process they shot a man to death and wounded his wife, although the couple's children escaped. Meanwhile, local residents scoured the bodies and camp at Beaver Creek for souvenirs.

After meeting with Ute leaders and US Army officers at Fort Lewis, near Durango, a party from the reservation made their way to the attack site or, as a newspaper in nearby Rico described it, "the place where the cowboys manufactured six good Indians to order." The Utes cremated the bodies, which that paper considered "a barbarous and inhuman way of disposing of the dead . . . much more becoming in savages than so-called civilized people." The Beaver Creek Massacre, as it came to be known, demonstrated that both old problems and hatreds died hard.

June 20, 1960

Former Farms into National Grasslands

For more than seven decades, the federal government gave away western land for free—too much land as it turned out, which fueled economic saturation and environmental exhaustion. To rectify that overabundant generosity and return some of the nation's physical bounty to its natural state, the US Department of Agriculture assigned nearly 4 million acres on the Great Plains to the US Forest Service on June 20, 1960, creating the national grasslands.

High crop prices and irrigation projects combined with the Homestead Act's free land policy to fuel agricultural settlement in eastern Colorado in the early twentieth century. But by the 1920s, profits declined and drought set in, turning much of the Great Plains into the Dust Bowl. Exposed earth formerly held in place by native grasses blew away, taking dreams of self-sufficiency with it. In 1935, President Franklin D. Roosevelt established the Resettlement Administration, renamed the Farm Security Administration two years later, to address the crisis. The program loaned or granted nearly $1 billion over a decade for farmers to relocate from marginal land to more suitable acreage or to move to towns and give up agriculture. Federal officials restored over 11 million acres to the national domain in the process. After attempting various restoration proposals during and after World War II, more than a third of that land was reclassified as twenty national grasslands in 1960. Like the national forests, they offer places to camp, hike, fish, and otherwise get in touch with nature in a prairie rather than a mountain setting.

Colorado embraces two of the tracts. Pawnee National Grasslands encompasses more than 193,000 acres in Weld County and boasts one of the most photographed spots on the high plains: the Pawnee Buttes. Comanche National Grasslands, the nation's fourth largest, extends over 443,000 acres in Baca, Las Animas, and Otero Counties. It includes the largest dinosaur track site in North America, carved and painted rock art of ancient American Indian cultures, and traces of the Santa Fe Trail, reflecting the complicated history of a seemingly quiet place.

June 21, 1997

Eight Men Talking in a Library

International attention focused on the Denver Public Library's recently expanded main building near Civic Center on June 21, 1997, when leaders from the world's most economically advanced countries gathered at a large round table there for the Summit of the Eight.

Such conferences, which commenced in the 1970s, grew in significance after the Cold War ended. Participants included the United States, United Kingdom, Canada, Germany, Italy, France, and Japan and expanded in 1997 to include Russia, with European Union officials as observers. Leaders arrived at Denver International Airport, where their airplanes parked in a row. For four days in late June, downtown Denver was transformed into a high-security world's fair, with almost every hotel and meeting area in use. President Bill Clinton stayed at the Brown Palace Hotel and met with several world leaders there. Other events during the summit included dinners at the governor's mansion and the former home of US senator Lawrence C. Phipps, hosted by Governor Roy Romer and Denver mayor Wellington Webb, respectively. The Fort Restaurant in Morrison offered the dignitaries delicious western fare. British prime minister Tony Blair gave a televised interview from the Colorado State Capitol. Spouses of the world leaders traveled to Winter Park on the Ski Train and had brunch at the Oxford Hotel. Musicians and American Indian dancers entertained the dignitaries at the National Western Stock Show complex one evening.

The ambitious agenda for the two-day library summit proved almost impossible to cover or resolve, but most sources considered the conference a triumph for the host city. One diplomat gushed: "We felt a genuine welcome from everyone in Denver. We were very happy here. The cab drivers, the hotel people, everyone was kind to us and polite. I can speak for the entire French delegation by saying thank you Denver, thank you Colorado." The summit table remains on display at the library, and many Coloradans retain memories of clustering behind barricades throughout downtown Denver hoping to spot a president or prime minister.

Ralston Finds Himself Up a Creek

The Pikes Peak gold rush of the late 1850s owed a great deal to an earlier American gold rush, one in northern Georgia a quarter century earlier. One of its veterans, Lewis Ralston, played an essential role in Colorado history when he made the first recorded discovery of gold on a tributary of Clear Creek in what is now Jefferson County on June 22, 1850.

In 1828, at age twenty-three, Ralston was working as a cowboy in northern Georgia on land that remained under Cherokee control. One of Ralston's partners found gold that year, instigating a rush that lasted nearly a decade, and Ralston traded cattle for prospecting. Five years later he married a Cherokee woman and started a family. Ralston remained in Georgia, but many of his wife's family members were forced out over the Trail of Tears in the late 1830s, relocating to present-day Oklahoma. A decade later, the California gold rush inspired many experienced hands in Georgia and among the Cherokees farther west to try their luck. Ralston joined a party that traveled to the new tribal land in early 1850. From there they followed the Cherokee Trail extending north from the Santa Fe Trail, then followed the eastern slope of the Rocky Mountains and cut through present-day southern Wyoming toward California-bound trails. They prospected along the way, and on June 22, Ralston spotted a few flakes of gold in a stream that now bears his name.

A trace of gold did not dissuade Ralston's party from their California quest. He reached the West Coast but returned soon after, preferring the life of a farmer in Georgia. He and his wife raised nine children but suffered along with the rest of the country during the Panic of 1857. Recalling his good fortune up Clear Creek, the fifty-two-year-old Ralston returned there in 1858 with some family and friends from Georgia and Cherokee country, including William G. Russell. Ralston headed back to Georgia empty-handed but Russell persevered, and his placer discoveries along Cherry Creek that summer instigated the Pikes Peak rush. Ralston Creek retains the name of its famous prospector, whose discovery site is commemorated at Arvada's Gold Strike Park.

A Diversion Deep under the Divide

The boundaries and geography of Colorado create a fundamental tension—most of the people and farms live east of the Continental Divide, but most of the water falls on the western side. Some eastern Coloradans have advocated diverting that water, earning ire from western slope residents who consider the resource theirs. On June 23, 1947, Governor W. Lee Knous pressed a button to start pumping water through the Colorado–Big Thompson Project's (C-BT) tunnels, one of Colorado's largest, most complicated, expensive water relocation efforts.

In the 1930s, diverting water to drought-stricken northeastern Colorado proved politically controversial. Advocates included US senator Alva B. Adams, the namesake and son of a former governor, and Governor Edwin C. Johnson. Opposition rallied to Congressman Edward T. Taylor, who insisted that water deposited by nature on the western slope should stay there and threatened to instigate lawsuits for violating the Colorado River Compact with downstream states. The project earned the support of President Franklin D. Roosevelt, whose Public Works Administration combated unemployment during the Great Depression through infrastructure projects.

The first trickle of western slope water emerges from the Alva B. Adams Tunnel near Estes Park during its dedication ceremony on June 23, 1947.

In 1938, construction began on 12 reservoirs, 21 dams and dikes, 7 hydroelectric plants, 95 miles of canals, and 35 miles of tunnels. Crews commenced the 13-mile-long Adams Tunnel (named for the senator) under Rocky Mountain National Park in 1940, with one portal at Grand Lake in Grand County and the other at Estes Park in Larimer County. World War II made labor and materials more expensive, but the C-BT continued. Workers holed through on June 10, 1944—four days after D-Day—and lined the 10-foot-wide tunnel with concrete. Knous presided over the 1947 ceremony that inaugurated the system by sending water through the Adams Tunnel. Within a decade, reservoirs filled and water flowed down the eastern slope. The success of C-BT inspired and at times conflicted with other diversion projects, reflecting both the contentious question of water in the West and the region's insatiable thirst.

June 24, 1889

The Wild Bunch in Telluride

At 10:00 a.m. on June 24, 1889, just as Telluride's San Miguel Valley Bank opened for business, three armed men overpowered the employees and confiscated more than $20,000. Another member of the gang stood watch outside to prevent anyone from interfering, but nothing seemed amiss to passersby. The robbers strolled out, mounted their horses, and took off. One newspaper called it "one of the most daring pieces of robbery recorded in criminal history, and [it] leaves traces of a thoroughly pre-concocted plan to execute the work without endangering the lives of the robbers and without failing to secure the funds of the bank."

Prospectors reached the San Miguel River in the mid-1870s after the Utes surrendered the San Juan Mountains. Transportation to the isolated region proved a challenge, but its high-grade ore demanded attention. Otto Mears constructed a road linking the Uncompahgre and San Miguel River valleys over Dallas Divide, and Telluride flourished as a respectable community rather than just another rambunctious mining town. Hydroelectric power came to Telluride through an 8-mile line from a generator near Ophir, demonstrating the benefits of scientist Nikola Tesla's work in alternating current. Throughout the 1880s, Telluride ranked as one of the wealthiest spots in Colorado and possessed a name synonymous with profit around the country, a moniker derived from the region's gold-rich tellurium ore. Little wonder that Butch Cassidy chose the town's largest bank as his career's first target, setting the stage for his life of crime.

Cassidy and his gang, the Wild Bunch, threatened employees if they sounded the alarm without giving them a ten-minute head start. Once the word was out,

San Miguel County sheriff J. A. Beattie set out with a posse in pursuit. The gang dashed by a stagecoach in Dolores County, and passengers marveled at the speed of their horses even after riding hard for a dozen miles. Cassidy evaded law enforcement all the way to his hideout in southeastern Utah. The bank's shareholders covered the loss, and Telluride's productive mines soon negated the money taken.

Harding Understands Colorado

Historians might consider Warren G. Harding one of the worst American presidents, but he found only adoration from thousands of people who saw him in Denver on June 25, 1923.

Escaping a plethora of scandals percolating in Washington, DC, Harding and his wife, Florence, set out on a "Voyage of Understanding." The long jaunt was intended to rejuvenate the beleaguered executive and connect him to a less critical public. Entering Colorado through the Arkansas River valley from Kansas, Harding's train arrived at Denver's Union Station on June 24. They visited with wounded World War I soldiers recuperating at Fitzsimons Army Hospital and then took a short drive into the mountains. The Hardings dined with US senator Lawrence C. Phipps at his home on Pearl Street and retired to their suite at the Brown Palace Hotel.

Harding's public events took place on June 25. A parade 8 miles long and witnessed by an estimated 100,000 people wound through Denver, including a stop in City Park to see the view from the grounds of the natural history museum. The presidential entourage paused to greet thousands of children gathered on the capitol grounds before making a circuit through downtown, ending at the City Auditorium. There Harding spoke to 12,000 spectators, while others gathered on the streets outside to listen through amplifiers. He insisted on national enforcement of Prohibition and touted the idea of a world court to keep the peace in the wake of World War I. In the only local aspect of his remarks, Harding praised the recent Colorado River Compact as a model for governmental cooperation at the state and national levels.

Following the speech, the presidential train proceeded toward Wyoming. It paused in Greeley for Harding to admire Colorado State Teachers College and the beet sugar industry. The "Voyage of Understanding" continued northwest to Alaska by rail and boat before returning down the Pacific coast. The president died in San Francisco on August 2, negating Florence's promise as they departed from Union Station: "We're coming back some day to see you again."

Long on the "Great American Desert"

An expedition of twenty-one men, led by Major Stephen H. Long, camped in present-day Logan County on June 26, 1820, the first American exploration of modern Colorado in over a decade.

The United States and Spain teetered on the brink of war after the Louisiana Purchase, but the Adams-Onís Treaty of 1819—which established the first clear border between the two countries—calmed tensions enough to allow a study of the Great Plains. Long's party of surveyors and naturalists commenced up the Platte River in early June 1820 and followed its southern branch toward the Rocky Mountains. The band groused at the treeless prairie, sandy hills, and grasses that proved poor fodder for their horses and mules. Four days after camping near present-day Sterling, they spotted a bluish peak on the horizon, later named Longs Peak in honor of their commander. Proceeding through what is now downtown Denver to Waterton Canyon, where the river emerges from the Rockies, the Long expedition abandoned their task of finding its source. Instead, they continued southward along the eastern slope, pausing in mid-July while three members made the first recorded ascent of Pikes Peak. They explored the Arkansas River as high as the Royal Gorge before turning downstream and meandering back to the states.

Long's 1823 report included botanical and zoological information and descriptions of native cultures. His impression of the region, however, proved dismissive. Long's map labeled eastern Colorado the "Great American Desert," giving a name to the same sentiment Zebulon M. Pike had expressed a dozen years earlier. Long called the region "almost wholly unfit for cultivation, and of course uninhabitable by a people depending upon agriculture for their subsistence." He argued that "the scarcity of wood and water, almost uniformly prevalent, will prove an insuperable obstacle in the way of settling the country." His report cast aspersions on what later became—through irrigation and new farming techniques—a prosperous place. It also inspired a vision of Colorado as a place to get through rather than to, for years to come.

Coloradans on the Highest Court

Byron R. White, Colorado's first native to sit on the United States Supreme Court, served his final day as an associate justice on June 27, 1993. Nearly a quarter century later, one of White's former law clerks, Neil M. Gorsuch, brought a touch of Colorado back to the bench.

Born in Fort Collins in 1917, White grew up in the sugar beet fields near Wellington. At the University of Colorado in the 1930s, White epitomized the scholar-athlete, achieving stellar grades and earning renown in athletics. His success on the football field won him the nickname "Whizzer White" and led to stints with two professional teams. White earned a law degree from Yale University and served in the US Navy during World War II. He clerked for Chief Justice Fred M. Vinson after the war and worked as a lawyer in Denver in the 1950s. White organized the Colorado branch of John F. Kennedy's presidential campaign in 1960, and although Kennedy lost the state, he appointed White deputy attorney general. In 1962, Kennedy nominated and the US Senate confirmed White as an associate justice of the Supreme Court.

White's liberal political ties contrasted with his conservative tendencies on the bench. He dissented from the majority in two prominent cases—*Miranda v. Arizona* (1966), which required law enforcement to inform suspects of their constitutional rights, and *Roe v. Wade* (1973), which legalized abortion. White tended liberal in civil rights cases, although he spoke for the majority in *Bowers v. Hardwick* (1986), which denied constitutional protections for homosexuality. His resignation after thirty-one years on the court took effect at the end of its term in 1993. In retirement, White served occasionally as a federal appeals court judge. He died in Denver in 2002.

Gorsuch, born in Denver in 1967, grew up in a politically active family. He taught at the University of Colorado law school and served on the Denver-based federal Tenth Circuit Court of Appeals. President Donald J. Trump appointed Gorsuch to the Supreme Court in 2017, and he was confirmed after a bitter partisan fight in the US Senate. Court observers expected Gorsuch, who had clerked for White just before his retirement, to follow the justice's conservative path, although Gorsuch has also emerged as an advocate for American Indian rights.

June 28, 1934

A New Approach to Federal Land

President Franklin D. Roosevelt signed a bill named for western Colorado's long-serving Democratic congressman Edward T. Taylor on June 28, 1934. The Taylor Grazing Act redefined the relationship between Americans and government-owned land, tracts that had been bought, negotiated for, or conquered from other countries and American Indian cultures.

Since the Land Ordinance of 1785, authorities had viewed western land as both a money-making proposition and a way to reinforce American claims to vast stretches of North America. By selling the land to settlers, the government raised money and filled the territory with people of common vision and desire. In 1862, the Homestead Act promoted western settlement by giving away land for free to those who would occupy and develop it, a practice generously expanded—as defined by increasing amounts of free acreage—throughout the late nineteenth century. Homesteading flourished into the early twentieth century, but a drought in the early 1930s compounded the Great Depression and demanded a new approach to using federal land.

The Taylor Grazing Act, named for its sponsor who represented a district composed in large part of open range, reorganized a patchwork swath of generally unfarmable tracts used primarily by cattle and sheep ranchers. Federal officials sold or leased a few isolated parcels, but most came under new management. Grazing districts controlled the private use of remaining public land. Ranchers paid a fee to feed their animals on it to regulate its viability. Roosevelt appointed Farrington R. Carpenter, a lawyer from Routt County with a ranch on the Yampa River near Hayden, as the first director of the grazing service, which became the Bureau of Land Management in 1946. Carpenter contended with decades-old friction between cattle and sheep interests and established a precedent of cooperation between government and private interests. Although tension lingers over the balance between access and control over the federal range, the Taylor Grazing Act provided a structure to encourage fair and balanced use among all parties.

June 29, 1975

"Everybody Welcome" in Colorado Springs

Readers of the *Colorado Springs Gazette* learned disappointing news on June 29, 1975, when the paper reported the imminent closing of the Cotton Club, a popular downtown nightclub that had challenged racial attitudes and divisions for more than a quarter century.

The Cotton Club was the result of years of dedicated work by Fannie Mae Duncan, an Oklahoma native whose family relocated to Colorado Springs in 1933. She graduated from high school and found employment at a café at Camp Carson. Reflecting the segregated military of World War II, the young African American woman worked at a canteen that served members of that ethnic group alone. In the late 1940s, she and her husband, Edward, opened a restaurant in downtown Colorado Springs. After they visited lively African American nightclubs in Denver's Five Points neighborhood, Fannie Mae Duncan decided to emulate those successful institutions.

Fannie Mae Duncan (standing at center) poses with friends and customers at the counter of her Cotton Club in Colorado Springs in 1958.

Duncan's nightclub did not discriminate by race, as did many statewide bars, restaurants, and hotels. Police chief Irvin "Dad" Bruce was shocked to hear that white, black, and Latino patrons mixed freely at the Cotton Club and demanded that Duncan serve African Americans only. Duncan responded that she had not been issued a racially restricted license, and non-black patrons protested their potential exclusion from a popular part of the Colorado Springs social scene. Bruce relented and became one of Duncan's strongest supporters. To reassure and welcome patrons, Duncan placed a large sign in the window that read "Everybody Welcome."

The Cotton Club drew some of the biggest names in music, including Louis Armstrong, Fats Domino, Duke Ellington, Billie Holliday, B. B. King, Fats Waller, and Dinah Washington. Flip Wilson started his career as an emcee there while serving in the US Air Force. Nonetheless, demolition billed as "urban renewal" silenced the club in the summer of 1975. Duncan died in 2005 at age eighty-seven, but memories endure: "People used to tell me that they loved to come to the Cotton Club because they felt so at home there. It was easy to find, and hard to leave." Her club exemplifies the potential for good food and music to break down barriers and bring people together.

June 30, 1765

Rivera Crosses the Line

European empires looked to the New World as a source of profit, and discoveries of rich societies like the Aztec and Inca fueled this desire. Although Spanish expeditions into the present-day United States in the mid-sixteenth century failed to locate similar wealth, the hope lingered. Juan María Antonio de Rivera, a military engineer, crossed the modern boundary between Colorado and New Mexico on June 30, 1765, on one of the last of these expeditions.

Governor Tomás Velez Cachupín ordered Rivera to head northwest from the Rio Grande valley in the summer of 1765, in search of rumored silver deposits and to locate the upper reaches of the Colorado River. The governor also sought reconnaissance about potential overland routes through the region to connect New Mexico to Spain's new settlements on the Pacific coast. Rivera faced opposition from the Utes, a native culture that traded with Spain and dominated the western slope of the Rocky Mountains. Suspicious of Spain's motives, the Utes sought to deflect the Spanish from their territory by guiding them around its southern reaches. Rivera entered Colorado near the modern town site of Edith in Archuleta County and crossed the Navajo, Los Piños, and Animas Rivers on his trek, noting Ancestral Puebloan ruins all the way. He named one river "El Río de Nuestra Señora de Dolores" (the River of Our Lady of Sorrows), today's Dolores River. But warnings about impassable waterways and terrifying beasts beyond, likely concocted by the Utes to get rid of the interlopers, kept Rivera from proceeding farther.

Rivera brought his small band back to southwestern Colorado in the fall of 1765. They reached the Colorado River in eastern Utah before returning to New Mexico. His expeditions taught the Spanish that establishing a connection to California over native trails might be feasible, but to do so they would need to build a trade and military alliance with the Utes—a group too strong, numerous, and widespread simply to ignore or conquer. Connections between western Colorado and New Mexico proved essential to both areas for decades to come.

July

Baking away in Bent County

Coloradans, like just about everyone else, claim that if the weather offends, just wait a few minutes for it to change. From droughts to floods, from bitter cold to scalding heat, from sunshine to whiteout conditions, a year in the Centennial State offers a spectrum of weather.

Colorado offers some incredible climate records. The Bent County seat of Las Animas reached a temperature of 114°F on July 1, 1933, Colorado's highest recorded to that time. Thermometers hit the same mark in Sedgwick, in the county of the same name, on July 11, 1954. A temperature of 118°F recorded in 1888 in the Adams County town of Bennett long endured in state lore, although scholars consider it a typo when compared with less dramatic highs reported nearby on the same day. Maybell, in Moffat County, secured the lowest recorded temperature when the mercury plummeted to negative 61°F on February 1, 1985. The tied high temperature record held until July 19, 2019, when verified sensors recorded 115°F at John Martin Reservoir, restoring Bent County's toasty supremacy. With climate change an increasing concern globally, Colorado's latest record will likely fall before long.

Storms in Colorado offer impressive precipitation and wind records. Holly, in Prowers County, endured over 11 inches of rain on June 17, 1965. Wolf Creek Pass, a break in the Continental Divide in Mineral County, registered the deepest snow levels in Colorado history on March 31, 1979, with 251 inches, just shy of 21 feet. Silver Lake Reservoir, near the Continental Divide in Boulder County, set a state, national, and global record for the most snow falling in twenty-four hours, with 7 feet, 3 inches overnight on April 14–15, 1921. Monarch Pass, on the Continental Divide between Chaffee and Gunnison Counties, registered a record 148-mile-per-hour wind gust on February 18, 2016. A tornado traveled nearly 200 miles in only five hours from Crowley to Phillips Counties in 1922, while another destroyed the town of Thurman in Washington County and killed ten people on August 10, 1924. Twisters devastated Limon in 1990, Holly in 2007, and Windsor in 2008. Mercifully, the sun prefers to shine on the Centennial State, and its climate helps make the state such an appealing place to live.

The Temporary End of the Line

In the fall of 1994, Denver cheered the inaugural run of the Regional Transportation District's (RTD) new light rail system. Yet the sleek white trains gliding through downtown represented an echo of the old rather than a harbinger of the new. Nearly half a century earlier, on July 2, 1950, Denver's decades-old urban rail service clattered to a halt.

The first horse-drawn trolley cars appeared in Denver in 1871. Soon, a series of private companies established lines extending from the city center in every direction. The Denver Tramway Company (DTC) inaugurated cable cars in 1888, and the following year a web of wires appeared above the streets to power cars with electricity. The DTC consolidated independent services into a city transit monopoly in 1900, managing 150 miles of track. It exercised political power as well, using nefarious means to protect its interests and undermine attempts at regulation. By the turn of the twentieth century, streetcars enabled urban sprawl and "white flight," as wealthy Denverites sought to move away from impoverished, blighted neighborhoods at the heart of the city. The DTC partnered with land speculators to foster new developments—including Berkeley, Curtis Park, Highlands, Montclair, and Park Hill—easily accessible from workplaces in downtown by the streetcar system. In 1901, the DTC opened its first of many inter-urban lines, serving the coal mining town of Leyden in Jefferson County to provide fuel for the company's power plant, a route that linked Arvada and other communities as well.

By the 1920s, buses started to replace trolleys. The DTC's woes piled on as its ridership struggled to afford fares during the Great Depression. After World War II, as Americans fell in love with the automobile, the DTC proved impossible to maintain. The last streetcar went out of service on June 3, 1950, and the last inter-urban line just under a month later. Denver purchased the DTC in 1971 and reorganized its bus service as the RTD. When light rail commenced forty-four years after the tramway service's abandonment, it proved that everything old is new again.

The Lake County War

Elias F. Dyer, a judge in Lake County—which then extended over most of southwestern Colorado—wrote a letter to his father, Methodist minister John L. Dyer, early on July 3, 1875: "I don't know that the sun will ever rise and set for me again, but I trust in God and his mercy. At eight o'clock I sit in court. The mob have me under guard." After adjourning a brief session that morning, five armed men rushed into the courtroom and killed the judge as he sat at the dais.

Mob rule on the upper Arkansas River emerged in the summer of 1874. Established ranchers resented competition from newcomers, who demanded their right to make a home. A feud between two men mushroomed into competing vigilante camps. One faction forced the other out and organized a Committee of Safety, intent on ruling Lake County. In January 1875, the committee ordered Judge Dyer to leave Granite, the county seat. He fled to Denver and requested territorial aid in restoring law and order, but newly appointed governor John L. Routt offered none, while the vigilantes terrorized or murdered anyone who opposed them.

Dyer returned to Lake County in the spring of 1875, traveling across the region to assess the situation. In early July, sitting in the county seat of Granite, he heard indictments against Committee of Safety members, who came to his courtroom armed to the teeth. Their accusers, understandably intimidated, failed to testify. Dyer dismissed the charges, but the vigilantes executed him anyway to rid them-selves of a meddlesome jurist. No one faced trial in Dyer's death for fear of retribu-tion, but the "Lake County War" fizzled after that dramatic moment.

The Committee of Safety dominated the river valley for years, even after their fiefdom—including Granite—was split off into Chaffee County in 1879. The epi-sode demonstrated the rough road toward the rule of law in early Colorado, and it long weighed on those affected. As Judge Dyer's father wrote in 1890: "God only knows how hard a trial this terrible tragedy was to me. After the lapse of all these years, the memory of it rushes over me like a flood."

July 4, 1891

Stratton Strikes Gold at Cripple Creek

On the same Independence Day in 1891 on which crowds celebrated the opening of the Mineral Palace in Pueblo, a prospector named Winfield S. Stratton made one of the greatest mineral discoveries in Colorado history with a gold strike on the southwest flank of Pikes Peak.

Born in Indiana in 1848, Stratton moved to Colorado Territory in 1872. He set-tled in Colorado Springs, hoping to cash in on the genteel community founded the previous year by William J. Palmer. Stratton earned a meager existence as a car-penter while prospecting through the Rocky Mountains for nearly two decades. In the summer of 1891, he joined other Colorado Springs residents in pursuing rumors of gold near Pikes Peak, in present-day Teller County. Stratton made several claims on July 4, most auspiciously a patch of earth that churned out valuable ore for years and anchored the lucrative Cripple Creek district. He named that site the Independence Mine in honor of the holiday. By the middle of the decade, in part as a result of the silver-crushing Panic of 1893, Stratton possessed more money than any other Coloradan.

The mercurial, philanthropic Stratton lived humbly in Colorado Springs, astonishing many people who expected him to relocate among the nation's elite. He bestowed money and gifts on his fellow residents, provided the city with land for public buildings and funded its streetcar system, and invested in mining and real estate across Colorado. Stratton gave large sums to Colorado College and the Colorado School of Mines and helped Horace A.W. Tabor after his fortune disappeared in the Silver Panic. His generosity contrasted with a stubborn, cranky, hermit-like existence, nurtured through years of poverty and fortune alike.

After Stratton sold the Independence Mine in 1899, he remained in Colorado Springs. Following his death in 1902, a legal battle developed over the estate, with various individuals and the city and state governments shamelessly jostling for cash. The bulk funded the Myron Stratton Home, named for his father, to provide a sanctuary for the indigent; it remains in operation.

July 5, 1893

Bates Comes to Colorado Springs

Off a train at a depot in Colorado Springs stepped an English literature professor on July 5, 1893, hired by Colorado College for a three-week summer program. The arrival of Katharine L. Bates set the stage for one of the most famous, beloved, patriotic US poems, one eventually set to music and sung today as "America the Beautiful."

One of the state's most respected institutions of higher education, the private Colorado College came about through the support of town founder and Denver & Rio Grande Railroad president William J. Palmer. Established in 1874, the core of its neo-Gothic campus rose in the early 1880s. Colorado College gained a reputation for academic excellence and physical beauty, for both the campus itself and the broader region, both of which it retains today. It also drew professors for both permanent and temporary postings, including Bates's assignment in 1893.

Bates, a Massachusetts native and graduate of Wellesley College in 1880, later joined the faculty of her alma mater. She traveled across the United States in 1893, a trip that opened her eyes to the country's vastness and beauty. Bates delivered lectures at Colorado College during her three-week tenure and took in the sights.

Most famously, she rode a wagon to the top of Pikes Peak toward the end of her stint, a journey she later credited with inspiring her most famous poem. The summer's continental experience and the mountain trek combined to form a lasting vision: "Our sojourn on the peak remains in memory hardly more than one ecstatic gaze. It was then and there, as I was looking out over the sea-like expanse of fertile country spreading away so far under those ample skies, that the opening lines of the hymn floated into my mind."

The poem was titled "America the Beautiful," and Bates published it in 1895. It went through several revisions before a final draft appeared in print in 1911. Bates selected one of seventy-four potential tunes to accompany it, creating one of the nation's best-loved songs of praise. A monument with plaques bearing the tribute to mountains and plains under spacious skies stands atop Pikes Peak.

July 6, 1994

A Deadly Day on Storm King Mountain

A small forest fire smoldering west of Glenwood Springs in Garfield County erupted on July 6, 1994, surrounding and killing fourteen firefighters on Storm King Mountain.

Tinder-dry conditions made 1994 one of Colorado's worst fire seasons on record. By midsummer, large fires burned in Delta and Larimer Counties, including one that damaged Colorado State University's mountain campus. In three weeks, eighty blazes scorched more than 8,000 acres across Colorado, some caused by human activity and others by nature. The South Canyon fire, started by lightning on July 2, threatened Interstate 70 on the west side of Glenwood Springs, and several hotshot teams arrived three days later to contain it. A weather front pushed through on July 6, and strong winds emerged seemingly from nowhere. Some firefighters escaped from the runaway flames, but fourteen found themselves trapped on Storm King Mountain without adequate protection. Governor Roy Romer rushed to the scene the following day, only to face petty accusations of grandstanding during an election year by his political opponents. Meanwhile, Congressman Scott McInnis and his wife, Lori, helped place the victims in body bags. Of the forty personnel killed fighting wildfires in Colorado from 1910 to the early 2010s, 35 percent perished on that summer day in Garfield County. A memorial trail leads from the Colorado River valley to a mountainside monument honoring the fallen firefighters.

The South Canyon fire inspired changes in firefighting techniques nationwide, including portable shelters and radios for all personnel to diminish the chances of another catastrophe. It also reflected the dangers of mountain life. As the *Denver Post* warned, "Forests in the Rockies have regenerated after such conflagrations for millions of years, and firefighters have only a limited capacity to protect people who stand in the way of such powerful natural forces." Residents must prepare for the worst, even while enjoying the best Colorado has to offer.

July 7, 1908

Democrats Convene in Denver

Tens of thousands of people filled Denver in early July 1908 for the city's first national political convention. Attendees outside the new City Auditorium frolicked in snow, which trains from the Moffat Road had brought from the Continental Divide. Meanwhile, a crowd of eager partisans thronged the building on July 7 to open the Democratic National Convention.

Democrats had lost the three previous presidential elections but pinned their hopes on perennial candidate William Jennings Bryan of Nebraska, who had been defeated by William McKinley in 1896 and 1900. He had won Colorado's

Crowds gather outside the City Auditorium in Denver to watch Democratic National Convention delegates enter for their presidential nominating convention in July 1908.

July

vote both times, aiding the decision to hold the 1908 convention in Denver. The city also touted its central location and railroad connections and benefited from the increasing appeal of tourism that drew Americans to the Rocky Mountains. Mayor Robert W. Speer sealed the deal with the auditorium, a massive meeting hall that survives as the Ellie Caulkins Opera House in the Denver Center for the Performing Arts. An advocate of the "City Beautiful" movement of grand public buildings and parks, Speer used the convention to prime the pump for civic improvements before and after the Democrats gathered in Denver.

Conventioneers praised the auditorium and the city, even as they battled over issues and strategies. The *Rocky Mountain News* described the average Democratic delegate as "a man wearing a lot of badges and yelling all the time." Their ranks included five women, the first to participate in a Democratic national meeting, as well as Matthew R. Denver of Ohio, son of James W. Denver, former Kansas governor and the city's namesake. Bryan—who remained at his Nebraska home during the meeting, per tradition—received a standing ovation lasting almost an hour and a half from 15,000 partisans when his nomination was proposed on July 8. The following day the party officially declared him its candidate and adjourned on July 10.

Bryan lost the 1908 contest to Republican William H. Taft, although once more he earned a majority of Colorado's votes. Denver waited a century to host another political convention.

July 8, 2013

"Restorationists" on the High Plains

Resentment toward government is nothing new in Colorado, but there are times when the burden seems too heavy to bear and frustrated citizens pursue dramatic options. A meeting held in the Washington County seat of Akron on July 8, 2013, reflected this simmering anger, not to mention the lengths to which disaffected Americans will go to redress their grievances.

Rural, generally conservative northeastern Coloradans found much about state authority to oppose in the spring of 2013. Democrats running the General Assembly approved regulations on oil and gas development, new demands on rural electric providers, and gun control measures, while Governor John Hickenlooper ruffled feathers with limits on subsurface water access and death row clemency. Feeling that their interests and values were dismissed by urban communities, some residents of the northeastern plains took the name "restorationists" and called for a reinvigorated rural voice. The Akron meeting debated two proposals offered by Weld County commissioners. Either they should secede to create a new state—named North Colorado, New Colorado, Liberty, or something else—or join a more politically appealing neighbor, such as Wyoming. Commissioners from Phillips County, meanwhile, suggested altering the legislature, dominated by the Denver metropolitan area, to have one house with equal representation for each county.

In the November 2013 election, eleven Colorado counties considered pursuing secession. Voters in five of those counties—Cheyenne, Kit Carson, Phillips, Washington, and Yuma—approved the idea, but the rest rejected it, including Weld, whose commissioners had instigated the talk of political divorce. Overall, 45 percent of voters in the eleven counties supported secession, with 55 percent opposed. The following year, the proposal by Phillips County commissioners to restructure the legislature failed to secure enough signatures to make it onto the ballot, preventing a legal challenge to an idea that conflicted with a half century of court rulings. Both defeats also failed to resolve the lingering resentment many rural Coloradans felt toward their urban-dominated state.

July 9, 1842

A Confluence of History

Several prominent individuals in western US history encountered one another along the South Platte River in present-day Morgan County on July 9, 1842. This series of remarkable interactions was caused and recorded by one of the most prolific US adventurers.

On his first of five western expeditions, Lieutenant John C. Frémont trekked up the South Platte River to map overland routes that summer and reported his first sighting of the Rocky Mountains (specifically Longs Peak) that morning. Proceeding up the river, he encountered a party led by James Beckwourth—a renowned trapper born in 1798 to a slave mother and her white owner, who freed his offspring—looking for stray horses. Leaving Beckwourth to his task, Frémont continued past a group of New England–born trappers with their American Indian wives and a "number of little fat buffalo-fed boys." A few miles farther upstream, he arrived at an island where lived one "Mr. Chabonard," as Frémont identified him. The man was actually Jean-Baptiste Charbonneau, known as "Pomp" after his birth in 1805 to guides Sacagawea and Toussaint Charbonneau during the Lewis and Clark expedition. In 1842 he worked for Bent, St. Vrain & Company, whose fur trade empire dominated the region. According to Frémont: "Mr. C. received us hospitably. One of the people was sent to gather mint, with the aid of which he concocted very good julep, and some boiled buffalo tongue, and coffee with the luxury of sugar were soon set before us. The people in his employ were generally Spaniards, and among them I saw a young Spanish woman from Taos, whom I found to be [Beckwourth's] wife."

Both Beckwourth and Charbonneau worked with the US Army during the conquests of New Mexico and California in 1846 and stayed for the gold rush. Beckwourth returned to Colorado in 1859, joined the territory's volunteer troops as a scout, and participated unwillingly in the Sand Creek Massacre. Both men died in 1866, Beckwourth in Denver and Charbonneau in Oregon. Frémont's account testifies to the diversity that has shaped much of Colorado's story.

July 10, 1694

A Spanish Foray into Colorado

At the dawn of the seventeenth century, the Spanish attempted to control the Rio Grande valley through colonization and conversion of the Puebloans of New Mexico to their culture. American Indian resistance led to sporadic conflicts, the largest of which started in 1680 and forced the Spanish out of the region. The Spanish returned in 1692, after which Governor Diego de Vargas demonstrated more consideration toward the Puebloans. He also became the first non–American Indian for whom clear historical proof exists to have set foot in what is now Colorado.

Some, or more likely many, non–American Indians traipsed across the Centennial State's invisible boundaries before Vargas, although records are vague, dubious, or nonexistent. In the summer of 1694, the governor sought to subdue rebel holdouts north of Santa Fe. His company included about a hundred Spanish soldiers and settlers and several dozen allied Puebloans. To avoid a suspected assault near Taos, Vargas detoured northward along the Rio Grande and crossed into present-day Colorado in the San Luis Valley. He described the region as "the land of the Yuttas"—the Utes, with whom the Spanish had peaceful relations before the 1680 uprising. The company reached Culebra Creek, a tributary flowing westward from the Sangre de Cristo Mountains, near the modern town of San Luis. From there, Vargas proceeded downstream to the Rio Grande, which he forded several miles south of its junction with the Culebra. He made this crossing at a spot popular for centuries, according to archaeological evidence, on July 10, 1694. From there, Vargas's expedition proceeded southwestward to the present site of Antonito and continued along the current route of US Highway 285 back to Santa Fe.

Vargas's brief excursion into modern Colorado is enough for him to claim the title of "first" among non–American Indians in the state, a testament more to the scant and imprecise historical records of early Spanish exploration than to the governor's wanderlust.

July 11, 1869

The Battle of Summit Springs

The last major conflict between American Indians and the US Army in eastern Colorado took place along what is now the Logan-Washington County line on July 11, 1869, when troops surprised a Cheyenne encampment at a watering hole called Summit Springs.

The Medicine Lodge treaty of 1867 required Cheyennes to accept reservation life in what is now Oklahoma, but northern factions known as the Dog Soldiers fought containment. In the spring of 1869, a band led by Tall Bull headed north to hunt with their Sioux allies. Major Eugene A. Carr's cavalry soldiers, based at Fort Lyon on the Arkansas River, pursued them into Nebraska. Pawnee scouts commanded by Major Frank J. North joined the effort, as did civilian William F. Cody. Tall Bull proceeded from the Republican River to the South Platte River and waited until it was low enough to cross. He led about 500 people, including just over 100 men of fighting age and two settlers kidnapped in Kansas, Susanna Alderdice and Maria Weichell.

Carr attacked in the afternoon of July 11, taking the Cheyennes by surprise. Pawnees and soldiers charged through the camp as their quarry fled across the plains or hid in nearby ravines. In the chaos, Alderdice fell dead, Weichell was rescued, and North killed Tall Bull. A storm built during the battle, and soldiers looted the village while it raged. The attackers killed 52 Cheyennes and captured 17; one soldier suffered a slight wound. Four days later, Carr's force arrived at Fort Sedgwick near Julesburg, his fame spreading nationally by telegraph.

Summit Springs ended native hegemony in eastern Colorado, but the battle took on a life of its own. In later years, scout "Buffalo Bill" Cody reenacted it with broad artistic license in his Wild West performances around the world. At least once, a retired Carr joined the reenactment, charging in at the last moment to rescue the hostages. Aside from barbed wire fences and a few small monuments, the battle site in southern Logan and northern Washington Counties appears much as it did on that bloody day.

Cruising down the Blue River

When Samuel Adams—whom the press described as either a captain or a commodore—set out on an expedition down the Blue River on July 12, 1869, intending eventually to reach the Gulf of California, the skeptical town of Breckenridge turned out to wish him well.

After the Civil War, the federal government needed information about the West to encourage mining and agricultural settlement. Adams sought the expedition awarded to John W. Powell in the spring of 1869 and attempted to hijack it before Powell arrived at the starting point of Green River, Wyoming. Chased from there, Adams tried again in Breckenridge, planning a trip down the Blue River to the Grand (Colorado) River and from there downstream to its mouth. He named his outfit the "Summit County and Colorado River Exploring and Prospecting Company" and intended to find new mineral sources and demonstrate the river's navigability to promote western development. Three boats with four occupants apiece set out from Breckenridge on July 12, laden with food and mining tools but not scientific instruments or mapmaking tools, reflecting Adams's vision of profit. Two weeks into the journey, one boat wrecked on the Blue River and the disillusioned party trudged back up to Breckenridge.

Adams set out again with four men, but the others returned after the boats sank with most of the supplies. He claimed to have reached the Grand Canyon on foot by the end of July. A month later Adams reappeared in Colorado Territory, informing a Golden newspaper of great farmland and minerals all along the river. Adams's reports conflicted dramatically with those of Powell, who completed his descent of the Green and Colorado Rivers in the fall of 1869, and people wondered if Adams had actually taken his trip. Two years later, he persuaded the US Congress to debate a bill compensating him $20,000 for his efforts, but he never received payment. Adams's tales of paradise in the American Southwest grew more elaborate with each passing year but never rang true, and most scholars consider him little more than an untalented huckster.

First Run of the Colorado Midland

The first railroads built into the Rocky Mountains of Colorado employed the narrow gauge, a 3-foot width between the rails that required smaller locomotives and cars than standard (4 feet 8½ inches in width) gauge but allowed for tighter turns to navigate the rugged landscape. The narrow gauge's monopoly ended on July 13, 1887, with the Colorado Midland Railway's inaugural run westward from Colorado Springs, over Wilkerson Pass into South Park, and across Trout Creek Pass to Buena Vista on the upper Arkansas River.

The Colorado Midland owed its existence to James J. Hagerman, an iron and railroad tycoon from Wisconsin. He came to Colorado Springs in 1884 to recuperate from tuberculosis in William J. Palmer's genteel community at the base of Pikes Peak. Hagerman found new sources of profit in precious metal and coal mining around Aspen, Cripple Creek, Glenwood Springs, and Leadville. He resurrected a stillborn idea of building a railroad west from Colorado Springs, one that challenged the popular notion of narrow gauge domination. Hagerman solicited funds from American and European investors for the expensive proposition, which demanded extensive tunneling to accommodate the less flexible standard gauge. The potential for new routes to wealthy mining districts helped his case, and construction commenced in 1886.

Service started over the Colorado Midland line in July 1887 and extended from Buena Vista to Leadville two months later. Crews holed through a tunnel—"the great artificial gateway through the backbone of the continent," according to a Leadville newspaper, reported in a Carbondale newspaper—under Hagerman Pass on the Continental Divide that summer. Trains reached Aspen by early 1888, and the line extended to coal deposits near Glenwood Springs and New Castle later that year. It survived the Panic of 1893 and remained an important part of Colorado's transportation network through World War I. The end of the war led to a drop in demand for service on the Colorado Midland, and in the early 1920s workers dismantled Colorado's first mountain standard gauge line.

July 14, 1938

Colorado's Version of Jurassic Park

President Franklin D. Roosevelt signed an executive order on July 14, 1938, expanding a tiny national monument of 80 acres in northeastern Utah into a massive preserve encompassing 318 square miles along the Green and Yampa Rivers primarily in Moffat County, extending the region known as Dinosaur National Monument across the boundary into Colorado.

Scientists exploring arid regions around the world fueled the public's insatiable demand for knowledge about prehistoric life, the awe-inspiring dinosaurs in particular. On his 1869 expedition down the Green River, John W. Powell noted fossilized remains in the area, but the site remained untouched by paleontologists for decades. Because of its remoteness, the region avoided the vandalism of the Great Dinosaur Wars that pillaged treasures in Fremont County and elsewhere around the world. Locals recognized its significance nonetheless; as a Steamboat Springs newspaper declared in 1915, "Monsters Dwelt in this Country during Past Ages."

Formal digs commenced in 1909 at a fossil quarry in Utah, which President Woodrow Wilson designated as Dinosaur National Monument six years later. Roosevelt's action in 1938 increased the monument 2,500 times over, making it three-quarters the size of Rocky Mountain National Park. The Moffat County town of Artesia changed its name to Dinosaur in 1966, a year after a tourist road opened from there into the monument. Dinosaur hosts the primary visitors' center, although another stands at the original quarry site across the state line in Utah.

Dinosaur National Monument's isolation affects its tourist numbers, but fascination with the prehistoric critters inspires plenty of visitors. The site witnessed controversy in the 1950s when Congressman Wayne Aspinall advocated building Echo Park Dam at the confluence of the Green and Yampa Rivers. He touted benefits including hydroelectricity, water storage, and tourism, but conservationists succeeded in preventing the inundation of the monument's core. Dinosaur remains an awe-inspiring landscape of value far beyond the incredible fossils that inspired it.

July 15, 1943

Soldiers on Skis at Camp Hale

A deal struck between the federal departments of agriculture and war on July 15, 1943, authorized the US Army to use of thousands of acres of the White River National Forest to train soldiers for winter mountain combat. The arrangement transformed Camp Hale, an outpost near Tennessee Pass on the Continental Divide, into a facility specializing in combat on skis.

As tensions escalated worldwide before World War II, the American military prepared to fight. It selected an Eagle County valley, served by the Denver & Rio Grande Western Railroad and accessible via US Highway 24, for a mountain combat training center. Work commenced near the small town of Pando in the spring of 1942. Laborers erected dozens of buildings for the offshoot of Camp Carson, named Camp Hale in honor of Colorado's Spanish-American War hero General Irving Hale. The site proved frigid and swampy, the ground often little more than frozen mud, and it suffered from pollution when air inversions trapped coal smoke in the narrow valley. Little wonder that many of its wartime occupants dubbed the post "Camp Hell."

In early 1943, soldiers attempted ski training but struggled from a lack of knowledge, organization, and discipline. Many grew unfit for duty as a result of

Lieutenant William J. Bourke trains soldiers in the Tenth Mountain Division to perform an about-face on skis at Camp Hale during World War II.

exhaustion, altitude sickness, and frostbite; and rumors circulated that soldiers even requested transfers to combat zones to escape Camp Hale. When the US Forest Service opened more land for mountain training space that summer and Olympics-class skiers joined the effort, the base's usefulness improved.

Camp Hale prepared soldiers for both summer and winter mountain combat until 1945, although few of the 14,000 soldiers who passed through it served in combat areas that demanded their special skills. The post's greatest legacy emerged after the war, when veterans returned to Colorado with visions of European-style resorts in the Rocky Mountains—including Friedrich Pfeifer and Peter W. Seibert, who founded Aspen and Vail ski areas, respectively. Although of limited use during World War II, Camp Hale inspired Colorado's winter sports industry.

July 16, 1945

Colorado Sets the Skies on Fire

Ore mined in Colorado helped inaugurate a new era in world history on July 16, 1945, when scientists with the top-secret Manhattan Project successfully tested the first atomic bomb in New Mexico. Fuel from western Colorado, in part, made this terrifying new weapon possible.

Prospectors discovered radioactive minerals including radium, uranium, and vanadium in several Colorado counties—Montrose especially—and across the Utah line in the 1890s. Without a market, however, the sources remained undisturbed. Scientists experimented with radium as a cancer cure in the 1910s, leading to a brief mining boom. Reduction plants arose near Naturita, and farmers in Nucla profited from selling crops to local markets. At the same time, vanadium proved popular with steel manufacturers as a strengthening element. By the late 1930s, competing firms operated in Montrose County—the Vanadium Corporation of America in Naturita and the United States Vanadium Corporation, which built a company town called Uravan (after uranium and vanadium) for its workers. The region prospered with industrial development nationwide that demanded vanadium from Colorado sources during World War II.

The Manhattan Project came to the region in 1943. Established the previous year, it bought tailings from mines across western Colorado. Processing plants made uranium sludge in Uravan and Durango at a rate of 3 tons per day, and a mill in Grand Junction refined the product. Locals drafted into military service were returned to the mines, where their expertise proved more important than on the battlefield. Secrecy remained paramount—unaware workers believed only that the federal government wanted their vanadium. The three atomic bombs built in the summer of 1945 used Colorado ore as fuel, in addition to deposits from Africa and Canada. The secret was out after August 1945, when two bombs obliterated Japanese cities. Mining in western Colorado remained an essential part of nuclear weaponry during the Cold War, as the federal government demanded ever more of the formerly worthless radioactive rocks.

July 17, 1880

What Grant Did on His Summer Vacation

On the heels of a three-year world tour, former president Ulysses S. Grant spent more than a month in the only state he had admitted into the Union. As Grant's party moved through southern Colorado on July 17, 1880, citizens once more cheered their former chief executive.

Leaving behind the scandals of his two terms, Grant and his family departed from the country in the spring of 1877. Tens of thousands of people greeted him across Europe, and he received warm receptions in Egypt, the Middle East, Southeast Asia, China, and Japan. Grant returned to San Francisco in late 1879.

His well-publicized exploits polished his image as Grant considered a third run for the presidency. On a western US tour in 1880, his party departed from Trinidad on July 17 after a reception there the night before and proceeded north on the Denver & Rio Grande Railroad. Grant greeted crowds at Pueblo and Colorado Springs, joined by Governors Alexander C. Hunt, John L. Routt (Grant's closest Colorado friend), and Frederick W. Pitkin. That evening the party arrived at Manitou Springs, which served as a base of operations for sightseeing.

On July 22, Grant's entourage returned to Pueblo and proceeded through the Royal Gorge to Leadville, pausing at Cañon City and Buena Vista. They spent a week and a half in Leadville, where Grant took in a show at the Tabor Opera House, attended receptions, and visited mines owned by Routt and Horace A.W. Tabor. From there, Grant and Routt traveled by coach to Gunnison via Saguache and over Cochetopa Pass. Unreconstructed Confederates plotted Grant's assassination in the mining camp of Irwin but were exposed. Grant and Routt crossed Schofield Pass to the Crystal River and eventually meandered their way back to the rest of the party at Manitou Springs. By mid-August, Grant arrived in Denver, where he spent a week making excursions to Boulder, Golden, and Idaho Springs. Grant's party left Colorado on August 23, five and a half weeks after they entered the state. He did not win re-nomination that year, but Grant won the hearts and minds of Coloradans during his long sojourn in the Centennial State.

July 18, 1955

Fort Collins Memories on Main Street

A day after its invitation-only dedication, Disneyland in California opened to the public on July 18, 1955. For Harper Goff, who designed many elements of the park's architecture, the first visitors who strolled under a railroad track and emerged onto Main Street, USA, might as well have been walking through his hometown of Fort Collins, Colorado.

Goff, an artist for the US Army during World War II and for Hollywood studios afterward, grew up in the Larimer County seat where his father edited a newspaper. While shopping in a model train store in London in 1951, Goff met Walt Disney when they both wanted to buy the same set. A fan of Goff's designs, Disney hired him to help plan a long-simmering idea for a themed amusement park near the cartoon studio. The concept evolved into the ambitious Disneyland, on which Goff worked as one of several leading concept artists. He collaborated on projects including the park's fairytale castle but poured his heart and memories into Main Street, which also incorporated aspects of Disney's hometown of

Marceline, Missouri. The quaint, turn-of-the-twentieth-century facades echoed the Fort Collins of Goff's childhood, in particular a city hall that Goff based on the old county courthouse. Although that structure no longer stands, today's Old Town Fort Collins retains much of the charm that Goff replicated; it also boasts a tribute mural in Harper Goff Alley.

Several amusement parks in Colorado, including Denver's Elitch Gardens and Lakeside, offer fun but not the cohesive plan of a theme park. Disneyland's success inspired construction of one in Jefferson County called Magic Mountain, which opened in 1959 with a layout that echoed the California park. Later scaled back and renamed Heritage Square, it boasted a Victorian-inspired main street, as well as shops and rides. The last vestiges of Heritage Square closed in 2018. Colorado's sole surviving theme park, the North Pole, debuted in El Paso County on the north flank of Pikes Peak in 1956. It remains in operation and has delighted generations of Coloradans with Christmas-themed rides and the chance to chat with Santa Claus.

July 19, 1879

Surveying the Last of Colorado's Lines

To the casual eye, Colorado seems simple—a giant rectangle among giant rectangles in the West. Yet the four geometric boundaries, approved in 1861 with the creation of Colorado Territory, tell a more complicated story. The southern and northern lines—37 degrees and 41 degrees of north latitude, respectively—intersect two meridians measured west of Washington, DC, the 25th to the east and the 32nd to the west. The former are parallel while the latter curve toward each other, making the northern boundary slightly shorter than the southern. Until surveyors marked the lines, however, they remained theoretical. When Rollin S. Reeves reached Colorado's northwestern corner on July 19, 1879, the Centennial State found its limits at last.

Federal survey teams started mapping Colorado's bounds in 1868, when Ehud N. Darling traced most of the Colorado–New Mexico line. The following year, Oliver Chaffee marked the separation between Colorado and Nebraska from the northwest corner of Kansas to the southeast corner of Wyoming. He used the telegraph in nearby Julesburg to coordinate with federal timekeepers while calculating Colorado's eastern longitude. In 1872, John Major proceeded down the Kansas line to Colorado's southeastern corner and the next year traced the Colorado-Oklahoma divide to Darling's line. Alonzo Richards extended Chaffee's work westward in 1873, splitting Colorado from Wyoming. Two years later, Chandler Robbins worked from Darling's line to Four Corners, the nation's most famous boundary spot. Reeves finished the task in 1879 when he surveyed from Four Corners northward along the edge of Utah Territory.

Surveyors erred while working through rugged terrain, so Colorado's straight boundaries are not actually straight. Significant jogs exist in Archuleta, Baca, Jackson, Montrose, and Weld Counties; thus all four edges meander from their declared course to some extent. A study in 2018 suggested that as a result of the challenges of surveying in the nineteenth century, Colorado has no fewer than 697 sides, technically making it a "hexahectaenneacontakaiheptagon." Courts have ruled, however, that surveyed lines rather than straight ones described in law represent true boundaries. Whether four or hundreds, Colorado's geometric limits define authority and create a cherished identity for all who live within them.

July 20, 2012

Sorrow Comes to Aurora Again

A movie theater in Aurora, Denver's largest suburb, filled with patrons for the debut of the latest film in the "Batman" franchise, *The Dark Knight Rises*, shortly after midnight on July 20, 2012. What started as exciting escapism turned into an infamous moment of domestic terrorism when a gunman opened fire on the crowd, killing twelve people and injuring seventy others.

James E. Holmes, a native of California, studied at the University of Colorado Anschutz Medical Campus in Aurora. He dressed in body armor and booby-trapped his apartment before driving to the nearby theater. Holmes entered as a ticketed patron, then sneaked out an emergency door he had propped open. After retrieving firearms from his car, Holmes returned to the theater and inflicted a nightmare under cover of the action film. In less than two minutes he unleashed a massacre and then left in the chaos. Law enforcement arrested him in the parking lot. Holmes's mug shot with a haunted expression and bright orange hair dominated the media. He went on trial in 2015, and a jury found him guilty and sentenced him to life in prison without parole.

The theater killings raised the specter of other crimes, including the Columbine High School Massacre thirteen years earlier. It also brought back memories of another shooting in Aurora. In 1993, former employee Nathan J. Dunlap entered a Chuck E. Cheese restaurant, killed four workers, and wounded another before fleeing with $1,500. Convicted and sentenced to death, Dunlap won a temporary reprieve from Governor John Hickenlooper—in office during the theater shootings—in 2013, which inspired a debate on capital punishment's future in Colorado.

In memory of the murdered victims of Aurora's twin tragedies—at the restaurant in 1993, Sylvia Crowell (age 19), Ben Grant (19), Marge Kohlberg (50), and Colleen O'Connor (17); and at the theater in 2012, Jon Blunk (26), A. J. Boik (18), Jesse Childress (29), Gordon W. Cowden (51), Jessica Ghawi (24), John Larimer (27), Matt McQuinn (27), Micayla Medek (23), Veronica Moser (6), Alex Sullivan (27), Alex Teves (24), and Rebecca Wingo (32).

July 21, 1880

A Fort on the Uncompahgre River

Within a generation, American competition reduced Ute influence on the western slope from dominance to desperation. Following the Meeker Incident in September 1879, many Coloradans demanded their expulsion from the region, including Governor Frederick W. Pitkin, who condoned vigilantism against the Utes. Federal officials and the diplomatic Ouray worked out a deal in early 1880—his Tabeguache band would relocate to present-day Grand Junction, while Parianuche and Yamparika Utes in northwestern Colorado had to surrender their territory along the White River and move to a reservation in Utah. To manage this expulsion, the US Army established a small outpost, or "cantonment," on the Uncompahgre River on July 21, 1880.

Colonel Ranald Mackenzie led several hundred soldiers from Fort Garland in the San Luis Valley to the Uncompahgre River, chafing at the rates charged by Otto

Soldiers of Company K, 10th United States Infantry, pose outside their barracks at Fort Crawford on November 5, 1886.

Mears to cross his toll roads through the San Juan Mountains. At the new post, erected near Colona on the present Montrose-Ouray County line, Mackenzie's soldiers attempted a delicate balance. They sought to encourage or force the Utes to move downstream while holding back nearly 2,000 Americans who desired the region and planned to settle there. Three-quarters of the Utes affected needed to consent, an impossibility until Mears bought each vote for two dollars apiece, improving Mackenzie's opinion of him. Nonetheless, some Utes attempted resistance. A Tabeguache faction led by Colorow planned an assault on the troops near Olathe, but Mackenzie had prepared for such an incident. Colorow employed discretion, and the Utes retreated in the face of a cavalry formation.

By the summer of 1881, the Utes were forced out of all but a small strip of southwestern Colorado. The cantonment was obsolete, but it remained in operation. In 1886 it was renamed Fort Crawford, after an officer killed while pursuing the Apache leader Geronimo in Mexico. The US Army finally abandoned the post in 1890, and local farmers bought its buildings and land, coveting the structures and irrigation ditches as they had much of the rest of Ute territory.

July 22, 1984

Laying to Rest the Solid Muldoon

One of the most bizarre funerals ever witnessed in Colorado took place on Muldoon Hill, along a highway between Pueblo and Beulah in Pueblo County, on July 22, 1984. There, local residents bade farewell to their most famous neighbor, a century-old ceramic composite of a prehistoric man nearly 8 feet tall and weighing half a ton, known as the Solid Muldoon.

In 1876, a Pennsylvania huckster named George Hull constructed a humanlike figure that he hoped would fool the world into believing he had found the "missing link" between man and monkeys, drawing on the fascination with Charles Darwin's recent theory of evolution. Hull molded and baked crushed rock, ground meat and bones, blood, and plaster to make his creation as confounding to science as possible. He partnered with infamous showman P. T. Barnum, who arranged for an associate in Colorado Springs to find a proper place to bury the figure. In the meantime, Hull manufactured turtles and fish in similar styles to plant with the petrified man, to bolster the hoax. The team installed the collection on Muldoon Hill, a known fossil source, in the spring of 1877. An orchestrated "discovery" took place on September 16, and the find earned the moniker "Solid Muldoon" in honor of a popular Irish song about a solid, stout man of that name. Barnum arrived in Pueblo four days later, ostensibly to negotiate its purchase for his museum in New York City, although he was in on the scheme and sought only publicity.

The Solid Muldoon, dismissed by scholars but fascinating all the same, toured cities across the country. It debuted in New York City in November, prior to a planned New England and European tour. David F. Day borrowed its name for his newspaper published in Ouray. People who knew of the ruse but were denied a cut of the profits exposed the fraud in February 1878, however. The maligned figure eventually made its way back to Pueblo County, where the Beulah Historical Society arranged for a reburial in 1984. An Irish wake took place on the hill next to Colorado Highway 78, where a tombstone declares "Long Live Our Solid Muldoon."

July 23, 1951

Cowboy Governor versus Cowboy Warden

Governor Dan Thornton requested that a state board ban the flogging of inmates at the penitentiary in Cañon City on July 23, 1951. The whipping of prisoners with a salt water–soaked leather strap as they lay over a wooden horse had long been employed by warden Roy Best.

The Republican Thornton—a Gunnison County cattleman who gave Colorado-made Jolly Rancher candies to his visitors—won election in 1950, defeating the incumbent Democrat, Walter W. Johnson. Best, a native of Rocky Ford, had toured with a rodeo, joined the Colorado State Patrol, and helped break a prison riot at Cañon City in 1929. Appointed warden by Governor William H. Adams in 1932, Best modernized the facility and its treatment of prisoners and instituted industrial labor to keep inmates busy and provide them with skills for the outside world.

Controversies swirled about Best, however. In addition to his brutal discipline—which made him a hero to some Coloradans and a sadist to others—the warden proved a sloppy bookkeeper, obscuring the penitentiary money he funneled into his own pocket. Upon Best's indictment for embezzlement in September 1950, Johnson failed to suspend the warden, a fellow Democrat. During that fall's gubernatorial campaign, Thornton pledged to get Best to step aside. The folksy warden refused and easily won acquittal. Nonetheless, pressure built for Best to resign, especially after news of six more beatings in the summer of 1951—five for a violent attempted breakout and one for disrespecting a guard. The criticism rolled off Best, who nonchalantly described the institution under his control as nothing more than a well-patrolled hotel.

In April 1952, a grand jury indicted Best and eight prison officers for violating the civil rights of inmates, a first in American history. The nine men escaped punishment in that trial as well, but that summer a state board voted a two-year suspension for Best. The infuriated, humbled warden railed against Thornton, but to no avail. Best died of a heart attack on May 27, 1954, three days before the end of his suspension and a planned triumphant return to the prison.

July 24, 2007

CU Shows Churchill the Door

Universities often walk a fine line between the academic freedom scholars require to explore divisive ideas and the need to maintain professional standards. One of the most bitter and public examples of this tension culminated on July 24, 2007, when the University of Colorado's (CU's) governing board dismissed ethnic studies professor Ward Churchill.

The university possessed a mixed record of intellectual liberty—its leaders allied with the Ku Klux Klan against Catholic and Jewish professors during the 1920s, yet a generation later, CU aided an effort to dismiss charges of seditious behavior during the Cold War. Churchill's case represented Boulder's most shocking and controversial test of academic freedom to date. Shortly after the September 11, 2001, terror attacks, he compared its victims to compliant citizens of Nazi Germany and defended the murderous hijackers. When Churchill's remarks found a wider audience in 2005, cable news networks and the internet pounced. His public events turned into media circuses, and many of his students rallied to their professor's defense. Republicans in particular eviscerated Churchill, including Governor Bill Owens and CU president Hank Brown, a former US senator. While the press fanned flames of hyperbole, the university investigated charges of academic dishonesty against the tenured professor.

After studying Churchill's sloppy scholarship, on July 24, 2007, CU's board of regents voted 8 to 1 to dismiss him. Brown stated: "The university has an obligation to ensure its faculty's work is above reproach. Academic freedom requires academic integrity, responsibility, and accountability." The decision met with bipartisan support, including from the new Democratic governor, Bill Ritter. A legal fight ensued, and a jury agreed in 2009 that his firing smacked of politics but awarded him only a single dollar in compensation, reflecting Colorado's exhaustion on the matter. State courts repeatedly rejected Churchill's attempts at reinstatement or retaliation against CU in the early 2010s, and the US Supreme Court refused to hear his case in 2013.

Everybody Comes to Fort St. Vrain

Fort St. Vrain, established in 1837 along the South Platte River near present-day Gilcrest in Weld County, existed for one reason—to kill off the competition. The firm of Bent, St. Vrain & Company, which dominated bison and beaver pelt trade from Bent's Fort on the Arkansas River, resented independent posts between that waterway and Fort Laramie on the North Platte River. To squeeze out interlopers along the Trapper's Trail—specifically Forts Jackson, Lupton, and Vasquez—the company built a post near the others and named it for company founder Ceran St. Vrain. His brother Marcellin operated the well-stocked post and put the smaller neighbors out of business by the early 1840s. It survived as a profitable destination and a magnet for travelers, best exemplified on July 25, 1843, when it welcomed a host of frontier notables.

Lieutenant John C. Frémont had stopped at Fort St. Vrain on Independence Day that year, and after a quick trip south to the Arkansas River, he returned to plan an epic expedition. On July 25, Frémont conferred with scout Christopher "Kit" Carson, cartographer Charles Preuss, scout Alexis Godey, and Thomas Fitzpatrick, a trapper familiar with the passes of the Rocky Mountains. All four contributed in diverse ways to the expanding American knowledge and control of the West. Leaving Fort St. Vrain the following day, Frémont's party set out to the northwest, proceeding up the Cache la Poudre River and down the Laramie River, by which they crossed Colorado's invisible northern line into Wyoming. Frémont's trip took him down the Snake and Columbia Rivers, over the Sierra Nevadas, past Lake Tahoe, and through the Great Basin and presaged his conquest of California during the Mexican-American War in 1846.

With the fur trade in decline, Bent, St. Vrain & Company abandoned Fort St. Vrain in 1847, although the site remained a gathering place for many years. A granite marker erected in 1911 commemorates the trading post, although its adobe ruins were bulldozed in the 1950s.

Holing through the Alpine Tunnel

As Colorado's mining economy boomed in the 1870s and 1880s, railroads competed to reach new towns and tap markets throughout the Rocky Mountains. The Denver, South Park & Pacific Railroad (DSP&P), for example, raced the Denver

& Rio Grande Railroad (D&RG) toward Gunnison County. On July 26, 1881, crews digging under the Continental Divide for the DSP&P met one another deep underground at the holing through of the Alpine Tunnel.

Former governor John Evans, a booster and investor in several railroad ventures, helped found the DSP&P in 1872. Construction halted near Morrison after the Panic of 1873 but proceeded by the late 1870s up the South Platte River, crossing Kenosha Pass into South Park. A spur led traffic over Boreas Pass to serve the mining towns of Breckenridge and Dillon and arced back over Fremont Pass to the silver empire of Leadville. The main line broached the Arkansas River valley at Trout Creek Pass and set its sights on the Continental Divide.

Gunnison emerged as the hub of a productive region in 1879, and the DSP&P and other lines wanted to harness it. The company laid track nearly to the summit of the divide and then punched a hole through near the crest. Work started on the Alpine Tunnel in January 1880, and a crew of approximately 400 workers spent a year and a half digging and blasting from both sides. They carved a tunnel over 1,700 feet long lined with California redwood. When they holed through in the summer of 1881, the teams were off by less than 2 inches. From the divide, the line ran to Gunnison, which the D&RG had reached a few months earlier via Marshall Pass. The DSP&P ultimately dead-ended a few miles to the northwest at the mining town of Baldwin.

A Denver, South Park & Pacific Railroad train descends from the west side of the Alpine Tunnel through the Continental Divide in the 1880s.

The Alpine Tunnel served railroad traffic until 1910. By then, the DSP&P had been bought and sold several times. The rest of the route was abandoned in the late 1930s, a victim of both the Great Depression and automobile competition. The tunnel entrances are covered today, but tourists still make the hike to visit one of Colorado's engineering marvels.

July 27, 1875

Construction Commences on Old Main

Fourteen years of wrangling culminated in a few inauspicious shovelfuls of dirt turned on a hill looming over the south side of Boulder on July 27, 1875. With those scoops, work started at last on the first building of the University of Colorado (CU), known today as Old Main.

Colorado's first territorial legislature designated Boulder as the site of a university in 1861, but a lack of funds and efforts by other communities to capture the school delayed work until 1875. Construction delays, recruiting faculty, and determining a balance between classical and modern educational styles further delayed the institution. Not until the fall of 1877, one year after Colorado joined the Union, did its university open. At the dedication ceremony, President Joseph A. Sewall declared: "If the State . . . has an interest in the well being and prosperity of her citizens, she must be interested in and foster higher institutions of learning. These tend to make good and strong citizens, and the State can have no higher interest, no better product."

CU struggled in its earliest years to build enrollment and find a purpose. Unlike the mining school in Golden, the agricultural college in Fort Collins, and the teachers' school in Greeley, the university's vague definition deprived it of clear goals. By the century's end, CU's enrollment grew and the campus developed into an attractive haven of learning. It flourished under the twenty-two-year presidency of James H. Baker, who envisioned the institution as an Ivy League school in the shadow of the Rocky Mountains. Two more decades of George Norlin's leadership created a campus of comfortable stone and terra cotta buildings, known as the "Colorado Style."

Growth continued after World War II, when so many former servicemen enrolled that many lived in a trailer park nicknamed "Vetsville." CU eventually erected satellite campuses in Denver and Colorado Springs, as well as a training hospital now known as the Anschutz Medical Campus, located at the former Fitzsimons Army Hospital in Aurora. The university emerged from shaky beginnings to hold a place of pride as Colorado's flagship institution of higher education.

First Tracks of the Denver & Rio Grande

A ceremony in Denver on July 28, 1871, accompanied the start of construction on the Denver & Rio Grande Railroad (D&RG), which boasted an inspirational vision for the future. As the *Rocky Mountain News* declared, "May the rails thus laid not end until we are bound by their iron embrace with the far distant valley of the Rio Grande; and united commercially with the trade, the resources, and the industries of the grand valley and New and Old Mexico."

By late 1870, three railroads had reached Denver—the Colorado Central from the west, the Kansas Pacific from the east, and the Denver Pacific from the north. William J. Palmer, who directed construction of the Kansas Pacific, envisioned a line stretching south from Colorado's capital city to the Rio Grande valley of New Mexico and perhaps as far as Mexico City, creating an international commercial route. Rejecting the nation's standard gauge of track width (4 feet 8½ inches) for the narrow gauge (3 feet), Palmer sought a smaller but more versatile line that could snake into mountain canyons inaccessible to broader railroads. He hoped to tap valuable markets in the Rocky Mountains and perhaps even find a route across the Continental Divide, challenges that stymied other lines. After the summer of 1871, iron rails extended south from Denver past landmarks named for the D&RG's founder, including Palmer Lake and Palmer Divide. The line connected Colorado Springs, Pueblo, and El Moro (near Trinidad) before abandoning its southward path to the Atchison, Topeka & Santa Fe Railroad. Instead, it focused on the mountains, connecting mining towns and spreading across the state.

The D&RG struggled in the early twentieth century. It merged with the Western Pacific Railroad in 1920 to create the Denver & Rio Grande Western Railroad. The line traded hands several times after that, most recently acquired by the Union Pacific Railroad in 1996. Some of its original routes remain in operation, but most in the mountains have been abandoned. A few remain in service as tourist attractions, offering a taste of the glory days of Colorado railroads.

A Spanish Escort across the Plains

The summer sun beat down on a party of 140 Spaniards, Puebloans, and Apaches, directed by native guides and commanded by General Juan de Ulibarri. On July 29, 1706, they reached the south bank of the Arkansas River in present-day Prowers

County, having trekked for two and a half weeks from Santa Fe toward a refugee settlement known as El Cuartelejo.

In the century since the Spanish arrived in New Mexico, relations with native cultures often proved contentious. Whenever the situation grew too intense, Puebloans fled to what is now western Kansas to live with their Apache allies until things calmed down at home. One of the last Puebloan uprisings took place in 1696, and for a decade its leaders hid at El Cuartelejo. When they asked the Spanish authorities for permission to return, Governor Francisco Cuervo y Valdés saw an opportunity to improve relations with his neighbors and locate their hiding place at the same time. He dispatched Ulibarri to lead the expedition, which set out in mid-July 1706.

The party crossed northeastern New Mexico, entered Colorado near the modern town of Branson, and proceeded northeastward across Las Animas, Baca, and Prowers Counties. Ulibarri described the prominent Two Buttes as "two little hills very much alike, sharp and pointed. I called them Las Tetas de [the breasts of] Domínguez." On July 29, when they reached the Arkansas River—known to native cultures as the Napestle—Ulibarri praised "the best and broadest valley discovered in New Spain" and its plentiful wild fruit. They crossed the river near what is now Granada, and the next day they struck out across the plains north of the Arkansas, reaching El Cuartelejo on August 4. Ulibarri's expedition and the refugees retraced their route through southeastern Colorado on the way home and returned to Santa Fe on September 2.

The Ulibarri expedition proved a success in strengthening ties among the Spanish, Puebloans, and Apaches. Yet the discovery of French-made goods at El Cuartelejo reminded the Spanish that their European competitors sought influence on the Great Plains as well.

July 30, 1861

Mark Twain Stops in Julesburg

In the mid-nineteenth century, few towns in Colorado Territory boasted the significance of Julesburg. It served as a station for overland mail and telegraph routes and as the diversion point between trails to the mining region and points farther west, linking Colorado to the rest of the country. On July 30, 1861, a twenty-five-year-old Missourian named Samuel Clemens—known later as the brilliant author Mark Twain—paused in Julesburg for an hour to change stagecoaches.

In the summer of 1861, to escape the Civil War in his home state, Clemens traveled west with his brother Orion, who had been appointed to the government of

Nevada Territory. Five days after leaving St. Joseph, the Clemens boys stopped at Julesburg, which Samuel described as "the strangest, quaintest, funniest frontier town that our untraveled eyes had ever stared at and been astonished with." In his tongue-in-cheek manner, Clemens marveled at the first community he saw since departing from Missouri as he strolled about sightseeing. Clemens looked askance at the "Great American Desert" and its river, "the shallow, yellow, muddy South Platte, with its low banks and its scattering flat sand-bars and pigmy islands—a melancholy stream straggling through the centre of the enormous flat plain . . . The Platte was 'up,' they said—which made me wish I could see it when it was down, if it could look any sicker and sorrier."

One resident of Julesburg fascinated Clemens—Joseph A. "Jack" Slade, a stage company agent with a deadly reputation. In 1859, trader Jules Beni set up shop at what became Julesburg, named for him, to take advantage of the gold rush traffic. Most accounts agree that Beni and Slade quarreled over accusations that Beni had stampeded livestock and then charged people to recapture them, inspiring Beni to shoot Slade and flee the town. After Slade recovered, he tracked down Beni in 1863, killing him and cutting off his ears to wear as a trophy. Slade met his maker in Montana Territory the following year when he was lynched for disturbing the peace. The quiet town of Julesburg, now the seat of Sedgwick County, belies its scandalous past.

July 31, 1976

The Big Thompson Flood

Coloradans prepared to mark their statehood centennial on August 1, 1976. The day before the state's 100th birthday, however, a deadly natural disaster undermined the celebratory atmosphere when a cloudburst flooded the Big Thompson River in Larimer County.

A thunderstorm built near Estes Park in the late afternoon of July 31, and rain fell on the upper reaches of the Big Thompson by 6:00. The small but concentrated storm raged for four hours, and more than a foot of rain fell. The river, which averaged a depth of 2 feet in the dry summer months, rose to 20 feet and swept away everything in its path, gaining strength and speed as it rushed through the gorge between Estes Park and Loveland. Residents and tourists found themselves in the flood's path without any warning, trapped by the steep canyon walls. Word spread erratically as the water wiped out telephone lines, and people who attempted to race ahead of the disaster down US Highway 34 found themselves in greater danger than those who abandoned their cars and scaled the mountainsides above the

Governor Richard Lamm (wearing tie) talks with residents affected by the Big Thompson River flood in 1976, with damage from the disaster in the background.

river. Deborah Watts, who lost her three-year-old son Aaron in the flood, recalled seeing a car in the torrent: "I caught a glimpse of the occupants. I could see the look of horror and terror in their eyes as the petrified couple plunged on down the river to their certain death." Most of US 34 washed away in the deluge, especially at the narrow east end of the canyon, hampering relief and recovery efforts.

The Big Thompson flood killed 143 people, including summer visitors and local residents. Damage totaled $35 million, including the loss of more than 400 houses and 50 businesses. Destruction extended from Estes Park downstream all the way to the South Platte River, as the water broadened after leaving the canyon and caused additional flooding on the plains. Survivors dedicated a memorial along US 34 on the 25th anniversary in 2001, and an annual commemoration takes place there to honor those lost in Colorado's deadliest flash flood.

August

Colorado Joins the Union

President Ulysses S. Grant signed a proclamation admitting Colorado into the Union on August 1, 1876. The first state admitted since Nebraska nine years earlier, Colorado earned the nickname "Centennial State" for its promotion in the US century birthday year. One might expect such news to have inspired fevered celebration in Colorado. If so, one would be wrong.

Coloradans had exhausted their cheers a month earlier when a vote on July 1 confirmed the state constitution drawn up the previous winter. Then, the *Rocky Mountain News* had preened that "another star is added to Columbia's galaxy, and Colorado is the Centennial State in good earnest. After weary years of waiting, we are at last to govern ourselves." A Pueblo newspaper employed a more sarcastic tone, noting that "now if we have any scoundrelly or incompetent officials we will have the satisfaction of knowing that we elected them ourselves."

By contrast, Grant's proclamation a month later inspired little emotion. Papers found a grasshopper plague on the eastern plains more worthy of attention. Merchants, however, discovered a unique opportunity to tout their wares. One press declared that "the proclamation laid at the door of every citizen of Boulder County by Henry C. Thompson is as significant to our welfare as that of Ulysses. Thompson tells you that he has the finest stock of groceries, provisions, and family supplies to be found in Boulder, and they are being daily sold at prices that defy competition. Heed this proclamation and buy your groceries at this cheap cash store."

The lack of interest in Colorado's statehood was echoed a century later. Until 1967, Colorado Day was a state holiday, commemorated on August 1. That year, officials moved the day off for state employees to the first Monday in August. In 1986, Colorado Day disappeared from the calendar altogether, replaced by Martin Luther King Jr.'s birthday. Yet as this book suggests, for those fascinated and entertained by the state's rich history, every day is Colorado Day.

Bloody Bridles on the National Stage

An older man with piercing eyes and a full white beard, looking and sounding more like a prophet than a politician, whipped a silver coinage convention in Chicago into hysterics on August 2, 1893. Davis Waite, the Populist governor of

Colorado, energized the crowd with his oratory. He employed his trademark line, arguing that "it is better, infinitely better, rather than our liberties should be destroyed by the tyranny which is oppressing humanity all over the world, that we should wade through seas of blood—yea, blood to the horses' bridles."

Waite served in the Wisconsin and Kansas legislatures before moving to Aspen in 1879. He prospected for silver and worked as a lawyer but found his voice in 1891 when he established the *Aspen Union Era*, a newspaper associated with the Populist movement. Populists sought greater government oversight (if not out-right ownership) of railroads, banks, and corporations and advocated the free coinage of silver to democratize the nation's currency.

Waite rode the Populist wave to the governor's office in 1892, its only occu-pant to hail from a third party. Nicknamed "Bloody Bridles" for his famous phrase, Waite's evangelical style earned him nationwide fame. But the Panic of 1893 dealt a body blow to the state, and Waite seemed unsuited to the task. His suggestion to have Mexico coin money with Colorado silver the federal government no longer wanted earned scorn, as did his near use of deadly force against Denver officials when he backed off an order for the Colorado National Guard to attack the city hall at the last minute. Waite sided with strikers during a labor dispute in Cripple Creek, a rare stance for a Colorado governor, but supporting labor unrest during an economic collapse made him seem out of touch to many Coloradans. He advo-cated women's suffrage, approved in 1893, and then blamed women for voting him out of office the next year. Waite's political fate had more to do with his inability to tackle the Panic of 1893, an overwhelming task for anyone, but the colorful chief executive often proved his own worst enemy.

August 3, 1964

Death of the Turnpike's Mascot

Drivers on the Denver-Boulder Turnpike, bearing bones and table scraps like always, learned sad news on August 3, 1964—Shep was dead. The sixteen-year-old shepherd-mix dog, a fixture at the toll booths on the road for as long as it had existed, had been euthanized.

Planned in the late 1940s as one of Colorado's first controlled-access highways, the Denver-Boulder Turnpike would replace a meandering trip on back roads between the capital city and the flagship university with a direct, fast toll road. In 1951, Shep meandered onto the toll booth construction site—at the US Highway 287 interchange in Broomfield today—and remained there for thirteen years. From the beginning, he served as the turnpike's mascot. He appeared at its dedication ceremony on January 19, 1952, and pictures of Shep even graced the company's annual reports. Toll booth operators cared for him, brought him home on cold nights, and paid his medical bills—including a time when a farmer mistook the dog for a coyote and fired a shotgun at him, injuring Shep's paw. Motorists joked that paying the dime fare to travel the road seemed less onerous when they caught a glimpse of Shep lying beside the booth, soaking in the sunshine. He received numerous tasty treats throughout each day from drivers but maintained a sleek physique all the same. In more than a decade, he never got hit by a car.

By the summer of 1964, old age had caught up with Shep, and on August 3 the toll booth operators asked his veterinarian, Clyde Brunner, to take away his pain. He was buried on a hillside just south of the toll booths that same day. In 1967, the turnpike paid off its debt and the road became free. Although the booths disappeared, Shep's grave—marked by a marble stone and iron fence—remained. When construction threatened the site in 2009, Shep was exhumed and his remains were cremated by Brunner, tending to his most famous patient one last time. Shep's grave, complete with an urn holding his ashes, was relocated to the Broomfield Depot Museum to protect and honor one of Colorado's best-loved canines.

August 4, 2010

Welcoming Back Pro Cycling

Decked out in riding attire, Governor Bill Ritter and Lance Armstrong—seven-time winner of the Tour de France bicycle race—appeared at a press conference at the state capitol on August 4, 2010, to announce the return of competitive cycling to the Centennial State.

The bicycle proved popular with late nineteenth-century Americans, who used the new vehicle for business and pleasure. One newspaper reported in 1879: "The velocipede mania has broken out in Boulder, and ambitious youth may be seen every evening weaving their winding way down the streets, struggling manfully to maintain their equipoise on the fractious bicycle. Broncho breakers are at a discount in subduing the new 'animile.'" Cycling allowed young people to escape parental clutches for fun and romance. Clubs organized excursions and events in towns throughout the state. The bicycle revolutionized travel and social interaction.

The Red Zinger Bicycle Classic, Colorado's first professional cycling competition, debuted in 1975 with sponsorship from Boulder's Celestial Seasonings tea company. It changed corporate affiliation in 1980 and became the Coors Classic, drawing cyclists from around the world to test their skills against Colorado's altitude and climate until it ended in 1988. The state lacked professional cycling until 2011—the race announced by Ritter and Armstrong the year before. Originally named the Quiznos Pro Challenge after its Denver-founded sandwich company sponsor, it became the USA Pro Cycling Challenge in 2012. The strenuous mountain contest folded after the 2015 race, but enthusiasm for a formal competition remained high. The Colorado Classic succeeded the Pro Cycling Challenge in 2017 and became one of the few women-only bicycle races in the United States two years later.

Colorado hosts several annual amateur competitions as well. Ride the Rockies debuted in 1986 and sends 2,000 riders on a week-long tour through the high country. In 2012, Pedal the Plains premiered, a less strenuous tour that promoted tourism on the prairies, too often overshadowed—literally and figuratively—by the Rocky Mountains. The state's myriad cycling events offer exercise, adventure, and a special way to experience the Centennial State.

August 5, 1920

Riots in Downtown Denver

Five days into a walkout against the Denver Tramway Company (DTC), the strike devolved into a riot. Mobs of union members attacked streetcars staffed by strikebreakers, toppling two in front of the Cathedral of the Immaculate Conception on Colfax Avenue, in which the replacement workers sought sanctuary. Strikers set other cars on fire and attacked the *Denver Post*'s offices for the paper's defense of the DTC. The tramway strike brought labor violence—all too familiar in mining communities across Colorado—to the heart of the capital.

Throughout the 1910s, DTC workers' salaries stagnated. Streetcar drivers and other employees lobbied for a union to negotiate collectively with the company, but—like many firms opposing the threat of organized labor—the company offered meager wage hikes to prevent unionization. During World War I, DTC workers organized a union chapter anyway, embracing drivers, mechanics, power plant operators, and other employees. A postwar economic downturn inspired the DTC to reduce wages in the summer of 1920, which the union fought in court.

Hoping to force the DTC to preserve wages, on August 1 members voted to strike by a tally of 887 in favor and 10 against. The company responded by barricading its property and hiring three dozen strikebreakers from out of state to fight for the DTC. Several hundred World War I veterans, members of the American Legion, joined them. The riots of August 5 served as prologue to a gun battle at

Denver Tramway Company cars lie toppled on Colfax Avenue with the Colorado State Capitol in the background during the August 1920 strike

a car barn the next day, in which six protestors died. More than eighty people on all sides suffered injuries during the strike. On August 7, Governor Oliver H. Shoup requested federal troops from Fort Logan to restore order. Less than two weeks after it started, the strike ended with most union leaders indicted for various offenses and members forced to return to work under the old wage system, if they were lucky enough to get their jobs back at all. The DTC strike reflected the challenge of fighting entrenched corporate interests with deep pockets and political allies, even in the heyday of organized labor in the United States.

August 6, 1846

Mormon Settlers "Bear" a Burden

While attempting in vain to locate the main body of the westward-bound Church of Jesus Christ of Latter-Day Saints in the summer of 1846, a group of forty-three Mormon colonists from Mississippi faced a more immediate problem in Pueblo County on August 6. Two members chased a wounded deer into some bushes, where they startled a grizzly bear. It attacked them, and one man suffered three bites to the head before rescuers killed the bruin. The wounded man survived, but the encounter reflected the myriad challenges faced by the small, meandering band.

In early 1846, church president Brigham Young prepared to lead his flock from Illinois to a new settlement in the West. He instructed the Mississippi party to rendezvous with the main group somewhere along the Platte River. The forty-three colonists headed up the Oregon Trail from Missouri as their compatriots straggled across Iowa. Unsure of Young's intentions and not expecting the Illinois party to catch up until the next year, the Mississippians decided to make a winter camp. In early July they met a trapper named John Reshaw at Fort Laramie, who escorted them southward to the Arkansas River. A few miles below the Hispano settlement at El Pueblo, they started construction on a log cabin camp a day after their tussle with the grizzly bear.

The Mormons passed a mild winter at peace with the region's population. They planted gardens, hunted wildlife, and erected a wooden temple for worship and communal gatherings. It hosted members of the Mormon Battalion, a group of volunteers sent by Young to join General Stephen W. Kearny's invasion of northern Mexico in the summer of 1846. The temple also sheltered people fleeing an anti-American uprising in New Mexico in early 1847. At its peak, the Mormon settlement housed about 275 people, making it by far the largest town in present-day Colorado.

In the summer of 1847, the Mormons left Pueblo County and followed Young's party toward the Great Salt Lake. Floods obliterated all traces of their settlement within a few decades, although Mormons returned to southern Colorado as colonists by the century's end.

August 7, 1904

Catastrophic Train Wreck at Eden

The deadliest railroad accident in Colorado history occurred on August 7, 1904, a few miles north of Pueblo, where the Denver & Rio Grande Railroad (D&RG) line crossed the misleadingly named Dry Creek near the similarly misleadingly named town of Eden.

A cloudburst that evening swelled creeks in Pueblo County, and the moisture undermined the railroad bed and bridges built on sandy foundations. Railroad worker Henry Eiten saw the dangerous conditions and walked north from Eden in the rain to flag down Train #11 heading south from Colorado Springs. Eiten stood a hundred yards south of the Dry Creek bridge when he saw the train approach and watched helplessly as its headlight disappeared from view. The locomotive, traveling at a cautious 15 miles an hour because of the weather, almost made it across before the bridge collapsed, pulling the engine, tender, baggage car, and several passenger cars into the torrential muck. A porter on the sleeping car at the end of the train managed to apply the brakes in time to prevent it from falling in, saving about two dozen people.

When news of the disaster reached Pueblo, a train set out for Eden packed with doctors and railroad officials, along with crews to rebuild the bridge and keep traffic moving. More than 200 volunteers joined 25 police officers and firefighters trying to rescue survivors and recover bodies of the dead. One car ended up a mile downstream from the accident site, and residents of the Arkansas River valley found human remains as far as 20 miles away. Some victims were swallowed up by the murky water and earth never to be seen again, making an official death count difficult to achieve, but estimates placed the total at more than 100 of the approximately 125 people on the train. A coroner's jury meeting in Pueblo blamed the crash on lackadaisical maintenance by the D&RG. It demanded that other spans like the failed bridge, which was built of wood three decades earlier, be replaced with ones of stone and steel. The Eden disaster offers a sobering reminder of the need for vigilance when it comes to infrastructure.

August 8, 1936

Annexing the Forgotten Empire

In the summer of 1936, a Breckenridge newspaper printed a "Special Flag-Raising Issue of the *Summit County Journal*" and stated "Tomorrow, August 8, We Become Part of the U.S.A." A grand ceremony, both patriotic and bizarre, took place on the grounds of the county courthouse that day when politicians claimed roughly 2,000 square miles in the heart of the country that, until then, supposedly did not belong to the United States.

With the Louisiana Purchase of 1803, the United States bought from France the claim to all land draining into the Mississippi River from the west, including Colorado east of the Continental Divide and the Sangre de Cristo Mountains. In 1819, federal officials worked out the Adams-Onís Treaty to establish a border with the Spanish empire. The line in Colorado followed the Arkansas River to its source near Leadville, then extended due north. Some sources argued, incorrectly, that these deals left a gap between the geometric line north of the Arkansas and west of the divide, embracing most of Grand and Summit Counties and a sliver of Eagle County.

When the Woman's Club of Breckenridge realized the supposed oversight, they lobbied for formal annexation to resolve the matter. Scholars pointed out that the Utes had surrendered the region to American officials in 1868, but club members retorted that the Utes were not a real nation, so the ceremony remained essential. Among the thousands of attendees were Governor Edwin C. Johnson, Congressman Edward T. Taylor, Adjutant General Neil W. Kimball, members of the Colorado National Guard and American Legion, a US Navy recruiting officer, and the state registrar of federal land, who "regards the affair as an unnecessary formality, but she plans to attend to be on the safe side." Kimball raised an American flag while guns fired a salute, and the country was whole at last. In addition to a dozen towns and some of the state's most popular winter resorts, the region had produced millions of dollars in gold, silver, and other resources over the years—wealth the Spanish or French would have loved to claim as their own.

August 9, 1859

Macomb at Mesa Verde

Captain John N. Macomb's US Army expedition, searching for a route to connect New Mexico and Utah Territories, skirted the northern flank of Mesa Verde on August 9, 1859, as they followed abandoned trails through modern southwestern Colorado.

In the late 1850s, the federal government and Mormon settlers clashed over authority in Utah, and the army sought new avenues to enter the territory in case it needed to restore control by force. Macomb organized a survey to reestablish the Old Spanish Trail, a route that had connected Santa Fe with California until Ute resistance forced its abandonment in the mid-1840s. His orders called for a survey between New Mexico and the Green and Grand (Colorado) Rivers' junction in present-day eastern Utah. Macomb set out in mid-July 1859 with a pack train and about sixty men, primarily a military escort for his surveyors, artists, engineers, and cooks.

The expedition passed through modern Archuleta, La Plata, Montezuma, and Dolores Counties over several weeks. It enjoyed cordial interactions with several Ute and Navajo bands. The group visited Pagosa Springs, noted Chimney Rock, and crossed the Animas River near the present site of Durango. Geologist John S. Newberry observed Ancestral Puebloan ruins on the north face of Mesa Verde on August 9. A few days later, on the Dolores River, he wrote: "Our Camp on the site of a ruined town. Present supply of water and grass very meager, these ruins very ancient. Could such a population be now sustained here—has the climate changed?"

The party recorded ruins throughout the region and noted some of the first dinosaur bones discovered in the West near modern Moab, Utah. The group proceeded to the confluence in late August and returned to New Mexico on a southerly branch of the braid-like Old Spanish Trail. Following the San Juan River, they camped near what is now Four Corners, a point created by law five years later. The 1859 Macomb expedition provided Americans with a taste of the West's wonders, although the impending Civil War deprived the survey of a greater audience.

August 10, 1972

It's Curtains for Rifle Gap

A massive work of art hung across Rifle Gap, a canyon formed by East Rifle Creek above the town of Rifle in Garfield County, on August 10, 1972. The design of husband-and wife artistic team Christo and Jean-Claude Javacheff, the striking, bright orange, nylon curtain offered an astonishing contrast to the landscape. It also proved no match for Colorado's winds.

The Javacheffs (known simply as Christo and Jean-Claude) commenced their project in 1970. After weather and logistical glitches delayed its October 1971 debut, Christo and Jean-Claude tried again in August 1972. Nearly 100 workers stretched a cable 1,368 feet across Rifle Gap, held in place by 864 tons of concrete foundations. The orange curtain unfurled from the cable, from which drooped more than 200,000 square feet of nylon connected at the bottom by twenty-seven anchors. Several times the artwork snagged as it unfurled, but breezes through the canyon worked it loose. A curved opening allowed vehicles on Colorado Highway 325 to pass underneath. Christo and Jean-Claude arranged for the curtain to hang until October 1, but less than a day and a half after its debut, winds shredded the orange fabric. While crews dismantled the shroud and its cables, a cheerful Jean-Claude expressed gratitude that they got it up at all while Christo sounded a haughtier note: "The project was over for me at 11:00 Thursday," referring to the moment it unfurled. "I promised I would get it up there, but I didn't promise how long it would stay."

Christo and Jean-Claude earned renown for dramatic public art erected around the world. Twenty years after *Valley Curtain*, they announced plans for a new Colorado project, *Over the River*, a series of silver shrouds suspended over the Arkansas River in Chaffee and Fremont Counties. Years of legal challenges by

Christo and Jean-Claude's orange curtain draped across Rifle Gap in Garfield County during its brief existence in August 1972

environmentalists and concerned locals—who organized under the name Rags over the River—failed to dissuade Christo, but he ultimately abandoned *Over the River* in 2017 to protest the Donald Trump administration, with which he would need to work to erect the temporary display on federal government–owned land.

August 11, 1861

Father Dyer Preaches in Fairplay

Thirty people gathered in the mining community of Fairplay—named in the hope that it would prove more respectable and trustworthy than earlier placer camps in South Park—for the town's first Sunday services on August 11, 1861. They listened to a message delivered by a circuit-riding Methodist preacher named John L. Dyer, one of Colorado's religious pioneers.

Born in Ohio in 1812, the young Dyer moved to Illinois with his family before settling in Wisconsin, where he joined the Methodist ministry in 1851. He served as a preacher in several communities in Wisconsin and Minnesota before traveling to the brand-new Colorado Territory a decade later. There he came under the leadership of the Reverend John M. Chivington, who soon traded in his Bible for a military uniform. Dyer was dispatched to South Park and marveled—as motorists on US Highway 285 still do—at the vista from Kenosha Pass, "a view of grandeur never to be forgotten. Prairies, surrounded with high mountains and interspersed with pine-groves and small peaks—a very Eden Park—are a sight seldom surpassed even in the Rocky Mountains." Dyer also preached from the Park County seat of Buckskin Joe (near present-day Alma) and traveled to many mining camps in the next few years. His circuit extended to Oro City at the Arkansas River headwaters, to which he carried the mail over Mosquito Pass. Dyer earned the nickname "Snowshoe Itinerant" for the handmade skis he used to navigate the route.

Assigned to New Mexico Territory in 1868, Dyer looked askance at Catholicism but praised the Hispano population. Two years later he returned to circuit riding in Colorado, based out of Breckenridge and his family's home in Castle Rock. After a half century of serving Methodism, Dyer died in 1901, shortly after viewing his stained glass portrait installed in the state capitol. His grand funeral took place at Trinity Methodist Church in Denver. A chapel dedicated to Dyer's memory stands in Fairplay's South Park City museum, and several towns and physical landmarks have borne his name, mostly in the area through which he used to ski.

August 12, 1892

Banqueting at the Brown Palace

The Knights Templar, a national fraternal organization, concluded their 1892 annual convention on August 12 with a grand banquet in the eighth-floor ballroom of Denver's newest and most impressive hostelry, the Brown Palace Hotel. The Knights' week-long gathering inaugurated one of Colorado's most historic edifices, host to the rich and powerful.

Henry C. Brown, who funded the hotel, donated 10 acres of his homestead for the state capitol in 1867 and made a fortune selling other parcels to people who wanted to live on Capitol Hill, a ridge known originally as Brown's Bluff.

Brown's fortune paid for an astonishing edifice of red sandstone and granite, cast-iron beams, and terra cotta and concrete walls, declared Colorado's first fireproof building. Prolific architect Frank E. Edbrooke designed the hotel on a triangular site, shaped by Denver's street layout, and incorporated the latest in Gilded Age engineering and technology. Exterior decorations included carvings of Colorado wildlife and the initials and profile of Brown himself. It earned fame for a massive atrium capped by a glass roof to admit natural light. As a result of the building's shape, guests could choose their rooms based on whether they preferred sun in their room in the morning or afternoon. A twenty-two-story tower addition, providing additional guest rooms and function halls, opened across Tremont Street in 1959.

The Brown Palace has hosted myriad prominent people. Many Presidents starting with Theodore Roosevelt have stayed there; Bill Clinton used it as his base of operations during the Summit of the Eight in 1997. Royal guests rubbed shoulders with famous actors, and several governors lived there during their terms. Even the Beatles enjoyed the Brown's accommodations when they came to Denver in 1964. For decades, Charles and Claude K. Boettcher owned the iconic institution. It hearkens to Colorado's ranching roots by hosting the National Western Stock Show's champion steer each January. The Brown Palace has witnessed a parade of history and continues to do so, serving as a dignified, welcoming host for the Centennial State.

August 13, 1997

A Colorado Cartoon Premieres

The longest-lasting and most controversial television show set in Colorado broadcast for the first time on August 13, 1997, on the then-obscure Comedy Central cable network. Created by Trey Parker and Matt Stone, who grew up in Jefferson County and met while attending film school at the University of Colorado in the early 1990s, *South Park* represents for some the epitome of satire and for others the voice of the lowest common denominator.

After graduation, Parker and Stone teamed up with other college friends to produce a film about one of Parker's fascinations: the sordid tale of Colorado cannibal Alfred Packer. Filmed on location at places central to the Packer story—including Lake City's Hinsdale County Courthouse, where he went on trial—and starring Parker as the carnivorous star, *Cannibal! The Musical* premiered in 1996. That gruesome romp and several short, crude cartoons starring a quartet of foul-mouthed children gained attention on college campuses and among Hollywood executives. Comedy Central commissioned a pilot featuring the young denizens of South Park, a small mountain town based on the Park County seat of Fairplay, and aired it in 1997.

South Park has carved out a niche as a topical, bitingly witty show that tackles issues other television programs dare not approach. It delights and infuriates liberals and conservatives alike, lampoons organized religion, skewers social trends, and generally targets any and every aspect of human existence. Lowbrow humor often veils thought-provoking critiques of contemporary issues. As behooves a Colorado-set show, the state features prominently, from familiar urban and mountain backdrops to visits to Casa Bonita and the Pepsi Center. South Park references legalized marijuana and the controversy surrounding Ward Churchill at the creators' alma mater. A movie version of the show premiered in 1999. Initially hesitant Fairplay residents have found opportunities to cash in on those who want to buy merchandise in the real South Park. Crude yet creative, South Park is Colorado to much of the world.

August 14, 1993

Papal Prayers in the Mile High City

Catholics from around the world converged on Denver in August 1993 when Pope (later Saint) John Paul II came to Denver to celebrate the eighth World Youth Day.

President Bill Clinton met the pontiff at Stapleton International Airport on August 12. They discussed global affairs at Regis University, a Catholic institution in northwest Denver founded in 1877. That evening, John Paul rode through Mile High Stadium in his glass-sided "popemobile" and waved to tens of thousands of cheering faithful. The pope welcomed all to "Denver, a stupendous setting in the heart of the United States of America." He stayed at the Cathedral of the Immaculate Conception during his visit and celebrated mass there for American bishops on August 13 before traveling to Camp St. Malo, a Catholic retreat in the mountains of Boulder County. The pope strolled through the forest and prayed at its Chapel on the Rock, a structure that survived fires and mudslides that destroyed much of the camp in the early 2010s.

On August 14, John Paul made several appearances in Denver. He celebrated mass at the cathedral with World Youth Day delegates and met with thousands of members of Denver's archdiocese at McNichols Arena. A 14-mile pilgrimage of youthful delegates from Civic Center park (temporarily renamed Celebration Plaza) to Cherry Creek State Park culminated in a prayer vigil with a gathering of more than 250,000. The celebration climaxed the following morning with a papal mass at Cherry Creek Reservoir, where crowds had camped overnight. With an audience in the park estimated at 375,000, the ceremony ranked as the largest gathering in Colorado to date. John Paul declared: "It is not just that the young people of today are the adults of the future who will step into our shoes and carry on the human adventure. No, the longing present in every heart for a full and free life that is worthy of the human person is particularly strong in them." When the pope's airplane departed from Denver later that day, Coloradans could only marvel at the manic, exhausting, inspirational events of the past four days.

August 15, 1870

A Transcontinental Link of Iron

Ten miles separated railroad construction crews in what is now eastern Arapahoe County on August 15, 1870. A keg of whiskey stood halfway between them, a prize to the team that reached it first. They both commenced at 5:00 a.m., and workers coming from the east won the reward around noon. The two lines linked at 2:53 p.m. near a bridge over Comanche Creek. The connection near the present town of Strasburg provided, in the words of one historian, "the first permanent, continuous, uninterrupted chain of railroads across the United States."

Less than two months after the Denver Pacific Railway linked Denver and the Union Pacific Railroad in Wyoming Territory, workers finished the Kansas Pacific Railway across the plains from Kansas City to Denver. The transportation links and new ore-processing smelters rescued a territory teetering on the brink of ruin. As the *Rocky Mountain News* declared: "The road is at last finished, thanks to the energy, the enterprise, the unyielding determination of those who have had the care of the great work. The difficulties encountered, however, are equaled only by the satisfaction we have at the final triumph. Welcome to the Kansas Pacific. Welcome to the new and brighter era which it opens for Denver and our Rocky Mountain territory."

A historical marker in Strasburg praises "the rail chain's final link" completed in 1870, but the claim that Colorado boasts the nation's true transcontinental railroad connection—rather than the previous year's joining of lines in Utah Territory—is misleading. The lack of a bridge over the Missouri River at Omaha, Nebraska, forced Union Pacific passengers to cross by boat before proceeding west. In theory, thanks to the Kansas Pacific, one could travel from New York City to a bridge over the Mississippi River at Rock Island, Illinois, meander toward Kansas City, cross the Missouri River and proceed west to Denver, turn north to Cheyenne, and from there make his or her way to San Francisco. Although no single train actually made such a circuitous journey, after the joining on August 15, 1870, the nation boasted its first complete iron bond.

Back to School at Columbine High

After spending nearly four months on their knees, students, faculty, and staff at Columbine High School in Jefferson County got back on their feet on August 16, 1999.

Two students had opened fire on their classmates and teachers the previous April 20, killing 13 and wounding 20 more, turning a sanctuary of life and learning into a nightmare. The deadliest school shooting in American history to that point horrified people around the world. The word *Columbine* ceased to refer solely to the state flower that spring day. It was hijacked into service as a point of comparison for every act of gun violence—especially in schools—that followed, including three more in Colorado. Fatal shootings took place at Platte Canyon High School in Park County in 2007, Arapahoe High School in Centennial in 2013, and STEM School Highlands Ranch in 2019, and global media raised the specter of nearby Columbine every time.

When about 2,700 students arrived at Columbine on the morning of August 16, 1999, they raised to full staff the American flag that had flown half that high since April. Alumni and families formed a human channel through which students proceeded into their building. At a pep rally, student body president Mike Sheehan declared: "Although we were surrounded by terror and destruction, we still stood strong. We have prevailed. We have overcome." But the mood angered some families of those murdered who argued that ceremonies did not acknowledge the lives lost the previous spring. Some students refused to return to the scene of carnage, no matter how much it had been repaired; emotional wounds lingered even as physical wounds healed. The Columbine shootings remain a communal trauma, a shadow over the Centennial State.

In memory of Colorado's school shooting victims and in the hope that the list will never grow longer—Cassie Bernall, Kendrick Castillo, Steven Curnow, Claire Davis, Corey DePooter, Kelly Fleming, Matt Kechter, Emily Keyes, Daniel Mauser, Daniel Rohrbaugh, Dave Sanders, Rachel Scott, Isaiah Shoels, John Tomlin, Lauren Townsend, and Kyle Velasquez.

Giving Germans the Cold Shoulder

Carl Wulsten's hopes for a German colony in the valley between Colorado's Wet and Sangre de Cristo Mountains came to a bitter end—bitter cold, that is—on August 17, 1870, when an early frost killed off many of the crops the settlement needed to survive.

After the Civil War, prospective homesteaders envisioned a self-sufficient life, some individually and others in communities. Of the two formal colonies founded in Colorado in 1870, Greeley flourished while Colfax, in what was then Fremont County, did not. Wulsten had envisioned a safe haven for his fellow German immigrants. Approximately 300 people left Chicago in the spring of 1870, having paid $250 per family to participate in the scheme. They rode a special train emblazoned "Westward the Star of Empire Takes Its Course—German Colonization Society of Colfax, Fremont County, Colorado Territory." After raucous welcomes from Germans in St. Louis and Kansas City, they took the Kansas Pacific Railway to the end of the track in western Kansas and continued overland to 40,000 acres reserved for them by Vice President Schuyler Colfax, for whom they named their colony. Territorial governor Edward M. McCook provided weapons and supplies to help the community, which raised hackles among established Coloradans who noted that they had not received such presents upon their arrival.

The settlers planted a crop but failed to work together effectively, largely because of Wulsten's inept leadership. The frost on August 17 made it unlikely that the Germans could support themselves through the winter, and many relocated to Pueblo and other nearby towns. Colfax's population dwindled steadily in the early 1870s. The valley proved excellent for grazing livestock, but Wulsten's colony was all but abandoned by the time Custer County was organized there in 1877. Even the opening of a distillery to produce alcohol from locally grown potatoes the following year failed to rescue Colfax. Although the German colony disappeared into the high valley grasses, Schuyler Colfax's name endures on Denver's longest avenue.

Colorado's Only Nuclear Power Plant

For a state with extensive connections to nuclear energy, Colorado has hosted only one nuclear power plant. The Fort St. Vrain Power Station operated for thirteen years before technological limitations forced an end to its production on August 18, 1989.

In 1965 the Public Service Company of Colorado announced plans to build a nuclear power station near Platteville, along the South Platte River in Weld County. It stood near the ruins of a fur trading post from which the facility took its name. Close enough to water sources and highways but far enough from major population centers to ease public fears, the station reflected a nationwide flirtation with commercial fission reactors. Construction commenced three years later, and in December 1973 crews loaded fuel into the reactor. A series of tests followed, and on December 11, 1976, the reactor first provided electrical power to customers. The optimism faded quickly, however. For more than a decade the station endured a series of problems that forced it to shut down temporarily for repairs. Not until November 6, 1981, did the reactor reach its full power output, yet only three days later crews took it offline for additional work. Leaks, small fires, and other woes prevented the station from meeting its potential. After a control rod malfunctioned during testing in early August 1989, inspectors discovered numerous structural flaws. Public Service Company shut the reactor down for good a week and a half later.

By that time the public's affection for nuclear power had soured. Incidents like the Three Mile Island accident in Pennsylvania in 1979 and the Chernobyl disaster in Russia in 1986 fueled fear of the concept. The remaining fuel was sent to a federal facility in Idaho, a transfer that ended on June 26, 1992, with a ceremony involving 700 current and former station employees. Four years later the Fort St. Vrain Power Station reopened as a natural gas–fired facility and remains so today. Across the street from the massive works stands a multipurpose building designed to evoke the namesake trading post, a meeting of furs and fission on the high plains.

August 19, 1887

The Town That Uses Its Melon

State officials approved the incorporation of a town in Otero County on August 19, 1887, one that developed into one of the most successful agricultural communities in Colorado.

Rocky Ford earned its name from a natural crossing of the Arkansas River used by American Indians and early Euro-American travelers in southeastern Colorado. In 1871, George W. Swink purchased land on the south bank from a fraudster claiming to have authority over the Vigil & St. Vrain land grant. Settlers primarily from Illinois—including Swink's wife and eleven children—arrived in the early 1870s; and the adobe village expanded through fertile soil, irrigation, and a good location, boasting more than fifty Anglo and Hispano residents. In 1875,

Rocky Ford relocated 2 miles to the south when the Atchison, Topeka & Santa Fe Railroad (AT&SF) announced its route between La Junta and Pueblo, and the town flourished.

Blessed with a green thumb, Swink experimented with many crops and found his calling in watermelon. His 1878 harvest was such a success that the town celebrated with a Watermelon Day festival, an annual tradition that drew thousands by the turn of the twentieth century, consuming heaps of free melons and leaving the ground covered with a carnage of seeds and rinds. As one newspaper described Watermelon Day in 1889: "Melons by the thousands were furnished, and they were melons. Large and sweet, none other can compare to a Rocky Ford melon." The AT&SF carried watermelons, muskmelons, and cantaloupes to markets nationwide; and Rocky Ford's name became synonymous with the finest that fields could offer.

After a beet sugar factory opened in 1900, the town's population doubled. The *Rocky Mountain News* reported: "The land is almost in the heart of what a few years ago appeared on the map as the 'Great American Desert.' Irrigation has made it one of the most fertile places in that section of the West." The sugar refinery closed in 1979, but the town endures. Americans still wait eagerly every year to see Rocky Ford cantaloupes at their grocery stores.

August 20, 2005

A Carousel Commemoration

Hundredth-birthday celebrations seem particularly appropriate in Colorado, the Centennial State. On August 20, 2005, the residents of Burlington cheered the 100-year mark for their town's most beloved and famous attraction: the Kit Carson County Carousel.

The Philadelphia Toboggan Company built seventy-four carousels in the early twentieth century. They sold their sixth to Elitch Gardens in Denver in 1905. It consists of forty-six wooden animals selected by Elitch's agents, including horses, camels, zebras, goats, deer, giraffes, a lion, a tiger, a hippopotamus, and other hand-carved critters, accompanied by four chariots. A Wurlitzer organ, played by 100 keys, performed the function of an entire orchestra, from woodwinds and brass to percussion instruments. Elitch's replaced its carousel in 1928, and the Kit Carson County commissioners paid $1,250 for the old one, a controversial choice in an agricultural area beset by drought and in the grasp of the Great Depression. The ride operated in Burlington until 1931. By the time it resumed in 1937, mice had destroyed the organ works, so recorded band music sufficed for decades. In the summer of

Louisa Everett, the author's daughter, takes a spin on the Kit Carson County Carousel in August 2019.

1981, thieves made off with four animals, but the pieces were recovered in Kansas five months after their disappearance. Preservation work in the late twentieth century restored the carousel's animals, landscape scenes, machinery, and organ. In 1987, the US Department of the Interior named it a national historic landmark.

The centennial celebration in 2005 featured a barbecue, carousel rides, and a brass band. Officials read congratulatory proclamations from the National Carousel Association, the city of Burlington, and Governor Bill Owens, who declared August 20 "Kit Carson County Carousel Day." A museum dedicated to the attraction's history and care opened in 2007. One of the few American carousels that still boast its original paint and one of the best preserved in the country, it remains a much-loved destination and a charming pastime on the high plains.

August 21, 1849

The End of Bent's Fort

Reports conflicted about what precisely happened in present-day Otero County on August 21, 1849. Some witnesses described a gunpowder explosion, while others suggested tar barrels set ablaze. Regardless of what William Bent actually did that day, the result was clear—the destruction of Bent's Fort, the commercial and social hub of the Santa Fe Trail.

St. Louis-based traders William and Charles Bent and Ceran St. Vrain partnered in 1830 to harvest beaver and bison pelts. They constructed a massive adobe trading post on the Santa Fe Trail in 1833. It stood on the Arkansas River border between the United States and Mexico and became a profitable institution where diverse cultures interacted. Native, American, and Mexican trappers brought pelts there to trade for high-quality goods imported over the trail. Well-funded and located, Bent, St. Vrain & Company quickly dominated the high plains economy.

The imposing, bustling structure impressed all who entered it. Susan S. Magoffin stayed at Bent's Fort in the summer of 1846 while recuperating from a miscarriage. She wrote that "the outside exactly fills my idea of an ancient castle . . . Here in the Fort, and who could have supposed such a thing, they have a regularly established billiard room! They have a regular race track. And I hear the cackling of chickens at such a rate sometimes I shall not be surprised to hear of a cock-pit . . . My health, though not good, is drank by [all the inhabitants], and sometimes a complimentary toast is slipped in. The Fort is not such a bad place after all."

The Mexican-American War disrupted trade, and American soldiers depleted the fort's supplies. Bent, St. Vrain & Company tried to sell the post to the US Army, but the federal government refused the $15,000 asking price. The partnership dissolved, and William Bent prevented anyone else from using the fort by destroying it in August 1849. He erected a smaller trading post downstream, but the glory days of the fur trade were long gone. A reconstruction—now a national historic site—arose on the foundations of the original Bent's Fort in the 1970s.

August 22, 1889

A Palace for Mineral Monarchs

City officials in Pueblo approved plans by a Swedish immigrant named Otto Bulow on August 22, 1889, for a showplace to commemorate Colorado's mining and quarrying industries.

Colorado's economy in the late nineteenth century flourished with wealth extracted from the ground, and the Mineral Palace celebrated that prosperity. Inspiration for the palace came from William H. "Coin" Harvey, an entrepreneur who had owned a silver mine in Ouray County. Bulow's edifice, which occupied a city block and boasted decorations of minerals and precious gems, employed an Egyptian style. The interior hall, capable of hosting 4,000 people, included display cases with ore samples from across the state, country, and world. Statues of "Queen Silver" and "King Coal," donated by mining interests in Aspen and Trinidad, respectively, presided over the scene, flanking a stage at the heart of the building. A dome above it stood 72 feet above the ground. The *Pueblo Chieftain* published a special twenty-page edition to celebrate the palace's opening on Independence Day in 1891, and media far and wide trumpeted the must-see destination. An Aspen newspaper, for example, praised "its manifold wonders [that] told a graphic story of the fabulous wealth stored in the mountains and valleys of Colorado."

Drawing on the era's affection for grand expositions, the Mineral Palace thrived for years. Harvey left Pueblo before the end of 1891 and defended silver as an essential part of the nation's economy, even after the end of federal silver purchase two years later. He managed William J. Bryan's pro-silver presidential campaign in 1896. The Mineral Palace remained a tourist attraction, but by the Great Depression it stood neglected and dilapidated. Condemned in 1935 and left to rot, demolition on the massive pile commenced in 1942. Many of its geological treasures went into smelting fires, but the Mineral Palace Park remains a lush oasis in the heart of Pueblo, where King Coal and Queen Silver once reigned supreme in a state built on mining.

August 23, 1883

Avenging the Grand County Commission

A grand jury, meeting on August 23, 1883, indicted three men on charges of murder in an infamous intersection of crime and politics earlier that summer. A shootout on the shore of Grand Lake the previous Independence Day had left all three Grand County commissioners dead.

The trouble started as a struggle between two county Republican politicians. John G. Mills of Teller City—a mining camp in present-day Jackson County, then claimed by both Grand and Larimer Counties—bore a checkered past, including accusations of responsibility for the deaths of two political opponents in Mississippi in 1875. Edward P. Weber, a lawyer from Illinois, settled in Grand Lake in 1879 and represented mining and smelting firms. The two men battled over the location of the county seat, then contested between Grand Lake and Hot Sulphur Springs, and which Republican gubernatorial candidate to support in 1882. Governor Frederick W. Pitkin appointed them both to vacancies on the Grand County commission, Mills in 1881 and Weber in early 1883. By the spring of 1883, Weber and a third commissioner, Barney Day—a survivor of the Beecher Island battle in 1868—allied to oust pro-Mills politicians in the county.

Mills sought his revenge on July 4, 1883. He and three armed men, including Sheriff Charles W. Royer, hid behind boulders near the shore of Grand Lake. Shots rang out as Weber, Day, and their friend Thomas J. Dean walked along a path. Mills hit Weber, and both sides exchanged gunfire. Day killed Mills before he, shot repeatedly, fell dead into the lake. When the smoke cleared, residents carried Weber and Dean to a hotel, where they died. Royer took his own life in Georgetown twelve days later, while Mills's other accomplices simply disappeared.

The gruesome story astonished the state. Governor James B. Grant gave thought to abolishing Grand County altogether but appointed a new commission instead. The August 1883 indictments against three men tangentially connected to the incident failed for a lack of evidence. The grisly Mills-Weber feud ranks as one of Colorado's most astonishing political scandals.

August 24, 1873

Jackson and the Mount of the Holy Cross

Photographer William H. Jackson stood precariously on a rocky ridge 13,000 feet in elevation on the morning of August 24, 1873. He hoped to capture with his camera a long-rumored but never proven sight—the Mount of the Holy Cross. A brief break in the clouds allowed Jackson to make eight negatives of the peak and its snow-formed icon, after which the exhausted artist and his assistants scrambled back down to the comfort of their valley camp.

A native of New York and a Civil War veteran, Jackson traveled across the West doing odd jobs and dabbling as a painter and photographer. Ferdinand V. Hayden, who coordinated the federal government's western surveys, hired him in 1870. Hayden reasoned that grand images reproduced cheaply could guarantee appropriations for the extensive, expensive task. Of the many photographs Jackson took for Hayden, the Mount of the Holy Cross most captured the public's imagination. Reproduced widely, it offered religious inspiration to some and proof of the nation's manifest destiny to others. Jackson expressed no such sentiment in his journal when describing the August 1873 adventure. He wrote instead of cold, misty conditions that made him feel "alone apparently in space, not being able to see anything except the rock I was sitting on." He and his team spent a miserable, hungry night and the following morning accomplished their task quickly and made their way down to the even more inspirational beans and bread in camp.

Jackson remained with the federal surveys until their end in 1879. Within a few years he relocated to Denver and built a thriving business taking promotional photographs for railroads in Colorado. By the 1890s, Jackson owned a studio with five assistants on Colfax Avenue but nearly lost his business in the Panic of 1893. He moved his family to Detroit, Michigan, in 1897 and explored new technologies in photography. In 1942, Jackson died in New York City at age ninety-nine. Befitting his status as a renowned artist and photographic innovator and as one of the last Civil War veterans, he was buried in Virginia's Arlington National Cemetery.

August 25, 1888

A Shootout in Stonewall

"What may prove a long and bloody struggle opened to-day on the Maxwell grant, at Stonewall," a town in the Sangre de Cristo Mountains of Las Animas County, reported the state press on August 25, 1888, as a decades-old conflict over land ownership turned violent.

As part of Mexico's attempt to strengthen its hold on its northern frontier, New Mexico's governor Manuel Armijo granted 1.7 million acres straddling the present Colorado–New Mexico boundary to Carlos Beaubien and Guadalupe Miranda in 1841. This land came to be known as the Maxwell Grant, for Beaubien's son-in-law Lucien B. Maxwell, who encouraged Hispano settlement on the vast claim. Lying primarily in modern New Mexico, the tract extended east of the Sangres and northward to the Spanish Peaks and upper Purgatoire River.

In 1869, Maxwell sold his fiefdom to a firm called the Maxwell Land Grant & Railway Company, which promoted agricultural and mineral development. The new owners resented the presence of those already settled on the grant. Defying the 1848 Treaty of Guadalupe Hidalgo, which demanded that the conquering Americans recognize Mexican property rights, the company sought to evict the inhabitants. To that end, a US Supreme Court ruling in 1887 voided all claims to the grant except those of the corporate owner. When Las Animas County officials sought to evict Hispano and Anglo residents of Stonewall the following year, a firefight broke out. Law enforcement and company agents barricaded themselves in a hotel as bullets flew, leading to the deaths of three settlers. A nearby barn fire distracted Stonewall's residents long enough to allow the pinned-down party in the hotel to flee to Trinidad by the end of the day.

Although the people of Stonewall won the skirmish, their victory proved hollow. Farming and ranching gave way to coal mining by the century's end, and the Colorado Fuel & Iron Company quickly dominated the region. Many residents became wage laborers down the mine shafts and, as they had long feared, ultimately lost their independence to corporate power.

Domínguez and Escalante at Montrose

A Spanish expedition consisting of two priests, a cartographer, two aristocrats, and five other men arrived on August 26, 1776, at a marshy area on the banks of the Uncompahgre River. Their campsite, which they named "La Ciénega de San Francisco" ("the Swamp of St. Francis"), stands today on the south side of Montrose, near History Colorado's Ute Indian Museum.

The Domínguez-Escalante expedition had set out from Santa Fe about a month earlier to scout an overland route between the Spanish settlements of New Mexico and missions on the California coast. Led by two priests—Francisco Domínguez and Silvestre Vélez de Escalante—the survey doubled as an effort to spread Catholicism to native cultures. The group entered the state in early August and traveled along or across the San Juan, Animas, Mancos, Dolores, and San Miguel Rivers in southwestern Colorado. Before reaching La Ciénega de San Francisco, they passed the future town sites of Ignacio, Durango, Dolores, Naturita, and Nucla.

Beyond present-day Montrose, the expedition meandered through the mountains along the Uncompahgre and Gunnison Rivers, crossed over Grand and Battlement Mesas, and waded through the Colorado River near modern Parachute. They left Colorado via the White River by mid-September, making their way toward the Great Salt Lake before turning south. Two months later they crossed back to the east bank of the Colorado River near what is now the Utah-Arizona boundary, and by the beginning of 1777 they had returned to Santa Fe.

Domínguez and Escalante considered their trip a disappointment, since the Utes and other cultures they encountered expressed little interest in converting to a new faith. That ambivalence disheartened the friars, who lost interest in finding a route to California. Nonetheless, their journals offer a fascinating glimpse into eighteenth-century western Colorado. Numerous natural features on the western slope bear the priests' names, and a stained glass window honoring their map maker, Bernardo Miera y Pacheco, stands in the Colorado State Capitol.

Amache's First Internees

A train bearing 192 men, 19 women, and 1 child arrived in the Prowers County town of Granada on August 27, 1942, the first group of Japanese Americans from

Barracks erected to house Japanese Americans incarcerated at the Amache concentration camp in Prowers County during World War II

Southern California whose involuntary migration to Colorado reflected the nation's paranoia during World War II.

In the wake of the Pearl Harbor attack, many Americans viewed immigrants from Japan and their descendants as potential traitors and saboteurs, without any real evidence. President Franklin D. Roosevelt authorized the forced removal of Japanese American citizens from the Pacific coast. The federal government established ten camps across the American West to house thousands of detainees. Colorado's camp, named Amache after the wife of pioneer cattle rancher John W. Prowers, opened after a frenzy of construction in the summer of 1942.

"Surreal" best describes life at Amache. At its peak in late 1942, the camp held more than 7,500 people, making it the tenth-largest town in Colorado. Prisoners lived in barracks with whatever possessions they had carried from home.

Amache's police, fire, and postal departments and a newspaper were all staffed by residents. It operated traditional and vocational training schools. Students played sports against local teams and organized chapters of the Boy Scouts and Campfire Girls. Amacheans could obtain permission to leave the camp to work or shop. While at times their day-to-day lives may have appeared to unfold much like those of people in other rural Colorado towns, the presence of barbed wire fences and guard towers were just some of the constant reminders that their civil rights had been suspended.

Amache's population waned after restrictions against Japanese Americans relaxed in 1943. It closed in mid-October 1945, with most of the people detained returning to the West Coast. Amache's buildings were distributed among farms and ranches, with Otero County appropriating its schools and some structures hauled as far away as the University of Denver. The camp faded back into the sagebrush from whence it came, with only a few concrete foundations surviving. Granada high school teacher John Hopper and his students have organized preservation efforts since the 1990s, intent on protecting and restoring the memory of Colorado's most controversial community.

August 28, 2008

Obama's Mile High Moment

Before an estimated 84,000 people at Denver's Invesco Field at Mile High, Senator Barack Obama of Illinois accepted the Democratic presidential nomination on August 28, 2008.

Although a major city with a central location, Denver had only hosted one other presidential nominating convention. A century earlier, in 1908, Democrats had met in Denver's City Auditorium to select William J. Bryan as their candidate for the third time. Denver mounted a determined effort to secure the 2008 convention, led by Democratic mayor John W. Hickenlooper. When delegates arrived at the Pepsi Center for five days of speeches and formal party business on August 23, the city basked in the spotlight. Hickenlooper spoke on August 25, calling for productivity over divisiveness. He declared that "there were a lot more barn raisings than there were shootings in the Old West." Prominent party leaders, including Senator Hillary R. Clinton of New York—whom Obama had defeated for the nomination—and her husband and former president, Bill Clinton, along with former Denver mayor and cabinet member Federico Peña, rallied the partisan faithful. On August 27, Senator Joe Biden of Delaware accepted the nomination for vice president, and Colorado senator Ken Salazar made a speech declaring Obama the party's candidate, confirmed by acclamation of the state delegations.

The following day, to accommodate tens of thousands of people who wanted to see the first African American accept a major party's candidacy for president, throngs filled Invesco Field. Colorado Democrats, including Governor Bill Ritter and Congressman Mark Udall, found an eager audience while warming up the crowd. Obama's acceptance speech sent the Denver Broncos' stadium into pandemonium, although Republicans later ridiculed the venue and its column-festooned stage as the "Temple of Obama." As a state nearly evenly divided among registered Democratic, Republican, and unaffiliated voters, Colorado proved a battleground in 2008 and 2012, although both times it cast a majority of its votes for the victorious Obama.

| August 29, 1965 |

Carpenter Makes a Long-Distance Call

M. Scott Carpenter, one of Colorado's most celebrated modern adventurers, spoke from the sea to space on August 29, 1965. At the start of a forty-five-day mission with nine other men in a metal tube 200 feet off the California coast, he chatted by radio with astronauts on the Gemini 5 capsule orbiting Earth. For Carpenter, the extraordinary was commonplace.

Born in Boulder in 1925, Carpenter graduated from the University of Colorado in 1949 with a degree in aeronautical engineering. He served as a pilot with the US Navy during the Korean War. The National Aeronautics and Space Administration (NASA) selected him as one of its seven Mercury program astronauts in 1959, and the team trained for the first manned US missions in space. On May 24, 1962, Carpenter became the second American to orbit the Earth, taking three trips around the planet in his Aurora 7 craft and splashing down in the Atlantic Ocean just under five hours after liftoff. In the 1983 film *The Right Stuff*, based on a book of the same name about the Mercury team, actor Charles Frank portrayed Carpenter.

Carpenter took a leave of absence from NASA to participate in experiments testing the body's underwater endurance. The SEALAB II program in the Pacific Ocean, from which he called his orbiting colleagues in 1965, allowed Carpenter to coordinate deep-sea dives and other scientific endeavors. His ocean-based work continued until his retirement from the navy in 1969. Carpenter founded an investment company that developed technologies for athletes and divers, supported innovations in pesticides and renewable energy, and wrote several books. He continued his submersible studies privately, often teaming up with renowned explorer Jacques Cousteau. When not above the atmosphere or under water, Carpenter enjoyed skiing at Vail.

The dynamic Carpenter—described as "the first person to conquer both outer and inner space"—died in 2013 at age eighty-eight in Boulder. City officials named a park after him, which boasts a playground complete with a four-level climbing tower shaped like a rocket ship.

August 30, 1931

Jack Swigert's Birthday

No Coloradan has ever had a better perspective of their state than Jack Swigert. Granted, as the command module pilot of the Apollo XIII mission, he had little time to enjoy the view.

John L. "Jack" Swigert Jr., born in Denver on August 30, 1931, attended Regis and East High Schools as well as the University of Colorado. He served in the US Air Force in the mid-1950s in Korea and Japan, in the air national guards of Connecticut and Massachusetts, and as a private test pilot. In 1966 the National Aeronautics and Space Administration (NASA) selected Swigert as an astronaut for the Apollo missions of manned flights to the moon. His big break came in April 1970, when NASA pulled the pilot of the Apollo XIII mission for medical reasons. Swigert joined Jim Lovell and Fred Haise on what was supposed to be the third mission to the lunar surface. On the way to the moon, however, a malfunction in the vessel's oxygen system caused an explosion that nearly crippled the ship. The three astronauts conserved enough power, water, and oxygen to return successfully to Earth six days after their launch.

Three years after his harrowing trip, Swigert took a job advising the US House of Representatives on scientific matters. By the late 1970s, he returned to Colorado to work in the aerospace industry and try his hand at politics. In 1982, Swigert ran for a US House seat as a Republican, winning handily the new sixth district of Denver's southern suburbs. During the campaign, doctors diagnosed him with bone cancer, and although their early prognoses looked promising, the illness spread rapidly. On December 27, 1982, Swigert died at age fifty-one in a Washington, DC, hospital, a week before his swearing-in as a member of Congress.

Swigert's contributions have been memorialized in unique ways. In the 1995 film *Apollo 13*, actor Kevin Bacon played the Coloradan's role. Two years later, a bronze statue of Swigert in his mission gear went on display in the US Capitol as part of the National Statuary Hall collection, and a copy of the likeness stands in Denver International Airport.

Architect Elijah E. Myers's depiction of the proposed Colorado State Capitol, as envisioned in the summer of 1885

A Plan for the State Capitol

"Where laws are enacted for the government of a great State, public records preserved, and accommodations provided for the executive and judiciary branches of the government, the character of the building should be such as to command respect for these high purposes." So wrote Elijah Myers, whose plan for the Colorado State Capitol was adopted on August 31, 1885.

Both practical and aesthetic needs inspired the statehouse—it would consolidate offices in one building, making government more efficient and cheaper, and at the same time provide a showplace for a rich, young state. Myers included large chambers for the legislature and courts and offices for everyone from the governor and secretary of state to the commissions of railroads and mines to the state geologist and engineer, as well as display space for Colorado's history and horticulture. A dome crowning the edifice offered visitors unparalleled views of the region.

A prolific architect, Myers offered his clients the best the Gilded Age had to offer. By the time the Board of Capitol Managers selected his plans, Myers already had two statehouses to his credit, in Michigan and Texas. The Arapahoe County Courthouse, which Myers also designed, towered over Denver from 1883 until its demolition in 1933, supplanted by the City and County Building. Myers made blueprints for schools, hospitals, churches, post offices, courthouses, city halls, and private homes across the country in the late 1800s.

Construction started on the capitol in 1886 and lasted fifteen years, although the building welcomed its first tenants in 1894. When the statehouse at last stood finished in 1901, Coloradans and visitors marveled at the granite, marble, brass, and oak edifice, as they do today. Since the late nineteenth century, the capitol has provided a stage for celebration and controversy alike, as befits the home of a representative government. As Myers wrote, "In our advanced American civilization there need be no apprehension that the Capitol Building of Colorado will not stand, a handsome and stately structure, the admiration of future ages."

September

Lucky Lindy in the Colorado Sky

The most popular man in the United States concluded a brief but enthusiastic visit to Colorado early on September 1, 1927, when Colonel Charles A. Lindbergh departed from Denver's airfield after having flown his famous "Spirit of St. Louis" airplane to the Centennial State.

In May 1927, Lindbergh tested the limits of human and technological endurance with a nonstop flight across the Atlantic Ocean, traveling from New York City to France in less than a day and a half. He earned nicknames including "Lucky Lindy," the "Lone Eagle" (for his solo trip), and the simple "We" for his first, exhausted words upon landing in Paris: "Well, here we are." After his return home, Americans feted Lindbergh across the country, a tour funded by a foundation established by Colorado's former US senator Simon Guggenheim. Lindbergh flew over Nebraska on August 31 and arrived in Denver early that afternoon, landing at Lowry Field, now an industrial area at 38th Avenue and Dahlia Street. A lengthy parade wound from there through the city, the pilot sharing a car with Governor William H. Adams and Mayor Benjamin F. Stapleton. Lindbergh paused to greet masses of fans at the University of Denver and the state capitol. Hundreds of prominent Coloradans attended a banquet in his honor, and thousands more listened to the remarks over radio speakers in downtown streets and at the City Auditorium. Lindberg touted the high-altitude city as a natural aviation hub: "With a good airport, Denver may expect to be one of the air centers, if not the air center of the West."

Lindbergh spent the night at the Brown Palace Hotel before returning to Lowry Field early on September 1. His plane buzzed infirm veterans at Fitzsimons Army Hospital in Aurora before heading north. Lindbergh circled Greeley before proceeding to South Dakota that afternoon. Coloradans heeded his call two years later by opening the Municipal Airport—later Stapleton International Airport—in east Denver. Lone Eagle Peak in Boulder County also honors the aviator whose feat gave Americans a reason to cheer in the Roaring Twenties.

Gunnison Crosses the Continental Divide

More than thirty soldiers and scholars, accompanied by eighteen wagons, an ambulance, and a carriage, crested Cochetopa Pass in present-day Saguache County on September 2, 1853. Led by Captain John W. Gunnison, the party hoped to chart a transcontinental railroad route through what is now Colorado and link the United States from coast to coast with iron rails.

Departing from Missouri on June 23, Gunnison and his second-in-command, Lieutenant Edward G. Beckwith, scouted the Santa Fe Trail and other Great Plains pathways. While Gunnison led his caravan in search of a viable course west, three other US Army expeditions scouted other potential passages. His party passed the ruins of Bent's Fort in late July and proceeded up the Huerfano and Apishapa Rivers. Near the modern town of Walsenburg, Gunnison wrote, "Pike's Peak to the north, the Spanish Peaks to the south, the Sierra Mojada [Wet Mountains] to the west, and the plains from the Arkansas . . . make the finest prospect it has ever fallen my lot to have seen." They crossed the Sangre de Cristo Mountains and camped at Fort Massachusetts, at the base of Blanca Peak in the San Luis Valley. After scouting several options, the band traversed Cochetopa Pass—one of the easiest gaps in the Continental Divide—at midday on September 2 as a thunderstorm developed, an ominous portent for the captain.

The Black Canyon of the Gunnison River forced the party to detour around its south rim and challenged the notion of building a transcontinental railroad through the region. Gunnison's party continued past the modern sites of Montrose, Delta, and Grand Junction. After Paiutes killed Gunnison and seven others in Utah Territory on October 26, Beckwith took command and completed the survey. Federal officials concluded that "the country is so broken, and the difficulties of construction so great, and the expense would be so enormous, that the building of a railroad over this portion may be pronounced impracticable." Although Gunnison did not survive the expedition, his name endures in Colorado with a namesake river, town, and county.

September 3, 1779

Spain versus Comanche in Pueblo County

A combined force of Spaniards, Puebloans, Utes, and Apaches, commanded by New Mexico's governor Juan Bautista de Anza, battled with a band of Comanche for control of modern Colorado on September 3, 1779, in what is today southern Pueblo County.

Comanche power over the southern Great Plains increased throughout the eighteenth century, in part through trade with the French in the Mississippi River valley, who cultivated a check against their Spanish competitors. On the northwestern fringe of Comanche territory—present-day southeastern Colorado—a faction led by Cuerno Verde (Greenhorn) led raids against Spain and its native allies. Anza, an experienced military commander, won appointment as New Mexico's governor in 1777 with orders to stabilize the region. In mid-August 1779, Anza organized nearly 800 fighters, including professional soldiers, colonial volunteers, and American Indians targeted by the Comanche. His force, one of the largest the Spanish ever dispatched from New Mexico, proceeded up the Rio Grande into the San Luis Valley in search of Cuerno Verde. They scoured the valley, the upper Arkansas River, and South Park before stumbling on the Comanches' camp along Fountain Creek near present-day downtown Colorado Springs. The allied army pursued the Comanche southward along ancient paths that paralleled modern Interstate 25 and caught up with Cuerno Verde again along Greenhorn Creek on September 2.

The battle that started that day ended the following morning with Cuerno Verde's death around 10:30 a.m. After the victory on September 3, Anza returned to Santa Fe through La Veta Pass and the San Luis Valley. Greenhorn Creek, where the Comanche leader died, bears his name, as does Greenhorn Peak, and a monument in Colorado City commemorates the battle. Comanche strength across the plains waned in the following years, from battle and disease. By the early 1780s, the Comanches sought more peaceful relations, and the Spanish and their native allies jumped at the opportunity to avoid the bloodshed they had endured during Cuerno Verde's time.

September 4, 1915

Dedicating Rocky Mountain National Park

Dignitaries both local and national stood in a light drizzle near Estes Park to dedicate Rocky Mountain National Park on the afternoon of September 4, 1915, as nature expressed its preference for scenic rather than oratorical grandeur. Once the officials finished their soggy remarks, a correspondent reported that "the clouds parted as if by the action of some mighty, unseen hand, and the sun of Colorado broke forth in rain-ringed splendor from across the newly laid snow on Longs Peak and made a new fairyland of the dazzling land of bewilderment."

Several factors motivated the creation of Rocky Mountain National Park. Estes Park residents advocated a tourist destination, especially naturalist and hotelier Enos Mills. He was joined by Freelan O. Stanley, co-founder of the Stanley Steamer automobile company and owner of the Stanley Hotel, which opened in 1909. Denver-area motor clubs supported the notion as well, eager to promote Colorado as a vacation spot with scenery easily accessible from the city and enjoyable from the seat of a car. To that end, work commenced on Fall River Road in

1913, two years before President Woodrow Wilson signed legislation establishing the park. Congressman Edward T. Taylor, the staunchest supporter of the park in Congress, pointed out that visitors cut off from the Alps of Europe during World War I could "see America first" by vacationing in their own country and enjoying a landscape just as beautiful, if not more so.

Fall River Road proved inadequate to accommodate increasing traffic, and construction started on Trail Ridge Road in 1926 to succeed it. Tourist numbers grew with each passing year, putting ever more strains on the park's infrastructure and natural landscape. It encompasses more than 400 square miles and extends over portions of Boulder, Grand, and Larimer Counties. Rocky Mountain National Park ranks as Colorado's most visited unit of the National Park Service and is among the top ten most visited parks in the country, with camping, hiking, fishing, wildlife viewing, and many other amenities enjoyed by several million people every year.

September 5, 1879

First Edition of the *Solid Muldoon*

Colorado communities in the late nineteenth century demanded one amenity above all others—a newspaper. The presence of a newspaper suggested permanence and prosperity for nascent towns. Part critic, part cheerleader, the press informed residents and cajoled elected officials while promoting local pride. One of the most successful small-town newspapers ever to grace the Centennial State, the *Solid Muldoon*, debuted in Ouray on September 5, 1879.

David F. Day, the cheerfully cantankerous editor of the *Muldoon*, hailed from Ohio. He had fought in the Civil War, earned the Medal of Honor at Vicksburg, and escaped from several Confederate prisons including Georgia's infamous Andersonville. Day and his wife, Victoria, settled in Missouri where he edited a newspaper. They relocated to the thriving mining region of Ouray County in 1878. The paper he founded the following year took its name from a famous hoax in 1877 involving a supposedly fossilized prehistoric man discovered in Pueblo County.

The *Solid Muldoon* informed readers about mining development, advocated the removal of Utes from western Colorado, and lobbied for civic improvements. Like many newspapers of the day, it wore its political allegiance proudly, touting Democrats and lambasting Republicans. In another common trait, the *Muldoon* boosted its own town and ridiculed others. "Ouray is the center of the universe," Day wrote, "and we hereby give notice that all other alleged centers are frauds and base imitations." Also, "If Silverton had a warmer climate and a little better brand of whiskey, almost any person could be content to live there who hadn't lived in a live town like Ouray." Meanwhile, Lake City was "just a little too far from Ouray to ever amount to much" and Montrose "the most forsaken, desolate, barren looking hole in all Colorado."

The *Muldoon* entertained Ouray and audiences nationwide thanks to Day's widely circulated wit, until he moved to Durango to take over a press there in 1892. After his death in 1914, rivals and friends alike remembered him as one of the state's most influential journalists.

September 6, 1920

The Manassa Mauler Defends His Title

In a small town in Michigan on September 6, 1920, fourteen months after claiming the title of world heavyweight champion, William H. "Jack" Dempsey defeated Billy Miske in the first boxing match broadcast by radio, proving that he deserved his hard-earned notoriety.

Dempsey hailed from Manassa, a Mormon farming colony in Conejos County, although he and his family strayed from the faith. Born in 1895, Dempsey lived a migratory childhood, as the large family meandered through various Colorado towns trying to make ends meet. They found their greatest success in Montrose, where mother Celia took the reins from her unreliable husband, Hyrum. She opened a boarding house catering to builders of the Gunnison Tunnel water diversion project, and the Dempseys prospered until the work was finished and crews moved elsewhere. The family relocated to Utah, but Dempsey returned to Montrose in 1911 to start a pugilistic career in a town he liked. Boxing under the name "Kid Blackie," Dempsey alternated between small local bouts and work in the mines. He sparred in Aspen, Durango, Gunnison, Leadville, Rico, Salida, Telluride, and Victor. In 1913, when Dempsey stood in for his brother Bernie in a fight in Cripple Creek, he inherited his older sibling's nickname "Jack."

Dempsey's fame grew in the late 1910s as he boxed to raise money during World War I. On Independence Day in 1919, Dempsey defeated Jess Willard in Ohio to capture the world heavyweight boxing championship and won international renown. In the 1920s, between defending his status in the ring, Dempsey pursued an acting career, appearing several times with Denver native Douglas Fairbanks. Even the loss of his boxing title in 1926 to Gene Tunney failed to tarnish Dempsey's appeal. He retained close ties to his native state; Dempsey often relaxed quietly in a motel on Denver's Colfax Avenue owned by sports enthusiast Eddie Bohn.

*Jack Dempsey, the "Manassa Mauler," photographed in 1919 shortly after
he claimed the title of the world's heavyweight boxing champion*

The "Manassa Mauler," nicknamed for his hometown, returned to the San Luis
Valley in 1966 to dedicate his birthplace as a museum. Dempsey died in New York
City in 1983.

September

Ouray County Shows Its Grit

Hundreds of people came to Ridgway, a town in Ouray County, to see it transformed into Fort Smith, Arkansas, on September 7, 1968. More than a mere case of mistaken identity, Ridgway adopted its alias while hosting crews shooting the western film *True Grit*.

True Grit starred John Wayne, Glen Campbell, and Kim Darby and earned Wayne—as irascible lawman Rooster Cogburn—his only Academy Award. Filming took place in Gunnison, Montrose, and Ouray Counties and lasted for several weeks in the fall of 1968. Locations included Ridgway, Owl Creek Pass (where Wayne filmed the climactic horseback gunfight scene), Blue Mesa Reservoir, and the county courthouse in Ouray. School boards gave students and staff permission to miss class for jobs related to the filming, ranging from extras to manual labor. The local press shadowed the filming, interviewed the actors, and photographed Wayne with a Montrose dentist who fixed one of the Duke's crowns. Wayne praised the "beautiful scenery" of the San Juans and raved about the steak at Montrose's Red Barn Restaurant. In between filming, he visited a mine in Aspen of which he was part owner.

Colorado-filmed movies run the gamut of genres. The list includes *About Schmidt* (2002), *Around the World in 80 Days* (1956), *City Slickers* (1991), *Dumb and Dumber* (1994), *How the West Was Won* (1962), *Indiana Jones and the Last Crusade* (1990), *National Lampoon's Christmas Vacation* (1989), *The Prestige* (2006), *The Searchers* (1956), *Snowball Express* (1972), and, obviously, *Things to Do in Denver When You're Dead* (1995). Clint Eastwood brawled with a gang in Georgetown in *Every Which Way but Loose* (1978) and shot scenes of *The Mule* (2018) in Fort Morgan, Manitou Springs, Trinidad, and Wiggins. *National Lampoon's Vacation* (1983) was filmed across southern Colorado, while its 2015 remake included an almost–sex scene at Four Corners. Bruce Willis battled terrorists at Denver's Stapleton International Airport in *Die Hard 2* (1990), and aliens attacked Peterson Air Force Base in *Independence Day* (1996). Colorado's diverse settings provide a touch of Centennial State charm to the silver screen.

A Survey in the San Juans

"One thing very peculiar about this particular part of the country is the deathlike stillness that almost oppresses one in passing through it." Thus described Franklin

Rhoda on September 8, 1874, as he led a small party along a remote Ute path in the San Juan Mountains.

Rhoda worked for federal surveyor Ferdinand V. Hayden in the early 1870s and traveled to the San Juans in the summer of 1874. The Utes had lost the region through the Brunot Treaty the previous year, and Rhoda's team sought to map its resources for American miners. Rhoda led six men from Colorado Springs through South Park, across the Arkansas River, and into the San Luis Valley. Their work commenced in July near Cochetopa Pass at the Ute reservation's Los Piños Agency. About a week into their work through the rugged region, the Rhoda party summited their first fourteener, Uncompahgre Peak. They climbed two more fourteeners that year—Mount Sneffels and Mount Wilson—to scout the basins and passes of southwestern Colorado Territory. Rhoda's team endured harsh weather, including downpours and lightning strikes, and visited several small mining camps, such as Howardsville, Silverton, and Animas City (now Durango) on the Animas River. On September 8, the seven men and their pack train crested the divide between the Animas and San Miguel Rivers, separating modern San Juan and San Miguel Counties, and made their way to a campsite just below today's Telluride.

The team arrived at Del Norte on October 10, ending their work for the season, and Rhoda returned to Washington, DC, to write his report. He noted the San Juan Mountains' uniqueness and challenges: "In describing a river or a simple range of mountains, the order of the sequence is laid down in nature; all you have to do is to commence at one end of the line and follow it. The mountains in the so-called San Juan country, however, are very complicated, and present no definite lines that may be followed in a description without leaving much untold."

September 9, 1916

Opportunity Knocks for Knowledge

A woman with an inspirational vision saw her dream come true in downtown Denver on September 9, 1916, when the Opportunity School opened with Emily K. Griffith at its helm.

Born in Ohio in 1868, Griffith and her family homesteaded in Nebraska sixteen years later. As a teacher in humble prairie schoolhouses, she supported her family. The Griffiths moved to Colorado in 1894, and Emily found work as a teacher in Denver. Her skill, generosity, and optimism aided students in the ethnically diverse Five Points neighborhood. Griffith alternated between service as a state official and a teacher from 1904 through 1912, often leaving her state capitol office to help students and their families. She dreamed of doing more, though, for "the boys and girls, their parents, too, whose education has been limited by poverty." Griffith wanted "to establish a school where the clock will be stopped from morning until midnight. I want the age limit for admission to be lifted and the classes so arranged that a boy or girl working in a bakery, store, laundry, or any kind of shop who has an hour or two to spare may come to school, study what he or she wants to learn to make life more useful. The same rule goes for older folks, too . . . I already have a name for that school. It is Opportunity."

With help from philanthropists, entrepreneurs, and journalists, Griffith opened the school in 1916. Her desk stood in the hallway where she could interact with people, and her family cooked soup daily to feed the students. Vocational programs aided thousands of pupils of all ages, and she changed course offerings to meet the latest demand. Griffith's school evoked the social optimism of the Progressive era and proved a triumph, earning her national praise.

In 1933, Griffith and her invalid sister Florence retired to a cabin in Pinecliffe, in the mountains of Boulder County. One of Colorado's most generous souls and her gentle sister were murdered there in 1947. A stained glass window in the state capitol and, most important, the school—now known as the Emily Griffith Technical College—preserve her remarkable legacy.

September 10, 1945

Mike Loses (Most of) His Head

A hatchet job gone wrong created a legend, one of the fowlest characters ever to call the Centennial State home. Lloyd and Clara Olsen, residents of the Mesa County town of Fruita, looked forward to a chicken dinner on September 10, 1945, and their rooster Mike was on the menu. But Lloyd's aim was a little off, and while removing most of Mike's head he left the brain stem intact, allowing Mike's body to continue to function. In addition, his jugular vein clotted before he bled to death. According to some accounts, Mike slept that first headless night with his cranium tucked safely under his wing. The Olsens sustained Mike with grain and water dispensed from an eyedropper, and he tripled in size after his almost-execution.

Before long, the Olsens' "Headless Wonder Chicken" took on new life as a side show attraction. He appeared before crowds from coast to coast, received a $10,000 insurance policy, and won fame in national magazines and even the Guinness Book of Records. The Olsens kept his dislocated head in a jar of ether, which traveled with the family on the freak show circuit. All the while, Mike behaved as normally as possible. In the words of one Fruita resident, "He was a big fat chicken who didn't know he didn't have a head."

Mike's reign as cock-of-the-walk lasted a year and a half. In 1947 he suffocated on a bit of grain lodged in his throat. The Olsens had lost a tool they used to extract obstructions, and he died in an Arizona motel. The fate of his various body parts remains a mystery—perhaps he finally graced the dinner table after all. But Mike's legacy lives on through a headless statue and an annual festival in Fruita. In 2012, Mike's fans even threw his head into the ring for president on the Free Range Party ticket, claiming his candidacy "a no-brainer." Fruita's fine feathered friend still stands head and shoulders above his clucking Colorado colleagues.

September 11, 1957

Nuclear Fire at Rocky Flats

Years of neglected safety procedures and the relentless demand for an ever greater output culminated at the Rocky Flats nuclear weapons plant in northern Jefferson County on September 11, 1957, when a plutonium fire threatened to spew radiation over the Denver metropolitan area.

Defense installations sprouted in Colorado during World War II, and that momentum continued into the Cold War. US senators Edwin C. Johnson and Eugene D. Millikin lobbied federal officials for a facility to construct plutonium triggers for nuclear weapons. Government agents chose Rocky Flats, a plateau at the base of the Rocky Mountains' eastern slope between Boulder and Golden. Work at the facility, touted as an economic boon, commenced in 1952. National advocates of Rocky Flats praised the construction of nuclear weapons to maintain the balance of power with the Soviet Union, and local media trumpeted the influx of federal dollars.

The fire in 1957 offered the first warning of the secretive plant's horrifying potential. An even bigger fire in 1969 spread airborne plutonium over nearby Arvada and Westminster and nearly caused a meltdown akin to the Chernobyl disaster seventeen years later. In 1973, radioactive waste leaking into the soil and water supply triggered warnings in downstream communities, Broomfield in particular. A liberal turn in Colorado's politics and the rise of environmentalism in the 1970s aroused protests that drew thousands of people. Yet President Ronald Reagan's militarization in the 1980s demanded ever more production at the flats and inspired a gathering of 15,000 anti-nuclear weapons activists who nearly encircled the perimeter fence in 1983.

Rumors of the plant's shoddy condition led to a Federal Bureau of Investigation raid in 1989. That and the end of the Cold War inspired its closing in 1992. Cleanup work lasted until 2005, four years after the site's designation as Rocky Flats National Wildlife Refuge. Health problems for former workers linger, as do doubts about the site's safety. Modern promises of clean air, water, and earth clash with the history of Rocky Flats, one filled with secrets and lies.

September 12, 1977

Fed-Up Farmers in Baca County

A group known as Partners in Action for Agriculture convened in the Baca County seat of Springfield on September 12, 1977. Around 500 farmers vented their frustrations about federal farm legislation in the high school gym. Eugene Schroeder told the assembled crowd: "We must have a fair price for our products plus enough to exist on. We can't feed the nation on cheap food with the American farmer who is producing that food going broke." Schroeder and others called for an agricultural strike and protests to raise awareness of their precarious situation.

Local residents talked of little else than the strike after the September 12 meeting. One correspondent to the Springfield newspaper wrote that it "set much of the Baca County world on its ear—hind legs—or whatever part of your anatomy the results of that meeting happened to hit the hardest." Ten days later, farmers visited Pueblo to lobby the federal secretary of agriculture and met with members of the US Congress and state legislators as well. The notion of an agricultural strike made headlines far beyond southeastern Colorado. Anger at low crop prices that made it difficult for farmers to survive struck a chord, and the strike proposal spread nationwide. Farmers from Delaware, Minnesota, Virginia, and other states attended a Pueblo rally on September 22, and others organized their own protests across the country. Leaders of the movement in Baca County conducted phone interviews with radio stations in various states and Canadian provinces and traveled to Washington, DC, to speak to politicians and the press on behalf of rural Americans. By the year's end, 10,000 farmers brought their tractors to rallies at the Colorado State Capitol, and similar "tractorcades" took place at government buildings nationwide.

The Baca County meeting in 1977 inspired a nationwide organization for farmers and ranchers known as the American Agriculture Movement (AAM). It coordinates testimony on farm-related legislation and organizes "tractorcade" protests to raise awareness of rural issues. The AAM's roots demonstrate the potential of small places to make a big difference.

Ute and American delegates in Washington, DC, after signing the Brunot Treaty in 1873, including Chipeta and Ouray (bottom row center) and Charles Adams and Otto Mears (right end of middle row)

September 13, 1873

The Utes Surrender the San Juans

American prospectors trespassed on the massive Ute reservation in western Colorado Territory in the early 1870s, but the federal government hesitated to restrain its own citizens, even though an 1868 treaty with the Utes demanded just that. To prevent conflict, Commissioner Felix R. Brunot negotiated a new deal that ceded the San Juan Mountains region to the United States. This proposal, made on September 13, 1873, became known as the Brunot Treaty.

Factors including smelting technology, the General Mining Act of 1872 that promoted mining on federal land, and the Panic of 1873 combined to fuel American interest in digging wealth out of the ground. Legal niceties like the boundaries of American Indian reservations offered little impediment. After Ute factions complained of the transgressions, federal agents sought to amend the reserve's limits. A council in August 1872 at the Los Piños Agency, near Cochetopa Pass in present-day Saguache County, involved Brunot and agents Lafayette Head and Charles Adams, but the Utes demanded enforcement of the 1868 treaty. That

November, Adams and Saguache businessman Otto Mears escorted prominent Utes including Tabeguaches Ouray, his wife, Chipeta, his sister, She-towich, and the Yamparika Nicaagat to the East Coast. The trip was intended to awe native cultures into submission. The Utes visited Washington, DC, New York City, and other major cities but once again rejected any new deal.

At another council at Los Piños in 1873, Brunot forced a Ute surrender to legalize the San Juan interlopers. Ouray, who sought peace at almost any cost, convinced members of other Ute factions to back the cession. Federal agents rewarded him with an annual annuity and a farm near present-day Montrose, which reinforced the view among many Utes that Ouray was an American puppet. The farm survives today as History Colorado's Ute Indian Museum, where Chipeta lies buried. The Brunot Treaty calmed the situation briefly, but further trespassing led to violence and the expulsion of most Utes from western Colorado by the decade's end.

September 14, 1978

An Alien Finds a Home in Boulder

In the 1960s, the University of Colorado UFO Project, chaired by physicist Edward U. Condon, dismissed the scientific benefits of research into strange sightings in the sky. Undaunted by this rejection, a decade later an alien from the planet Ork came to live in the university town of Boulder when *Mork and Mindy* premiered on ABC on September 14, 1978.

A spinoff of the *Happy Days* television show, *Mork and Mindy* related the zany antics of Mork from Ork, an alien played by the uninhibited Robin Williams. After Mork landed near Boulder in his egg-shaped spaceship, town resident Mindy McConnell, played by Pam Dawber, allowed him to live in the attic of her Victorian house apartment. The sitcom centered around Mork's attempts to understand Earthlings, often with bizarre, hilarious results and some Orkan profanity: "Shazbot!" The opening credits featured scenes around Boulder, including Williams and Dawber flying a kite in front of the Flatirons, strolling down the Pearl Street Mall, standing on the goal posts at Folsom Field, and their house at 1619 Pine Street. In November 1979, Williams dressed as a Denver Broncos cheerleader and danced as Mork before the crowds at Mile High Stadium. After four seasons, including Mork and Mindy's marriage and the birth of their child Mearth, played by comedian Jonathan Winters, the series ended in 1982.

As surreal as sitcoms could get, *Mork and Mindy* reflected Boulder's reputation as a place unlike any other in Colorado, at times described sarcastically as a town surrounded by reality. The show allowed Williams to display his formidable comic talent and launched his career as a major television and film star. After his death in 2014, mourners gathered for an impromptu tribute at the Pine Street house. Congressman and Boulder resident Jared Polis dressed as Mork in tribute to the actor. Each episode ended with Mork reporting to his Orkan superior Orson on what he had learned about life on Earth. What better way to remember the show and the genius of Robin Williams than to grab one's ears and bid a hearty "Nanu, nanu."

September 15, 1879

First Meeting of the Historical Society

"The attention of old timers and all interested in the early history of Denver and Colorado, is called to the meeting of the State Historical Society," the *Rocky Mountain News* informed its readers. Established by the General Assembly in the spring of 1879 to protect and preserve the nascent state's story, organizational sessions took place that summer. Colorado's historical society held its first official meeting in Denver on September 15. Members discussed the military and educational history of their community and heard bombastic remarks by Mayor Richard Sopris about the glory of the state and its capital city over the previous two decades.

The Colorado Historical Society and its slumgullion collection occupied space in hotels, office buildings, and the Arapahoe County Courthouse until 1895, when it moved to the capitol's basement. Visitors marveled at exhibits overflowing with taxidermied animals, geological specimens, pottery from Ancestral Puebloan sites, and the desiccated remains of those who lived in the ancient cities of southwestern Colorado. The society proved so popular that it soon merited a separate building, a marble museum across Fourteenth Avenue from the state capitol, designed by Frank E. Edbrooke and opened in 1915. Its collections grew in size and scope, from dioramas of historic scenes made by the Works Progress Administration during the Great Depression to "Baby Doe" Tabor's wedding dress. The crowded edifice also proved insufficient, and in 1977 the society moved to the Colorado Heritage Center, a modernistic, sloping structure of brown brick erected on Thirteenth Avenue between Lincoln Street and Broadway. This structure and the state's judicial building north of it came down to make way for the Ralph L. Carr Colorado Judicial Center, and a sleek new museum opened a block to the south in 2011.

Now known as History Colorado, the historical society operates the flagship facility in Denver and museums and sites across the state. It interprets Colorado's complicated, dynamic, often controversial story and provides a meeting ground for the state's past, present, and future.

Breaking Ground for the Coliseum

City dignitaries gathered on the south side of the National Western Stock Show grounds in northeast Denver on September 16, 1949, shovels at the ready. They broke ground for a "mammoth new municipal stockyards stadium," as the *Denver Post* described, "a modern, shell-shaped stadium of concrete construction, long-needed, long-planned, and long-awaited." Coloradans today know the gray structure with a graceful curved roof as the Denver Coliseum.

Since the early twentieth century, the stock show had boasted its own arena, but its iron framework obstructed views and made the attractive structure feel cramped. To better serve the stock show and lure additional business, the city approved an 8,000-seat, $3 million structure. It opened on January 10, 1952, with a program celebrating farming and ranching, as befit its connection to the stock show. Governor Dan Thornton, a cattleman from Gunnison County, presided at the inaugural event. For nearly a quarter century it hosted musical acts including Black Sabbath, Eric Clapton, Creedence Clearwater Revival, Bob Dylan, the Eagles, Led Zeppelin, the Moody Blues, Elvis Presley, Cat Stevens, the Rolling Stones, Ike and Tina Turner, and the Who. By the mid-1970s, musicians had moved to McNichols Arena, named for Mayor Bill McNichols, and then the Pepsi Center, which replaced the arena in 1999. The coliseum remained an active venue, however, hosting events ranging from ice shows and circuses to American Indian powwows, from high school graduations and sporting competitions to motocross and monster truck rallies and, most important, the National Western Stock Show.

Interstate 70, built in the early 1960s, severed the coliseum from the stock show grounds, but they remain linked in purpose. Work to lower the interstate below grade in the late 2010s promised to reunite the coliseum with the rest of the complex, while the stock show facility underwent a dramatic modernization and expansion in partnership with Colorado State University. Whatever the coliseum's future may hold, its past is as solid as its concrete.

The Battle of Beecher Island

A group of about fifty volunteer troops from Kansas and Colorado Territory, commanded by Major George A. Forsyth and Lieutenant Frederick H. Beecher, awoke early on September 17, 1868, thinking that a herd of bison was about to stampede through their camp. In short order, the band on the Arikaree River in present-day Yuma County realized their deadly error.

The bloodshed that followed the Sand Creek Massacre in late 1864 calmed as several native groups signed treaties with the federal government, agreeing to relocate to reservations in modern Oklahoma. Yet a campaign in the spring of 1868 against a faction of the Northern Cheyennes known as the Dog Soldiers fanned the flames once more. General Philip Sheridan attempted to stop the Dog Soldiers' raids on Kansas settlements by recruiting locals to scout and distract the Cheyennes, giving the US Army time to deal a crippling blow. That September, Forsyth's volunteer unit found itself surrounded and outnumbered by several hundred Dog Soldiers, other Cheyennes and Arapahos, and some Brulé Sioux on the banks of the Arikaree. For nine days the party hunkered on a sandbar in the middle of the river, later named Beecher Island after the officer who was killed during the drawn-out battle. Four other soldiers died and many suffered serious wounds. A scout slipped through the American Indians' line to get help. By the time relief arrived on September 25, the warriors had wearied of their sport and departed, having lost nine of their fighters including the inspirational, vengeful leader Roman Nose.

The near-destruction of Forsyth's command achieved epic status. Lieutenant Colonel George A. Custer forebodingly declared that "there will never occur in our future hostilities with the savage tribes of the West a struggle the equal of that in which were engaged the heroic men who defended so bravely 'Beecher's Island.'" Survivors gathered at the site in 1905 to erect a monument to the Americans killed, and a newer panel describing the battle honors both Beecher and Roman Nose. The island itself disappeared in a flood of the Arikaree River in 1935.

September 18, 1891

Mustering Out at Fort Lewis

Contrary to popular opinion, the US Army did not operate in the West to fight American Indians. Instead of making war, troops most often sought to prevent war by providing a buffer between native groups and outsiders. By the end of the nineteenth century, conflict and disease had overwhelmed American Indians, and the army's presence struck many as both excessive and expensive. To that end, the US Department of War abandoned many posts, including Fort Lewis in La Plata County, from which troops marched out for the last time on September 18, 1891.

Miners in the San Juan Mountains asked for military protection as they moved onto land taken from the Utes in the mid-1870s, whose authority endured to the south, west, and north. In the fall of 1878, the army created a post on the San Juan River in present-day Archuleta County, at a Ute thermal water source called Pagosa Springs. It took the name Fort Lewis after an officer killed in Kansas that same year. The bastion proved too isolated to be useful, especially after the Meeker Massacre that terrified American settlers in western Colorado. In the fall of 1880, it relocated to the La Plata River near the mining town of Animas City (now Durango). Fort Lewis represented a barrier between that community and the Ute reservation to the south and west. Soldiers investigated accusations of livestock theft by Utes and Navajos, whose reservation stood to the south in New Mexico and Arizona Territories. They also restored order after American settlers killed Utes hunting off the reservation in the Beaver Creek Massacre of 1885.

By the late 1880s, the need for Fort Lewis waned, and the federal government ordered its closure in 1891. After twenty years as an American Indian boarding school, the fort repurposed as a vocational school in 1911. Promoted to higher education in the 1930s, Fort Lewis College moved to a site overlooking Durango in 1956. It offers both free tuition to American Indian students and acclaimed programs on southwestern America. The college preserves the name, although few traces survive of the historic forts at Pagosa Springs or on the La Plata River.

September 19, 1953

In the Mood for Glenn Miller

A swing band conducted by Dick Jurgens performed the first concert at a new ballroom in the student center at the University of Colorado (CU) in Boulder, dedicated on September 19, 1953. The hall boasted the name of the school's most famous dropout: band leader Glenn Miller.

Born in Iowa in 1904, Alton Glenn Miller took his name from the Democratic candidate for president that year. The Millers lived in Nebraska and Missouri before moving to Morgan County in 1918. As a teenager, Glenn—who loathed his first name—found employment as a soda jerk at a drugstore and in the town's beet sugar factory. He played football for the Fort Morgan High School team, where his grades suffered from his greatest distraction—the trombone. Years later, Miller's mother, Lou, recalled: "Glenn used to work on the beet drys and at lunch hour he'd go yonder down the railroad tracks and play that horn. He just played on that horn all the time. It got to where Pop and I used to wonder if he'd ever amount to anything." Miller graduated in 1921 and looked for work in bands, without success. He enrolled at CU in January 1923, where again academics and music clashed; Miller even failed a course in music harmony. His roommate, Greeley native and future media personality Ted Mack, helped make connections in the musical world. Miller dropped out of CU at the end of 1923 and slowly but surely built a thriving career. In 1928 he married Boulder native and former CU classmate Helen Burger. They visited family in Colorado regularly during his brief but internationally renowned career.

Miller's swing band, known for hits like "In the Mood," "The Chattanooga Choo Choo," "Little Brown Jug," "American Patrol," and many more, boosted spirits during the Great Depression and World War II. His plane disappeared over the English Channel in 1944, but the band played on. A biographical film starring James Stewart and June Allyson, filmed in part on the CU campus, premiered in 1954, a year after Miller's mother and other family members had gathered to dedicate the ballroom to the memory of a poor student and brilliant musical talent.

September 20, 1877

Anthony Speaks Suffrage in Lake City

The mining town of Lake City, high in the San Juan Mountains, buzzed with activity on September 20, 1877, as a crowd packed the Hinsdale County Courthouse past capacity. The crowd proved so large that the featured speaker, renowned women's suffrage advocate Susan B. Anthony, agreed to deliver her remarks on the grounds outside to accommodate everyone.

In 1876, Colorado's constitutional authors chose to extend voting rights to women in school board elections only. The General Assembly authorized a ballot measure the next year to determine how far the state's franchise should extend. The election drew attention from around the country. A Pennsylvania newspaper, quoted in a Colorado Springs paper, noted that "while only the men will have access to the ballot-box, the women, who constitute the most interested party, are conducting the campaign with matchless spirit and enterprise." The most prominent national suffragist to visit Colorado before the election, Anthony arrived in Denver on September 11. She focused her efforts on miners and ranchers in the southern part of the state, including remarks in Las Animas and Saguache, while other advocates canvassed the eastern slope cities. Anthony made two speeches in Lake City, each lasting several hours and drawing sizable crowds.

From Lake City, Anthony traveled to the boomtown of Leadville, where Governor John L. Routt stood at her side in support of equal suffrage, although the audience proved more interested in their cigars and whiskey. A correspondent from Pueblo responded to her point that, as taxpayers, women deserved to vote: "Idiots, lunatics, and aliens, though they may pay taxes, ought not to vote and can't vote." Anthony's tour culminated with a speech in Denver shortly before the early October election. The eager campaign notwithstanding, men rejected equal voting rights by more than a two-to-one margin. Some in the press considered the matter of women's suffrage settled nationally as a result. Advocates kept up the pressure regardless, and when male voters considered the question again in 1893, the outcome proved decidedly different.

September 21, 2012

Recognition for Chimney Rock

At the turn of the second millennium AD, a culture known as Chacoan dominated the Four Corners region from a cluster of cities in Chaco Canyon in today's northwestern New Mexico. Satellite communities with allegiance to the canyon extended for a hundred miles in every direction. On the northern Chacoan frontier stood a community known today as Chimney Rock, named for one of two stone spires that towered above it, in present-day Archuleta County.

Starting around AD 900, Chacoans colonized the region, erecting towns in the shadow of Chimney and Companion Rocks. Higher in elevation than any other Ancestral Puebloan settlement, archaeologists believe Chacoans used the Chimney Rock site as an astronomical calendar, with important buildings aligned with both the stones and celestial bodies at important times of the year, including solstices, equinoxes, and phases of the moon. For two and a half centuries, several hundred Chacoans inhabited eight communities clustered below the pinnacles. For reasons unknown, around AD 1150 the residents burned and abandoned the site, although competition from groups to the west (such as Mesa Verde) might have contributed to its decline.

Archaeological work at Chimney Rock, now located in the San Juan National Forest, occurred sporadically in the twentieth century. Although surveys are still made, American Indian descendants of the community's inhabitants have requested that no further excavations disturb the site. In 1970, Chimney Rock earned a listing in the National Register of Historic Places, spurring further attempts to protect and recognize it. Bipartisan support for designating it a national monument failed to overcome congressional lethargy, however. To better preserve and interpret the historic landmark, President Barack Obama used his authority under the Antiquities Act to declare Chimney Rock National Monument on September 21, 2012.

A United States Air Force jet parked on the parade ground of the Air Force Academy, with the cadet chapel in the background, as seen in the 1960s

A Wing and a Prayer at the Academy

A ceremony in El Paso County on September 22, 1963, dedicated one of Colorado's most impressive buildings: the cadet chapel at the United States Air Force Academy (USAFA), described by one critic as "seventeen aluminum tetrahedrons set on end to resemble both a small Gothic cathedral and a squadron of fighter planes ready to zoom into the stratosphere."

In part because of the efforts of President Dwight D. Eisenhower, a regular visitor to Colorado, the state secured the USAFA in 1954. A federal commission that included renowned aviator Charles A. Lindbergh chose a tract north of Colorado Springs, near Fort Carson and Peterson Air Force Base. Chicago architectural firm Skidmore, Owings, and Merrill produced designs for a sleek, modern campus to reflect a military academy dedicated to new technology. Critics compared it negatively to the army and navy academies, suggesting that the plan suited Disneyland more than the armed forces. Cadets studied in temporary facilities at Denver's Lowry Air Force Base as construction commenced. By 1958, when the facility opened for classes, striking rectangular structures of steel, concrete, and glass stood on granite terraces, contrasting with the pine-covered slopes west of the campus. One of the architects declared that "this academy, tucked in among the mountains, proudly standing on our modern Acropolis, will create a vibrant cultural and spiritual sense of forward-looking accomplishment in these young people."

With the United States locked in the Cold War with the atheistic Soviet Union, a chapel was essential for the USAFA. The modern Gothic design of spires interspersed with stained glass offered spaces for Protestant, Catholic, and Jewish services. One member of Congress called it an "aluminum monstrosity that will look like a row of polished teepees," while another suggested that "the boys fight and die in aluminum planes. They can worship in aluminum if they can die in it, can they not?" The building has overcome such opposition and added room for other faiths, and it stands today as one of Colorado's most beloved, inspirational structures.

September 23, 1909

Taft and the Gunnison Tunnel

When President William H. Taft, standing on a stage in Montrose County, set a golden bell down on a silver plate on September 23, 1909, an electric current opened gates holding back the Gunnison River. Water flowed through a 6-mile tunnel to the Uncompahgre River valley. As a local newspaper declared, "President Taft Smites the Rock and the Waters Gush Forth."

Settlers who moved into the Uncompahgre River valley in the late nineteenth century saw potential in the broad but dry region, but they needed water to turn it into a success. The nearby Gunnison River had plenty of water but lacked open land for farms, so diverting water to the Uncompahgre seemed a sensible option. The General Assembly pledged support for a tunnel and canal to water the Uncompahgre valley in 1901, but funds ran out before the project's completion. The federal government took over in 1903, selecting the Uncompahgre Project as one of the first for its new Reclamation Service, which built irrigation systems to encourage agriculture and homesteading in arid regions of the American West. The Uncompahgre Project boasted allies including President Theodore Roosevelt and Congressman John F. Shafroth.

As befit the first completed federal reclamation project, Taft traveled to Montrose in 1909 to dedicate it. Five minutes after his bell touched the plate, water started flowing out of the tunnel's mouth. Spectators at the president's reviewing stand and at the county fairgrounds cheered the trickling sound. Taft predicted that "this valley, with an unpronounceable name, is going to blossom like the rose." Within a few years, engineers built 470 miles of canals to transform Delta and Montrose Counties, encouraging diverse agricultural products. In the decades to come, the renamed Bureau of Reclamation erected many irrigation systems to re-plumb Colorado, fostering agricultural development on both sides of the Rocky Mountains. Environmental concerns eventually dampened the nation's enthusiasm for reclamation, but in the early twentieth century Americans praised the assistance to turn arid land into prosperous farms.

September 24, 1955

Ike's Heart Skips a Beat

Around 2:30 a.m. on September 24, 1955, Mamie Doud Eisenhower heard her husband, President Dwight D. Eisenhower, stirring in his bedroom in her family's home at 750 Lafayette Street in Denver. He looked pale, and she called for a doctor. For the first known time, a sitting chief executive had suffered a heart attack, and a nervous world turned its attention to Colorado.

The Doud house offered Ike and Mamie a haven from his military career. They married there in 1916 and took leaves in Colorado. As president, Eisenhower made Denver his base of operations during extended summer vacations. He fished on the Fraser River in Grand County, golfed at Denver's Cherry Hills Country Club, and painted wherever he could find a spot for his easel. Eisenhower worked at Lowry Air Force Base, and the staff at Fitzsimons Army Hospital in Aurora administered regular tests and provided preventive care. The president endured persistent rumors about his health, but aside from severe indigestion brought on by poor eating habits and the legacy of chain smoking, which he quit in the late 1940s, he proved relatively hale.

The physician called to Eisenhower's bedside that September morning mistook the heart attack for a digestive complaint. Not until almost twelve hours had passed did the president go to Fitzsimons for treatment. He remained at the Aurora facility for seven weeks and informed his first official visitor—Vice President Richard Nixon—on October 8: "It hurt like hell, Dick. I never let Mamie know how much it hurt." A heroic parade in Washington, DC, welcomed the presidential party back on Veterans Day, November 11, 1955, although he did not resume a full schedule until early the next year. Worried that altitude might cause another attack, doctors limited Eisenhower's later trips to Colorado, forbidding him from golfing or fishing in the state.

Although the Doud house remains in private hands, a commemorative plaque recalls its most famous occupants. Eisenhower's eighth-floor suite at Fitzsimons—now the University of Colorado Anschutz Medical Campus—was restored and opened as a museum in 2000.

September

Woodrow Wilson's Final Word

President Woodrow Wilson delivered what scholars consider the most impressive public address of his long career in Pueblo on September 25, 1919. It also proved to be his last.

Congress balked at the Treaty of Versailles that Wilson helped write during the spring of 1919, ending World War I with Germany. Wilson set out in early September on a national speaking tour, hoping to inspire crowds to demand its ratification. During the trip, his tone shifted from logical, persuasive arguments to combative propaganda, branding anyone who opposed the treaty as a traitor and a warmonger. Late on September 24, he arrived in Denver to cheering crowds and slept at the Brown Palace Hotel. A parade through downtown the following morning preceded his speech at the City Auditorium, after which his train departed for Pueblo.

Wilson delivered the tour's thirty-fourth formal address at Pueblo's city hall on the afternoon of September 25. After praising the auditorium, which allowed him to stand close to his audience, Wilson railed against the notion of "Irish-Americans," "German-Americans," and other split identities, arguing that "any man who carries a hyphen about with him carries a dagger that he is ready to plunge into the vitals of this republic whenever he gets the chance." The crowd cheered his bombastic words, and the president basked in their adoration before returning to his train.

A headache Wilson had endured most of the day intensified as his party headed east. His train stopped in eastern Pueblo County to let the president, his wife, and his doctor stroll in the evening air. Wilson accepted produce from a farmer and spoke to a World War I veteran before proceeding to Rocky Ford, where he greeted a crowd from the train. Farther down the Arkansas River, Wilson's condition worsened, and his aides canceled the tour. After his return to Washington, DC, he suffered a major stroke that handicapped his presidency; the US Senate rejected the treaty soon afterward. A plaque in Pueblo's city hall commemorates that spot as the scene of Wilson's last public oration and the abrupt end of a prolific, successful career.

Staking a Claim for Grand Junction

George A. Crawford, whose election as governor of Kansas in 1861 was declared invalid by the courts, came to western Colorado two decades later to locate a new town. Scouts praised the land at the confluence of the Grand (now Colorado) and Gunnison Rivers. On September 26, 1881, Crawford filed paperwork to establish a community there. Originally named Ute for the culture that until recently had dominated the region, it now bears the title Grand Junction.

The Grand Valley's scarce game offered little to the Utes, who preferred more forested mountains and mesas. After the Meeker Massacre in September 1879, public sentiment demanded Ute removal from western Colorado. The Tabeguache band, based at Ouray's farm near present-day Montrose, hoped to relocate to the Grand-Gunnison Rivers junction. Dismissing the notion was Otto Mears, famed for his toll roads through former Ute territory in the San Juan Mountains and a counselor to the Utes, who described the region as unsuitable for native cultures. At the same time he warned the Utes away, Mears saw potential for American settlement: "It was in my blood to want to see new furrows writhing from the plow ripping through the warm earth that had lain undisturbed since creation." Coordinating his efforts with pro-removal politicians including Senator Henry M. Teller and Governor Frederick W. Pitkin, Mears ensured that the Tabeguaches and most other Utes departed for a Utah reservation under an 1880 treaty.

Settlement at Grand Junction—named after the river confluence—proceeded slowly because of a lack of timber for construction and fuel. Irrigation opened the Grand Valley to agriculture, and by the century's end it earned national praise for specialty crops including fruit orchards and sugar beets. Grand Junction's sugar factory was transformed into a processing center for nuclear ore during the mid-twentieth century. The town boasts Colorado Mesa University, founded as a junior college in 1925 and promoted to university status in 2011. It captured the seat of the new Mesa County in 1883 and remains the western slope's political, educational, and economic hub.

September 27, 1865

From Camp Rankin to Fort Sedgwick

A military post, established near the vital crossroads town of Julesburg a year earlier, earned a new title on September 27, 1865, when the US Army renamed Camp Rankin as Fort Sedgwick, in honor of a general killed in Virginia a year and a half earlier.

Located in the modern county that bears the same name, Fort Sedgwick had its origins in the panic-stricken summer of 1864. Governor John Evans begged President Abraham Lincoln for troops to defend Colorado Territory against a supposedly imminent annihilation by American Indians. Failing that, Evans secured several new military posts staffed by volunteers in the South Platte River valley. Soldiers arrived at Julesburg late that summer to construct buildings of sod with wooden beam roofs covered in turf, the entire complex surrounded by a low sod defensive wall. A garrison of ninety soldiers patrolled the nearby trails in Colorado and Nebraska Territories.

The post faced a major challenge in early 1865, in the wake of the Sand Creek Massacre. Native cultures across the plains sought revenge, and Julesburg endured attacks in January and February. Expansion of the bastion followed quickly, with several hundred professional soldiers fresh from the Civil War in place by the summer. Fort Sedgwick, renamed in September, proved vital to restoring peace through force, but its setting impressed few visitors. On an inspection tour in 1866, General William T. Sherman declared, "It is impossible to conceive of a more dreary waste than this whole road is, without tree or bush, grass thin, and the [South] Platte running over its wide, shallow bottom with its rapid current; no game or birds; nothing but the long dusty road, with its occasional ox team, and the everlasting line of telegraph poles."

By the decade's end, conflict in eastern Colorado diminished. The army ordered Fort Sedgwick abandoned in May 1871, and homesteaders turned the military base into farm fields. A flagpole marks the location where the fort once stood, and its name—although little else about the real post—appeared as Kevin Costner's abandoned bivouac in the 1990 film *Dances with Wolves*.

September 28, 1719

Spain Finds Purgatory in Colorado

Hunkered on the eastern slope of the Sangre de Cristo Mountains, a massive expedition of Spaniards, Puebloans, and Apaches endured an early winter storm and feared whether they had enough food for everyone. Little wonder that this beleaguered company, which prepared to depart from its camp near present-day Trinidad on September 28, 1719, referred to a nearby river as "El Río de las Animas Perdidas en Purgatorio," the River of the Lost Souls in Purgatory.

Antonio Valverde y Cosío, the Spanish governor of New Mexico, undertook a daunting task in September 1719. French traders in the Mississippi River valley had supplied Comanches on the southern plains with weapons to raid the Spanish and their native allies, and a massive force organized by Valverde y Cosío planned retaliation. About 100 Spanish soldiers and settlers joined 500 Puebloans from the Rio Grande valley and 200 Apaches, whose culture dominated eastern Colorado at the time. Seeking battle with the Comanche, the host trekked northeastward from Santa Fe. The group made an arduous crossing of Raton Pass before an early burst of winter weather halted them on the forebodingly named river.

Valverde y Cosío's party continued north along ancient pathways that roughly paralleled present-day Interstate 25, passing the future sites of Walsenburg, Pueblo, and Colorado Springs. They skirted the Black Forest and arced back to the Arkansas River near modern Las Animas. They battled grizzly bears, mountain lions, and the weather but no Comanches. Ascending the Arkansas and Huerfano Rivers, they crossed the Sangre de Cristo Mountains near La Veta Pass and returned to Santa Fe by way of the Rio Grande, having traveled 800 miles in two months.

Valverde y Cosío sent out a smaller expedition under Pedro de Villasur in the summer of 1720. That force met a grisly end in eastern Nebraska at the hands of the Pawnee, a native group loyal to their French trading partners. By that time, what is now the Purgatoire River seemed a proper buffer between the heaven of New Mexico and the hell of the contested plains.

September 29, 1879

The Meeker Incident

For three decades, Ute bands in present-day western Colorado resisted the encroachment of Mexican and American interlopers. When faced with no alternative, they surrendered one tract after another and listened to the promises of federal agents who pledged to improve their lives by transforming them into farmers. Their communal frustration and despair found a gruesome outlet on September 29, 1879, when members of the Yamparika faction killed agent Nathan C. Meeker and ten other men at the White River Agency in modern Rio Blanco County.

Well-known as the founder of Greeley, Colorado's most prosperous farming community, Meeker accepted appointment as the White River agent in 1878. He envisioned remaking the Utes as Americans, but his disdain for native culture and paternalist behavior caused animosity among the Yamparika. Meeker ordered the Utes' horse racing course plowed under to end the sin of gambling and to prepare the fields and his charges for agrarian life. Recognizing the friction, however, Meeker also asked for support from the US Army. When troops ignored the pleas of prominent Yamparikas like Nicaagat—who had scouted for the army during campaigns against the Sioux—and entered the reservation on September 29, some Utes raided the agency. Meeker and ten other men at the agency were killed, their attackers mutilating the bodies.

Artist's depiction of the "Meeker Massacre" site along the White River, as portrayed in Frank Leslie's Illustrated Newspaper *on December 6, 1879*

The Yamparika took hostage Meeker's wife, Arvilla, their daughter, Josephine, and the wife of an agency employee and her two young children. Over the next several weeks, the prisoners moved with Nicaagat and other Utes southward to Grand Mesa. She-towich, sister of Tabeguaches peacemaker Ouray and wife of a prominent Yamparika, convinced the group to release the hostages nearly a month after the "Meeker Massacre." Charles Adams, a longtime ally and interpreter on the Ute reservation, escorted the Meekers back to Greeley. The brutal episode convinced many state residents that the time had come to expel the Utes from western Colorado.

September 30, 1873

A British Bird atop Longs Peak

Tourists have flocked to the Centennial State since the mid-nineteenth century. On September 30, 1873, a remarkable visitor achieved her goal of reaching the summit of Longs Peak, one of the most challenging mountains in Colorado.

Isabella Bird, a globetrotting Briton whose journeys included stops in Canada, Japan, China, Korea, Southeast Asia, India, Persia, and places throughout the Mediterranean, came to Colorado on her way home from a visit to Hawaii. Bird's stops in Colorado included Fort Collins, Denver, Colorado Springs, and South Park; but she exhausted her vocabulary in lavishing praise on Estes Park and present-day Rocky Mountain National Park. She claimed that "in this glorious upper world, with the mountain pines behind and the clear lake in front, in the 'blue hollow at the foot of Long's Peak' . . . I have found far more than I have ever dared to hope for."

Upon her approach to Estes Park, Bird praised what she considered "a landmark in purple glory," Longs Peak. With trapper and scout "Mountain Jim" Nugent— with whom Bird seemed more than a little smitten—as her guide and two students along for the adventure, she set out to ascend the fourteener. When they reached the top after an arduous two-day climb, Bird marveled: "From the summit were seen in unrivaled combination all the views which had rejoiced our eyes during the ascent. It was something at last to stand upon the storm-rent crown of this lonely sentinel of the Rocky range, on one of the mightiest of the vertebrae of the backbone of the North American continent, and to see the waters start for both oceans."

Bird wrote prolifically, and her observations about meandering to various corners of the world remain in print. Her narrative of Colorado, *A Lady's Life in the Rocky Mountains*, published six years after her visit to the region, remains one of the most enjoyable travel accounts ever produced by the myriad visitors drawn to the state over the years.

October

Rolling the Dice on Gambling

Thousands of people flocked to Gilpin and Teller Counties on October 1, 1991, lured by more than a dozen casinos that opened that day in hopes of reinvigorating former mining towns.

Games of chance flourished throughout the Rocky Mountains during Colorado's mining boom in the late nineteenth century, yet another way to separate prospectors and wage workers from their hard-earned money. Territorial legislators had banned gambling in the mid-1860s, and the law remained in force for over a century. Yet scofflaws flourished, often with the tacit approval of law enforcement and elected officials. To end the corruption, laws loosened starting in the 1970s, with repeated and unsuccessful efforts to adopt some form of casinos. Voters at last permitted limited stakes casino gaming in three communities—Black Hawk, Central City, and Cripple Creek—in 1990. The amendment earmarked a portion of the proceeds to create the State Historical Fund, which has provided millions of dollars for preservation projects. Since the early 1990s, many Colorado structures and landscapes have benefited from a more reliable source of funding than most other states enjoy, promoting historic preservation statewide. The law also enabled Utes in southwestern Colorado to build their own casinos in the 1990s.

Small casinos opened to great fanfare in restored buildings in the three towns in October 1991. "Big Dave" Mura, standing over 7 feet tall and dressed in buckskins, fired a shot down Cripple Creek's main street to signal the start of legal gambling. Crowds packed Black Hawk and Central City as well. Some visitors expressed disappointment at the small scale of Colorado's casinos, however, including a Californian who thought "they've done a nice job of saving the history here and it's a very charming place, but it seems a bit quiet" in comparison to casinos in Nevada and New Jersey. Casinos have since grown in number and size, transforming Gilpin County's towns in particular. A skyscraper over thirty stories tall looms over Black Hawk, and Central City built its own parkway to provide direct access from Interstate 70. While Coloradans debate the impact of casino gambling, the new boom continues in the old towns.

Silver's Last Boomtown

Prospectors Nicholas C. Creede and Charles F. Nelson, clambering down a hillside in what is now Mineral County on October 2, 1889, located their third and

A street scene in the silver mining town of Creede, high in the San Juan Mountains, in the boom days of the early 1890s

final vein of silver in the area for the year. Their lucrative discoveries inspired Colorado's last great silver rush.

Miners had scoured the San Juan Mountains for valuable minerals since the early 1870s. The upper reaches of the Rio Grande proved disappointing until Creede, Nelson, and others found silver deposits in 1889 and 1890. Nelson recalled that "we were high up on the mountains, in the midst of the most beautiful scenery in Colorado . . . that would send a Bierstadt or a Moran into an ecstasy of artistic delight." Their timing proved excellent—the US Congress adopted bimetallism via the Sherman Silver Purchase Act in 1890 and guaranteed an inflated market for the mineral. By the spring of 1891, a town named for Creede had expanded to a city of 1,200 residents. Investment poured in from sources like banker David H. Moffat and US senators Thomas M. Bowen and Edward O. Wolcott. When the Denver & Rio Grande Railroad (D&RG) balked at extending a line to Creede, Moffat paid for the work himself. Completed by the end of 1891, he sold the line a few months later to the D&RG. In 1893 the General Assembly organized the region into Mineral County, and Creede hijacked its seat from a nearby hamlet by the year's end.

Prosperity in Creede proved short-lived. When the federal government abandoned bimetallism during the Panic of 1893, most of the new silver mines slashed their workforce or closed completely. The community limped through the early twentieth century but perked up with a new mining boom in the mid-1900s and through tourism. Yet it never quite recaptured the heady atmosphere described

October

290

by poet Cy Warman in 1892: "It's day all day in the daytime, and there is no night in Creede." Nonetheless, Mineral County's name recalls the late nineteenth-century glory days when silver glinted brighter there than anywhere else in Colorado.

Honoring the Best Dam Politician

President Jimmy Carter signed legislation on October 3, 1980, to declare three reservoirs on the Gunnison River the Wayne N. Aspinall Storage Unit of the Colorado River Storage Project (CRSP). By naming the manipulated stretch of waterway in honor of the former congressman, the federal government recognized Aspinall's far-reaching impact.

Born in Ohio in 1896, Aspinall and his family moved to Colorado eight years later, first to Wray in Yuma County and then to Palisade in Mesa County. In 1914, Aspinall enrolled at the University of Denver (DU). After a stint in the US Army during World War I, he graduated and returned to Palisade as a teacher with his wife, Julia. Aspinall reenrolled at DU to earn a law degree in 1925 and established a practice on the western slope. With the support of Grand Junction newspaper editor and Democratic kingmaker Walter Walker, the conservative Aspinall won election to the General Assembly in 1930. The legislator earned prominence as an advocate of water reclamation projects and served in leadership positions in both chambers.

Aspinall won the western slope's seat in the US House of Representatives in 1948. He called for re-plumbing the West's rivers for irrigated farms, hydroelectric power, flood control, and tourism. Opponents quipped, "He never met a dam he didn't like." In the 1950s, Aspinall clashed with environmentalists over the Echo Park Dam, which would have inundated much of Dinosaur National Monument. Although that part of the Colorado River Storage Project never came to pass, he secured many other dams, including those later named in his honor. Aspinall also touted the Fryingpan-Arkansas Project to divert water for southeastern Colorado farmers.

Although Aspinall supported some conservation measures, battles with environmentalists and the liberal turn of the Democratic Party led to his political downfall. Upon Aspinall's death in 1983, a decade after he left Congress, liberal Democrat and critic Governor Richard Lamm conceded, "You can't take a drink of water in Colorado without thinking of Wayne Aspinall."

Reinventing Sixteenth Street

An estimated 200,000 people—roughly 40 percent of Denver's population—thronged Sixteenth Street at lunchtime on October 4, 1982, to celebrate the transformation of the former commercial hub of the city and, it was hoped, the revitalization of a decaying downtown.

In the early twentieth century, Sixteenth Street represented the commercial heart of the capital. Shoppers strolled through locally owned department stores including Daniels and Fisher, Denver Dry Goods, the Golden Eagle, Joslin's, the May Company, and Neusteters. By the mid-century, sprawl lured customers to multi-store facilities that catered to automobiles, such as the Cherry Creek Shopping Center. One of the nation's first malls, it was designed by Temple H. Buell and completed in 1955. Meanwhile, the downtown icons merged, franchised to suburban malls, or closed. Meanwhile, urban renewal—a euphemism for demolishing historic structures to create parking lots—destroyed much of Denver's architectural legacy. Only through the work of dedicated preservationists like Dana Crawford, who in 1963 coordinated the rescue of a block of Larimer Street to make Larimer Square, did any of the city's physical heritage survive.

Politicians and developers in the 1970s proposed reinventing Sixteenth Street as a pedestrian mall. In 1980 the street closed to traffic, replacing asphalt with granite paving stones that resembled a snakeskin from above, along with flowering planters and distinctive lighting. The Regional Transportation District offered a free shuttle and anchored each end of the mall with a bus terminal to serve the metropolitan area's northern and southern halves.

The October 1982 ceremony offered a much-needed moment of joy after the oil shale bust earlier that year. The dedication took place at the Daniels and Fisher clock tower, an iconic shard of the store that had survived the wrecking ball. The Sixteenth Street Mall offered the hope of real urban renewal. It remains a gathering place for shoppers, diners, buskers, tourists, and more and helped fuel a reawakening of interest in and affection for downtown Denver.

Rescuing Soldiers at Milk Creek

A bugle call pierced the pre-dawn sky along Milk Creek in today's Rio Blanco County on October 5, 1879. It was a welcome signal to a party of besieged soldiers that help had arrived.

Nathan C. Meeker, head of the White River Agency on the Ute reservation since 1878, infuriated his charges through his attitude and actions. In September 1879, a nervous Meeker requested support from the US Army. Lieutenant General William T. Sherman ordered to the agency Major Thomas T. Thornburgh, commander of Fort Fred Steele on the Union Pacific Railroad line in Wyoming Territory. Thornburgh departed with over 200 troops and civilians on September 21. Six days later in today's Moffat County, he conferred with Colorow, a prominent Yamparika Ute. Thornburgh promised not to cross Milk Creek, the reserve's unofficial northern boundary. Colorow returned to the agency to confer with Nicaagat, another leading Yamparika.

Thornburgh's command arrived at Milk Creek on September 29, and he chose to proceed to the White River in search of sufficient forage. Colorow and Nicaagat perceived his actions as an attack, and a battle ensued. Thornburgh and a dozen Americans died, in addition to nearly 40 Utes, during the conflict that lasted for seven days. In the meantime, Utes struck the agency as well, killing Meeker and 10 other men. A party of 45 African American cavalry soldiers on patrol from Fort Lewis, in southwestern Colorado, arrived on October 2 and bolstered the besieged troops. When Colonel Wesley Merritt's command of more than 250 troops arrived at dawn three days later, the Utes dispersed. Merritt tended to the wounded and buried the dead and discovered the "Meeker Massacre" upon his arrival at the White River Agency on October 11. Eleven soldiers later received the Medal of Honor for valor during the conflict at Milk Creek.

Although the events of 1879 led to Ute removal from most of western Colorado, Colorow returned with hunting parties from a Utah Territory reservation through the 1880s. To interpret the site, the Rio Blanco County Historical Society dedicated Milk Creek Battlefield Park in 2015.

October 6, 1838

The End of Fort Jackson

For entrepreneurs in the early nineteenth-century West, one industry offered greater profits and more bitter competition than any other, as it had for centuries in North America—the fur trade. One of the trade's casualties, Fort Jackson, met its end on October 6, 1838, when its largest competitor bought it out, removed its goods, and closed it down.

Most early American fur companies focused on the upper Missouri River valley, with easy access from St. Louis. The American Fur Company (AFC), founded in 1808 by John Jacob Astor, proved one of the most successful. By the 1830s it boasted a large trading post, Fort Laramie, on the North Platte River in present-day Wyoming. Trade in beaver and bison pelts also took place farther south on the eastern slope of modern Colorado, dominated by Bent, St. Vrain & Company (BSV&C). Challengers to the BSV&C's Bent's Fort on the Arkansas River opened small posts along the South Platte River in today's Weld County, including Forts Vasquez and Lupton. In response, BSV&C opened Fort St. Vrain nearby in 1837. To stop infringement on its trading territory to the north, that spring the AFC established a small adobe outpost amid the other three. The company named it Fort Jackson after the recently retired President Andrew Jackson.

Forts Jackson and St. Vrain offered each other a greater challenge than the smaller posts, as both possessed greater capital and access to quality goods. Merchants based at Fort Jackson sought out American Indian camps on the high plains, hoping to do business with them before they could reach the BSV&C posts. Eager to protect his firm, William Bent purchased Fort Jackson from the AFC in the fall of 1838. It was a practical decision for the AFC, considering the declining beaver trade and cost of competition. On October 6, Bent's employees stripped the post of its trade goods and useful materials and transferred them to nearby Fort St. Vrain.

In contrast to its three neighbors, scholars dispute the location of Fort Jackson, although historian LeRoy R. Hafen claimed to locate its ruins near the small town of Ione in the 1920s.

October 7, 1863

Treaty Making in the San Luis Valley

Prominent Utes—including Ouray of the Tabeguache and Colorow of the Yamparika—signed a treaty in Conejos County on October 7, 1863, one that intended to prevent conflict before it started by renouncing Ute claims to Colorado Territory east of the Continental Divide.

More than a half dozen Ute factions dominated much of modern Colorado in the eighteenth and early nineteenth centuries. They traded with the Spanish and Mexican settlers in New Mexico but retained their autonomy and resisted when the influence of outsiders grew onerous. Hispano settlement on Mexican land grants in the 1850s fueled the tension, as the newcomers occupied Ute hunting territory in the San Luis Valley. The Pikes Peak gold rush further complicated the situation. To some Utes, the notion of ceding their easternmost claims to protect the Rocky Mountains' western slope seemed sensible. In early October 1863, rancher Lafayette Head hosted a parley at his spread in Conejos, one of the controversial communities in the valley. A prominent figure in political and economic circles, Head had earned the respect of Anglos and Hispanos alike. He built relationships with American Indian groups as well, serving as a federal agent negotiating with Apache bands and, since 1860, the Tabeguache Utes.

Governor John Evans attended the event, as did Colonel John M. Chivington, commander of Colorado's armed forces, and Lieutenant Colonel Samuel F. Tappan, in charge of nearby Fort Garland. The deal struck on October 7 ceded Ute claims east of the divide and in Middle Park and promised supplies and livestock as compensation. It also presaged the vital role Ouray came to play as the most compromising Ute. The lack of attendance by most Ute bands limited the treaty's effect, however. Although the Civil War distracted federal officials from carrying it out, the 1863 agreement survived in theory if not law. Five years later a more comprehensive treaty formalized the 1863 deal and heralded the beginning of the end of Ute autonomy in Colorado.

October 8, 1991

Schroeder Speaks against Harassment

Patricia Schroeder, a longtime member of Congress from Denver, rallied fellow elected women to demand an investigation of sexual harassment charges against Clarence Thomas, President George H.W. Bush's nominee to the US Supreme Court, on October 8, 1991.

Schroeder and her husband, Jim, came to Colorado in the mid-1960s after law school. She practiced and taught at the University of Colorado and Regis College. A Democrat, Schroeder reflected the party's transition in Colorado, as young liberals supplanted aging conservatives. Her fellow partisans nominated her to run for Denver's congressional seat in 1972, the first woman in Colorado history to seek such an office. Schroeder's victory that November was the first of twelve wins for the first district seat, which she held for just shy of a quarter century.

Schroeder made waves in the US Congress as a new member challenging party hierarchies and institutional practices and as a rare voice speaking out on behalf of women's issues, including the right to have an abortion. She faced dismissive treatment and sexual harassment from colleagues but earned fame for her verbal barbs. Schroeder nicknamed Ronald Reagan—whose military spending she opposed—the "Teflon president" for his ability to dodge responsibility for controversial matters. In opposing the Vietnam War and supporting nuclear disarmament, Schroeder clashed with more hawkish politicians. She challenged conservatives who touted family values but opposed her proposals to establish paid family leave.

Her protest in 1991 represented one of many dramatic public statements in favor of sex and gender equality. Schroeder supported fellow Coloradan Gary Hart's pursuit of the 1988 Democratic presidential nomination, and after he withdrew she briefly considered running for the office herself.

One of Colorado's most prominent liberal voices and successful politicians, Schroeder left Congress after twelve terms. In 1997, another long-serving Democratic woman from Denver, Diana DeGette, succeeded her. The Schroeders moved to Florida after her retirement.

October 9, 1992

From Weapons to Wildlife

When President George H.W. Bush signed legislation creating the Rocky Mountain Arsenal National Wildlife Refuge in Adams County on October 9, 1992, he declared: "The very idea of converting the Rocky Mountain Arsenal into a national wildlife refuge would have been inconceivable a few years ago. Our success in doing so demonstrates that, when we focus on opportunities rather than problems, we can match the resilience of nature with human ingenuity."

World War I demonstrated the horrors of chemical weapons, and the fear that enemies might use them in World War II inspired the federal government to produce its own stockpile. In May 1942, officials selected 28 square miles—farmland confiscated from 200 families for the project—northeast of downtown Denver as a chemical fabrication site. By the end of the year the Rocky Mountain Arsenal stood operational. It produced mustard and chlorine gases during the war, and afterward the federal government leased space at the arsenal to private companies for experimentation and construction. For four decades the arsenal produced sarin and napalm gases, among many other deadly chemicals, and bombs to deliver them. It also endangered its neighbors by burning or evaporating chemicals and pumping toxic waste thousands of feet under the city, which caused the "Denver series" of earthquakes in the 1960s. Popular outcry, legal battles, and treaties banning the use of chemical weapons led to the end of production in 1982.

As the Cold War ended, the arsenal found a new purpose. The discovery of nesting bald eagles in 1986 initially inspired panic; one biologist remembered thinking "'oh, my God, we've got an endangered species on a Superfund site.' I thought we would have to chase them away." Congresswoman Patricia Schroeder lobbied for the wildlife refuge, noting that the vast tract buffered the most toxic areas from outsiders and attracted diverse animals and birds. Although some parts of the refuge will remain forever sealed to contain their toxins, the arsenal offers an urban haven for lovers of eagles, hawks, deer, bison, coyotes, prairie dogs, badgers, and more.

First Run of the Rio Grande Southern

The San Juan Mountains of southwestern Colorado are some of the most rugged, snowiest, intimidating peaks of the Rockies. After trespassing miners forced the Utes to surrender the region in 1873, Otto Mears constructed 300 miles of toll roads through the mountains to link burgeoning communities. Moving with the times, on October 10, 1890, the iron horse replaced real horses on his toll road from Ridgway in Ouray County to Placerville in San Miguel County when the first scheduled train ran on the Rio Grande Southern Railroad (RGS).

In the 1880s the Denver & Rio Grande Railroad (D&RG) served the north, east, and south flanks of the San Juans, but the western reaches were inaccessible. Mears thus employed 1,500 men to turn his route over Dallas Divide into a railroad grade. The RGS operated from Ridgway on the D&RG to Placerville by October 1890 and reached Telluride on December 1. From there, crews built a serpentine route called the Ophir Loop to climb up toward Lizard Head Pass and served Rico in Dolores County by September 1891. In the meantime, laborers building from the D&RG at Durango worked west to Dolores and curved back into the mountains. The lines met 11 miles southwest of Rico in Montezuma County on December 17, 1891.

The Panic of 1893 hit shortly after the RGS commenced operation. The line lost much of its business but endured nonetheless. During the Great Depression it introduced the Galloping Geese, a cost-efficient bus-truck-locomotive hybrid known for its awkward waddle down the tracks. Over the years the line transported precious metals, cattle, and even radioactive ore mined in the San Miguel River valley. The RGS went out of business in 1951, supplanted by automobiles, and the Geese dismantled the tracks they once used. Six original, restored Geese survive—three at the Colorado Railroad Museum in Golden, one each on display in Dolores and Telluride, and one that serves tourists at Knott's Berry Farm in California. In a state rife with railroad history, the RGS and especially the Galloping Geese offer a remarkable chapter.

Finding Fossils at Florissant

Arthur C. Peale, a geologist employed by Ferdinand V. Hayden's epic western surveys, gathered specimens of ancient plant fossils from a prehistoric lakebed in present-day Teller County on October 11, 1873. His modest collection and

Tourists from a Colorado Midland Railway excursion perch atop a petrified redwood tree stump at Florissant in 1900.

descriptions of several dozen petrified tree stumps offered the first evidence of the treasures known as the Florissant fossil beds.

Described as a prehistoric Pompeii, Florissant owes its existence to a volcano that erupted about 34 million years ago. Ash from an eruption in what is now Park County buried a lush landscape, preserving it for scholars and treasure seekers alike. Within forty years of Peale's visit, scientists gathered more than 30,000 insect fossils of more than a thousand species, as well as thousands of fish, birds, small mammals, and so many fossilized plants that the Smithsonian Institution could not count them all in their collections. The wonders brought looters as well—the Colorado Midland Railway sponsored fossil-collecting excursions, with countless scientific wonders destroyed or lost. Walt Disney came to Florissant in 1956 to buy a redwood stump as an anniversary present for his wife, Lillian, and it remains on display at Disneyland in California.

By the 1960s, development threatened to obliterate much of the site. Land-owners who owned the fossil area supported protection of Florissant, but others coveted the beautiful region for mountain homes. Scientists and environmental activists such as Estella B. Leopold, daughter of conservationist Aldo Leopold, joined forces with Coloradans including Denver lawyer and legislator Richard

Lamm. Along with Florissant residents, they created an advocacy group to lobby the federal government and gave tours of the area to members of the US Congress. Preservation of the site enjoyed bipartisan support among Colorado's delegation, and President Richard M. Nixon signed a bill establishing Florissant Fossil Beds National Monument in 1969. The site remains a biological marvel and high country oasis for visitors of all kinds.

October 12, 1972

Denver's Schools before the Bench

Oral arguments took place at the US Supreme Court in Washington, DC, on October 12, 1972, in a case with wide-ranging implications for race relations and public education, as Denver's school board stood accused of orchestrating an unofficial system of segregation.

The high court declared state-sponsored school segregation unconstitutional in 1954, and the bitter and lengthy process of diversifying public education commenced. For students in predominantly African American and Latino neighborhoods in northeast Denver, frustrations felt in the Deep South echoed in Colorado. In 1969, advocates for ethnic equality filed a lawsuit claiming that Denver officials had drawn school attendance boundaries to concentrate minority students and assigned most white teachers to other schools. As a result, school segregation existed in the city. A federal court found that the district purposely assigned African Americans and Latinos to seven poorly equipped schools and that another twenty-five schools demonstrated de facto segregation as a result of other policies. The case worked its way through the judicial system to Washington, DC, when attorneys argued both sides at the Supreme Court in October 1972.

The following summer, justices ruled 7 to 1 in *Keyes v. School District No. 1, Denver, Colorado*; Justice Byron R. White, a Colorado native, sat out the case. The justices found intent to isolate minority students and demanded a more equitable distribution of pupils and resources. *Keyes* struck a blow against segregation by practice rather than law, in contrast to other decisions that had invalidated statutes. It demonstrated the obstacles Latinos and African Americans faced in the United States and expanded the scope of civil rights reform nationwide. Denver used busing to diversify by spreading out the school population, a process that had started in 1969 and expanded after *Keyes*. That controversial policy ended in the 1990s, when federal courts ruled that African Americans and Latinos possessed enough influence to secure adequate facilities and resources, even though many schools remained mired in de facto segregation.

Laying the Line to Pagosa Springs

Many early Colorado towns longed for a railroad connection to the wider world. The benefits of passenger and freight service often represented a make-or-break prospect. Pagosa Springs, named for thermal waters nearby, offered an example of this steel salvation when the Rio Grande, Pagosa & Northern Railroad (RGP&N) laid tracks into the town on October 13, 1900.

The timber industry inspired this spur off the Denver & Rio Grande Railroad (D&RG) between Chama, New Mexico, and Durango. Pine and aspen trees could benefit not only the local community but, with a rail connection, the wider region. Construction started in the fall of 1899 from the D&RG line at Pagosa Junction, about 30 miles down the San Juan River from Pagosa Springs. Grading and track laying proceeded for the next year through rugged mountain country along the river. In August 1900, as the line neared completion, a newspaper reported on the excitement: "It will be time to celebrate, for a railroad means a great deal to this place. Pagosa will soon be in the swim." When the new line reached the seat of Archuleta County that fall, it benefited the scattered timber camps in the region and led to the construction of new lumber mills as well, with easier access to markets, supplies, and workers.

For years, rumors swirled about extending the RGP&N line over Wolf Creek Pass and linking it with the D&RG at Del Norte. One newspaper suggested that the idea "will give the Rio Grande another Glenwood, as the curative properties of the waters are well known and have been the basis of an Indian tradition for hundreds of years." Keeping a railroad clear over one of the snowiest passes in the state proved an insurmountable challenge, however, and Pagosa Springs remained an end-of-track town. In 1906, the D&RG acquired the RGP&N and operated it for thirty years, until the Great Depression forced the line's abandonment. Eventually, the tracks came up and automobile traffic replaced the absent railroad line into Pagosa Springs.

A Marvel of Highway Engineering

Governor Roy Romer cut a ribbon inside the Hidden Lake Tunnel in Garfield County on October 14, 1992, marking the completion of Interstate 70 in Colorado. Romer compared Glenwood Canyon's highway design to the skills of the Aztec empire, while federal officials declared it "the most difficult project in the inter-state system" and "a capstone achievement for the United States," as the nation's road plans approved in the 1950s came to fruition at last.

After World War II, engineers advocated controlled-access highways to manage traffic and promote city development and expansion. Federal officials approved a network of roads without intersections in 1956. In Colorado, plans included a route paralleling the eastern slope of the Rocky Mountains, one extending from Denver out to Kansas, and a link down the South Platte River to a transcontinental highway across Nebraska. The first segment, just over 11 miles between 48th and Evans Avenues in Denver, was named the Valley Highway for its route along the South Platte. It sliced through the capital by 1958. Similar routes through Colorado Springs and Pueblo were completed by 1960, and work through the next decade linked them to create Interstate 25. Interstate 80–South, completed in 1970, was renamed Interstate 76 in 1976 in recognition of the nation's bicentennial and Colorado's centennial.

Federal planners intended I-70 to end at Denver, but resentful Coloradans lobbied President Dwight D. Eisenhower, a frequent visitor, to intervene and order I-70's extension. Business groups like Club 20 lobbied for an innovative tiered design in Glenwood Canyon, while environmentalists objected to irreparable damage to the landscape. Even the Colorado Historical Society helped negotiate, as it had done to protect the Georgetown Loop. The ceremony in October 1992 reflected this collaboration. One Aspen resident, who overcame his opposition to the project, remarked: "If I were the canyon, I'd be saying, 'I'm about 40 million years old today, and I'm cooking on all burners. I'm the proud owner of a new four-lane highway.'"

October 15, 1906

Making Tracks to Marble

A team of Japanese immigrant laborers commenced work on one of many short line railways in the Colorado high country on October 15, 1906, laying track from the coal mines of Placita up the Crystal River to a quarry town named for its pure white stone: Marble. This 10-mile-long route, the Crystal River & San Juan Railroad (CR&SJ), inspired boom times in Marble, as its gleaming product found use in projects across the state, the country, and the world.

A geologist located the vast marble deposits in 1873, but the source remained undisturbed until after Americans forced the Utes to surrender most of western Colorado by the decade's end. Interest in the stone grew in the 1880s, but a lack of transportation made development difficult. The quarry along Yule Creek received its first major project in 1895 when state officials chose it to supply flooring stone for the capitol. The rock's quality and abundance earned praise, but it proved difficult to extract and move. Without adequate transportation, marble from other states and even Europe was cheaper on the American market. Construction of the CR&SJ—nicknamed the Can't Run and Seldom Jumps—removed Marble's greatest obstacle.

Marble's heyday came in the early twentieth century as the City Beautiful movement swept the nation. Governments of every kind replaced old, crumbling structures with massive new edifices, and Colorado's marble offered the perfect stone for grand architectural vision. Hundreds of buildings and monuments used the Yule Creek rock, most notably the Lincoln Memorial in Washington, DC, the largest marble project in American history. It also provided the massive capstone for the Tomb of the Unknown Soldier at Arlington National Cemetery.

During World War I, many of the skilled Italian immigrants who worked at Marble left to fight, and a postwar recession posed further challenges. Recovery in the 1920s proved short-lived, and the Great Depression sealed the town's fate. The quarry and railroad were abandoned in 1941. The stone works reopened in 1990 and supplies decorative and monument stone to a global market.

October 16, 1891

Colorado's First National Forest

Economic development in the Gilded Age created unprecedented profits, often at the expense of the country's natural resources. Forests in mining areas suffered extensive damage—clear-cutting wasted trees, destroyed animal habitats, and caused flooding and pollution. To slow this destruction, the US Congress passed the Forest Reserve Act in 1891, allowing presidents to designate national forests unilaterally. President Benjamin Harrison created Colorado's first and the country's second national forest in portions of Eagle, Garfield, Moffat, Rio Blanco, and Routt Counties on October 16, 1891, when he proclaimed the White River Plateau Timberland Reserve.

Support for such a designation had started two years earlier when Colorado's legislature memorialized the federal government to protect a relatively undisturbed portion of Rocky Mountain scenery. The White River reserve initially encompassed 1.1 million acres and promised to draw campers, fishers, hunters, and other tourists who might shun the denuded parts of Colorado's high country. One newspaper called the designation "a grand thing for Colorado, and in fact for the entire Union, as it will perpetuate various kinds of wild animals, and keep large tracts of timber from being destroyed; at the same time it will maintain a never-failing flow of water in the numerous streams which head in this reservation."

Forest reserves often proved contentious, as residents and politicians railed against federal interference in economic development. Contrary to fears at the time, the designation did not prevent timber harvesting, dam construction, or other activities but merely managed them to ensure the long-term health and utility of the region and resources. As one press stated, forests "are designed to promote, not to interfere with, Colorado's welfare." Expanded over the years to 2.3 million acres across eight counties, White River sees more visitors than any other national forest in the country. Beyond the myriad summer activities, thousands of tourists come every winter to play at snowbound resorts including Aspen, Beaver Creek, Snowmass, and Vail.

October 17, 1906

Turning Smelters into Scholars

A ceremony in Golden dedicated a new administration building made of stone, capped with a gold-domed cupola, at the Colorado School of Mines on October 17, 1906. It bore the name of Simon Guggenheim, a mining and smelter magnate who had donated $80,000 for the structure. The gesture reflected both his philanthropic spirit and a desire to boost his public image.

Guggenheim was the sixth son of Meyer Guggenheim, a Philadelphia textile importer who invested in two silver mines in Leadville in 1881. One struck a rich vein that August, and money poured out of the mountains. By the decade's end, Meyer Guggenheim funded a smelter in Pueblo to process his ore, and the fortune grew exponentially. The Guggenheims parlayed their wealth into a monopoly called the American Smelting and Refining Company. Simon Guggenheim traveled west to manage the family's investments and saw opportunities for his own advancement in Colorado. He unashamedly bribed state legislators in 1907 to secure a seat in the US Senate, where he served until 1913. His largesse continued, especially in academic architecture—buildings bearing his name also stand at the University of Colorado, Colorado State University, and the University of Northern Colorado. In later years he and his wife, Olga, established the Guggenheim Fellowships to support American cultural development.

The Colorado School of Mines, founded by the territorial legislature in 1874, promotes work in engineering and the sciences in a state that serves as the perfect laboratory for students. It remains an internationally renowned institution whose graduates seek to balance resource development with environmental sustainability, and Guggenheim Hall dominates as a campus icon visible across Golden. Its students and faculty challenge the declaration of one speaker at the building's dedication in 1906, who compared "men to ores, and admitted with regret that a majority of souls were of the low grade, refractory variety." The school of mines boasts one of the best reputations of any institution of higher education in Colorado.

October 18, 1988

Something Brewing in LoDo

Beer represents an essential aspect of Colorado's international reputation. In addition to the long-lived Coors, the historic Tivoli and Zang's, and other brands, an ever-increasing number of microbreweries sate the demand for ales and lagers. The Wynkoop Brewing Company, which opened its doors on October 18, 1988, set the stage for the fermented revolution.

Like many others, John W. Hickenlooper and Jerry and Martha Williams hoped to cash in on Colorado's oil shale boom in the late 1970s and early 1980s. Their dreams evaporated when the industry collapsed in 1982. With their severance pay as seed money, they raised nearly a million dollars to renovate a stone and brick warehouse in Denver's Lower Downtown (LoDo) district, then a run-down neighborhood. As Hickenlooper stated: "Old buildings and brewpubs are a great fit. Strong masonry walls, sturdy timbers, high ceilings, and structures saturated with history are perfect." Attempting such a venture in a long-neglected area seemed risky to many, but following its 1988 grand opening, the Wynkoop Brewing Company proved a success for its owners and the start of major change in LoDo. Other brewpubs and businesses opened in the area, which blossomed after Coors Field debuted in 1995. The economic renaissance combined modern tastes with historic preservation and rejuvenated LoDo, which in turn inspired similar restoration and new construction in many older Denver neighborhoods. The Wynkoop convinced investors that the past and present could combine to create a promising future.

Hickenlooper parlayed his success into politics, drawing on his reputation and folksy image to win election as Denver's mayor in 2003 and 2007. He captured the governor's office in 2010 and 2014 and took a run at the Democratic nomination for president leading up to the 2020 election, at times struggling to maintain his businessman's make-no-enemies demeanor. In the summer of 2014, he met a fellow Democrat, President Barack Obama, for a beer and a game of pool at the Wynkoop, inspiring a brewery director to declare that "a visit from the president and the governor is an exciting testament to the elevated status of craft beer in America."

Environmental Terrorism at Vail

Colorado's environmental consciousness increased steadily from the 1960s onward, as frenetic population growth cluttered the state's landscape and put ever greater pressure on its resources. Those individuals who feared the consequences of such development often turned to politics and peaceful protest, but some occasionally crossed the line of violence. When residents of Vail awoke to smoke rising from the ridge high above town on October 19, 1998, they saw firsthand the willingness of some environmental activists to fight with fire.

Although winter sports blossomed throughout the Rocky Mountains in the late twentieth century, few places enjoyed the international reputation of Vail. The Eagle County resort boasted ties to President Gerald R. Ford and his family, enjoyed easy access from Interstate 70, and flourished as an icon of the state's snowiest industry. In 1998, the resort planned an 885-acre expansion into White River National Forest, on land designated as part of Vail since its founding in the 1950s. The proposal earned the enmity of an international, decentralized movement known as the Earth Liberation Front (ELF) for its potential impact on lynx in the region. After setting up caches of gasoline, early on October 19, 1988, seven ELF supporters calling themselves "the Family" set three buildings and four chairlifts ablaze. No one was injured, and a structure housing two sleeping hunters was unharmed, but the fires caused an estimated $12 million in damages.

Later that day, media outlets received messages from "the Family" declaring: "Putting profits ahead of Colorado's wildlife will not be tolerated. This action is just a warning. We will be back if this greedy corporation continues to trespass into wild and unroaded areas." The Federal Bureau of Investigation labeled the crime "eco-terrorism" and pursued the perpetrators. Six members of "the Family" eventually went to prison; one remains at large. Vail Resort opened temporary structures amid the ruins by Christmas 1998, and construction continued in the new year. Inflicting destruction to resist destruction rarely offers a productive result.

Creating a Place of Peace

Juan Bautista de Anza, the Spanish governor of New Mexico, reported to his superiors on October 20, 1787, about a remarkable endeavor under way in present-day Colorado, a town built to bring together former enemies to live at a place of peace.

October

The community, named San Carlos de los Jupes, stood at the Arkansas-St. Charles Rivers junction in modern Pueblo County.

The Comanches, who exercised complete authority over the southern plains in the eighteenth century, found their power undermined by attacks from neighboring Kiowas and Pawnees, as well as by a food shortage. In the summer of 1787, the Jupe Comanche faction—numbering 2,000 and led by Paruanarimuca—appealed to Anza, whose victory over a Comanche band eight years earlier inspired this loss of status. Paruanarimuca hoped that a settlement could provide reliable food, and Anza saw the opportunity to entrench this newfound stability. The chosen site along the Arkansas River—known to native cultures as the Napestle—proved of interest to many groups. Although construction required lots of Spanish money and used primarily Spanish labor, Jupes, Apaches, Puebloans, and Utes participated as well. The town took the name San Carlos de los Jupes, in reference to the stream that joined the Arkansas there, as well as to Paruanarimuca's band, whose request made it possible. When Anza described the budding community in October 1787, he expressed well-earned pride and optimism.

This community offered remarkable potential as a site to overcome past hatreds, yet it lasted less than a year. In January 1788, Paruanarimuca's most favored wife died of an illness at San Carlos de los Jupes, and other Comanches interpreted her passing as a sign of danger. When they left, the other native and Spanish inhabitants had little reason to remain in a town so far removed from their own cultures. Abandoned by that spring, it quickly faded from memory. Within several decades, the Comanche presence shifted southward out of Colorado, as did the Apaches, and new groups from the north—like the Cheyennes and Arapahos—took their place.

October 21, 1999

A Promotion for the Black Canyon

President Bill Clinton re-designated a site in Montrose County as the Black Canyon of the Gunnison National Park on October 21, 1999, in recognition of "the unique combination of geologic and biologic features that make the canyon such an awe-inspiring place."

A deep, dark, intimidating gash in the earth, stretching over 50 miles through Gunnison, Montrose, and Delta Counties, the Black Canyon offers one of Colorado's most dramatic landscapes. Deep in the heart of Ute territory, the gorge remained unknown to outsiders until 1853, when Captain John W. Gunnison led a survey team through it in search of a route for a transcontinental railroad. Although

The Black Canyon of the Gunnison River, photographed by William W. Torrence in September 1900 during his harrowing journey through the gorge

his report dissuaded most builders, William J. Palmer tried to lay iron rails through the canyon in 1882. His Denver & Rio Grande Railroad worked west from Gunnison but eventually pulled out of a side canyon when the gorge grew too steep.

Farmers in the nearby Uncompahgre River valley saw the Gunnison River as an untapped resource and sought its water for their valley. Farmer John Pelton attempted to traverse the canyon with four companions in two wooden boats in 1900, hoping to locate a diversion tunnel site. After one craft wrecked, the party climbed out through a side canyon three weeks into their effort. One of the participants, William W. Torrence, tried again the following year with Abraham L. Fellows. Floating on rubber mattresses, Fellows and Torrence rode the rapids for ten deafening days but came out alive at the canyon's mouth. Drawing on their survey, the Bureau of Reclamation dug the Gunnison Tunnel under Vernal Mesa by the decade's end.

President Herbert Hoover designated part of the chasm as a national monument in 1932, and the Civilian Conservation Corps built tourist roads during the Great Depression. Clinton's signature in 1999 elevated the Black Canyon to a national park. It also established the Gunnison Gorge National Recreation Area downstream and authorized a study of the Curecanti National Recreation Area above the park, recognizing the region's popularity and potential.

October 22, 1976

The Nuggets Join the NBA

Two teams from the defunct American Basketball Association (ABA), the Indiana Pacers and the Denver Nuggets, met in Indiana on October 22, 1976. In their first game as members of the National Basketball Association (NBA), which remains the sport's largest organization, the Nuggets celebrated their new affiliation in fine style, defeating the Pacers by a score of 123 to 110.

The first Denver Nuggets team, also affiliated with the NBA, took its name from the Pikes Peak gold rush that inspired American settlement in present-day Colorado. They played in the late 1940s in Denver's Auditorium Arena, an annex to the City Auditorium, which now houses the Temple Buell Theatre in the Denver Center for the Performing Arts. The Nuggets disbanded after two losing seasons, and professional basketball remained absent from Colorado until the ABA debuted in 1967. The Denver Rockets premiered that fall in the league designed to compete for attention with the NBA. The new team took its name from owner Bill Ringsby, whose trucking fleet of Ringsby Rockets operated out of Colorado. It also reflected the state's role in the aerospace industry during the Cold War, building rockets for space vehicles and missiles. Renamed the Nuggets in 1974, the team moved to McNichols Arena the following year and performed ably even as the ABA faltered. They joined the NBA in the fall of 1976, starting with the game against the Pacers, a transition one *Denver Post* reporter considered "more like welcoming old times than saying hello to a new era in professional basketball."

Although the Nuggets have yet to win a national championship, they have secured several division championships. Star player Dan Issel, a member of the team during both its ABA and NBA days, returned as a head coach in the early 1990s, and the Nuggets eventually retired his number in tribute to his role. The Nuggets and the Colorado Avalanche hockey team moved to the Pepsi Center in 1999 and remain fixtures of the state's sports community, playing just steps away from where gold seekers scoured for nuggets of their own in the mid-nineteenth century.

October 23, 2004

Building a New Fort Lupton

A ceremony on October 23, 2004, marked the start of construction on a replica of Fort Lupton, a fur trading post near the town of the same name in southeastern Weld County.

While on a US Army expedition through present-day eastern Colorado in 1835, Lieutenant Lancaster P. Lupton marveled at the wealth of Bent, St. Vrain & Company's post on the Arkansas River. He determined to enter the lucrative fur trade himself and resigned his commission. In the fall of 1836, Lupton hired Hispano laborers to build an adobe structure on the model of Bent's Fort. Lupton's rectangular bastion stood on the east side of the South Platte River along the Trapper's Trail, a route between Taos, New Mexico, and Fort Laramie on the North Platte River in modern Wyoming. The new post took advantage of the lack of competition nearby, but its isolated location made re-supplying the fort a challenge. Nonetheless, Lupton did a bustling business, exchanging metal and glass goods, vegetables, and eggs with Cheyennes, Arapahos, Utes, and American trappers for beaver and bison pelts he sold in St. Louis.

Lupton's success inspired others, including trappers and fur companies that erected Forts Vasquez, Jackson, and St. Vrain within a few miles of Lupton's post. Lupton sold his business in 1844, and the post closed a year later as the fur trade waned. He moved to El Pueblo and opened a store, then farmed in present-day Fremont County before moving to California during the gold rush. The post fell into ruins, although it sheltered Pikes Peak gold seekers in the late 1850s. An agricultural town founded just south of the decaying fort in 1882 adopted its name.

A visit to Fort Lupton by a descendant of Lancaster P. Lupton in 1987 inspired talk of building a replica. The 2004 groundbreaking ceremony consisted of speeches and an American Indian blessing. Completed in 2011 near the original site, the new Fort Lupton houses the South Platte Valley Historical Society, hosts annual fur trade commemorations, and offers visitors a glimpse at life in the profitable, competitive mid-nineteenth century in Weld County.

October 24, 1859

The Government That Never Was

An election took place in the westernmost reaches of Kansas and Nebraska Territories on October 24, 1859, to select officers for a provisional Jefferson Territory. Designed to protect land and mining claims in the relatively ungoverned Pikes Peak gold rush region, Jefferson presaged the creation of Colorado. The extra-legal polity, unrecognized by any actual authority, also reflected the frustrated lengths to which disaffected, desperate Americans will go.

Prospecting in the late 1850s took place on the edges of Kansas and Nebraska Territories, and neither exercised much control over the miners. To fill the vacuum, meetings in Denver in 1859 created a constitution for a Jefferson Territory, named for the president whose Louisiana Purchase brought much of the region into American hands. The polity would exist only until the federal government—then distracted by sectional tensions over slavery's future—provided real organization. Jefferson claimed a vast swath of land including all of modern Colorado, slices of Kansas and Utah, almost half of Wyoming, and the Nebraska panhandle, although it existed scarcely beyond the imaginations of a few people in the mining districts. In the October 24 election, Robert W. Steele won the governor's office, and he convened a legislature two weeks later. The extra-legal body's inability to levy taxes, however, doomed the Jefferson experiment.

For a year and a half, supporters of Jefferson Territory used their imagined powers to insure property claims in the area. When Congress and President James Buchanan established Colorado Territory in February 1861, Jefferson's reason for being ended. More than a week after William Gilpin, appointed the first governor, arrived in Denver that May, Steele issued a proclamation ceding control to the recognized authority. He encouraged those who had served Jefferson to return "to their proper and legitimate avocations, whether agriculture or mining." Thus the bizarre existence of Jefferson Territory ended, with as much dignity as displayed by a group of youngsters who turn over their tree house to the person who owns the land on which it stands.

Denver Hosts the Reorganized Army

By the 1880s, American Indian autonomy had faded in the United States, broken by conquest and loss of territory. The US Army no longer needed as many forts. It consolidated scattered posts into large new ones near urban centers with rail links to move soldiers wherever they might need to go. To that end, Company A of the 18th US Infantry set up camp at a new fort site near the South Platte River 8 miles southwest of Denver on October 25, 1887.

Lieutenant General Philip Sheridan selected the site near Denver, and locals organized a town named Sheridan nearby in his honor. They referred to the post as Fort Sheridan, although that name went to a base near Chicago. Other proposed monikers included Fort McClellan, after Union General George B. McClellan, and Fort Denver. In 1889 it earned the name Fort Logan in honor of General John A. Logan. He had advocated a holiday to honor soldiers killed during the Civil War, now known as Memorial Day. Logan County in northeastern Colorado also bears the officer's name. Troops from Fort Logan headed to South Dakota after the Wounded Knee Massacre in 1890 and kept the peace during strikes and Denver's "City Hall War" in 1894. The demand for troops dropped by the century's end, and in 1909 the fort became a recruitment depot for citizens interested in joining the military. The post remained in operation during World War I and World War II as a training center, with a population of over 5,000 during the latter conflict, but by that time Fort Logan had served its purpose as an active installation.

Fort Logan operated as a veterans' hospital after World War II, and the post burial ground became a national cemetery in 1950. Later that decade, Governor Steve McNichols negotiated with the federal government to turn the fort into a state mental health hospital, which opened in 1961. Additional facilities designed by Temple H. Buell opened within a few years, and one of the officers' quarters became a museum. Fort Logan proved more functional than famous over the years, but its name still evokes an image of useful respectability.

False Start for Animas–La Plata

Western settlement often depends on harnessing scarce water resources, an expensive and complicated prospect. One of the best examples stands in La Plata and Montezuma Counties, where the Animas–La Plata Project (A-LP) veered between construction and litigation starting in the 1960s. Its groundbreaking ceremony, held near Durango on October 26, 1991, culminated decades of work but also proved premature, as lawsuits and legislation reshaped the project.

After years of discussion at the local and national levels, the US Congress authorized A-LP for southwestern Colorado and northwestern New Mexico in 1968. Planning and environmental studies continued for more than two decades. Residents of the nearby Southern Ute and Ute Mountain Ute Reservations lobbied for access to the A-LP's water as well, securing rights promised them at the beginning of the twentieth century. Not until 1991 did federal officials finalize the background work, allowing for groundbreaking that October. Environmental groups sued to halt the project in 1992, however, and it languished in the courts. Another round of reports followed, and finally, in 2002, construction resumed on two reservoirs and pumps and canals to divert water between the Animas and La Plata Rivers. Work finished on the then-largest earthen dam in the world south of Durango in 2008. The filling of Lake Nighthorse—named for Colorado's US senator Ben Nighthorse Campbell, whose advocacy in Congress got A-LP moving again—commenced, and the reservoir filled for the first time in the summer of 2011.

Various issues continued to delay A-LP's completion, including the reservoir's proximity to uranium tailings from Durango's Cold War–era mill, the logistics of pumping water to tribal communities, and determining how to provide recreational access to Lake Nighthorse. The ongoing work and controversy reflect the scope of water projects and the challenges inherent in balancing myriad concerns as diverse groups seek to advocate their interests over the precious resource.

October 27, 1972

Michener Honored at UNC

A thousand people gathered on the University of Northern Colorado (UNC) campus in Greeley on October 27, 1972, to dedicate a new library building to arguably the most famous person ever to serve on the school's faculty—internationally renowned author James A. Michener.

In 1936, Michener accepted an invitation to join the faculty at Greeley's teacher training school against the advice of a professor: "Don't accept the job, Michener. The sands of the desert are white with the bones of promising young men who went West and perished trying to get back East." The literary-minded man afflicted with wanderlust paid no heed, although he left Greeley in 1941 to serve in the US Navy during World War II. Michener's experiences inspired his first book, *Tales of the South Pacific*, in 1947, which won the Pulitzer Prize for fiction. His affection for writing carried him around the world, studying regions in depth and then writing stories of generations who lived in a specific, exhaustively portrayed place.

When UNC named its library for Michener in 1972, he was living in Colorado compiling information for perhaps his best-known work, *Centennial*, published two years later. It offers a fictionalized account of life along the South Platte River from prehistoric times through the 1970s. *Centennial* portrays many elements vital to the region's story, albeit with altered names, including the fur trading firm Bent, St. Vrain & Company, the Sand Creek Massacre, cattleman John W. Iliff, conflict between cattle and sheep ranchers, and the Great Western Sugar Company. Michener even alluded to the state's contemporary environmental challenges: "Pretty soon, if you want to see the unspoiled grandeur of Colorado you'll have to go to Wyoming."

The UNC library, which displays a bust of its namesake, stands as the perfect tribute, as Michener himself declared in 1989: "My life has been affiliated with libraries. I couldn't live without them, and for me to think that on the campus where I worked so diligently a noble library will commemorate those years when I grew up intellectually is delightful."

October 28, 1925

The Great Rattlesnake Massacre

Katherine M. Slaughterback lived up to her intimidating last name—and earned the nickname "Rattlesnake Kate"—when she defended herself and her young son from a bevy of rattlesnakes outside their small farmhouse near Ione in Weld County on October 28, 1925.

Slaughterback and her son, Ernie, arose early that morning to the sound of duck hunters, and she set out to see if they had left any of their quarry behind. Her horse, Brownie, proved skittish as she saddled him. Brownie continued to shy and snort as they approached the gate of their farm. When Slaughterback dismounted to open it, she noticed a rattlesnake near her feet, which explained Brownie's behavior. Her rifle made short work of the rattler, but she saw more snakes nearby and kept firing. After a few moments, Slaughterback realized that the farmyard was covered with rattlesnakes, likely heading to a nearby prairie dog colony to hole up for the winter. When she ran out of ammunition, she grabbed a sign post and fended off the slitherers by hand. Slaughterback battered away at the threatening critters for more than two hours, by which time her hands were raw and bloodied from the ordeal. All the while, three-year-old Ernie wailed from Brownie's back, terrified for his mother and himself.

After they returned safely to the house, the pair took a much-needed nap. Slaughterback went back out later that day to collect her kill, totaling 140 rattle-snakes. She harvested the meat, which proved just as welcome to their stomachs as the ducks she set out to find that morning, and debated what to do with the skins. Ultimately, Slaughterback made a dress, the envy of flappers everywhere, from her trophies. The story of "Rattlesnake Kate" spread nationwide, and she appeared at many social events in her snakeskin finery. Before her death in 1969 at age seventy-six, Slaughterback donated her dress and other souvenirs to Greeley's historical society. The dress and her small, restored farmhouse now occupy a place of honor at Greeley's Centennial Village museum, memorials to an uncommonly brave woman.

October 29, 1860

Catholicism Comes to Cherry Creek

Priests Joseph P. Machebeuf and John B. Raverdy arrived in Denver on October 29, 1860, assigned to tend to Catholics during the Pikes Peak gold rush. They set to work erecting a church building that stood ready to receive parishioners for Christmas services that year.

The first non–American Indian faith practiced in present-day Colorado, Catholicism came to the region via Spanish explorers as early as the seventeenth century. Its permanent presence commenced in the 1850s, with services for Hispano settlements in the San Luis Valley led by Santa Fe–based priests. Gold rush settlements rested primarily within the boundaries of Kansas Territory's diocese, but visits by priests from across the plains in the summer of 1860 demonstrated the difficulties of serving the community. The diocese in New Mexico Territory proved closer and better equipped to provide for Catholics in the region, and Bishop Jean-Baptiste Lamy sent Machebeuf and Raverdy north to tend the flock. Machebeuf led services, organized schools, and erected houses of worship across Colorado until his death in 1889. Historian Wilbur Fisk Stone said that Machebeuf was "responsible for the establishment of the denomination in its strength in practically every locality in the state, and his efforts and kindly work have made a glorious chapter in the religious history of the Columbine State."

Catholicism represented the state's single largest denomination by the early twentieth century. Its adherents have included Governors Steve McNichols, Bill

Owens, and Bill Ritter; astronaut John "Jack" Swigert; Horace and Elizabeth "Baby Doe" Tabor; and the unsinkable Margaret Brown. Colorado Catholics demonstrated their faith through architecture as well. Miller John K. Mullen earned such a fortune from flour that he paid for a library at the Catholic University of America in Washington, DC. Denver's Cathedral of the Immaculate Conception, completed in 1911, hosted services led by Pope John Paul II in 1993. Its neo-Gothic design reflects the inspiration that Colorado Catholics take from the building and their faith alike.

October 30, 2010 and 2019

Studying Ancient Colorado Critters

Colorado has been at the forefront of paleontology since the late nineteenth century and continues to illuminate our global story in diverse, exciting, pioneering ways. Two October 30ths in the bookend years of the 2010s have gone a long way to enlighten Coloradans and the world at large about the ancient animals that once called our state and our planet home.

Hundreds of residents of Pitkin County came to the Snowmass Water and Sanitation District office on October 30, 2010, to view artifacts recently extracted from a nearby construction site. A few weeks earlier, crews expanding Ziegler Reservoir near Snowmass Village had exposed the bones of a juvenile mastodon, an ancient pachyderm. The Denver Museum of Nature & Science (DMNS) sent scientists to Pitkin County to study the remains and determine what additional discoveries might await them at the "Snowmastodon" site. Within a few months, scholars extracted nearly 5,000 fossils from twenty-six species, including mastodons and mammoths, camels, horses, bison, and a ground sloth. The animals had inhabited the shore of a glacial lake high in the Rocky Mountains approximately 100,000 years ago, roughly the same time humans began migrating out of the African heartland where our species evolved.

Audiences watching a documentary that premiered on the Public Broadcasting Service on October 30, 2019, learned of another essential Colorado contribution to the understanding of life on Earth. Starting in 2016, paleontologists from the DMNS had conducted the very definition of groundbreaking work at Corral Bluffs Open Space in El Paso County, just east of Colorado Springs. Excavations there have offered scientists the greatest trove of early mammalian fossils ever discovered, dating from just after an asteroid impact annihilated the dinosaurs 66 million years ago. Paleontologist Tyler Lyson, one of the DMNS team leaders, declared: "Our understanding of the asteroid's aftermath has been spotty. These fossils tell us for the first time how exactly our planet recovered from this global cataclysm." Ongoing work at the Corral Bluffs site will help explain how mammals have endured and thrived globally ever since.

October 31, 1880

Race Riot in the Streets of Denver

Halloween calls to mind sweet treats and good-natured frights, but on October 31, 1880, the screams in Denver were real as a drunken mob attacked the city's Chinese population.

Immigrants and ethnic minorities have often inspired nativist suspicion and resentment among the general American population. Grumbles over Irish labor shifted to complaints about the Chinese after the Civil War. California politicians whipped up an anti-Chinese frenzy, warning of a future where cheap Chinese labor would push native-born Americans out of jobs.

Denver boasted a Chinese population of about 500 in 1880, clustered in the area now known as Lower Downtown. The simmering tension boiled over as a bar fight spilled into the dirt streets in the early afternoon of October 31. Firefighters tried to disperse the mob with water hoses, but the situation escaped the control of Mayor Richard Sopris. Beatings and looting spread, with surprising results. Some of the city's criminal figures defended their Chinese friends, and many houses of prostitution served as refuges for those fleeing the melee. Police officers fought back, and Governor Frederick W. Pitkin called in the state militia. The crowd beat a man named Look Young, who died of his injuries. Astonishingly, he was the only fatality.

Calm prevailed the following day, as many Chinese residents emerged from safe havens including hotels and the city jail. About 100 left the city, but the rest remained to rebuild their community. With a presidential election only days away, anti-Chinese Democrats cheered the riot, but the scene helped tip the scales toward the Republicans in the 1880 contest. Congress passed the Chinese Exclusion Act two years later nonetheless, with the support of sympathetic Republican senator Henry M. Teller: "The Caucasian race has a right, considering its superiority of intellectual force and mental vigor, to look down upon every other branch of the human family." The Denver riot exposed ethnic fractures within the city and state, demonstrating to the rest of the country that thriving, prosperous Colorado could be just as vicious as anyplace else.

Artist's depiction of a riot against Chinese immigrants in Denver, as portrayed in Frank Leslie's Illustrated Newspaper *on November 20, 1880*

November

FLORENCE RENA SABIN 1871-1953

Terrorism in the Colorado Sky

A starry sky blanketed sugar beet farms in Weld County on the evening of November 1, 1955. Suddenly, a streak of fire appeared, and pieces of metal, chairs, utensils, suitcases, and bodies rained down as Mainliner Denver—one of the jewels of the United Airlines fleet—plummeted to the ground, the victim of the first terrorist attack on an American airplane.

Colorado dominated that fall's headlines, especially as President Dwight D. Eisenhower recuperated at Fitzsimons Army Hospital after suffering a heart attack in September. The news took a darker turn after the explosion of Mainliner Denver five weeks later. The Weld County coroner identified the forty-four passengers and crew at a makeshift morgue in Greeley, and teams from the Federal Bureau of Investigation rebuilt the mangled airplane at Stapleton Airfield, from which the craft had departed on its way to Seattle. The investigation focused on passengers who had purchased flight insurance from kiosks at the airport before departure, a common practice of the era. Attention centered on one of the insured passengers, Daisie E. King, and her son, John G. "Jack" Graham, a man with a quick temper and a criminal record. King owned a Denver drive-in where Graham worked, and the two had had a fractious relationship since his childhood. Having driven his mother to Stapleton with his wife and children, Graham placed a bomb made of twenty-five sticks of dynamite in King's suitcase before she checked in. Eleven days after the crash, law enforcement declared Graham the culprit behind the airplane's destruction.

A trial in Denver's City and County Building in early 1956 drew large crowds. After deliberating for an hour, the jury returned a guilty verdict and a death penalty sentence. On January 11, 1957, Graham strode confidently from his cell to the gas chamber at the state penitentiary in Cañon City for his execution. In rejecting an appeal for clemency the previous October, the state supreme court declared, "Nowhere in the reports of criminal cases have we found a counterpart to this case, and we doubt if anything approaching it can be found in fiction."

Fighting the Flu in Silverton

The Spanish influenza, the deadliest epidemic disease in recorded history, beset the planet in 1918. Although the strain of flu originated in Kansas, it traveled the globe rapidly as World War I raged and earned its moniker after hitting Spain early and hard. No Colorado community, and perhaps no American town, suffered from the influenza more than Silverton, high in the San Juan Mountains. On November 2, 1918, as the epidemic built to a crescendo, the *Silverton Standard* tallied 128 deaths and perhaps as many as 600 additional cases reported, a toll roughly equal to half of the town's population. The press declared of the San Juan County seat, "In no city, town, or village has the epidemic of Spanish influenza proved more fatal."

Influenza first appeared in the state in September 1918 at the University of Colorado (CU), where military students contracted the disease. Doctors from Fort Logan and Washington, DC, attempted to contain the epidemic, to no avail. Health officials in Denver demanded that people in regular contact with others—clerks, deliverymen, grocers, and so on—wear surgical masks to limit the contagion. Customers shied away from stores, which hesitated to put on sales for fear of spreading disease. Some colleges, including Colorado A&M in Fort Collins and the School of Mines in Golden, quarantined their campuses and placed themselves under the control of the American Red Cross. Many public schools and even CU closed completely for a time. Governor Julius C. Gunter encouraged local governments to restrict public gatherings.

The disease raged statewide. Mountain towns with scant medical facilities—including Nederland, Rico, and Sargents—saw particularly high rates of disease. Forty people succumbed on the Southern Ute Reservation. Gunnison blockaded itself against the outside world, screening railroad passengers and forbidding automobile traffic through town, and thus managed to stave off the worst of the epidemic. Colorado lost 7,783 residents to influenza between the fall of 1918 and the summer of 1919 and tallied nearly 50,000 cases before the crisis abated.

November 3, 1872

Debunking the Diamond Hoax

A team of federal surveyors scoured the sage-covered hills of northwestern Colorado Territory on November 3, 1872, investigating rumors of a rich source of precious gems, rare in the United States. As they dug through ant hills and studied the specimens of diamonds and rubies spread across the landscape, the team declared the site an elaborate hoax.

The federal government authorized several studies of western resources after the Civil War. Geologist Clarence King secured appointment to lead a survey of the region along the 40th parallel of north latitude in 1867, a task that occupied him and a small team for the next five years. As their work concluded, chatter about a profitable diamond strike percolated in the West. The rumored location meandered from Arizona and New Mexico Territories to the San Luis Valley throughout 1872. In October, several prospectors announced that they had found nearly 300 diamonds and other gems in northwestern Colorado. This worried King, whose teams had found no geological evidence to support the claim. If it was true, King's work would be repudiated. Most sources believed the strike was fake, however, even as they dreamed of wealth, and King saw an opportunity to burnish his credentials. As a late addition to their schedule, King and his team returned to present-day Moffat County and found the obviously salted claim, with cheap gems strewn about in an unnatural fashion. King managed to warn investors in San Francisco before they paid exorbitant fees to nefarious people for a worthless plot of land.

King's exposure of the hoax earned him wide praise. One San Francisco press stated, "We have escaped, thanks to God and Clarence King, a great financial calamity." Another newspaper decried "one of the most craftily designed and thoroughly executed swindles of which the world has any record, and had it occurred in the spring instead of at the close of autumn, would have deluded thousands into a long, weary pilgrimage to the new Golconda [a gem mining region in India]. As it is, Colorado has suffered but little, and we are grateful for the escape."

November 4, 1924

The Ku Klux Klan Triumphant

Although Colorado Republicans tallied the most votes in an election held on November 4, 1924, the Ku Klux Klan declared itself the real winner. An organization that declared itself the voice of all true Americans, the white, Protestant Klan advocated ethnic and religious unity against the perceived threats of African Americans, Jews, Catholics, and immigrants. Unlike the shadowy post–Civil War Klan, this new nativist version proudly paraded itself in public.

Colorado's branch of the Klan emerged from a meeting at Denver's Brown Palace Hotel in 1921. Attendees announced that "we are not only active now, but we were here yesterday, we are here today, and we shall be here forever." As many as one in seven Denverites joined the Klan, which gained followers statewide. Grand Dragon John G. Locke led rallies at a stadium near the University of Denver, sponsored events at Denver amusement parks, and held cross burnings atop South Table Mountain near Golden. Chapters held bake sales and food drives for people who shared their views. Members in Cañon City railed against a rumored papal retreat at a nearby Catholic abbey, and those in Kit Carson County hosted events at Flagler's country club.

Members of the Ku Klux Klan in full regalia ride a Ferris wheel at the Fremont County fairgrounds in 1926.

Locke allied with Democrat Benjamin F. Stapleton to take Denver's mayoralty in 1923. By the November 1924 election, Klan members had infiltrated the Republican Party and elected Clarence J. Morley and Rice Means to the governor's office and to fill a vacancy in the US Senate, respectively. Nonmember US senator Lawrence C. Phipps bankrolled the Klan to aid his own reelection. It won a majority of the Colorado House of Representatives, but Democrats and non-Klan Republicans stymied the Klan in the state Senate. Resistance in the General

Assembly limited the group's power in early 1925, as did Denver judge Benjamin B. Lindsey and district attorney Philip S. Van Cise. Resenting his treatment by Locke, Stapleton turned against the Klan. He used World War I veterans in the American Legion to raid illegal bars and gambling dens that funded the group. In the face of such legal and moral embarrassments, Klan membership dissipated even as its attitudes lingered.

November 5, 1911

A Rocky Mountain White House

Readers of the *Denver Post* found an astonishing sight in the Sunday magazine on November 5, 1911—a sketch of an elaborate, towering castle in the mountains, the envy of any alpine monarch, mad scientist, or Disney princess. The headline proved even more remarkable: "A Summer Palace for Our Presidents: How Colorado Proposes to Build on a High Mountain Top a Great Granite Castle to Be the Nation's Capitol When the Hot Months Come."

In the days before air conditioning, presidents often spent part of the summer away from the heat and humidity of Washington, DC. Entrepreneur John B. Walker concocted the scheme for a permanent summer residence on his 4,000-acre estate near Morrison in Jefferson County. By providing facilities for the chief executive to vacation in Colorado, Walker hoped to bolster the status of the West. He set aside 100 acres of his property on Mount Falcon for the project. Architect Jacques Benedict concocted the vision that appeared in the *Post*, with private and public spaces including a 3,000-seat dining room, office and meeting space, and quarters for the first family and their guests. Schoolchildren across the state donated coins to raise money for the idea. In the summer of 1914, Walker invited President Woodrow Wilson to lay the cornerstone, but the onset of World War I prevented Wilson from attending. Construction continued in fits and starts until the mid-1920s, when Walker's meager funds ran out. By the decade's end, forest fires started by lightning strikes destroyed much of the work, as well as Walker's own home nearby.

Although Colorado's castle proved a failure, Walker found success with other schemes, including the Denver Mountain Parks system to protect high country wonders for city residents to enjoy. In 1927 he sold part of his property—which he called the "Garden of the Titans"—to Denver; it now goes by the simpler name of Red Rocks Park. Jefferson County bought the rest of Walker's tract in 1974 and designated it as open space. The 1914 cornerstone of the presidential castle remains in place, a reminder of Walker's grand, unrealized vision.

Polar Bear Pandemonium

Bears have played an outsized role in the Denver Zoo's history. Its collection origininated in 1896 with a black bear named Billy Bryan, named for presidential candidate William J. Bryan. Two decades later, the zoo pioneered realistic exhibits by replacing simple cages with a concrete and steel structure called Bear Mountain, made with plaster casts of hillsides near Morrison in Jefferson County. But a pair of polar bears named Klondike and Snow, born at the Denver Zoo on November 6, 1994, set a new standard for ursine influence at the world-renowned facility.

Shortly after the cubs' birth, their mother, Ulu, abandoned them. Staff whisked the cold, neglected newborns, weighing just over a pound apiece, to the on-site medical facility. Although stabilized with a formula of half-and-half, supplements, and simulated dog milk, Klondike and Snow needed round-the-clock care. Several members of the zoo staff stepped in as surrogate polar bear parents, and for weeks they exchanged exhausting duties of trying to keep the rapidly growing cubs fed, clean, and calm. Both animals faced medical challenges including nursing troubles and rickets from inadequate nourishment, all part of the learning process for zoo workers. By the early months of 1995, Klondike and Snow could stand and walk, and the team leashed them for lumbering strolls through the snow on the zoo property.

The experience became a media sensation, as television viewers watched Klondike and Snow's struggle to survive. Unprecedented numbers of visitors came to see them, leading to a 37 percent increase in zoo attendance from the previous year. Donations poured in to support the cubs, and merchandising soared as well. As the critters matured, the zoo faced a problem—it did not have room for two more adult polar bears. In November 1995 the pair left for Sea World in Florida, where Klondike died in 2013. Snow had died the previous year at a zoo in Arizona, where she went in the hope that the drier air would ease her skin allergies. A bronze statue of young Klondike and Snow now stands near the polar bear exhibit at the Denver Zoo.

Adopting Women's Suffrage

Years of patient, insistent lobbying bore fruit on November 7, 1893, when most men who cast their ballots in Colorado agreed to extend the franchise to the women in their communities.

The debate over equal suffrage for both sexes simmered from the earliest days of the United States. Many men considered women voters unnecessary, as fathers, husbands, brothers, and sons handled their families' political needs while mothers, wives, sisters, and daughters managed the household. In western polities, where new institutions and attitudes proved more malleable, women first found success in fighting for political equality. Wyoming Territory's legislature adopted equal voting rights in 1869, a policy included in the state constitution when it joined the Union in 1890. Colorado's constitution, adopted in 1876, extended the franchise to women in school board elections, to aid their power over family affairs. Women's suffragists recruited national figures like Susan B. Anthony to rally support in Colorado for a broader measure in 1877, but male voters balked, opposing the idea by more than a two-to-one margin.

Advocates shifted their strategy to a quiet campaign of education. In some communities, they suggested that women voters would help check the influence of immigrants and assert American values. In others, they paired the franchise with the temperance movement, promoting health and public safety by suggesting that women at the polls could protect families from the evils of alcohol. By 1893, prominent supporters of equal suffrage included Governor Davis Waite and former governor John L. Routt. The measure passed by a margin of 6,000 votes, inspiring supporter Caroline N. Churchill to declare: "Come ye disconsolates wherever you languish, come to Colorado and cast in your lot, here the sun shines brightest and there is hope for all women." In a sense, Colorado's vote in 1893 proved even more impressive than Wyoming's constitution—for the first time in the United States, male voters considered the question of equal suffrage unfettered by any other issue and agreed that women deserved the same rights as men.

November 8, 1887

The Most Infamous Lunger

Contrary to expectations of a violent demise, a newspaper reported in November 1887: "Doc Holliday died in Glenwood on the 8th with his boots off." The passing of John H. "Doc" Holliday, a notorious gambler and gunslinger, brought to a quiet end a short, bloody life.

Born in Georgia in 1851, Holliday came of age as his state endured invasion and defeat in the Civil War. He earned a degree in dentistry in Philadelphia but found alcohol and cards more enjoyable and was drifting through the West by the early 1870s. Holliday visited Colorado for the first time in 1876, just after voters approved the state constitution on Independence Day, and he dealt cards at a gambling house in Denver. He left town shortly after wounding a dissatisfied customer in a knife fight later that year. In the spring of 1879 he helped William B. "Bat" Masterson recruit fighters for the Atchison, Topeka & Santa Fe Railroad as they feuded with the Denver & Rio Grande Railroad over access to Leadville during the Royal Gorge War.

Holliday earned his notoriety at a gun battle in Tombstone, Arizona Territory, in October 1881. After pursuing lawbreakers with Wyatt Earp in early 1882, Holliday dealt cards in Trinidad and Pueblo before coming to Denver, where he was seized on May 15 to face trial in Arizona. Sympathetic authorities in Pueblo trumped up charges against him to delay the process, a tactic Colorado lawyers thereafter called "Hollidaying." Governor Frederick W. Pitkin rejected extradition, and Holliday eventually joined up with Earp in the boomtown of Gunnison.

In the summer of 1882, Holliday settled in Leadville, where he dealt cards and clashed with old foes on occasion. His lifelong battle with tuberculosis worsened with altitude and his liberal consumption of alcohol. Holliday met up with Earp and Masterson in Silverton in 1883 and last saw Earp in Denver in 1885. He alternated between there and Leadville until May 1887, when he moved to a Glenwood Springs sanatorium in hopes of easing his symptoms. Wheezing constantly and prematurely gray, Holliday died at age thirty-six and was buried in Pioneer Cemetery.

November 9, 1871

Florence Sabin's Birthday

Amid the statues of American icons in the US Capitol's National Statuary Hall collection resides a seated bronze figure of a humble, determined woman, Dr. Florence R. Sabin. Mere words scarcely do justice to Sabin, who made Colorado and the world a better place.

Born in the mining town of Central City on November 9, 1871, Sabin grew up there and in Denver. While visiting a school, her mother recoiled at the common use of a single cup for all students to drink water, a hygiene lesson Sabin recalled for the rest of her life. She attended several New England schools and taught in Denver before enrolling in Johns Hopkins Medical School in Baltimore, Maryland, in 1896. Sabin battled skepticism about women doctors through tenacious work, quietly demonstrating her skills rather than crusading.

After graduation in 1900, Sabin focused on laboratory work as the first woman faculty member at her alma mater. There, she reinvented knowledge of the lymphatic system, blood flow, and tuberculosis, a disease she knew well from her Colorado childhood. Sabin earned such renown that she was selected to represent

Statue of Florence Rena Sabin in the US Capitol in Washington, DC, part of the National Statuary Hall collection, as photographed in 2016

all women scientists in the United States at a ceremony honoring Marie Curie in 1921. Four years later she accepted a position as the first woman hired by the Rockefeller Institute in New York City, where she continued her studies until an age-mandated retirement in 1938. The sixty-seven-year-old returned to Denver to live with her sister Mary.

Sabin's retirement ended in 1944 when Governor John C. Vivian asked her to chair a state commission on health, part of a campaign to prepare Colorado for the post–World War II era. Studies demonstrated Colorado's shockingly high rates of disease, poor controls over milk production, and lack of adequate sewage treatment. She authored legislation passed by the General Assembly in 1947 that rectified many of these problems. At her behest, lawmakers also established a medical training school, now the University of Colorado Anschutz Medical Campus in Aurora. When Sabin died in 1953 at age eighty-one, she left behind a healthier, grateful state.

November 10, 1978

Taking a High-Altitude Hike

When President Jimmy Carter signed a bill amending the National Park Service and recreation on public land on November 10, 1978, he designated a new scenic hiking route: the Continental Divide National Scenic Trail (CDNST). Stretching more than 3,000 miles between the Canadian and Mexican borders, the CDNST remains a work in progress, with perennially outdoorsy Coloradans playing a leading role in its designation, construction, and use.

The Continental Divide emerged as a geographical concept in the nineteenth century, evolving from a central point from which all western waters radiated to a ridge separating the Mississippi River and Pacific Ocean drainages. In 1869 Samuel Bowles, a Massachusetts newspaperman, described the divide as "the back-bone, the stiffening of the Republic" and Colorado Territory's location on it as "the key-stone in the grand continental formation." It posed challenges to those who sought to conquer it with railroads and water diversion projects and remains at times a psychological as well as a physical barrier in Colorado and the West.

The idea of a recreational route following the divide originated in the 1920s, with advocates calling for similar trails in the Appalachian and Cascade Mountains and Sierra Nevadas. In 1962, enthusiasts marked a potential route along the Continental Divide in Colorado with blue cans nailed to trees. Six years later, the US Congress designated sixteen routes to study, including the Oregon, Pony Express, and Santa Fe Trails and the Continental Divide. A 1977 study defined the latter route, which Carter signed into existence the following year. Between the

New Mexico and Wyoming boundaries, the trail passes through or along the edge of twenty Colorado counties.

In the early 1980s, surveys identified the CDNST route, although financial and logistical challenges slowed its construction. It coincided with the Colorado Trail, a route connecting Denver and Durango, designated in 1974 and dedicated in 1988. Those two—and countless other—hiking paths make Colorado a destination for many Americans seeking a sublime stroll.

Striking Oil at the Wellington Dome

According to one Larimer County resident, "Practically everybody is excited over the discovery of a large gas well" on November 11, 1923. "Even the championship football game of the season between the Aggies and Colorado University gave way in popular interest to talk of tremendous fortunes to be made in oil and gas." The gusher blew for forty days before crews could cap it and harness the tremendous fuel reserve centered on the town of Wellington.

Colorado's first oil production took place in Fremont County in the 1860s, and a refinery at Florence processed the fuel. Drilling in eastern Boulder County at the turn of the twentieth century proved successful as well. With increasing automobile ownership by the 1920s, the need for fuel increased. The Wellington Dome helped sate the demand, and Fort Collins flourished as the new industry's hub. One newspaper declared, "Towns in northern Colorado have been experiencing the greatest excitement known in the state since the early days of gold mining booms." In the late 1920s, new oil fields in Moffat and Rio Blanco Counties invigorated northwestern Colorado's economy through oil and natural gas. By then, the Continental Oil Company (Conoco) emerged as the state's most successful corporate investor in liquid fuel. Conoco bought the Wellington wells, among others, and opened a large refinery in Adams County in 1931 to move fuel production closer to the Denver market. Several other refineries opened nearby, which remain the central feature of Commerce City's skyline.

Oil and natural gas production remains an integral part of the economy in several Colorado counties. Extracting the remaining fuel from permeated shale has offered challenges in recent years, however. Hydraulic fracturing, or "fracking," fostered an oil boom in the early 2010s, but some residents in Boulder and Larimer Counties sought to restrict the subterranean activity. Oil wells—some active, some dormant—dot the landscape across much of Colorado, reminders of the profit and controversy alike inherent in the development and use of fossil fuels.

From Tanning to Brewing in Golden

A Golden newspaper announced on November 12, 1873, that partners Adolph Coors, a German brewer, and Jacob Schueler, a Denver candy maker, had purchased a tannery on the east side of town to house a brewery. "We welcome these energetic gentlemen among us," the press declared, "and trust they will be as successful as they anticipate." The facility overcame myriad challenges to rank today as the world's largest beer-making complex: the Coors Brewery.

In early 1874, Coors and Schueler opened their Golden Lager Beer works and struggled through tough times caused by the Panic of 1873. By the time Colorado achieved statehood in 1876, the economic ship had righted again, and the brewery flourished. Additions to the structure reflected the beer's popularity, especially in mining towns where the Colorado Central Railroad delivered it, competing for customers with the larger Philip Zang Brewing Company in Denver. A garden on the property proved Golden's most popular gathering spot by the decade's end. Coors bought out Schueler in 1880 and turned the park into his home, a white wooden building that survives amid the hulking concrete structures that house the modern brewery.

Coors diversified during Prohibition by making malted milk and porcelain. It weathered the Great Depression—which put its competitor Zang out of business—and sold across the West by the mid-twentieth century. Coors's popularity and limited availability inspired the 1977 film *Smokey and the Bandit*, in which Burt Reynolds smuggles a truck full of the beer to eastern customers. President Gerald Ford, a frequent Colorado vacationer, stocked Coors beer on Air Force One when he returned to Washington, DC. Coors merged with several competitors in the early twenty-first century, although the family maintains influence over the Golden plant. Coors has endured the suicide of its namesake in 1929, the murder of his grandson during a botched kidnapping in 1960, numerous bitter disputes with labor unions, and competition from microbreweries to remain one of Colorado's great economic success stories.

Cabrini's Step toward Sainthood

When Pope Pius XI beatified the late Frances X. Cabrini on November 13, 1938, the Catholic Church recognized one of its most generous modern members, a person whose legacy resonates in Colorado and around the world as a voice for immigrants and ethnic laborers.

Born in Italy in 1850, Cabrini founded the Missionary Sisters of the Sacred Heart of Jesus in 1880. The order immigrated to the United States nine years later, arriving in New York City eager to aid its fellow newcomers. She marveled at American urban life, shuddered at ethnic slurs, and dedicated herself to improving the lot of immigrants. The sisters founded benevolent organizations in nine states across the country. In less than three decades, Cabrini traveled throughout the Western Hemisphere and left her mark of generosity in many communities.

At the turn of the twentieth century, nuns in Colorado contacted Cabrini to ask for her help on behalf of Italian immigrants working in coal mines and living in destitute conditions. She came to Denver in the fall of 1902 to open a parochial school and aided the poor in improving their status through vocational training. Her orphanage in Denver broke with the tradition of releasing its charges at age fourteen, to prevent young women from turning to a life of ill repute; instead, they remained with the sisters until they could marry or provide for themselves.

Cabrini purchased a mountaintop spot in Jefferson County to build a summer camp for the orphanage. During her last visit to Colorado in 1912, Cabrini relieved the parched sisters by pointing out a heretofore unknown spring that still flows. She also laid out a heart and cross in stones, preserved at what is now the Mother Cabrini Shrine. A statue of Jesus Christ, erected in the 1950s, towers over the shrine, a place of pilgrimage and spectacular views. The Catholic Church beatified Cabrini in 1938, more than two decades after her death, and canonized her in 1946, the first American citizen—following her naturalization in 1909—so recognized. Saint Francis Cabrini holds the well-earned distinction of patron saint of immigrants.

November 14, 1910

The C-Spangled Banner

A meeting of Denver's chapter of the Daughters of the American Revolution (DAR) on November 14, 1910, called on Colorado's leaders to remake its most visible symbol: the state flag. Since the mid-nineteenth century, Colorado had used a blue banner with the state seal, which the society ladies considered an uninspiring choice, and they insisted on a new emblem.

The DAR argued that "state loyalty is too precious ever to be lost" and thought that a more impressive flag, displayed with the patriotism that accompanied the Star-Spangled Banner, would encourage Colorado unity. Yet the members' suggested replacement—red with a central horizontal white stripe and also bearing the seal—proved just as humdrum to legislators in the spring of 1911. Andrew C. Carson, a Denver theater manager who wrote about Colorado's natural and human history, offered a simple alternative—a blue field crossed by a horizontal white stripe overlaid by a red "C" with a golden center. Carson's colors represented those of the Rocky Mountain columbine (the state flower since 1899), gold and silver mining, sunshine and snowfall, and the Spanish origins of the state's name.

Few Coloradans boasted more state pride than Carson, who wrote that "the sun rises at the west line of Kansas and sets before it gets to Utah" and portrayed the ideal state resident as one whose "heart is so big he has to keep his vest buttoned, and he wants everybody to come and help drink the finest refrigerated ozone that ever tickled a pair of lungs into ecstasy."

The design authorized by the General Assembly and Governor John F. Shafroth on April 25, 1911, proved remarkably difficult to define. Amendments in 1929 and 1964 clarified the size, color, and position of the flag's elements, whose vague proportions had led to myriad banners, all claiming to be Colorado's official flag. Since 1964, the straightforward, attractive design has represented Colorado to the rest of the nation and the world. In the early twenty-first century, it appears on diverse merchandising and expresses state affection to myriad audiences.

November 15, 1806

Pike Gets a Peek at His Peak

"At two o'clock in the afternoon I thought I could distinguish a mountain to our right, which appeared like a small blue cloud; viewed it with the spy glass, and was still more confirmed in my conjecture . . . When our small party arrived on the hill they with one accord gave three cheers to the Mexican mountains." Thus wrote Lieutenant Zebulon M. Pike on November 15, 1806, in present-day Bent County, when his small expedition sighted what he named Grand Peak. To the Utes it was Tava (Sun Mountain), since the morning sun touched it before other nearby heights. The Spanish initially called it Montaña del Sol for similar reasons, but since the early nineteenth century it has been predominantly known as Pikes Peak.

Pike set out that summer on the fifth American expedition into the Louisiana Purchase, seeking knowledge of geography and resources and to build relationships with American Indian cultures, whose allegiance the United States needed to control its new claim. Pike's primary goal was to find the headwaters and route of the Red River, which roughly divided American and Spanish claims on the southern plains. The party entered modern Colorado by way of the Arkansas River and built a small stockade near the site of Pueblo as a base of operations.

Tava, Montaña del Sol, El Capitán, Grand Peak, Pikes Peak, James Peak—a mountain of many names, as viewed in 2012 from Colorado Springs, with the Garden of the Gods in the foreground

Fascinated by the mountain, Pike set out with two soldiers and the party's doctor to climb it later that month. As they gained elevation, Pike marveled at the view: "The unbounded prairie was overhung with clouds, which appeared like the ocean in a storm; wave piled on wave and foaming, whilst the sky was perfectly clear where we were." The task proved tougher than he expected, as Pike wrote on November 27: "The summit of the Grand Peak, which was entirely bare of vegetation and covered with snow, now appeared at a distance of 15 or 16 miles from us, and as high again as what we had ascended, and would have taken a whole day's march to have arrived at its base, when I believe no human being could have ascended to its pinical."

The trek to the top grew easier by the end of the century with the completion of the Pikes Peak Cog Railway in 1891. In 1915, booster Spencer Penrose built a road to the summit and sponsored the Pikes Peak Hill Climb the following year to promote the route. If only Pike had known the quality of the doughnuts at the Pikes Peak Summit House, he might have tried harder to reach it.

November 16, 1900

A Lynching in Lincoln County

Bound by rope and chains to an upright rail, wood soaked in kerosene strewn at his feet, John P. Porter Jr. burned to death in front of a bloodthirsty, maniacal crowd near Limon in Lincoln County on November 16, 1900, in one of Colorado's most gruesome murders.

Eight days earlier, twelve-year-old Louise Frost was found raped and mortally injured between her home and her school. Members of every ethnic minority—including African Americans, Hispanos, and American Indians—fell under suspicion for little reason other than the majority white population disliked them. The Frost family buried Louise on November 11, and their thoughts turned toward vengeance; her father, Robert, sought to find her killer and "look into his dead face." Nonetheless, the press noted that even after the arrest of suspects on circumstantial evidence, including the African American Porter, "the authorities have been unable to secure any reliable clue to the identity of the real murderer." When law enforcement threatened the sixteen-year-old Porter's father and brother, he confessed to the crime, and officers stood aside when a mob seized him from Limon and took him to a pyre erected near the site of Louise's attack. Her father lit the wood and the crowd watched as Porter burned to death, pleading for mercy. By the time the fire died out the next morning, only ash and charred bones remained.

Porter's death capped decades of vigilantism in Colorado, which had one of the nation's highest rates of mob violence. Newspapers defended the action and the sheriff's decision not to waste taxpayer money on an inquest. Some blamed the General Assembly and former governor Alva Adams for repealing the death penalty in 1897, forcing vengeful citizens to take matters into their own hands. Legislators restored capital punishment in 1901, and lynchings declined precipitously. National audiences cringed, however—even Mark Twain lambasted Colorado in an essay written shortly after Porter's death. The incident demonstrated that Colorado's penchant for mob justice survived long after the frontier era had supposedly passed into history.

November 17, 1926

Great Western's Final Factory

Hundreds of residents of northeastern Colorado gathered in the Sedgwick County town of Ovid on November 17, 1926, as the Great Western Sugar Company dedicated a towering factory where workers refined beets into sugar. The twenty-second and final beet sugar factory erected by all companies in Colorado, the Ovid works reflected the prosperity and power of Great Western.

Beet sugar offered an economic lifeline to the state after the Panic of 1893 eviscerated the mining industry. No company proved more successful than

Great Western, founded by investors including John F. Campion and Charles Boettcher. In 1901 it opened a factory in Loveland, the first of thirteen Great Western erected in northeastern Colorado over the next quarter century, along with nine more in Montana, Nebraska, and Wyoming. The company contracted with thousands of beet growers in the South Platte River valley and recruited laborers—including Germans from Russia, Japanese, Belgians, Hispanos, American Indians, and Mexicans—to cultivate the valuable but finicky crop. By the time the Ovid works opened in 1926, sugar beets grew in nearly half of Colorado's counties. The state produced a quarter of all beets grown in the country and led the United States in beet sugar production. A lucrative industry, by the mid-1920s the value of Colorado's sugar beets outpaced the state's gold, silver, copper, lead, and zinc mines combined. As a newspaper in Fort Collins—which boasted its own Great Western works—averred in 1905, "Stand by the sugar beet and the sugar beet will stand by you."

Beet sugar remained vital to Colorado's economy into the 1970s. Federal trade policies and competition from sweeteners like high-fructose corn syrup weakened the industry, however, and led to the closure of most of the factories. Some industrial ruins dot the landscape today, while others have fallen to demolition; Ovid's impressive factory came down in 2016. Only Fort Morgan's works remain in operation, whose sickly sweet odor during the annual sugar campaign offers a reminder of the economic juggernaut that once dominated towns across Colorado.

November 18, 2005

Remembering a Native Activist

"One of the finest things about being an Indian is that people are always interested in you and your 'plight.' Other groups have difficulties, predicaments, quandaries, problems, or troubles. Traditionally we Indians have had a 'plight.'" Thus stated Vine Deloria Jr., one of the most prominent voices among American Indians in the twentieth century, in *Custer Died for Your Sins: An Indian Manifesto*, published at the height of the civil rights movement in 1969.

Born in South Dakota in 1933, Deloria hailed from the Sioux culture that once dominated the northern Great Plains. He served in the US Marines and earned degrees from several colleges, including the University of Colorado's law school. Deloria also worked on behalf of the American Indian Movement, inspiring a moribund native organization. After teaching for a dozen years in Arizona, he returned to Boulder in 1990 for a decade-long stint on the faculty of his alma mater. There, Deloria fostered his reputation as "a great leader and writer, probably the most influential American Indian of the past century," in the words of a colleague.

American Indians, like many groups in the 1960s, spoke out against generations of misery. Deloria offered native cultures in the United States a philosophy of resistance, presented in engaged, sarcastic, brilliant prose. He ridiculed the federal government as inept and arrogant in its dealings with American Indians, bemoaned the intrusions of scholars and missionaries, and contrasted the Cold War promotion of American values against historical treatment of distinct cultures within the country's boundaries. Deloria quipped that "practically the only thing the white men ever gave the Indian was disease and poverty." He also praised American Indians' hard-earned sense of humor, especially aimed at the perennial butt of jokes, George A. Custer.

On November 18, 2005, five days after his death at age seventy-two, a memorial service for Deloria took place in Golden. Friends and admirers gathered to celebrate a man who reinvigorated American Indians, infusing hope through his sharp mind and even sharper tongue.

November 19, 1867

Colorado's First Railroad

Colorado Territory seemed a desperate place in the mid-1860s. The mining boom had fizzled as investors looked elsewhere for profits. The Sand Creek Massacre ruined relations with American Indians and caused the rest of the country to view Colorado as barbarous. News that the first transcontinental railroad would bypass the territory to the north added insult to injury. To prevent Colorado from withering into obsolescence, a group of Denver investors built their own railroad, which would connect to the transcontinental line at Cheyenne, Wyoming Territory. On November 19, 1867, they incorporated the Denver Pacific Railway & Telegraph Company.

Plans existed already for the Colorado Central Railroad, which would connect Cheyenne with Golden, then the territorial capital. Denverites like John Evans, David H. Moffat, and Walter S. Cheesman prevented the bypass of their city through the Denver Pacific. Surveyors chose a 106-mile route in 1868, and grading commenced that summer. Crews laid rails southward from Wyoming on ties cut from logs floated down the Cache la Poudre River. The line extended from Cheyenne to the Cache la Poudre–South Platte Rivers junction, where farming colonists established Greeley along the railroad-in-progress in early 1870.

It continued past the ruins of the fur trading Forts Jackson, Lupton, St. Vrain, and Vasquez, abandoned only three decades earlier. Construction crews arrived in Denver on June 22, 1870, and a formal, enthusiastic dedication ceremony took place two days later. Colorado Territory's largest city—and capital after December 1867—possessed an iron link to the rest of the country and the world at last.

In 1880 the Denver Pacific merged with the Kansas Pacific Railway, which ran across the plains to Denver, as part of the Union Pacific Railroad empire. The route rescued Colorado from oblivion—easing transportation of people, supplies, and ore—and invigorated a faltering economy. The line remains in operation for freight but is best known for the Cheyenne Frontier Days train that uses historic equipment to carry tourists to Wyoming for the rodeo every July.

November 20, 1879

Culture Comes to the Cloud City

Horace and Augusta Tabor sat in their plush box at the Tabor Opera House in Leadville on November 20, 1879, opening night for the grand edifice. The state's second opera house—after Central City's, which had opened the previous year—boasted a range of backdrops behind a curtain decorated with an image of the Royal Gorge. Within its first few months, the house put on productions of Shakespeare and Gilbert and Sullivan and hosted guests including former president Ulysses S. Grant and former governor John L. Routt. In April 1882, Irish author Oscar Wilde battled altitude sickness to deliver a lecture from its stage. The Tabor Opera House reflected a mining town eager to demonstrate its respectability to itself and others.

Prospectors came to the headwaters of the Arkansas River in the fall of 1859 and found color in an area they named California Gulch. The gold dwindled quickly, but a community with the similarly optimistic title of Oro City clung to life for nearly two decades. A nearby silver strike in the spring of 1877 inspired the boomtown of Leadville, to which Oro City's residents—including the Tabors—relocated that summer. Investors included Routt, who worked his mine whenever he could escape political duties in Denver, and Horace Tabor, who moved his small store from Oro City and prospered, winning election as Leadville's first mayor in February 1878. Two months later, Tabor grubstaked two prospectors—supplying them with tools, food, and whiskey—who struck a rich silver vein. He and Denver banker David H. Moffat bought them out by the year's end and in short order became two of the richest men in Colorado.

Leadville—nicknamed the Cloud City for its 10,000-foot-plus elevation—grew faster than almost any other Colorado boomtown. The city and its hinterland boasted 20,000 people of almost every conceivable ethnicity by early 1879. Its sordid, drunken reputation inspired the more genteel residents to push for cultured entertainment, hence the Tabor Opera House. By the 1880s, the name Leadville was synonymous worldwide with prosperity.

November 21, 1927

Carnage at the Columbine Mine

Around 500 striking coal miners gathered outside the town of Serene and its neighboring Columbine Mine, located in southwestern Weld County, on the morning of November 21, 1927. More than a month into a statewide coal strike, the day's picketing turned deadly when strikers stormed a gate into the town. Guards beat one laborer, and when others tried to rescue him, they opened fire, killing six men. The "Columbine Massacre"—a title seized by a Jefferson County high school seven decades later—reflected the state's ongoing penchant for labor violence.

Declining demand for coal in the 1920s cut into corporate profits and wages for those who mined it. Half of the state's 12,000 coal miners went on strike against the Colorado Fuel & Iron Company and the Rocky Mountain Fuel Company (RMFC) on October 18, 1927. Picketing generally proved peaceful in a state accustomed to such labor disputes. Worried about a repeat of the Ludlow Massacre, Governor William H. Adams ordered the Colorado State Rangers—the state's law enforcement agency before the Colorado State Patrol was organized in 1935—to the strike zone. Louis N. Scherf, who had participated in the bloodshed at Ludlow as a ranger in 1914, commanded the force at the RMFC's Columbine Mine. The violence Adams had hoped to avoid broke out on the first morning that strikers and rangers faced one another, on November 21. The rangers fired into the unarmed crowd, killing six strikers and wounding several dozen others. RMFC board member Josephine A. Roche rushed to the site when she heard of the violence and ordered the rangers to disarm and throw their weapons down the mine shaft.

The strike lingered until February 1928, when the strikers returned to work. Scherf and the rangers faced no legal consequences for the strikers' deaths. Roche assumed the RMFC's presidency in March 1928 and instituted generous policies toward its workers to prevent future disputes. A landfill stands today atop the Columbine Mine site and its misnamed company town of Serene, and a memorial in nearby Lafayette's cemetery honors the murdered miners.

Artist's depiction of Auraria and Denver with Longs Peak in the distance, as portrayed in Frank Leslie's Illustrated Newspaper *on December 15, 1860*

November 22, 1858

Colorado's Capital, Kansas's Governor

To prevent anyone else from doing what they did—hijacking the claim to a town site at the heart of the gold prospecting region in western Kansas Territory—a party of Kansans led by William H. Larimer Jr. organized the Denver City Town Company on November 22, 1858.

Word spread quickly of gold discoveries made along the South Platte River upstream from modern Denver, in today's Denver and Arapahoe Counties, in the summer of 1858. By the autumn, parties of fortune seekers set out from western settlements in the United States. One group of Kansans organized Montana City on the east bank of the river near the most promising site for prospectors, between what are now Evans and Iliff Avenues. In September, another party set up St. Charles on the east bank of Cherry Creek, just above its confluence with the South Platte. A band led by William G. Russell, whose discoveries had ignited the Pikes Peak gold rush, established a camp called Auraria across Cherry Creek from St. Charles two months later.

Larimer's group arrived at St. Charles on November 16 and took control of the almost abandoned site, threatening to hang any remaining residents who resisted.

November

To enforce his control, Larimer chartered a new town six days later. Hoping to curry favor, his party named their community for James W. Denver, who had been the territorial governor when they set out westward, although he had resigned by the time they arrived at Cherry Creek. An experienced town planner, Larimer designed an orderly community with a main street named for himself; Larimer County later inherited his name as well. Auraria and Denver competed for businesses and residents, but the latter won a major victory by securing stagecoach service in March 1859. Transportation and communication lines ensured Denver's prominence, and it annexed Auraria just over a year later. Like a snowball rolling down a Rocky Mountain slope, Denver grew steadily as the commercial and political center of the region. The city remains Colorado's hub, having overcome its nefarious origin to serve the state and much of the American West.

November 23, 1939

A Tale of Two Thanksgivings

In 1932, Franklin D. Roosevelt won his first of four presidential elections by pledging to try anything, no matter how farfetched, to combat the Great Depression. Seven years later, with the economic crisis lingering and World War II raging in Europe and Asia, the president took the advice of American merchants who asked him to move Thanksgiving forward a week and extend the Christmas shopping season. To that end, instead of the traditional last Thursday in November—the 30th that year—Roosevelt declared November 23, 1939, as Thanksgiving.

Roosevelt's proclamation inspired a blend of confusion, amusement, and anger. Many Americans accepted the idea as one worth trying, although college football teams complained about the holiday's impact on their schedules. Yet at the time, state executives also had the power to declare Thanksgiving's date, and Colorado governor Ralph L. Carr selected November 30 instead of Roosevelt's choice. Under public pressure, however, Carr agreed to accommodate either Thanksgiving. Ultimately, twenty-two states followed the president's lead, while twenty-three stuck with tradition, and three—Colorado, Mississippi, and Texas—celebrated both. Government offices, banks, and schools in Colorado closed on both days, while department stores shuttered for the first but remained open for the second. Grocery stores expected to cash in on families hosting two big meals instead of one. The *Denver Post* observed: "The American people have so much to be thankful for that they are justified in devoting two days to Thanksgiving this year. Just the fact that we have kept out of the European war, have no reason to become involved in it, and are so firmly determined to stay out is enough to justify a special Thanksgiving day."

Regardless of the economic benefits, the prospect of competing Thanksgiving holidays proved too much for the nation to bear. In 1941, after two years of confusion, Congress passed and Roosevelt signed a bill designating the fourth Thursday in November as the thankful day.

November 24, 1922

Sharing the Colorado River's Water

Delegates from seven western states signed the Colorado River Compact (CRC) in Santa Fe, New Mexico, on November 24, 1922, in an attempt to replace costly legal battles over interstate water resources with cooperation and negotiation. The deal they struck set precedent for further compromises but often inspired as many court challenges as it sought to prevent.

The CRC owes much to Delphus E. Carpenter, a native of Greeley who earned a law degree from the University of Denver and won election to the General Assembly. Appointed the state's water litigator in the early 1910s, Carpenter feared a federal takeover of water rights by regionalizing Colorado's doctrine of prior appropriation. Such a policy would allow residents of other states to challenge Coloradans for water within their own boundaries and complicate a US Supreme Court precedent that demanded equitable apportionment of the resource between states. Carpenter envisioned diplomatic compacts between states to resolve water arguments outside the expensive, contentious courtrooms in which such disputes often boiled.

Appointed to the CRC commission by Governor Oliver H. Shoup, Carpenter brought together representatives from Arizona, California, Colorado, Nevada, New Mexico, Utah, and Wyoming—the Colorado River drainage states—in the early 1920s. Regional meetings took place for more than two years, starting with a session in the Colorado State Capitol in August 1920. The compact signed by Carpenter, Secretary of Commerce Herbert Hoover, and other commissioners in Santa Fe in 1922 laid out a framework for water apportionment. It divided the river into upper and lower basins, each sharing 7.5 million acre-feet of water per year, with another 1.5 million continuing downstream to Mexico. Diversion projects and population growth complicated the CRC in subsequent years, leading to ever more legal battles. Nonetheless, it offered the hope for a more productive and peaceful way to manage the West's scarce water.

Lindsey Back at the Bar

The Colorado Supreme Court reinstated a disbarred former Denver judge on November 25, 1935, his sixty-sixth birthday. Since Benjamin B. Lindsey had lived in California for years, the court's action proved mostly symbolic but recognized his unparalleled impact all the same.

A native of Tennessee, Lindsey and his family moved to Denver in 1880. He attended out-of-state schools before returning to Colorado late in the decade, taking odd jobs to help his impoverished family make ends meet. While working in a lawyer's office, Lindsey studied law and passed the bar examination in 1894. Appointed by Governor Charles S. Thomas to a Denver court position, Lindsey's responsibilities included orphaned children. His knowledge of and sympathy for children in challenging circumstances increased after he secured a judgeship in 1901. Lindsey used his authority to establish a special juvenile court to remove young offenders from the general criminal population in hopes of preventing recidivism. For a quarter century, the popular jurist won reelection as his juvenile court system caught on nationwide.

Lindsey worked with Progressive advocates in the early twentieth century, including reformers Edward P. Costigan, Upton Sinclair, and Theodore Roosevelt. In 1910 he exposed corruption in Mayor Robert W. Speer's administration in a series of national magazine articles. Lindsey later joined Denver district attorney Philip S. Van Cise to battle the Ku Klux Klan, which sought Lindsey's court records to embarrass families whose children had run afoul of the law. Lindsey won a disputed election in 1924, although the state supreme court ousted him three years later. To protect a career's worth of youths, Lindsey burned his records in his backyard.

Disbarred in Colorado at the urging of his former friend Van Cise, who opposed the fiery departure, Lindsey moved to Los Angeles and served as a judge there until his death at age seventy-three in 1943. The names of Lindsey and Van Cise survive on a Denver courthouse and jail, respectively. The "Kid's Judge" holds a place of honor in the annals of Colorado jurisprudence.

The Press Turns on Trumbo

On November 26, 1947, Hollywood newspapers announced the firing of screenwriter Dalton Trumbo and others on suspicion of anti-American sentiments and political ties. The Colorado native, one of the silver screen's best and most popular creative minds, found himself caught up in the panic-fueled dragnet of blacklisting during the early Cold War.

Born in Montrose in 1905, Trumbo and his family moved to Grand Junction three years later. His father worked as a credit collection agent, constable, and shoe salesman—all without success. Following the American entrance into World War I, Trumbo joined his peers in harassing Grand Junction kids of German ancestry. Yet his empathy grew after the war, when he worked with a blind veteran in a bookstore and would heat the man's glass eyes in a pan of water each winter morning to prevent them from freezing to his eyelids. During high school, Trumbo worked as a cub reporter for the *Grand Junction Sentinel* and earned the respect of its editor, Walter Walker. Walker encouraged Trumbo's storytelling nature, which paved the way for his career.

Trumbo briefly attended the University of Colorado before his father lost yet another job and the family moved to California in 1925. A decade later, he published his first novel. *Eclipse*, set in the fictional town of Shale City, offered a thinly veiled satire of his hometown. Residents of Grand Junction alternately read, tittered about, and denounced the work; its reaction virtually ensured that Trumbo would never return there. A semi-autobiographical work, *Johnny Got His Gun*, also set in Shale City, came out in 1939 and earned renown for its anti-war message. Those sentiments earned him the suspicion of supposedly more patriotic members of the Hollywood elite, who orchestrated his blacklisting and that of other entertainment figures.

Nonetheless, Trumbo wrote screenplays including *Roman Holiday* and *Spartacus*, aided by opponents of the witch hunt, and his reputation rebounded. Grand Junction forgave him as well; a statue of Trumbo writing while seated in a bathtub was installed on Main Street in 2005.

November 27, 1900

Sweet Beets in Sugar City

Twin brick pillars stand on the south side of Sugar City, a sweetly named town in Crowley County. For six and a half decades, these sentinels guarded the entrance to a massive factory where the National Beet Sugar Company (NBSC) processed root vegetables into sugar. The neglected site's silence today contrasts markedly with the excitement of November 27, 1900, when Sugar City's factory started work on the town's first campaign.

Part of the beet sugar boom at the turn of the twentieth century, Sugar City's refinery rose the same year as Rocky Ford's, a year after Grand Junction's, and a year before Loveland's. Unlike those towns, Sugar City did not exist until that year, and aside from the setting, it looked and felt much like a mining boomtown. In the 1880s, what is now Crowley County remained open prairie, but the construction of the Colorado Canal and the Missouri Pacific Railroad presaged a burst of settlement. Irrigation and transportation proved alluring, and the NBSC bought over 12,000 acres near two reservoirs along the railroad line. The company imported beet seed and machinery for a factory, and farmers and builders came to the site by late 1899. They lived in tents for months, as planting and factory construction took precedence over erecting a town. Most of the early residents consisted of Germans from Russia, the immigrant group most familiar with beet sugar. Sugar City's population increased from zero to 2,000 in the year before the first beets met the slicer in November 1900, a boomtown indeed.

In choosing the "saccharinely suggestive name of Sugar City," as one Denver press quipped, the NBSC created an optimistic vision for the future. The boom calmed by the 1910s, and the town boasted a stable population of about 800 into the Great Depression. A steady decline followed, and the factory closed in 1966, with demolition soon afterward. Now a community of fewer than 300 residents, the town's name, a metal sign bearing a picture of the factory, and the brick pillars are all that remain of the sweet, heady days of Sugar City.

November 28, 1901

Peacemaking at Telluride

After months of intransigence, Arthur L. Collins—a manager at the Smuggler-Union Mine above Telluride in San Miguel County—signed a deal with members of the Western Federation of Miners (WFM) labor union on November 28, 1901. Conceding to the demands of a bitter, deadly strike earlier that year, Collins sought to restore peace and profit alike.

Tension built among gold and silver miners near Telluride in the spring of 1901 over new pay rates announced by mine owners that changed the definition of a day's work and resulted in dramatically lower wages. Miners asked Collins, who represented the dominant Smuggler-Union mine, to submit the new deal to state authorities for arbitration, but he dismissed the need for any negotiations and forced the new rates on workers. The WFM, which had struck with success at Cripple Creek and with failure at Leadville in recent years, called out its members on May 2. Collins imported non-unionized workers to reopen the Smuggler-Union in mid-June, leading to friction between the outsiders and the picketing miners. To make matters worse, Collins hired the replacements under the old pay system rather than his new one, adding insult to injury.

Strikers clashed with the imported workers on July 3 in a gun battle that lasted through the morning, killing four men and wounding six. The strikers then rounded up eighty-eight company workers and marched them at gunpoint over the San Juan Mountains into Ouray County, with admonitions never to return on pain of death. Governor James B. Orman considered ordering the Colorado National Guard to the strike zone, but three days after the clash, Collins and the WFM settled the dispute and work at the Smuggler-Union resumed. Many of the recently evicted replacement laborers returned to Telluride and worked peaceably alongside union members.

Collins and the union agreed the following November to restore the old pay rate, and the crisis dissipated. Nonetheless, on November 19, 1902, a gunshot fired through a window killed Collins as he played cards with friends at his home near the mine. His murder remains unsolved.

November 29, 1864

The Sand Creek Massacre

Colorado has witnessed its share of good days and bad, but November 29, 1864, holds the record for the lowest point in the state's history when volunteer forces carried out a brutal attack on a Cheyenne and Arapaho camp in present-day Kiowa County, known as the Sand Creek Massacre.

Panic and paranoia gripped Colorado Territory's American population in 1864, fueled by dwindling mining profits and raids by American Indian groups from the northern Great Plains. Governor John Evans fanned the flames of fear, advocating unrestrained violence against native people suspected of attacks that summer. The Southern Cheyenne and Arapaho, who had maintained peaceful relations with outsiders during the Pikes Peak gold rush, met with Evans and Colonel John M. Chivington—commander of Colorado's militia—at Camp Weld near Denver in September. Both Evans and Chivington hoped to secure their political futures in a territory then attempting a bid for statehood, and the latter in particular sought to add a victory over American Indians to his triumph against Confederates at Glorieta Pass two years earlier.

Chivington led as many as 700 troops to a peaceful Cheyenne and Arapaho camp on Big Sandy Creek, arriving at dawn on November 29. Artillery fire and a cavalry charge shattered the morning air as Colorado's volunteer force set upon the camp. Some people fled up the creek bed, only to be trampled and battered

Colorado volunteers attacking a Cheyenne and Arapaho camp during the Sand Creek Massacre, as depicted in the twentieth century by artist Robert Lindneux

with rifle butts or slashed with bayonets. Estimates vary, but it is likely that more than 200 people died. Chivington's troops plundered the camp and scalped and mutilated the victims, going so far as to carve out women's genitalia to wear on their hats and saddles. They returned to a hero's welcome in Denver. In the months that followed, however, the massacre inspired bloody reprisals across the West and a congressional investigation.

Long neglected, the site earned protection in 2007 as the Sand Creek Massacre National Historic Site. Governor John Hickenlooper issued a formal apology for the bloodshed on behalf of the state during the anniversary ceremony in 2014. Descendants of those attacked remember the victims with a two-day "healing run" from Kiowa County to the state capitol every November. Today, the site commemorates the most indefensible moment in Colorado history, one that continues to haunt and horrify.

November 30, 1994

Alcatraz of the Rockies

The federal government's highest-security prison, known as Supermax and located near Florence in Fremont County, admitted its first inmates on November

30, 1994. Nicknamed the "Alcatraz of the Rockies," it secures the nation's worst offenders under lock and key.

The US Congress approved the United States Penitentiary Administrative Maximum Facility in 1989 and designated Fremont County—already home to several prisons, including Colorado's state penitentiary—to house it. Residents wanted the economically valuable facility so badly that they bought and donated to the federal government 400 acres for the site. Governor Roy Romer participated at groundbreaking ceremonies in July 1990. For the next four years, hundreds of workers erected the forbidding, triangular, $60 million structure on the sagebrush flats south of Florence. Concrete walls, fences, and fourteen rows of razor wire protect civilians from the men locked within the institution, as do guards watching from towers, trucks, and helicopters.

Residents of Supermax offer a who's who of mayhem and misery. The roster has included Joaquín "El Chapo" Guzmán (drug cartel kingpin), Robert Hanssen (federal agent turned Russian spy), Theodore Kaczysnki (the "Unabomber" who killed through mail-delivered explosives), Timothy McVeigh and Terry Nichols (architects of the 1995 Oklahoma City bombing), Zacarias Moussaoui (architect of the September 11, 2001, terror attacks), Richard Reid (the "shoe bomber" who attempted to blow up an airplane in 2001), Eric Rudolph (serial bomber who attacked the 1996 Summer Olympic Games in Atlanta, Georgia), Faizal Shahzad (attempted to detonate a bomb in New York City's Times Square in 2010), Thomas Silverstein (a multiple murderer held in solitary confinement from 1983 until his death in 2019), Dzhokhar Tsarnaev (bombed the finish line of the Boston Marathon in 2013), John Walker Lindh (US citizen who fought against American forces in Afghanistan), and Ramzi Yousef (planned the World Trade Center bombing in 1993). The United States has no more infamous address than Supermax.

December

Francis Lowry's Birthday

Francis B. Lowry, born in Denver on December 1, 1894, joined the US Army during World War I and trained in the brand-new field of aerial reconnaissance. He arrived in France in February 1918 and served as a photographer and observer of artillery positions from aircraft, an innovative technology on the field of battle. On September 26, during Lowry's thirty-third mission, German guns shot down his plane and he died in the crash. Buried in France initially, his remains were returned to Colorado for interment in September 1921, three years after his death.

Memorials for Lowry commenced with a Colorado National Guard airfield at 38th Avenue and Dahlia Street, opened in 1924. It also served as Denver's municipal terminal before the future Stapleton International Airport debuted in 1929. In the 1930s, the US Army planned a new aerial reconnaissance facility at Agnes Memorial Sanitorium, a tuberculosis hospital east of Denver founded by US senator Lawrence C. Phipps. The Works Progress Administration transformed the 880-acre facility into a military base starting in 1937, and the site took Lowry's name. An additional 960 acres east of Lowry Field, used as an auxiliary landing strip, was later named for John H. Buckley, a Longmont native also killed in aerial combat during World War I.

Lowry and Buckley fields flourished during World War II, instructing tens of thousands of trainees each year; they also offered military, economic, and social benefits. Both facilities shifted to the US Air Force in the late 1940s. Lowry housed the Air Force Academy from 1955 until it moved to El Paso County in 1958. It also served as President Dwight D. Eisenhower's base of operations during his Colorado vacations in the 1950s and as a nuclear missile base in the early 1960s. By then, encroaching neighborhoods made flight training impractical. Downgraded in 1994, Lowry Air Force Base remains an administrative center. Buckley Air Force Base in Aurora continues to serve the national defense, best known for its radar systems housed in massive white "golf balls" that dominate the eastern Denver metropolitan area's skyline.

The Colorado State Forest

The patchwork quilt of land division in the United States, seen as a checkerboard from high above, originated in a law that predates the US Constitution: the Land Ordinance of 1785. As surveyors parceled out the landscape into geometric units, they reserved 2 out of every 36 square miles for state governments to sell to fund public education. The rest remained property of the federal government, to be sold, given away as homesteads, or retained for future use. The creation of national forests in the Rocky Mountains starting in the late 1800s posed a challenge, with isolated pockets of state land surrounded by the reserves. During the Great Depression, this confusing system improved markedly with the creation of the Colorado State Forest.

In 1931, the General Assembly approved exchanging state lands trapped within national forests to create a cohesive tract that the state could run itself as a place of forestry education, timber cultivation, and tourism. In exchange for nearly 71,000 acres Colorado transferred to federal jurisdiction, foresters selected a portion of the Routt and Roosevelt National Forests near the Wyoming boundary. State forester W. J. Morrill, a professor at the Colorado Agricultural College in Fort Collins, declared, "A state forest of this size properly protected and regulated should develop into a property of which the state will be proud."

Swapping tracts with the federal government commenced in 1934, and on December 2, 1938, President Franklin D. Roosevelt signed a land patent that created the Colorado State Forest. It extends along the Medicine Bow Range, along the eastern edge of North Park in Jackson County with a few acres of Larimer County thrown in, and is the state's premier moose-viewing destination. For over thirty years a series of logging camps operated in the forest, part of its healthful management, but increasing environmental concerns led to their closure in the early 1970s. To promote the vast region as a tourist destination, it was designated State Forest State Park in 1971, reinforcing its status as a place of special beauty and tranquility.

December 3, 2011

Piloting Paoli for Half a Century

Virgil Harms, an octogenarian farmer and square dance aficionado, celebrated a remarkable milestone on December 3, 2011. A surprise party held to honor the resident of Phillips County commemorated his fifty years of service as the mayor of Paoli, a record unmatched in Colorado history.

Born on a farm north of Paoli in 1927, Harms served in the US Army during World War II before returning to Phillips County. He supported the generally conservative Democratic Party of the mid-twentieth century and remained with that party even as his community embraced the Republican Party and its conservative turn in the late 1900s. Mayor Oscar Lohn nominated Harms to serve on the town board in 1954 and named him mayor pro tempore in 1961 so that Lohn would not have to approve an application for a liquor license for the town's pool hall. Lohn died in November of that year, and Harms inherited Paoli's mayoralty. In the five decades that followed, no other resident sought the position, and with mayoral elections an expensive proposition for such a small town, the community simply stopped having them. The town board—over which Harms had presided for more than 600 meetings by 2011—canceled the mayor's term limits as well, and Harms carried on, balancing his political and agricultural duties.

With fewer than fifty residents, Paoli was content with the status quo. At the 2011 party, Harms observed: "I suppose if they didn't want me, they'd tell me. If someone else wanted the job, I'd let them have it." Meanwhile, his wife, Eloise, joked, "I don't want him to end up like the last mayor; he got out by dying," while Virgil quipped, "I'm not going to serve fifty more years, I'll tell ya." Harms's half century of leading his close-knit community exemplifies the character of many small Colorado towns. As he told one reporter: "We have no controversies, no school, no police, no fire department. When you don't have a lot to do, you just get along."

December 4, 2002

Remembering the Old Spanish Trail

As Spain's influence expanded in the late 1700s, the empire sought to connect its settlements in New Mexico and California. Expeditions like that of Domínguez and Escalante in 1776 searched for a route between the Rio Grande and the Pacific Ocean. The task then fell to Mexico after it won independence from Spain in 1821. By the end of the decade, a series of interconnected paths arced from Santa Fe to Los Angeles, known today as the Old Spanish Trail.

The name is problematic—instead of an old Spanish trail, the path blazed in the 1820s was new, Mexican, and a series of trails. Several routes extended across southwestern Colorado. Two ran north into the San Luis Valley, one from Taos and another paralleling modern US Highway 285. They met at Saguache and proceeded over Cochetopa Pass to the Gunnison River, around the Black Canyon, downstream to the Colorado River, and thence westward. Another trail followed in the footsteps of Domínguez and Escalante across the canyons of Archuleta, La Plata, Montezuma, and Dolores Counties into present-day Utah. Variations on these main paths wound through the mountains and around the plateaus of the western slope.

These trails, suitable for animals more than wagons, proved essential for several decades. They provided access to much of the interior of North America, and the globally profitable fur trade flourished as a result. Antoine Robidoux built three trading posts—including Delta County's Fort Uncompahgre—along one branch of the route and provided diverse cultures with valuable goods. The trails served as an extension of the Santa Fe Trail as well, creating a transcontinental trade route. Ute frustration at the presence of outsiders in their territory, through which the trails passed in western Colorado, inspired violence by the mid-1840s, however, and use of the trail routes waned.

In 2002, US senator Ben Nighthorse Campbell introduced a bill to add the Old Spanish Trail to the roster of federally designated National Historic Trails. That fall the US Congress passed, and on December 4 President George W. Bush signed, the Old Spanish Trail Recognition Act.

December 5, 1913

Colorado's Biggest Blizzard

"Colorado is snowbound," proclaimed the *Rocky Mountain News* on December 5, 1913, as the most intense blizzard ever recorded in the Centennial State drew to an end.

The storm hit with a strength unusual for the time of year. Snowfall started on December 1 and continued for five days, burying much of the state east of the Continental Divide under wet, white powder measured in feet. The infant science of meteorology proved incapable of forecasting the storm, and few could imagine its potential. Denver totaled nearly 4 feet of snow, while Georgetown amassed over 7 feet. Towns on the eastern plains missed the snow altogether but endured heavy rains from the storm fueled by moisture from the Gulf of Mexico.

Life as usual stopped. Trains across eastern Colorado were mired in snowdrifts, halting traffic from Pueblo to Fort Collins and as far east as Sterling. Rotary plows and thousands of workers with shovels toiled around the clock to free stranded trains and more than 200 Denver Tramway Company streetcars. Skis and snowshoes replaced motorized vehicles, telephone and electrical lines snapped, schools closed, and thousands of people found themselves stranded. Striking coal miners and their families living in tent colonies in Huerfano and Las Animas Counties endured particular misery. Disposing of the snow proved another problem. A hole cut in Denver's Sixteenth Street viaduct allowed flatbed cars to dump their load into the South Platte River. The new Civic Center park served as a depository, where mountains of slush lingered into the following summer. Denver's jail put its inmates to work helping dig the city out, and the fire department used hoses to spray snow off sidewalks until the streets grew saturated with water.

A Denver resident skis down an otherwise impassable Sixteenth Street during the December 1913 blizzard.

Although several people lost their lives in the storm, for most it proved an amusing nuisance. One store in Denver placed a sign in the street: "This Pile of Snow Free Today—Help Yourself—Plenty in Stock." Skiing enthusiast Carl Howelsen encouraged Denverites to schuss down the gentle slope on the west front of the state capitol. Like many big storms—but never quite as big—in the years since, the 1913 blizzard offered frozen fun to many Coloradans.

December 6, 1848

Fateful Choices in the San Luis Valley

In the broad, snowy, cold San Luis Valley on December 6, 1848, a group of men led by John C. Frémont pondered how to cross the Continental Divide. Their decision would cast a pall on the region—and Frémont's reputation—and cost nearly a third of the party their lives.

Americans wanted a transcontinental railroad immediately after conquering California from Mexico in 1848. To that end, renowned scout Frémont traveled up the Santa Fe Trail that fall. At El Pueblo, his party of thirty-three men—including Frémont expedition regulars Charles Preuss and Alexis Godey, cartographer and scout, respectively—took on trapper Bill Williams as a guide, who led them into the area now named Fremont County. The party made a miserable climb through the Wet Mountains and straggled over Mosca Pass in the Sangre de Cristo Mountains. After traversing the Great Sand Dunes, they camped in modern Saguache County to consider a railroad route across the Continental Divide. Williams and Frémont debated skirting the snowy peaks to the south or making a direct assault and, unfortunately, selected the latter.

With supplies dwindling, animals exhausted, forbidding mountains ahead, and winter's fury unleashed, Frémont's party headed up Carnero Creek. Some days they advanced only a few hundred yards, cutting down trees for firewood. Surviving stumps, some standing 30 feet tall, testify to the depth of the snow. The men ate their mules, candles, rawhide, and eventually each other—ten members of the expedition died, and the others survived through cannibalism. The bedraggled party trudged back out of the mountains in January 1849. Preuss reflected: "I am here, as poor as Job. But to have saved one's life is the best; the rest may be retrieved again."

In Taos, New Mexico, Godey organized rescue parties while Frémont sought to rescue his reputation in letters sent east. Nonetheless, the gruesome failure haunted his life. Frémont served as one of California's first senators in 1850, led another railroad survey in 1853, ran as the first Republican presidential candidate in 1856, and commanded Union troops during the Civil War. Yet the specter of his disastrous 1848 expedition always hovered nearby.

December 7, 1908

Colorado's First National Monument

National parks and monuments protect and promote tourism to unique features across the United States. On December 7, 1908, using authority bestowed by the US Congress through the Antiquities Act two years earlier, President Theodore Roosevelt declared Colorado's first national monument, Wheeler, high in the San Juan Mountains of Mineral County.

Wheeler National Monument, named for Lieutenant George M. Wheeler, who surveyed the area in 1874, consisted of 300 acres of geologic wonder. Spires of yellow and white stone stretch through the thin air toward the skies, and the area proved popular with visitors to the nearby town of Creede. As a newspaper stated in 1908, "The region set aside contains wide can[y]ons, broken ridges, pinnacles and buttes, forming such striking and varied scenes." Roosevelt's designation was expected to foster tourism, both for the natural landscape and for its haunting past, considering its proximity to where John C. Frémont's 1848 expedition got stuck in the snow. "Skeletons of mules, bits of harness and camp equipage found near this spot" spoke to the sorrowful tale of Frémont's survey, one report declared. Locals compared the vista at Wheeler to national parks like Yellowstone or the Grand Canyon, albeit on a much smaller scale.

In the 1910s, a trail built from Creede promised to boost attendance at the monument, and talk of automobile access increased. In-state competition for tourist dollars fueled the chatter, especially after the 1915 designation of Rocky Mountain National Park, which was more easily reached from large cities and transcontinental railroad lines. Plans for a highway from Creede fell through, however, because of financial and logistical obstacles. By the 1940s, annual visitors to the isolated geologic marvel numbered only in the dozens, and Congress decommissioned the site in 1950. Part of the La Garita Wilderness today, what is now known as the Wheeler Geologic Area never achieved the status that boosters in the early twentieth century had hoped it would attain.

December 8, 1929

Dedicating the Royal Gorge Bridge

An estimated crowd of 10,000 people gathered atop the Royal Gorge in Fremont County on December 8, 1929, to dedicate the world's highest bridge—a steel suspension span 1,260 feet in length and 956 feet above the Arkansas River that had carved the famous canyon.

In the early nineteenth century, Lieutenant Zebulon M. Pike found the Royal Gorge an obstacle to exploration. By the 1870s, it offered a route into the mining districts, battled over by several railroad lines. At the turn of the twentieth century, officials in nearby Cañon City imagined the gorge as a tourist attraction, hoping to cash in on visitors like other Colorado towns. The federal government ceded the Royal Gorge and its environs to Cañon City on June 11, 1906. After more than two decades of debate and planning, construction started in the summer of 1929 on a simple but elegant steel suspension bridge linking the north and south sides of the gorge. The project wrapped up by November, without the loss of a single worker. At the ceremony on December 8, officials read statements from Governor William H. Adams and Denver mayor Benjamin F. Stapleton, and local politicians speechified. Cañon City's mayor, T. Lee Witcher, dedicated the bridge to "those whose heartbeats respond to the grandeur of Nature."

Over the years, the attraction expanded to include a miniature train, gondola, funicular, carousel, water clock, theater, zipline, and several viewing platforms and drew visitors from around the world. The Royal Gorge Bridge held the record as the world's highest suspension bridge until 2001, when a span in China surpassed it by nearly 50 feet. On June 11, 2013—107 years to the day since Cañon City secured ownership of the gorge—a forest fire burned 90 percent of the park and destroyed most buildings on both sides of the gorge. Aside from a few singed planks, however, the famous span endured. The park reopened two years later after extensive reconstruction, which allowed its owners to modernize the experience while reconstructing popular attractions. The Royal Gorge Bridge remains one of Colorado's iconic structures.

December 9, 1867

Denver Secures the Capital

Colorado's territorial government meandered like a mountain stream for six years. Governor William Gilpin convened the first legislature in Denver in September 1861, but members from other parts of the territory resented Denver's influence. They relocated the seat of authority to Colorado City, a town later absorbed into Colorado Springs. When the legislature met in July 1862, it and the territorial courts called Colorado City home. Yet the new governor, John Evans, considered Denver "really the only tolerable place" in Colorado and refused to move. Legislators found Colorado City lacking as well and returned to Denver after five days.

Suspicion of Denver remained high, however, and the legislature revised the capital to Golden. Members convened there in February 1864 but found accommodations unsuitable and returned down Clear Creek. A year later they held another abortive session in Golden. When legislators met in January 1866, they used a structure built by William A.H. Loveland, which survives today as the Old Capitol Grill. Politicians nonetheless adjourned to Denver before the end of the session's first day. When the same thing happened in December 1866, the *Rocky Mountain News* reported: "Nearly all the members . . . testify that the same time spent in prison would be equally pleasant as at Golden City." By then a new governor, Alexander Cummings, had moved the executive office to Golden in an attempt to break Denver's influence. Cummings ruffled so many feathers while in office, though, that President Andrew Johnson was pressured to replace him with Alexander Hunt in the spring of 1867, making Hunt the fourth governor in six years.

The legislature, meeting in Loveland's edifice, resolved the matter in December 1867. Many hopeful towns competed for the designation, but members ultimately approved Denver as the capital. Territorial secretary Frank Hall approved the bill for Hunt on December 9, 1867. State voters formalized the choice in an 1881 election, when Denver won five times as many votes as the second-place finisher, Pueblo. It has remained the seat of government ever since.

December 10, 1941

Carr Asks Colorado for Tolerance

"As governor of Colorado," Ralph L. Carr declared via radio on December 10, 1941, three days after the attack on Pearl Harbor, "I want to express my pride in the people of this state for the manner in which they have received the news of the happenings in the Pacific. Not by hysterical expressions nor panic-stricken public demonstrations . . . but quietly, calmly, and as intelligent citizens . . . And it is my urgent request that no person may say or do anything which might cause embarrassment to some individual who is as truly American by reason either of birth or adoption of this country and unselfish in his patriotism as you or I." Carr's declaration and his subsequent actions rank him as one of Colorado's most respected governors.

Born in 1887 in Rosita, a mining town in Custer County, Carr grew up in the booming region of Cripple Creek. He earned a law degree from the University of Colorado and moved to Antonito, in Conejos County, where he built a reputation as one of the state's best water lawyers. Appointed the federal government's attorney in Colorado in 1929, Carr's renown for fairness and effectiveness flourished. He won election as governor in 1938 over incumbent Democrat Teller Ammons, and the efficient Republican secured a second term two years later.

Carr's plea for tolerance after Pearl Harbor echoed a lifetime of fighting for citizens regardless of background. Against significant opposition, Carr accepted Japanese Americans expelled from the West Coast into the Amache concentration camp. He told a group of farmers in Otero County: "I was brought up in small towns where I know the shame and dishonor of race hatred. I grew to despise it because it threatened the happiness of you, and you, and you." Carr lost a close US Senate race to the less tolerant incumbent Edwin C. Johnson in 1942 and resumed his legal practice. He died in the fall of 1950 while campaigning to return to the governor's office.

Ralph L. Carr Colorado Judicial Center, home to the state supreme court, bears his name; and memorials to him stand at the state capitol, in Denver's Sakura Square, and aside US Highway 285 on Kenosha Pass in Park County, designated the Ralph Carr Memorial Highway.

African Americans Demand Equality

A delegation of African Americans came to territorial governor Alexander Cummings's office on December 11, 1865, to present him with a petition signed by 137 members of the territory's black community. It implored the chief executive to send their demands to the US Congress, objecting to Colorado's proposed statehood in light of local attempts to deny black suffrage.

For a territory organized during the Civil War and led by Republicans, Colorado proved remarkably opposed to African Americans. In 1864, the legislature passed and Governor John Evans signed a bill forbidding black Coloradans from voting. The insults piled on in September 1865 when voters considered a state constitution. It passed by a narrow margin, with the strongest opposition in southern, predominantly Hispano counties that feared domination from Anglo communities. In the same election, voters considered African American suffrage, which they rejected by nearly 90 percent. The end of the Civil War that spring and the impending abolition of slavery apparently made few inroads in the territory. William J. Hardin, born free in Kentucky and a wartime arrival in Colorado, organized protests from the small but infuriated black community. Hardin and Henry O. Wagoner circulated the equality petition in late 1865 and secured the support of nearly all of Colorado's small African American population.

In Cummings, black Coloradans found an ally. An abolitionist from Pennsylvania, he advocated political equality and demanded desegregation of public schools, earning the enmity of many white Coloradans. Cummings fought statehood advocates who considered themselves winners in 1865, even though President Andrew Johnson vetoed a law admitting Colorado to the Union in May 1866. A year later, inspired by Colorado's discriminatory legislation, Republicans in Congress passed the Territorial Suffrage Act, which guaranteed African Americans the right to vote in western territories. His equal rights activism, among other contentious issues, earned Cummings so many enemies in Colorado that he lost his post in the spring of 1867.

A Partnership in Little London

Colorado Springs residents considered themselves genteel and respectable from the beginning. Established by Denver & Rio Grande Railroad founder William J. Palmer in 1871, "Little London" contrasted with the territory's hardscrabble mining communities. Two young men—Charles L. Tutt and Spencer Penrose—partnered on December 12, 1892, and went on to enjoy prosperous careers and lives, a success they shared with their fellow Colorado Springs residents.

Childhood friends from wealthy Philadelphia families, Tutt and Penrose grew up with the city. Tutt arrived in the late 1880s and encouraged Penrose to come in December 1892, amid the gold mining craze in nearby Cripple Creek. Hours after debarking from his train, Penrose got into a drunken fight at the country club, inspiring Tutt to remark, "Colorado Springs now knows that Spencer Penrose has arrived." The two young men officially started their partnership two days after the fracas. Over the next few years they invested in real estate, often alongside magnate Winfield S. Stratton. Tutt and Penrose made fortunes in mining and ore processing in Colorado and Utah and parlayed those fortunes into railroads, ranches, and prize fights featuring Jack Dempsey.

Tutt died in 1909, but Penrose carried on the partners' profitable and charitable work. Starting in the 1910s, Penrose poured his fortune into developing his adopted home of Colorado Springs. He built a road to the summit of Pikes Peak in 1915 and sponsored the first Pikes Peak Hill Climb the following year. In 1918 Penrose revitalized an old casino and hotel along a lake south of Colorado Springs into the Broadmoor, which remains the state's swankiest resort. Seals and flamingos imported to help dedicate the Broadmoor on June 29 of that year found the festivities so appealing that they escaped the hotel's lake and mingled with guests on verandas and in the lobby. Penrose opened the Cheyenne Mountain Zoo in 1926 and eleven years later founded the philanthropic El Pomar Foundation with his wife, Julie. Penrose was interred in a memorial observation tower above the mountainside zoo following his death in 1939.

December 13, 1908

Moffat Builds into Steamboat Springs

"Last Sunday was the great day in Steamboat Springs' history. On that day, December 13, 1908, old things passed away and all became new so far as Steamboat was concerned, for it was then that David H. Moffat's gang of railroad workers entered the city limits, leaving two shining rows of steel behind them that connected that place directly with Denver." This declaration by a Routt County press exemplified a grand moment for northwestern Colorado.

James H. and Margaret Crawford and their three children came to Colorado Territory in 1873. The following year, after living temporarily at Hot Sulphur Springs in Middle Park, they homesteaded along the Yampa River. The Crawfords

"Moffat Road" engine #302 prepares to pull a passenger train from the Steamboat Springs station in the 1910s.

enjoyed cordial relations with neighboring Utes, especially the Yamparika leader Colorow, into the 1880s. Other settlers joined them in building a community called Steamboat Springs, named for the chugging sound of a hot spring that reminded some of a riverboat's engine. A new noise arrived in 1908 with the Denver, Northwestern & Pacific Railroad, nicknamed the Moffat Road for its founder. The route connected the region to the outside world by rail, although one man who grew up in the town recalled later in life, "I can hardly remember a Moffat train that came in on schedule."

Steamboat Springs won the seat of Routt County—named for Governor John L. Routt—from Hahns Peak in 1912. Two years later, Norwegian ski jumper Carl Howelsen astonished a crowd of 2,000 people with his acrobatics. Once the tools of doctors and mail carriers, skis emerged as a popular pastime as a result of the inspiration of Howelsen and others. His jumping site evolved into the state's oldest continuously operated ski area, Howelsen Hill. James Temple, who grew up on a nearby ranch, opened a ski hill on Storm Mountain in late 1958, which grew into the Steamboat Ski Resort. Since 1935, the high school has boasted a "marching" band that skis down the street and uses plastic mouthpieces to cope with the cold. Snow shapes the character of Steamboat Springs in ways few Colorado communities can match.

December

Divvying up the Arkansas River

Aside from garish highway signs, most western state boundaries look like any other dirt road, fence line, or other nondescript part of the landscape. Nonetheless, they represent divergent communities and institutions, at times in conflict with one another. The line between Colorado and Kansas has inspired generations of tension, particularly over the water that passes from the former into the latter. An attempt to end decades of court battles and resentment culminated on December 14, 1948, when commissioners from both states signed the Arkansas River Compact.

At the turn of the twentieth century, agricultural settlement along the Arkansas River in southeastern Colorado flourished. Specialty crops like melons and sugar beets grew alongside hay and grains, made possible by extensive irrigation that re-plumbed the region. Farmers in Kansas protested that Coloradans exhausted the river and made it impossible for them to survive. The US Supreme Court adjudicated lawsuits between the states in 1902 and 1907, confirming the right of both states to their own water laws, including Colorado's complicated but entrenched doctrine of prior appropriation. Yet the court also insisted that water must flow from one state to another, a gesture of goodwill and cooperation that trumped the power of boundaries.

Enforcement proved challenging, as irrigation firms, municipalities, and influential corporations like the Colorado Fuel & Iron Company demanded their share. To better manage the resource, federal crews erected the massive John Martin Reservoir in Bent County. Another lawsuit in 1943 led to new negotiations between Colorado and Kansas, which culminated five years later. The Arkansas River Compact created intricate calculations to divide water and eased tensions between the states. The Fryingpan-Arkansas diversion project, approved in 1962 to move water east of the Continental Divide from five reservoirs through twenty-two tunnels, added a new layer of complication. More lawsuits at the turn of the twenty-first century demonstrated the limits of complicated agreements and the ever contentious nature of western water.

An Inauspicious Start for Vail

When Colorado's newest winter sports resort opened in Eagle County on December 15, 1962, it boasted the nation's first gondola, ski areas ranging from a beginner's slope to extensive backcountry bowls, and an Alpine-style community at the base of 3,000-foot-tall Vail Mountain. What the Vail Lodge and Inn lacked on opening day, unfortunately, was snow.

Vail's development started in the mid-1950s as a partnership between local resident and uranium prospector Earl V. Eaton and Peter W. Seibert, a World War II veteran who had trained at nearby Camp Hale and worked at nascent ski resorts in Aspen and at the base of Loveland Pass after the war. Eaton and Seibert recognized the skiing potential on Vail Mountain, which—like nearby Vail Pass—took its name from Charles D. Vail, the state's highway engineer in the 1930s. Lacking in mineral or timber resources, Vail found its fortune in tourism instead.

By the late 1950s, Seibert led the effort to develop a former high-altitude ranch into a ski resort. He secured support from the US Forest Service to build in the White River National Forest and touted plans for Interstate 70 that would connect the region to Denver and points beyond. Construction commenced on the lifts and a quaint, pseudo-Swiss village at the base of the mountain in the spring of 1962, while crews cleared slopes on its north flank. The resort's opening that December proved frustratingly dry, although a snowstorm on Christmas Eve more than a week later offered reason for holiday cheer, and guests soon flocked to the Vail valley.

With much of Interstate 70 complete through the Rocky Mountains by the 1970s, Vail flourished. Gerald and Betty Ford vacationed there during his presidency and maintained a home nearby after their retirement. Vail's success inspired other large-scale resorts, bringing economic development and environmental challenges to the high country. It remains one of Colorado's most prominent and popular winter destinations for locals and the world at large.

December 16, 1918

Colorado Goes Bone Dry

Governor Julius C. Gunter signed a proclamation on December 16, 1918, enacting a provision adopted by voters the previous month, one that seems incomprehensible in the age of microbreweries. After rejecting various ballot measures over the preceding fourteen years, Coloradans had finally approved a full prohibition on the manufacture, sale, and consumption of alcohol.

Pressure to ban alcohol built across the country in the late nineteenth century. Advocates argued that crime, especially domestic violence, would decrease without beer, wine, and spirits. Anti-booze groups touted "dry" candidates— those who supported their efforts toward prohibition—over "wets." Colorado's General Assembly adopted a law in 1907 permitting local governments to ban alcohol. Most agricultural areas approved prohibition, as did some cities, but booze still flowed freely in the mountain towns. In November 1914, voters approved a statewide alcohol ban, to take effect on January 1, 1916. The General Assembly enacted laws to carry out the measure, including enforcement and restrictions on advertising. Denver saloon owners tried to exempt their city, but the state supreme court overruled a measure approved by Denver voters. When prohibition took effect in 1916, seventeen breweries across the state shut down while others adapted to new industries, and 1,800 saloons closed. In response, beer enthusiasts pushed for an exemption for their beverage, leading to passage in November 1918 of a "bone dry" amendment banning all forms of alcohol, which Gunter affirmed the following month.

Nationwide Prohibition took effect in January 1919 and remained popular with state officials and voters alike. Governor Oliver H. Shoup's secretary reported in 1921 that its effect "on the social, moral, and economic life of the community has been favorable," while the mayor of Trinidad prophesied that within fifty years "the question of liquor will have almost ceased to excite public discussion." The proliferation of speakeasies, bootlegging, and organized crime in the 1920s undermined Prohibition, however, leading to its state and national repeal in 1933.

December 17, 2008

A Coloradan in the Cabinet

A smiling man wearing a cowboy hat stood beside US senator Barack Obama, who had been elected president six weeks earlier, in a hotel ballroom in Chicago on December 17, 2008. Ken Salazar, a politico from one of Colorado's oldest families, stepped to the podium to accept Obama's nomination as secretary of the Department of the Interior in the upcoming administration.

Born in the San Luis Valley in 1955, Salazar grew up in a region occupied by generations of his ancestors, lured by Mexican land grants that promoted Euro-American settlement on the upper Rio Grande in the mid-nineteenth century. He attended Colorado College and earned a law degree in Michigan, returning to the lucrative industry of water law. Governor Roy Romer hired Salazar for the first of several positions within the state executive branch in 1987. The Democratic rancher and lawyer won election as Colorado's attorney general in 1998 and served in that role until he ran successfully for a US Senate seat in 2004. There he met Obama, who chose Salazar to restore conservation over resource extraction as interior department policy. Salazar retired from the position in 2013 and returned to Denver to practice law.

Compared to many states, Colorado has sent quite a few of its residents to work as federal department heads. Seven state residents, including Salazar, have served as interior secretary—Henry M. Teller (1882–85), Hubert Work (1923–28), Oscar L. Chapman (1949–53), James G. Watt (1981–83), Gale A. Norton (2001–6), and David Bernhardt (2019–). Two Coloradans served in more than one cabinet office, Work also as postmaster general (1922–23) and Federico Peña as transportation secretary (1993–97) and energy secretary (1997–98). Despite the state's thriving farms and ranches, only one Coloradan, Charles F. Brannan, has held the post of agriculture secretary (1948–53). As the state grows in population and political influence, with its evenly split partisan allegiances, more Coloradans might find presidents calling for their services.

December 18, 1888

Stray Cattle Lead to Cliff Palace

Centuries after Ancestral Puebloans abandoned today's southwestern Colorado, Spanish and American expeditions marveled at their impressive ruins, including Rivera in 1765, Domínguez and Escalante in 1776, and Macomb in 1859. William H. Jackson photographed the area in 1874, and correspondent Virginia D. McClurg visited in the 1880s. But the most dramatic rediscovery took place on December 18, 1888, when local ranchers Richard Wetherill and Charles Mason were looking for stray cattle. While standing on a ledge, they saw instead the ruins of Cliff Palace, the most famous remnant in what is now Mesa Verde National Park.

Colorado's earliest sedentary inhabitants domesticated wild plants and developed irrigation systems to harness the scarce water of the Four Corners region. By about AD 750 their settlements spread widely, including to the top of Mesa Verde, a sloping flatland with a cliff face overlooking the Mancos River. Ancestral Puebloan communities flourished in the early 1000s, shifting from adobe to stone structures with features like subterranean kivas and towers. For reasons still debated, Mesa Verde's residents moved from its flat top to its sheltered flanks around the 1100s, erecting hundreds of cliff dwellings, of which Cliff Palace—with 200 rooms including 23 kivas—ranked first in size. This thriving region suffered an extended drought in the late 1200s, and survivors fled to the better-watered Rio Grande valley of modern New Mexico.

The Wetherill family collected baskets, pottery, and desiccated human remains, later displayed at the state capitol. A Swedish tuberculosis patient named Gustaf Nordenskiold pillaged the site in 1891, shipping relics to Europe. Outraged over the loss, McClurg and others lobbied for federal protection. President Theodore Roosevelt signed a bill creating Mesa Verde National Park in 1906, the first reserve for a manmade rather than natural landscape. The federal government carved more acreage out of the Ute Mountain Ute Reservation—including the Cliff Palace area—in 1913. Mesa Verde protects some of Colorado's greatest pre-historic heritage.

Protecting Yucca House

The plethora of Ancestral Puebloan sites in southwestern Colorado offers a great deal to scholars, American Indians, and the country at large. One of the largest communities erected by Colorado's earliest cultures, Yucca House, earned protection on December 19, 1919, when President Woodrow Wilson declared the site a national monument.

Wilson's proclamation described the 10 acres on the eastern slope of Sleeping Ute Mountain, southwest of Cortez, as "an imposing pile of masonry of great archeological value, a relic of the prehistoric inhabitants of that part of the country." Unlike the famous cliff dwellings that drew attention to nearby Mesa Verde National Park, Yucca House was one of the largest towns ever constructed by the Ancestral Puebloans in an open valley. Occupied from the AD 1100s to the 1300s, the ruins sheltered perhaps more than 10,000 people before their abandonment. Two primary structures stand within Yucca House National Monument, most notably the massive "West Complex" building of approximately 600 rooms and 100 kivas (subterranean religious structures), which stands 20 feet above ground level.

In 1878, William H. Holmes of the US Geological Survey conducted the first scientific studies of Yucca House. Other surveys took place in 1918, 1964, and 2000. Hallie Ismay, who for eighty years owned land abutting the monument and served as an unofficial guide, donated 24 acres in the late 1990s to increase its size and accessibility. The monument designation in 1919 promised increased attention and tourism, since Yucca House did not receive the snows that closed Mesa Verde in winter. Yet few visitors make their way to Yucca House because of its lack of interpretive facilities and its unexcavated condition. What the monument lacks in tourist amenities it makes up for in the promise of discovery, however, as Yucca House awaits the careful exploration of its cultural and historical riches in the generations to come.

Changing Claims to the Plains

A solemn ceremony in the Cabildo, a government building still standing in the historic French Quarter of New Orleans, Louisiana, transferred a vast yet vaguely defined land claim to the United States on December 20, 1803, formalizing the Louisiana Purchase.

Claims over eastern Colorado had alternated among several global powers since the late seventeenth century. In 1682, Robert Cavalier, Sieur de la Salle, declared—in the impossible-to-enforce style of the time—French ownership of the entire Mississippi River drainage. France sought to control the area between the Appalachian and Rocky Mountains—named "Louisiana" after King Louis XIV—through trade. In 1762, France transferred its claim to the western half of Louisiana to the Spanish. France forced Spain to return the province in 1800 as Napoleon Bonaparte sought to restore the French empire, but he proved unable to accomplish that task.

The United States stumbled into the Louisiana Purchase by accident. President Thomas Jefferson hoped to buy New Orleans, which controlled access to everything upstream from that point, to protect American interests in the trans-Appalachian West. Bonaparte saw his chance to get much-needed cash to fight European wars and rid himself of something he had no hope of controlling anyway. For 60,000,000 francs, the US land claim doubled in size.

The transfer included roughly half of modern Colorado, everything east of the Continental Divide and the Sangre de Cristo Mountains—in other words, the Mississippi River drainage coveted by La Salle more than a century earlier. To gain a better understanding of his acquisition, Jefferson authorized five expeditions into the purchase—including two led by Zebulon M. Pike—to scout the geography and resources and make contact with American Indian groups who controlled the area the United States now claimed. The Louisiana Purchase, however ill-defined, marked the first declaration of American authority in present-day Colorado.

Big Holes for Ike and Big Ed

Governor Richard Lamm rode in an antique Colorado State Patrol car through a tunnel high in the Rocky Mountains on December 21, 1979, as part of a ceremony to dedicate the completed twin bores of a corridor for Interstate 70 piercing the Continental Divide.

A truck enters the Eisenhower-Johnson Tunnel on Interstate 70 through the Continental Divide on November 12, 2007.

Initial plans for I-70, drawn up by federal engineers in the 1950s, dead-ended the road at Denver, dismissing the central Rockies as too convoluted to accommodate an interstate highway. Colorado politicians railed against the perceived dismissal, none more so than Edwin C. "Big Ed" Johnson, a three-term governor and US senator and one of the state's most popular leaders.

With the support of President Dwight D. Eisenhower, an extension of I-70 won approval, but determining the route proved challenging. Johnson dismissed the objections of engineers and portrayed the project as one worthy of the pioneer spirit. Planners proposed two tunnels, one breaching the Continental Divide separating Clear Creek and Summit Counties and another under the formidable Gore Range between Summit and Eagle Counties. Environmental activists successfully fought the latter proposal, but the former proceeded in the early 1970s.

Construction on the first tunnel bore, eventually used for westbound I-70, ended in 1973, and its name honored the president who had signed the interstate system into law. Work on the second bore started in 1975 and lasted four years. It took Johnson's name, in honor of the politician who had died in 1970. The completed project includes twin tunnels 1.7 miles long, emergency exit tunnels for pedestrians, and ventilation corridors above the roadway. Estimated to cost about

$250 million, the Eisenhower-Johnson Tunnel ranked as the most expensive highway project in American history to date. The ease of transportation enabled dramatic population and economic growth, especially for the more accessible winter sports industry, but also inspired myriad environmental consequences in the decades that followed. The tunnels both reflect and inspire the diverse opportunities and challenges faced by modern Coloradans.

December 22, 1909

Donating the Garden of the Gods

Officials in Colorado Springs approved an ordinance on December 22, 1909, to accept a bequest from Charles E. Perkins, a director of the Chicago, Burlington & Quincy Railroad. He left to the city 480 acres on its western edge, known for decades as the Garden of the Gods.

Settlers had marveled at the sandstone spires on the edge of the high plains, framing the view of Pikes Peak, since the 1850s gold rush. No one knew where the name came from, but some argued that William Gilpin inspired its moniker with his suggestion "The Garden of the Immortal God." Not everyone considered the site sacred, however, and threats to it varied over the years. The lack of water around the rock marvels prevented farmers or ranchers from settling the area, but countless prospectors sought precious minerals, oil, natural gas, and coal. In 1903, a Colorado Springs resident proposed carving likenesses of the then-three assassinated presidents—Abraham Lincoln, James Garfield, and William McKinley—into the rocks.

The idea of preserving the Garden of the Gods as a public park emerged in the 1870s. Perkins bought 240 acres—the core of the site—and considered developing it into a vacation home, like his friend and fellow railroad magnate William J. Palmer, whose mansion stood a couple of miles to the north. In 1886, the US Congress rejected a proposal to turn the Garden of the Gods and Pikes Peak region into the country's second national park, one measuring 900 square miles, The area remained in Perkins's hands, and his local holdings had doubled by his death in November 1907. In 1932, Colorado Springs added 275 acres—including the famous Balanced Rock—to the tract Perkins's estate bestowed to the city in 1909. The donation was met with praise; one press story described the Garden of the Gods as "a natural park known throughout the United States and indeed all over the civilized world for its curious rock formations and beautiful scenery." The park remains one of Colorado's most popular and photographed natural wonders.

Organizing the Union Colony

Agricultural innovator Nathan C. Meeker convened a meeting in New York City's Cooper Union—a renowned institution where Abraham Lincoln once spoke—on December 23, 1869, to organize a farming colony in Colorado Territory. Meeker worked for *New York Tribune* editor Horace Greeley, who supported the effort to recruit residents for this Union Colony.

Having organized successful colonies in other states, Meeker traveled by rail to Colorado in 1869 to scout a proper site. Accompanied by *Rocky Mountain News* founder William N. Byers, Meeker arranged to buy nearly 12,000 acres along the Denver Pacific Railway at the junction of the South Platte and Cache la Poudre Rivers in Weld County. The company also claimed 60,000 acres in homesteads around the site to insulate their community from dangers like gambling and alcohol. Meeker restricted membership to what he considered respectable individuals who abstained from drinking and had money—he charged $155 in fees plus $25 to $50 per town lot, with the proceeds going to land purchase and expenses to establish the colony.

Settlers first arrived in the spring of 1870 and set to work digging irrigation ditches and building a town, named after sponsor Horace Greeley. The new town even boasted a newspaper named after his press in New York City. A report in November 1871 stated: "Greeley is Greeley still, only a little worse so—sobered down into the stern and solemn realities of living in earnest, and for a purpose, and that purpose looking to and meaning something substantial in the future. Like a faithful beast of burden after its coltish antics and frivolous freaks are over, they are settling into the traces for heavy work." Colonists threatened violence to prevent residents from making alcohol, rejected the construction of a billiard hall, and chastised members who strayed to the scandalous nearby town of Evans while supporting schools, a library, and a theater. Greeley permitted outsiders to settle by the late 1870s, by which time it represented the pinnacle of agricultural settlement in Colorado, the standard to which all other farming towns aspired.

Gate-Crashers at El Pueblo

A group of Mouache Utes led by Tierra Blanca arrived at the gate of El Pueblo, a small fort-like community at what is now downtown Pueblo, on December 24, 1854. They asked to enter, ostensibly to join the dozen or so Hispano residents for the Christmas celebration. Suddenly, Tierra Blanca's party forced their way in and killed or wounded most of El Pueblo's inhabitants, part of a campaign they had waged against non-native people for several days. They captured a woman and two children, and with them the Utes disappeared into the night.

El Pueblo arose in the spring of 1842 near the Arkansas River–Fountain Creek junction, a popular location for native and American campsites; both the Pike and Long expeditions had operated from stockades near there earlier in the century. An American visitor in 1846 called El Pueblo "a wretched species of fort, of most primitive construction, being nothing more than a large square enclosure, surrounded by a wall of mud, miserably cracked and dilapidated." Yet the humble appearance of the adobe structure, with a few rooms arranged in a U-shape and a gated wall facing the Arkansas River, belied its significance. It served as a hub for trappers, settlers, and explorers like Charles Autobees, James Beckwourth, Christopher "Kit" Carson, John C. Frémont, Bill Williams, and Richens L. Wootton. By 1854, however, few people remained at El Pueblo, fearing Ute resentment toward the increasing numbers of interlopers.

Tierra Blanca's party committed similar depredations against non-native inhabitants of present-day southern Colorado after the bloodshed at El Pueblo, which inspired a military campaign against the group in 1855. Settlers shied away from the site after the Christmas Eve attack, but the gold rush at the end of the decade led to a resurgence. The modern city of Pueblo dates to 1858, and the site of the crumbling adobe ruins disappeared until archaeological excavations uncovered them in 1989. A reconstruction of the outpost followed, and today a museum run by History Colorado celebrates one of the most important communities in the state.

December 25, 1867

A Wrestling Match Leads to War

A diverse crowd of several hundred Anglo and Hispano residents gathered in Trinidad to celebrate Christmas on December 25, 1867. During the revelry, a stagecoach driver challenged a local Hispano resident to a wrestling match, and the masses cheered their respective champions. When the driver broke his competitor's leg, Hispanos charged the ring. The Las Animas County sheriff, a Hispano, arrested the coachman after one man died in the post-match riot, and a weeks-long free-for-all ensued, fueled by simmering ethnic tensions in southern Colorado Territory.

Established in 1862 by Anglos and Hispanos, Trinidad balanced its cultural diversity with shared political and economic influence. Yet problems percolated.

Disputes arose among Mexican land grant claimants and American homesteaders. Hispanos also worried about losing their influence after gold discoveries in northern New Mexico doubled the region's Anglo population. Meanwhile, American Indians only recently forced out sought to reclaim the region.

On December 31, the driver escaped from the jail and barricaded himself with several Anglos in a nearby hotel, exchanging fire with Hispanos outside. A band of Mouache Utes offered to intervene, but Anglos and Hispanos alike asked the native group to stay out of the fight. The *Rocky Mountain News* reported on January 6, 1868: "The affair of Christmas seems to have grown into a war of races . . . The strife is bloody enough already, but of its termination no one can predict." By that time the driver had fled the town, and both sides stood down. Ten Hispanos died in the so-called Trinidad War, and several dozen people sustained injuries.

At the end of January 1868, acting governor Frank Hall visited Trinidad to pledge territorial assistance in restoring order. In the meantime, Coloradans awoke to the agricultural and mining potential of the heretofore overlooked region. Corporate investment and railroads transformed the area by the century's end, creating a new set of challenges, but in the immediate wake of the Trinidad riots, Anglos and Hispanos reclaimed their fragile ethnic peace.

December 26, 1996

Death of a Pageant Princess

The sound of a father's horror echoed in a basement in Boulder on December 26, 1996, when he discovered the murdered body of his daughter, six-year-old JonBenét Ramsey. Her death remains perhaps the most infamous, sensationalized unsolved crime in Colorado history.

The Ramsey family lived in an affluent neighborhood on the west side of Boulder, although they maintained vacation homes in and family ties to Michigan and Georgia. Parents John and Patsy and children Blake and JonBenét enjoyed a comfortable lifestyle, afforded by the father's job with a computer company affiliated with Lockheed Martin, an aerospace firm that had moved to Jefferson County during the Cold War. JonBenét, a precocious and pretty child, appeared in pageants and won the Little Miss Colorado competition in 1995 at the age of five.

A day after celebrating Christmas, Patsy Ramsey discovered a rambling ransom note supposedly from a foreign faction, threatening JonBenét if the family did not pay $118,000. What started as a kidnapping morphed into homicide when John Ramsey found JonBenét's body in the basement wine cellar. The little girl died from strangulation, with a cord still wrapped around her neck, and her body bore evidence of sexual assault. The investigation soon took on a farcical tone, as personality feuds and egos among Boulder County law enforcement and judicial officers made an already confused situation worse. The media transformed JonBenét's killing into a sensation, with speculation and accusation often trumping journalistic integrity.

Questions about the home invasion shifted suspicion to members of the Ramsey family, who left Colorado for Michigan to escape a media circus that all but declared their guilt. Patsy Ramsey died of cancer in 2006, two years before officials announced that forensic evidence had cleared the family. The case remains a topic of morbid fascination, plagued by the incompetence of the early investigation. JonBenét lies buried next to her mother in a Georgia cemetery.

December 27, 1858

A Feast for Masonic Miners

A group of prospectors gathered at the cabin of Oscar E. Lehow and Andrew Sagendorf on what is now the Auraria Campus in downtown Denver on December 27, 1858. There they celebrated the feast day of St. John the Evangelist, a prominent date on the Masonic calendar.

Freemasonry, a fraternal and benevolent society, flourished in the nineteenth century. Its pageantry and secrecy appealed to some members, while its social and economic connections drew others. The feast day offered the founding members of the local fraternity—who had already held several small meetings—a chance to celebrate. The grand master of Kansas Territory, under whose jurisdiction the Pikes Peak gold rush country lay, praised the extension of Freemasonry, noting new chapters "located within the newly discovered Gold regions of the West and literally amidst the highest hills and lowest valleys, where the sun, reflecting from perpetual snow, warms the rich vale in its constant verdure. Truly, this is an age of penetration and progression, and the genial influence of Masonry, cementing and warming the hearts of its members, keeps pace with the march of civilization." Within a few months, followers of the craft erected the area's first Masonic temple at Central City in modern Gilpin County. When Colorado Territory received its own grand lodge designation in the summer of 1861, Methodist minister John M. Chivington secured the leadership post of grand master.

Masons emerged as prominent political and business leaders in Colorado, and the group grew in number and stature. In 1890 they dedicated in Denver a massive temple built of orange sandstone and designed by Frank E. Edbrooke, which endured a fire in 1984 and remains a prominent feature on the Sixteenth Street

Mall. Masonic lodges operate in communities across the state and continue to promote social and philanthropic endeavors, although membership in all secret societies has declined since the early twentieth century. Nonetheless, the architecturally based Freemasonry remains—literally and figuratively—a cornerstone of Colorado history.

Cragmor's Last Gasp

The director of Cragmor Sanatorium, once the state's most exclusive destination for health seekers, announced on December 28, 1961, that the facility's remaining patients would depart by the following summer, bringing its long and prosperous history to a close.

People suffering from lung ailments, tuberculosis in particular, flocked to Colorado in the late nineteenth century, hoping that the high elevation, thin air, and plentiful sunshine might restore them to health. Dozens of sanatoriums,

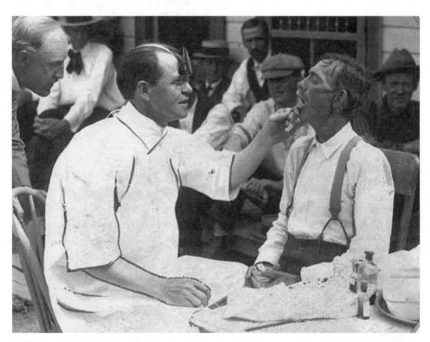

A doctor examines a tuberculosis patient at the Craig Colony sanatorium in Jefferson County in the early twentieth century.

some founded by religious or ethnic groups and others funded by generous benefactors, opened across the state. They offered long-term and occasionally permanent residency for medical refugees. No sanatorium compared to Cragmor, however, a destination for rich and powerful "lungers" from around the country and the world.

As befit Colorado Springs' reputation as a genteel community, Cragmor offered afflicted members of the upper crust an exclusive resort in which to recuperate. Dr. S. Edwin Solly, whose skills drew patients to Colorado Springs, sought support from town founder William J. Palmer and others to fund Cragmor in the summer of 1905. Within a decade, a massive new facility opened to expand the number of patients—and amount of money—flowing in. The elite residents of Cragmor led to an economic boom in Colorado Springs as they enjoyed the tourist amenities and patronized local stores. Forced to accept indigent patients during World War I, the sanatorium reclaimed its wealthy reputation after the conflict. It won recognition as "the most desirable sanatorium in the world" by an international tuberculosis association in 1924.

Cragmor declined during the Great Depression and World War II. It won a respite in 1952 when the federal government paid for Navajos from Arizona to recuperate there, but that program ended nine years later. Cragmor found a new purpose in 1965 as the University of Colorado at Colorado Springs, which occupies the sanatorium's renovated buildings and benefits from its commanding site overlooking the city, Pikes Peak, and the Garden of the Gods.

December 29, 1845

When Texas Tried to Claim Colorado

Texans are known for thinking big, but sometimes even they stretch things too far. Their grandness found particular expression in the 1830s, when Americans in the Mexican province of Texas declared their independence. Texas and Mexico argued over their common limit for nine years, and the republic existed in political limbo. The United States finally acquiesced to Texas's requests for annexation in 1845, and on December 29, Texas joined the Union. Its legal limits at the time of admission included all or part of thirty-one of the sixty-four counties in modern Colorado.

Before Texans rebelled, the US-Mexico border stood along the Adams-Onís Treaty line established in 1819. In Colorado, it followed the Arkansas River upstream to its source near Leadville and extended due north from there into present-day Wyoming. Taking a page from President Thomas Jefferson, who had unsuccessfully suggested the Rio Grande as the southern reach of the Louisiana Purchase, Texans declared that river as their border with Mexico. As such, their claimed limit before and after admission to the Union extended up it from the Gulf of Mexico to its source in today's San Juan County and due north from the headwaters into what is now Wyoming. This placed Santa Fe within Texas's control, although it held no authority over New Mexico. It also meant that, after December 1845, traders at Bent's Fort and settlers at El Pueblo supposedly looked across the Arkansas River into an American state rather than Mexico.

Considering the distance from Texas's government, the republic and the state exercised no control over modern Colorado, even though their claimed authority extended through it. The border controversy helped inspire the war between the United States and Mexico in the late 1840s. After five years of dispute, Texas accepted its current boundaries through the Compromise of 1850, and the contested claim over Colorado disappeared with as little local interest as its declaration had inspired. Only in recent decades have large numbers of Texans come to colonize Colorado.

December 30, 1911

Winter Sports in Middle Park

"A perfect panorama of innocent sports, good feeling, and unbridled enthusiasm" commenced in the Grand County seat of Hot Sulphur Springs on December 30, 1911, according to a local newspaper, a "labyrinth of merriment . . . on land, on ice, on snow, as well as in the air." The town's carnival presaged modern Colorado's prosperous, profitable winter sports industry.

Trappers and early settlers used skis, sleds, and the like, but only for practical purposes—getting from one community to another, hauling goods through the mountains in winter, and rescuing people caught in storms. In the 1880s, communities organized skiing clubs in Aspen, Ouray, and several Gunnison County towns including Crested Butte, Gunnison, and Irwin. "Norwegian snowshoes" remained functional rather than fun items well into the twentieth century, however. The 1911 festivities in Hot Sulphur Springs changed that.

The carnival included men's and women's sled and toboggan races, skating competitions and performances, and a grand ball in the evening. Organizers announced a special event for the following day, New Year's Eve, involving a pair of visiting Norwegians, Carl Howelsen and Angell Schmidt. Howelsen had earned renown in Norway, Sweden, and Germany for his ski jumping abilities. He emigrated to the United States in 1905 and found work as a stone mason and bricklayer in Chicago. There and in New York City, he amazed audiences by jumping on tracks with soaped skis. Howelsen traveled to Denver in 1909, lured by the Rocky Mountains. He and his friend Schmidt explored the mountains during the winter, a slow time for construction work, and favored the powder of Middle Park. They built a jump and demonstrated their skill for the Hot Sulphur Springs carnival, astonishing the crowd with distances of nearly 80 feet.

Howelsen returned to Grand County two months later for another carnival. In 1914 he organized one in the Routt County seat of Steamboat Springs, on what is now called Howelsen Hill. His efforts fueled interest in winter sports and laid the foundation for a vital industry.

December 31, 1943

John Denver's Birthday

Henry J. Deutschendorf Jr., born in New Mexico on December 31, 1943, earned international popularity through his mellow, romantic, naturally inspired songs—recorded and performed for more than three decades under his stage name, John Denver.

Denver grew up in a military family and moved often as a young man. His wandering ways continued after he dropped out of college in 1964. Three years later, Denver achieved his first hit as a songwriter with "Leaving on a Jet Plane," recorded by the folk group Peter, Paul, and Mary. He toured college campuses, singing protest songs about the Vietnam War and the Richard Nixon administration. Success allowed Denver and his wife, Annie, to move to Aspen in 1970, although their relationship strained because of his travel and temperament. After one bitter exchange in 1974, Denver went skiing on Aspen Mountain and during the chairlift ride composed "Annie's Song" in his estranged wife's honor. Nonetheless, they divorced in 1982.

Colorado's landscape often inspired Denver's music, never more than a camping trip in Pitkin County in the early 1970s that led to "Rocky Mountain High." The song debuted in 1972 and endured in the state's mythos; Colorado leaders named it the state's second official song in 2007. Denver recalled: "Some people had the idea that the song was about getting stoned in the mountains, and it's true that was going on, but the song was about how exhilarating it was to *be* there, to feel free, to have come to such a place, both personally and geographically. And it was a reflection on mortality." Denver's environmentalism led him to establish the Windstar Foundation at Snowmass in 1976 to advocate sustainable living. He died piloting a small plane that crashed in the Pacific Ocean off California in 1997. After

Windstar closed in 2012, a statue of Denver at the foundation was relocated to the Red Rocks amphitheatre in Jefferson County.

Speaking of a Rocky Mountain high, it's time to return to January 1 and start the calendar again. Here's to another happy, healthy, historic year in the great state of Colorado.

IMAGE CREDITS

Introduction

PAGE 4   Author's collection

January

PAGE 9   *Courtesy*, History Colorado, Stephen H. Hart Research Center, Denver, object I.D. 2000.129.847

PAGE 16   Author's collection

PAGE 26   *Courtesy*, History Colorado, Stephen H. Hart Research Center, Denver, object I.D. 89.451.3383

PAGE 33   *Courtesy*, History Colorado, Stephen H. Hart Research Center, Denver, object I.D. 89.451.2614

February

PAGE 43   *Courtesy*, History Colorado, Stephen H. Hart Research Center, Denver, object I.D. 92.209.4

PAGE 48   Author's collection

PAGE 55   *Courtesy*, Denver Public Library, Western History Collection, call number X-33812

PAGE 62   *Courtesy*, History Colorado, Stephen H. Hart Research Center, Denver, object I.D. PH.PROP.3791

March

PAGE 72   *Courtesy*, History Colorado, Stephen H. Hart Research Center, Denver, object I.D. 84.193.302

PAGE 78   *Courtesy*, History Colorado, Stephen H. Hart Research Center, Denver, object I.D. 86.200.2093

PAGE 84   *Courtesy*, Denver Public Library, Western History Collection, call number RMN-041–7224

PAGE 90   Author's collection

PAGE 95   *Courtesy*, Denver Public Library, Western History Collection, call number Z-66

April

PAGE 105   *Courtesy*, Denver Public Library, Western History Collection, call number AUR-2102

PAGE 111   *Courtesy*, History Colorado, Stephen H. Hart Research Center, Denver, object I.D. 2019.41.1

PAGE 118   *Courtesy*, History Colorado, Stephen H. Hart Research Center, Denver, object I.D. 89.451.4271

PAGE 126   *Courtesy*, History Colorado, Stephen H. Hart Research Center, Denver, object I.D. 2014.148.23

May

PAGE 135   *Courtesy*, Denver Public Library, Western History Collection, call number RMN-055–1559

PAGE 140   *Courtesy*, History Colorado, Stephen H. Hart Research Center, Denver, object I.D. 96.186.8

PAGE 148   *Courtesy*, History Colorado, Stephen H. Hart Research Center, Denver, object I.D. 92.3.42

PAGE 155   *Courtesy*, History Colorado, Stephen H. Hart Research Center, Denver, object I.D. 89.451.893

June

PAGE 165   *Courtesy*, History Colorado, Stephen H. Hart Research Center, Denver, object I.D. 85.313.5

PAGE 171   Author's collection

PAGE 176   *Courtesy*, History Colorado, Stephen H. Hart Research Center, Denver, object I.D. PH.PROP.5265

PAGE 183   *Courtesy*, History Colorado, Stephen H. Hart Research Center, Denver, object I.D. 96.174.4614

PAGE 189   *Courtesy*, Colorado Springs Pioneers Museum, Lew Tilley Collection, catalog number S995.0333.0004

July

PAGE 200   *Courtesy*, History Colorado, Stephen H. Hart Research Center, Denver, object I.D. 86.296.10227

PAGE 208   *Courtesy*, Denver Public Library, Western History Collection, call number TMD-389

PAGE 213   *Courtesy*, History Colorado, Stephen H. Hart Research Center, Denver, object I.D. 2000.129.1256

Image Credits

PAGE 218 *Courtesy*, History Colorado, Stephen H. Hart Research Center, Denver, object I.D. 86.200.6658

PAGE 223 *Courtesy*, Denver Public Library, Western History Collection, Rocky Mountain News Photo Archives

August

PAGE 231 *Courtesy*, History Colorado, Stephen H. Hart Research Center, Denver, object I.D. PH.PROP.3040

PAGE 236 *Courtesy*, History Colorado, Stephen H. Hart Research Center, Denver, object I.D. 98.227.1

PAGE 245 Author's collection

PAGE 251 *Courtesy*, History Colorado, Stephen H. Hart Research Center, Denver, object I.D. PH.PROP.2326

PAGE 255 Author's collection

September

PAGE 264 *Courtesy*, History Colorado, Stephen H. Hart Research Center, Denver, object I.D. 89.451.5784

PAGE 270 *Courtesy*, Denver Public Library, Western History Collection, call number X-30679

PAGE 278 *Courtesy*, History Colorado, Stephen H. Hart Research Center, Denver, object I.D. 88.526.3

PAGE 285 *Courtesy*, Denver Public Library, Western History Collection, call number X-30669

October

PAGE 290 *Courtesy*, History Colorado, Stephen H. Hart Research Center, Denver, object I.D. 86.200.1562

PAGE 298 *Courtesy*, History Colorado, Stephen H. Hart Research Center, Denver, object I.D. 90.156.980

PAGE 307 *Courtesy*, Denver Public Library, Western History Collection, call number Z-7377

PAGE 317 *Courtesy*, History Colorado, Stephen H. Hart Research Center, Denver, object I.D. 2001.149.9

November

PAGE 324 *Courtesy*, Royal Gorge Regional Museum and History Center, Cañon City, call number 1991.032.003

PAGE 329 Author's collection

Image Credits

Image Credits

SOURCES

Introduction

Samuel Bowles, *The Parks and Mountains of Colorado: A Summer Vacation in the Switzerland of America* (Norman: University of Oklahoma Press, 1991 [1869]), 36 (quotation).

January

1. Nick Johnson, "Rocky Mountain High: A History of Cannabis in Colorado," *Colorado Heritage* (January–February 2015), 24–31 (quotation 27); "Colorado Amendment 2012 Election Results," *Denver Post*, http://data.denverpost.com/election/results/amendment/2012/, accessed February 4, 2016.

2. Derek R. Everett, *The Colorado State Capitol: History, Politics, Preservation* (Boulder: University Press of Colorado, 2005); *Castle Rock Journal*, January 9, 1895, 3; *Denver Post*, October 11, 1950, 1 (quotation).

3. William J. May Jr., "The Colorado Sugar Manufacturing Company: Grand Junction Plant," *Colorado Magazine* 55: 1 (Winter 1978), 15–45; *Denver Times*, December 31, 1899, 5 (quotation); *The Valley of Opportunity: A History of West-Central Colorado*, Bureau of Land Management Cultural Resource Series, Colorado #12, http://www.nps.gov/parkhistory/online_books/blm/cultresser/co/12/chap7.htm, accessed March 18, 2015.

4. *Rocky Mountain News*, January 4, 1941, 1, 14; *Denver Post*, January 4, 1941, 1, 3; "Denver Ordnance Plant/Remington Arms Company," Jefferson County Historical Commission, http://jeffco.us/placenames/search3.cfm?ps_oid=1371029&search=, accessed February 5, 2016; Carl Ubbelohde, Maxine Benson, and Duane A. Smith, *A Colorado History* (Boulder: Pruett, 2006).

5. LeRoy R. Hafen, "George A. Jackson's Diary, 1858–1859," *Colorado Magazine* 12: 6 (November 1935), 201–14 (quotations 205); Historical Society of Idaho Springs, *History of Clear Creek County: Tailings, Tracks, and Tommy Knockers* (Denver: Specialty Publishing, Inc., 1986).

6. *Colorado Springs Gazette*, January 7, 1942, 1–2, 4 (quotation); "Fort Carson—Garrison," US Army, http://www.carson.army.mil/garrison/fort-carson-history.html, accessed November 25, 2015.

7. Dallas Williams, *Fort Sedgwick, Colorado Territory: Hell Hole on the Platte* (Julesburg, CO: Fort Sedgwick Historical Society, 1993), 11 (quotation); Doris Monahan, *Julesburg and Fort Sedgwick: Wicked City, Scandalous Fort* (Sterling, CO: self-published, 2009).

8. *Vail Trail*, January 2, 1976, 1, 21; January 16, 1976, 8, 56; "January 1976," Elvis-History.com, http://www.elvis-history.com/english/year1976/januar.htm, accessed May 28, 2015; "Ford Had Deep Connections to Vail, Colorado," *Denver Post*, www.denverpost.com, July 8, 2011.

9. "Missing Rocks Traveled from the Moon to Former Governor's Home Office," *Denver Post*, www.denverpost.com, June 2, 2010; "Gov. Ritter, Mines Unveil New Home for Moon Rock," Colorado School of Mines, http://www.mines.edu/Gov.-Ritter-Mines -unveil-new-home-for-moon-rock, accessed December 17, 2013.

10. Louis S. Warren, *Buffalo Bill's America: William Cody and the Wild West Show* (New York: Alfred A. Knopf, 2005); *Fort Collins Express*, October 15, 1887, 1 (quotation); *Rocky Mountain News*, January 15, 1917, 1, 3.

11. *Colorado Transcript* (Golden), January 16, 1901, 3; February 20, 1901, 2 (quotation); *Steamboat Pilot*, January 16, 1901, 1; January 30, 1901, 1; February 13, 1901, 1.

12. "Dynasty," TV.com, www.tv.com/dynasty, accessed March 19, 2015; "TV Acres: Real Estate," TV Acres, www.tvacres.com/homes_dynasty.htm, accessed March 19, 2015.

13. Bill Hosokawa, *Thunder in the Rockies: The Incredible Denver Post* (New York: William Morrow, 1976), 23 (quotation).

14. Gary Morgan, *Three Foot Rails: A Quick History of the Colorado Central Railroad* (Colorado Springs: Little London, 1974); "Colorado Central Railroad," UtahRails.net, http://utahrails.net/up/colorado-central.php, accessed June 23, 2015.

15. Perry Eberhart, *Guide to the Colorado Ghost Towns and Mining Camps* (Athens, OH: Swallow, 1969); Dave Southworth, *Colorado Mining Camps* (Las Cruces, NM: Wild Horse, 1997); Donald F. Danker (ed.), *Mollie: The Journal of Mollie Dorsey Sanford in Nebraska and Colorado Territories, 1857–1866* (Lincoln: University of Nebraska Press, 1976) (first quotation); *Rocky Mountain News*, November 11, 1873, 4 (second quotation).

16. "Sex-Change Industry a Boon to Small City," *New York Times*, www.nytimes.com, November 8, 1998; "Stanley H. Biber, 82, Surgeon among First to Do Sex Changes, Dies," *New York Times*, www.nytimes.com, January 21, 2006.

17. LeRoy R. Hafen, "The Coming of the Automobile and Improved Roads to Colorado," *Colorado Magazine* 8: 1 (January 1931), 1–16 (quotations 4); Associated Cultural Resource Experts, *Highways to the Sky: A Context and History of Colorado's Highway System* (Denver: Colorado Department of Transportation, 2002).

18. Mary Ellen Gilliland, *Summit: A Gold Rush History of Summit County, Colorado* (Silverthorne, CO: Alpenrose, 1980), 266 (quotation); "2010 Community Profile," Town of Silverthorne, http://www.silverthorne.org/Modules/ShowDocument.aspx?document id=463, accessed July 6, 2015.

19. Duane A. Smith, "A Social History of McPhee: Colorado's Largest Lumber Town," in *Forests under Fire: A Century of Ecosystem Mismanagement in the Southwest*, ed. Christopher J. Huggard and Arthur R. Gómez (Tucson: University of Arizona Press, 2001), 41–65.

20. *Rocky Mountain News*, January 16–20, 1872, 1; January 21, 1872, 4 (quotation).

21. Paul H. Gantt, *The Case of Alferd Packer: The Man Eater* (Denver: University of Denver Press, 1952).

22. *Rocky Mountain News*, January 23, 1935, 3; Elinor McGinn, *A Wide-Awake Woman: Josephine Roche in the Age of Reform* (Denver: Colorado Historical Society, 2002), 71, 92 (quotations).

23. F. Carl Schumacher and George C. Wilson, *Bridge of No Return: The Ordeal of the USS Pueblo* (New York: Harcourt Brace Jovanovich, 1971), 101 (quotation); "USS *Pueblo*

(AGER-2)," USS *Pueblo* Veterans Association, http://www.usspueblo.org/index.html, accessed July 25, 2015.

24. *Rocky Mountain News*, January 24, 2008, 7 (quotation); January 25, 2008, 7, 39; *Denver Post*, January 25, 2008, 1B–2B; Daniel A. Smith, "Populist Entrepreneur: Douglas Bruce and the Tax and Government Limitation Moment in Colorado, 1986–1992," *Great Plains Research* 6: 2 (Fall 1996), 269–94; Christine R. Martell and Paul Teske, "Fiscal Management Implications of the TABOR Bind," *Public Administration Review* 67: 4 (July–August 2007), 673–87.

25. *Denver Post*, January 26, 1998, section AA (quotation 2AA); "Denver Broncos," Sports Ecyclopedia, http://www.sportsecyclopedia.com/nfl/denver/broncos.html, accessed November 21, 2015.

26. *New York Times*, January 26, 1875, 4 (quotation); Diane Abraham, "Bloody Grass: Western Colorado Range Wars, 1881–1934," *Journal of the Western Slope* 6: 2 (Spring 1991), 1–23.

27. Charles J. Bayard, "A Notice of Silver Ore on the Upper Platte in 1808," *Colorado Magazine* 51: 1 (Winter 1974), 43–51 (quotations 46–47).

28. *Rocky Mountain News*, January 28, 1885, 4 (quotation); January 29, 1885, 2, 4; January 30, 1885, 2, 4, 8; January 31, 1885, 2, 4, 8; Harold U. Faulkner, *1890–1900: Politics, Reform, and Expansion* (New York: Harper and Row, 1959).

29. Willard E. Simms, *Ten Days Every January: A History of the National Western Stock Show* (Wheat Ridge, CO: Record Stockman, 1980); Thomas J. Noel, *Riding High: Colorado Ranchers and 100 Years of the National Western Stock Show* (Golden, CO: Fulcrum, 2005).

30. "Station's Archived Memories," Rocky Mountain PBS, http://www.rmpbs.org /volunteer/sam/about-stations-archived-memories-sam/, accessed May 11, 2015.

31. *Metropolitan*, January 31, 1992, 3, 6; Margaret Coel, Jane Barker, and Karen Gilleland, *The Tivoli: Bavaria in the Rockies* (Boulder: Colorado and West, 1985); "Auraria Neighborhood History," Denver Public Library, https://history.denverlibrary.org/auraria -neighborhood, accessed September 3, 2015.

February

1. Stephen Harding Hart and Archer Butler Hulbert (eds.), *The Southwestern Journals of Zebulon Pike, 1806–1807* (Albuquerque: University of New Mexico Press, 2006); Thomas J. Noel, *Buildings of Colorado* (New York: Oxford University Press, 1997).

2. Carl Abbott, Stephen J. Leonard, and Thomas J. Noel, *Colorado: A History of the Centennial State* (Boulder: University Press of Colorado, 2005); *Bent's Old Fort* (Denver: State Historical Society of Colorado, 1979); Stella M. Drumm (ed.), *Down the Santa Fe Trail and into New Mexico: The Diary of Susan Shelby Magoffin, 1846–1847* (Lincoln: University of Nebraska Press, 1962), 67 (quotation).

3. Deer Trail Pioneer Historical Society, *Deer Trail Rodeo Centennial, 1869–1969* (publication information unknown); "Hittson, John," Texas State Historical Society, https://tshaonline.org/handbook/online/articles/fhi38, accessed May 19, 2015; "Rodeo Education," Pro Rodeo Hall of Fame, http://www.prorodeohalloffame.com/rodeo-history/,

accessed May 19, 2015; "Drone Hunting Measure Rejected Tuesday in Deer Trail," *Denver Post*, www.denverpost.com, April 1, 2014.

4. *Rocky Mountain News*, February 5, 1954, 24 (quotation), 30; James O. Chipman, "Billy Adams," Adams State University, http://www.adams.edu/lutherbean/billyadams.php, accessed September 18, 2015.

5. *Rocky Mountain News*, February 13, 1868, 1; Charles J. Kappler (ed.), *Indian Affairs: Laws and Treaties*, vol. 2 (Washington, DC: Government Printing Office, 1904), 990–96; Virginia McConnell Simmons, *The Ute Indians of Utah, Colorado, and New Mexico* (Boulder: University Press of Colorado, 2000).

6. "North American Aerospace Defense Command," http://www.norad.mil/Home .aspx, accessed February 6, 2016.

7. *Steamboat Pilot*, February 11, 1937, 2, 4; February 18, 1937, 1; March 4, 1937, 1; June 3, 1937, 1; *Aspen Daily Times*, April 1, 1937, 1 (quotations); Abbott Fay, *A History of Skiing in Colorado* (Lake City, CO: Western Reflections, 2008); "Berthoud Pass Ski Area," Coloradoskihistory.com, http://www.coloradoskihistory.com/lost/bpass.html, accessed June 13, 2015.

8. Session Laws of Colorado, Second General Assembly, 1879 (first quotation 87, second quotation 89); *Colorado Weekly Chieftain* (Pueblo), October 23, 1879, 1 (third quotation); "CMHI Pueblo Museum," Colorado Mental Health Institute at Pueblo Museum Foundation, http://www.cmhipmuseum.org/, accessed August 27, 2015.

9. *Denver Daily Tribune*, February 10, 1878, 4 (quotations); Thomas J. Noel, *Riding High: Colorado Ranchers and 100 Years of the National Western Stock Show* (Golden, CO: Fulcrum, 2005).

10. "Fort Vasquez Site, National Register of Historic Places Inventory-Nomination Form," National Park Service, http://focus.nps.gov/pdfhost/docs/NRHP/ Text/70000169.pdf, accessed September 18, 2015; William B. Butler, *The Fur Trade in Colorado* (Lake City, CO: Western Reflections, 2012), 152 (quotations).

11. James E. Hansen II, *Democracy's College in the Centennial State: A History of Colorado State University* (Fort Collins: Colorado State University, 1977); *Fort Collins Courier*, October 2, 1879, 1 (quotation).

12. Lisa Lindell, "'No Greater Menace': Verne Sankey and the Kidnapping of Charles Boettcher II," *Colorado History* 10 (Denver: Colorado Historical Society, 2004), 37–56; Edward Butts, *Wrong Side of the Law: True Stories of Crime* (Toronto, ON: Dundurn, 2013).

13. *Aspen Times*, February 9, 1950, 1; February 16, 1950, 1; *Rocky Mountain News*, February 14, 1950, 39–40; February 19, 1950, 37, 43; William Philpott, *Vacationland: Tourism and Environment in the Colorado High Country* (Seattle: University of Washington Press, 2013).

14. C. W. Hurd, *Boggsville: Cradle of the Colorado Cattle Industry* (Las Animas, CO: Boggsville Committee, 1957); "Prowers, John W.," Otero County Genealogy and History, http://www.coloradoplains.com/otero/history/bent1881_bio39.htm, accessed May 24, 2015.

15. Stephen J. Leonard, Thomas J. Noel, and Donald L. Walker Jr., *Honest John Shafroth: A Colorado Reformer* (Denver: Colorado Historical Society, 2003); *Colorado Transcript* (Golden), February 18, 1904, 4 (quotation).

Sources

16. *Report of the Secretary of War*, United States Serial Set, vol. 1277, 39th Congress, 2nd session, S. Ex. Doc. 26, February 14, 1867; C. A. Prentice, "Captain Silas S. Soule, a Pioneer Martyr," *Colorado Magazine* 12: 6 (November 1935), 224–28; "The Life of Silas Soule," National Park Service, http://www.nps.gov/sand/learn/historyculture/the-life-of-silas-soule.htm, accessed July 1, 2015 (quotation).

17. Jerome C. Smiley, *History of Denver* (Denver: Times-Sun, 1901); Stephen J. Leonard and Thomas J. Noel, *Denver: Mining Camp to Metropolis* (Niwot: University Press of Colorado, 1990).

18. Charles J. Kappler (ed.), *Indian Affairs: Laws and Treaties*, vol. 2 (Washington, DC: Government Printing Office, 1904), 807–11; Robert W. Frazer, *Forts of the West* (Norman: University of Oklahoma Press, 1972); Stan Hoig, *White Man's Paper Trail: Grand Councils and Treaty-Making on the Central Plains* (Boulder: University Press of Colorado, 2006).

19. "Friends of Browns Canyon, Colorado—Browns Canyon National Monument," brownscanyon.org, accessed February 19, 2015 (quotation); "Obama to Declare Browns Canyon in Colorado a National Monument," *Denver Post*, www.denverpost.com, February 18, 2015.

20. Charles J. Kappler (ed.), *Indian Affairs: Laws and Treaties*, vol. 1 (Washington, DC: Government Printing Office, 1904), 555–57; "History of the Southern Ute," Southern Ute Indian Tribe, https://www.southernute-nsn.gov/history/, accessed March 25, 2015.

21. Janet Lecompte, "Charles Autobees," *Colorado Magazine* 34: 3 (July 1957), 163–79; 34: 4 (October 1957), 274–89; 35: 1 (January 1958), 51–70; 35: 2 (April 1958), 139–53; 35: 3 (July 1958), 219–25; 35: 4 (October 1958), 303–8; 36: 1 (January 1959), 58–66; 36: 3 (July 1959), 202–13.

22. David J. Weber, *The Spanish Frontier in North America* (New Haven, CT: Yale University Press, 1992); Carl Ubbelohde, Maxine Benson, and Duane A. Smith, *A Colorado History* (Boulder: Pruett, 2006); Stella M. Drumm, *Down the Santa Fe Trail and into New Mexico: The Diary of Susan Shelby Magoffin, 1846–1847* (Lincoln: University of Nebraska Press, 1962), 72 (quotation).

23. Stephen Singular, *Talked to Death: The Life and Murder of Alan Berg* (New York: Birch Tree Books, 1987), 311 (quotation).

24. Franklin K. Van Zandt, *Boundaries of the United States and the Several States*, Geological Survey Bulletin 1212 (Washington, DC: Government Printing Office, 1966), 257–58 (quotations).

25. *Denver Post*, October 21, 1981, 1C; October 29, 1988, 1A, 15A.

26. Betty L. Hodge, "Fort Garland: A Window onto Southwest History," entire issue of *San Luis Valley Historian* 24: 2 (1992); *Solid Muldoon Weekly* (Ouray, CO), December 14, 1883, 2 (quotation); "Costilla County," History Colorado, http://www.historycolorado.org/oahp/costilla-county, accessed November 20, 2015.

27. Dick Kreck, *Anton Woode; The Boy Murderer* (Golden, CO: Fulcrum, 2006); *Boulder Daily Camera*, April 6, 1893, 2 (quotation).

28. Eugene H. Berwanger, *The Rise of the Centennial State: Colorado Territory, 1861–1876* (Urbana: University of Illinois Press, 2007); Derek R. Everett, *The Colorado State Capitol: History, Politics, Preservation* (Boulder: University Press of Colorado, 2005).

29. William Swilling Wallace, *Antoine Robidoux, 1794–1860: A Biography of a Western Venturer* (Los Angeles: Glen Dawson, 1953); Ken Reyher, *Antoine Robidoux and Fort Uncompahgre* (Ouray, CO: Western Reflections, 1998).

March

1. Duane A. Smith, *Horace Tabor: His Life and the Legend* (Niwot: University Press of Colorado, 1989); Duane A. Smith, *Henry M. Teller: Colorado's Grand Old Man* (Boulder: University Press of Colorado, 2002), 117 (quotation).

2. Elting E. Morison, *The Letters of Theodore Roosevelt*, vol. 5 (Cambridge, MA: Harvard University Press, 1952), 604 (first quotation); *Aspen Daily Times*, March 6, 1907, 1; *Castle Rock Journal*, March 8, 1907, 4 (second quotation); *Mancos Times-Tribune*, April 5, 1907, 1 (third quotation); "Find a Forest by State," United States Forest Service, http://www.fs.fed.us/recreation/map/state_list.shtml, accessed July 14, 2015.

3. "Biography," Minoru Yasui Tribute Project, http://www.minoruyasuitribute.org/#!blank/c1qyu, accessed November 21, 2015.

4. L. Ray Burrola, "Casimiro Barela: The First Chicano State Senator, 1876–1915; with an Historical Overview of Chicanos in Early Colorado," MA thesis. Colorado State University, Fort Collins, 1975; José E. Fernández, *The Biography of Casimiro Barela*, trans. A. Gabriel Meléndez (Albuquerque: University of New Mexico Press, 2003).

5. "Dorothy Ballast Jarrett, Who Ran the Drive-in with the First Cheeseburgers, Dies at 94," *Denver Post*, www.denverpost.com, March 20, 2011.

6. Roger Baker, *Clara: An Ex-Slave in Gold Rush Colorado* (Central City, CO: Black Hawk Publishing, 2003); *Rocky Mountain News*, March 7, 1884, 5 (quotation).

7. *Denver Post*, March 7, 1968, 49, 64; "Buell, Temple H.," History Colorado, Office of Archaeology and Historic Preservation, http://www.historycolorado.org/sites/default/files/files/OAHP/Guides/Architects_buell.pdf, accessed February 5, 2016; "History of Cinderella City Mall," City of Englewood, Colorado, http://www.englewoodgov.org/inside-city-hall/city-departments/community-development/redevelopment-projects/citycenter-englewood/history-of-cinderella-city-mall, accessed February 5, 2016.

8. Mark Thompson, "The Politician Who Bridged the 37th Parallel," New Mexico Office of the State Historian, http://newmexicohistory.org/people/lafayette-head, accessed November 27, 2015; Virginia McConnell Simmons, *The San Luis Valley: Land of the Six-Armed Cross* (Niwot: University Press of Colorado, 1999); *Colorado Springs Gazette*, August 26, 1876, 2 (quotation).

9. *Mountain-Ear* (Nederland), March 7, 2002, 8–11, 13–16 (quotations 8); March 14, 2002, 1, 4; "Frozen Dead Guy Days," http://frozendeadguydays.org/, accessed July 20, 2015.

10. Gary Morgan, *The Georgetown Loop: Colorado's Scenic Wonder* (Fort Collins, CO: Centennial Publications, 1984).

11. Derek Carlson, "World War II Comes to Delta," *Journal of the Western Slope* 15: 1 (Winter 2000), 1–17; Robert C. Mikesh, *Japan's World War II Balloon Bomb Attacks on North America* (Washington, DC: Smithsonian Institution Press, 1973); Carl Abbott, Stephen J. Leonard, and Thomas J. Noel, *Colorado: A History of the Centennial State* (Boulder: University Press of Colorado, 2005).

12. *Leadville Herald Democrat*, March 13, 1895, 1; March 17, 1895, 10 (quotation); *Boulder Daily Camera*, March 13, 1895, 1; Stephen J. Leonard, *Lynching in Colorado, 1859–1919* (Boulder: University Press of Colorado, 2002).

13. "National Register of Historic Places Listings—March 21, 1997," National Park Service, http://www.nps.gov/nr/listings/970321.htm, accessed December 7, 2015; Douglas Brown, "Douglas County's Lamb Spring Archaeological Dig Could Rewrite Human History," *Denver Post*, www.denverpost.com, April 15, 2012; "History of Lamb Spring," Lamb Spring Archaeological Preserve, http://lambspring.org/?page_id=158, accessed December 7, 2015.

14. Wilson Rockwell, *Uncompahgre Country* (Denver: Sage Books, 1965).

15. *Denver Daily Times*, March 22, 1877, 4; "State Seal," Colorado State Archives, https://www.colorado.gov/pacific/archives/state-seal, accessed July 19, 2015, "Colorado Symbols and Emblems," Colorado Legislative Council, 2013.

16. Richard D. Lamm and Duane A. Smith, *Pioneers and Politicians: 10 Colorado Governors in Profile* (Boulder: Pruett, 1984), 81 (quotation).

17. Stephen Harding Hart and Archer Butler Hulbert (eds.), *The Southwestern Journals of Zebulon Pike, 1806–1807* (Albuquerque: University of New Mexico Press, 2006), 168 (first quotation); Session Laws of Colorado, 1931, Twenty-eighth General Assembly, 883 (second quotation); *Record-Journal of Douglas County*, February 27, 1931, 2, 6; "History and Culture—Great Sand Dunes National Park and Preserve," National Park Service, http://www.nps.gov/grsa/learn/historyculture/index.htm, accessed April 12, 2015.

18. *Pueblo Chieftain*, March 17, 1998, 4A; March 19, 1998, 1A–2A; "Pueblo Home of Heroes," Pueblo Home of Heroes Association, http://www.pueblohomeofheroes.org/, accessed October 8, 2015 (quotation).

19. LeRoy R. Hafen, "The Fort Pueblo Massacre and the Punitive Expedition against the Utes," *Colorado Magazine* 4: 2 (March 1927), 49–58 (first quotation 49; second quotation 55; third quotation 58).

20. *Alamosa Journal*, March 20, 1914, 1; Ruben Donato, Gonzalo Gúzman, and Jarrod Hanson, "*Francisco Maestas et al. v. George H. Shone et al.*: Mexican American Resistance to School Segregation in the Hispano Homeland, 1912–1914," *Journal of Latinos and Education* 16: 1 (January–March 2017), 3–17; Sylvia Lobato, "School Lawsuit from 1914 Remembered," *Alamosa News*, www.alamosanews.com, accessed July 12, 2018 (quotation).

21. *Congressional Globe*, 38th Congress, 1st session, March 22, 1864, 1228; Eugene H. Berwanger, *The Rise of the Centennial State: Colorado Territory, 1861–1876* (Urbana: University of Illinois Press, 2007); Derek R. Everett, *Creating the American West: Boundaries and Borderlands* (Norman: University of Oklahoma Press, 2014).

22. *Kiowa County Press*, March 18, 1921, 2; *Silverton Standard*, March 26, 1921, 2 (quotation); *Carbonate Chronicle*, March 28, 1921, 6; "USS *Colorado* BB-45," USS *Colorado* Alumni Association, http://usscolorado.org/wordpress/, accessed November 25, 2015; "USS *Colorado* (SSN-788) Commissioning Committee," http://usscoloradocommittee. org/, accessed November 25, 2015.

23. Thomas J. Noel, Stephen J. Leonard, and Kevin E. Rucker, *Colorado Givers: A History of Philanthropic Heroes* (Niwot: University Press of Colorado, 1998); *Rocky Mountain News*, November 4, 1892, 9 (quotation).

24. *Change Name of Grand River to Colorado River*, United States Serial Set, vol. 7920, 67th Congress, 1st session, H. Rep. 97, May 25, 1921, 5 (quotation); *Renaming of the Grand River, Colo.* (Washington, DC: Government Printing Office, 1921); Donald Worster, *A River Running West: The Life of John Wesley Powell* (New York: Oxford University Press, 2001).

25. Duane A. Smith, *Rocky Mountain Boom Town: A History of Durango, Colorado* (Niwot: University Press of Colorado, 1992); *Leadville Daily Herald*, September 30, 1882, 4 (quotation); "Train History," Durango & Silverton Narrow Gauge Railroad Train, http://www.durangotrain.com/history#.VhA35uxViko, accessed October 3, 2015.

26. *Rocky Mountain News*, March 27, 1931, 1; March 29, 1931, 1–4; March 30, 1931, 1, 7–8; *Denver Post*, March 28, 1931, 1, 3; March 29, 1931, 1–3, 7; March 30, 1931, 1, 4.

27. Michael F. Kohl and John Ostrom (eds.), *Discovering Dinosaurs in the Old West: The Field Journals of Arthur Lakes* (Washington, DC: Smithsonian Institution Press, 1997), 10 (first quotation); *Colorado Transcript* (Golden), April 10, 1878, 1 (second and third quotations); "Welcome to Dinosaur Ridge," http://www.dinoridge.org/, accessed July 25, 2015.

28. Don E. Alberts, *The Battle of Glorieta: Union Victory in the West* (College Station: Texas A&M University Press, 1998), 173 (first quotation); William C. Whitford, *Colorado Volunteers in the Civil War: The New Mexico Campaign in 1862* (Glorieta, NM: Rio Grande, 1971), 94 (second quotation).

29. *Sierra Journal* (Rosita), March 29, 1883, 2 (quotation); Joanne West Dodds, *Custer County at a Glance* (Pueblo, CO: Focal Plain, 2007).

30. John Cope, Martin Hatcher, and Charles Miller (eds.), *Looking Back: 100 Years of Western State College* (Gunnison, CO: B&B Printers, 2001); *Top o' the World* (Gunnison), April 11, 2001, 4–5 (quotation).

31. Session Laws of Colorado, Twenty-ninth General Assembly, 1933, 421 (first quotation); *Glenwood Post*, March 27, 1897, 2 (second quotation); *Herald Democrat* (Leadville), March 26, 1897, 1 (third quotation); *Silverton Standard*, March 27, 1897, 4 (fourth quotation); Michael R. Radelet, "Capital Punishment in Colorado: 1859–1972," http://pdweb.coloradodefenders.us/index.php?option=com_content&view=article&id=151&Itemid=103, accessed September 24, 2015.

April

1. Robert W. Larson, *Shaping Educational Change: The First Century of the University of Northern Colorado at Greeley* (Boulder: Colorado Associated University Press, 1989); Session Laws of Colorado, Seventh General Assembly, 1889, 409 (first quotation); *Fort Morgan Times*, April 12, 1889, 1 (second quotation).

2. *Denver Post*, April 3, 2007, 1A, 4A; *Rocky Mountain News*, April 3, 2007, 26–27; Tom Tancredo, *In Mortal Danger: The Battle for America's Border and Security* (Nashville, TN: WND Books, 2006); "Tancredo, Thomas G.," Biographical Directory of the United States Congress, http://bioguide.congress.gov/scripts/biodisplay.pl?index=T000458, accessed February 9, 2016.

3. Nell Brown Propst, *The Boys from Joes: A Colorado Basketball Legend* (Boulder: Pruett, 1988); *Steamboat Pilot*, April 12, 1929, 4 (quotation).

Sources

4. *Rocky Mountain News*, April 5, 1870, 1; John D.W. Guice, "Moses Hallett, Chief Justice," *Colorado Magazine* 47: 2 (Spring 1970), 136–51 (quotation 142).

5. Virginia McConnell Simmons, *The San Luis Valley: Land of the Six-Armed Cross* (Niwot: University Press of Colorado, 1999); *Denver Post*, April 6, 2001, 4B (quotation).

6. Robert K. DeArment, *Bat Masterson: The Man and the Legend* (Norman: University of Oklahoma Press, 1979), 292, 378 (quotations).

7. *Glenwood Post*, April 11, 1903, 1, 4 (first quotation); Jim Nelson, *Glenwood Springs: The History of a Rocky Mountain Resort* (Ouray, CO: Western Reflections, 1999); *Rocky Mountain Sun* (Aspen), June 10, 1893, 3 (second quotation).

8. Geraldine B. Bean, *Charles Boettcher: A Study in Pioneer Western Enterprise* (Boulder: Westview, 1976), 159 (quotation).

9. *Denver Post*, April 10, 1993, 1A (quotation), 9A–12A, 18A–20A; "Rockies History," Colorado Rockies, http://colorado.rockies.mlb.com/col/history/, accessed October 1, 2015.

10. Tim Pollard, "The Birth and Early Years of Club 20," *Journal of the Western Slope* 11: 2 (Spring 1996), 25–37; "Who We Are," Club 20, http://www.club20.org/about/who-we-are, accessed June 18, 2015 (quotation).

11. *Rocky Mountain News*, April 16, 1863, 2 (quotation); Charles F. Price, *Season of Terror: The Espinosas in Central Colorado, March–October 1863* (Boulder: University Press of Colorado, 2013).

12. *Rocky Mountain News*, April 13, 2005, 7A, 14A; *Denver Post*, April 13, 2005, 1A, 17A; April 14, 2005, 6B (quotation); Christine Marín, *A Spokesman of the Mexican American Movement: Rodolfo "Corky" Gonzales and the Fight for Chicano Liberation, 1966–1972* (San Francisco: R&E Research Associates, 1977).

13. Derek R. Everett, *Creating the American West: Boundaries and Borderlands* (Norman: University of Oklahoma Press, 2014); *Daily Colorado Chieftain* (Pueblo), July 7, 1877, 4 (quotation).

14. *Rocky Mountain News*, April 15, 1935, 1 (quotation), 6; *Denver Post*, April 15, 1935, 1, 3; Donald Worster, *Dust Bowl: The Southern Plains in the 1930s* (New York: Oxford University Press, 2004).

15. Kristen Iversen, *Molly Brown: Unraveling the Myth* (Boulder: Johnson Books, 1999), 42 (quotation).

16. *Solid Muldoon* (Ouray, CO), April 16, 1880, 2 (first quotation); August 28, 1885, 1; Mark I. West (ed.), *Westward to a High Mountain: The Colorado Writings of Helen Hunt Jackson* (Denver: Colorado Historical Society, 1994); Helen Hunt Jackson, *A Century of Dishonor: A Sketch of the United States Government's Dealings with Some of the Indian Tribes* (Norman: University of Oklahoma Press, 1995), 27 (second quotation), 337–38 (third quotation).

17. *Leadville Daily Herald*, April 18, 1882, 1; *Denver Express*, February 23, 1914, 1 (quotation); Duane A. Smith, *Henry M. Teller: Colorado's Grand Old Man* (Boulder: University Press of Colorado, 2002).

18. *Rocky Mountain News*, April 19, 1936, 1–2; April 23, 1936, 1; April 30, 1936, 1–2; Alice Marshall to Edwin C. Johnson, April 20, 1936, Governor Edwin C. Johnson Papers, box 26916, folder 4, Colorado State Archives, Denver (quotation).

19. Session Laws of Colorado, Seventh General Assembly, 1889, 424 (first quotation); *Aspen Daily Times*, May 21, 1889, 1; *Buena Vista Democrat*, May 23, 1889, 1; *Rocky Mountain Sun* (Aspen), May 25, 1889, 2 (second quotation); "Buena Vista Correctional Complex," Colorado Department of Corrections, http://www.doc.state.co.us/facility/bvcc-buena -vista-correctional-complex, accessed April 1, 2015.

20. George S. McGovern and Leonard F. Guttridge, *The Great Coalfield War* (Boston: Houghton Mifflin, 1972); Thomas G. Andrews, *Killing for Coal: America's Deadliest Labor War* (Cambridge, MA: Harvard University Press, 2008); F. Darrell Munsell, *From Redstone to Ludlow: John Cleveland Osgood's Struggle against the United Mine Workers of America* (Boulder: University Press of Colorado, 2009).

21. Robert G. Athearn, "Origins of the Royal Gorge Railroad War," *Colorado Magazine* 36: 1 (January 1959), 37–57; Robert G. Athearn, *The Denver and Rio Grande Western Railroad* (Lincoln: University of Nebraska Press, 1977).

22. "United States Mint in Denver, National Register of Historic Places Inventory-Nomination Form," National Park Service, http://focus.nps.gov/pdfhost/docs/nrhp /text/72000270.PDF, accessed March 2, 2016; *Aspen Democrat*, February 2, 1906, 1; *Daily Journal* (Telluride), February 2, 1906, 3; Louisa Ward Arps, *Denver in Slices: A Historical Guide to the City* (Athens, OH: Swallow, 1998).

23. *Rocky Mountain News*, April 23, 1859, 2 (quotation); Michael Madigan, *Heroes, Villains, Dames, and Disasters: 150 Years of Front-Page Stories from the Rocky Mountain News* (Denver: MadIdeas LLC, 2009).

24. "Colorado Earthquake History," United States Geological Survey, http://earth quake.usgs.gov/earthquakes/states/colorado/history.php, accessed October 27, 2015.

25. Session Laws of Colorado, Forty-sixth General Assembly, First Regular Session, 1967, 285 (first quotation); *Rocky Mountain News*, April 26, 1967, 5 (second quotation); *Denver Post*, April 26, 1967, 1, 3, 22; Richard D. Lamm and Duane A. Smith, *Pioneers and Politicians: 10 Colorado Governors in Profile* (Boulder: Pruett, 1984).

26. "Harry S. Truman: Proclamation 2924—Enlarging Hovenweep National Monument, Colorado and Utah," the American Presidency Project, http://www.presidency .ucsb.edu/ws/?pid=76663, accessed December 13, 2015 (quotation); "History and Culture," Hovenweep National Monument, National Park Service, http://www.nps.gov /hove/learn/historyculture/index.htm, accessed December 13, 2015; "BLM CO Canyons of the Ancients National Monument," Bureau of Land Management, http://www.blm .gov/co/st/en/nm/canm.html, accessed December 13, 2015.

27. "The Hastings Mine Disaster," http://hastingsmine1917.wixsite.com/minersremem bered, accessed May 20, 2017; *Montrose Daily Press*, April 30, 1917, 1; *Wray Rattler*, May 3, 1917, 2; *Eagle Valley Enterprise*, May 4, 1917, 7 (quotation).

28. *Colorado Daily Chieftain* (Pueblo), April 23, 1873, 4 (first quotation); *Denver Daily Times*, April 25, 1873, 4; April 28, 1873, 4; *Rocky Mountain News*, April 27, 1873, 4; April 29, 1873, 4 (second quotation); April 30, 1873, 4; *Daily Register Call* (Central City), April 29, 1873, 3.

29. *Denver Post*, April 29, 1922, 1, 6; *Rocky Mountain News*, April 30, 1922, 1 (quotation), 2; Session Laws of Colorado, Twenty-third General Assembly, extraordinary session,

1922; Charles Albi and Kenton Forrest, *The Moffat Tunnel: A Brief History* (Golden: Colorado Railroad Museum, 2002).

30. *Denver Post*, April 30, 1898, 2; *Rocky Mountain News*, May 1, 1898, 9; Geoffrey R. Hunt, *Colorado's Volunteer Infantry in the Philippine Wars* (Albuquerque: University of New Mexico Press, 2006).

May

1. *Rocky Mountain News*, May 2, 1890, 6 (quotations); Jack Gurtler and Corrine Hunt, *The Elitch Gardens Story: Memories of Jack Gurtler* (Boulder: Rocky Mountain Writers Guild, 1982).

2. Andrew Gulliford, *Boomtown Blues: Colorado Oil Shale* (Boulder: University Press of Colorado, 2003), x (quotation).

3. Matt Bai, "How Gary Hart's Downfall Forever Changed American Politics," *New York Times Magazine*, www.nytimes.com, September 18, 2014; "Hart, Gary Warren," Biographical Directory of the United States Congress, http://bioguide.congress.gov/scripts/biodisplay.pl?index=H000287, accessed February 24, 2016.

4. *Denver Post*, May 4, 1903, 1 (quotations); *Rocky Mountain News*, May 5, 1903, 16.

5. Melvin E. Norris Jr., "Dearfield, Colorado—the Evolution of a Rural Black Settlement: An Historical Geography of Black Colonization on the Great Plains," PhD dissertation, University of Colorado, Boulder, 1980, 185 (quotation).

6 Donald C. Kemp, *Colorado's Little Kingdom* (Denver: Sage Books, 1949), 5 (quotation); Alan Granuth, *The Little Kingdom of Gilpin: Gilpin County, Colorado* (Central City, CO: Gilpin Historical Society, 2000).

7. *Castle Rock Journal*, May 14, 1897, 2; Sharon Randall, Tracy Dixon, and Patty Horan, *The Night the Dam Gave Way: A Diary of Personal Accounts* (Franktown, CO: Castlewood Canyon State Park, 1997).

8. *Rocky Mountain News*, May 9, 1970, 1, 8; May 10, 1970, 5 (quotations), 8; *Denver Post*, May 9, 1970, 1, 3; May 10, 1970, 22; James E. Hansen II, *Democracy's College in the Centennial State: A History of Colorado State University* (Fort Collins: Colorado State University, 1977).

9. Charles A. Johnson, *Denver's Mayor Speer* (Denver: Green Mountain, 1969).

10. Stephen M. Voynick, *Climax: The History of Colorado's Climax Molybdenum Mine* (Missoula, MT: Mountain Press, 2014); *Steamboat Pilot*, November 9, 1944, 8 (quotation).

11. Charles Hedges (ed.), *Speeches of Benjamin Harrison* (New York: United States Book Company, 1892), 443, 444, 447 (quotations).

12. Adam Rovner, "When Jewish Colonists Prospected for Utopia in Colorado," http://forward.com/culture/211609/when-jewish-colonists-prospected-for-utopia-in-col/, January 6, 2015; *Leadville Daily Herald*, May 7, 1882, 2 (quotation).

13. Mark S. Foster, "Colorado's Defeat of the 1976 Winter Olympics," *Colorado Magazine* 53: 2 (Spring 1976), 163–86 (quotation 176).

14. "Colorado's Water Plan," https://www.colorado.gov/cowaterplan, xvii, xxvi (quotations), accessed December 4, 2016.

15. "Historic Water Pact Counts on Cooperation, Conservation, and Reuse," *Denver Post*, www.denverpost.com, April 28, 2011; "Colorado River Cooperative Agreement 2012," Grand County BOCC, www.youtube.com, posted May 29, 2012; "Colorado River Cooperative Agreement—Is It Working?" *Sky-Hi News*, www.skyhidailynews.com, June 4, 2013 (quotation).

16. "Voters in Denver Approve a New $2.3 Billion Airport," *New York Times*, http://www.nytimes.com/1989/05/17/us/voters-in-denver-approve-a-new-2.3-billion-airport.html, accessed May 13, 2015; Benjamin Bearup, "Denver International Airport: A 20-Year History," Airways News, http://airwaysnews.com/blog/2015/03/02/denver-internatio nal-airport-a-20-year-history/, accessed May 13, 2015.

17. *Denver Post*, May 17, 1973, 1 (quotation), 20, 96; Scott Kaufman, *Project Plowshare: The Peaceful Use of Nuclear Explosives in Cold War America* (Ithaca, NY: Cornell University Press, 2013).

18. Robert W. Frazer, *Forts of the West* (Norman: University of Oklahoma Press, 1972); Don English, *The Early History of Fort Morgan, Colorado* (Fort Morgan, CO: The Print Shop, 1975); Dee Brown, *The Galvanized Yankees* (Lincoln: University of Nebraska Press, 1986); *Rocky Mountain News*, May 20, 1868, 4; May 21, 1868, 4 (quotation).

19. *Daily Commonwealth* (Denver), May 24, 1864, 2; *Weekly Commonwealth* (Denver), May 25, 1864, 2 (quotation), 3; William C. Jones and Kenton Forrest, *Denver: A Pictorial History* (Boulder: Pruett, 1973).

20. *Romer v. Evans*, 517 US 620 (1996), 624, 635 (quotations); Stephen M. Rich, "Ruling by Numbers: Political Restructuring and the Reconsideration of Democratic Commitments after *Romer v. Evans*," *Yale Law Journal* 109: 3 (December 1999), 587–626.

21. *Weekly Commonwealth* (Denver), May 21, 1863, 3 (first quotation); March 19, 1863, 2 (second quotation); Thomas C. Jepsen, "The Telegraph Comes to Colorado: A New Technology and Its Consequences," *Essays in Colorado History* 7 (1987), 1–25.

22. Robert C. Black III, *Railroad Pathfinder: The Life and Times of Edward L. Berthoud* (Evergreen, CO: Cordillera, 1988).

23. David Remley, *Kit Carson: The Life of an American Border Man* (Norman: University of Oklahoma Press, 2011).

24. Alan J. Kania, *John Otto: Trials and Trails* (Niwot: University Press of Colorado, 1996), 139 (quotations); "Colorado National Monument," National Park Service, http://www.nps.gov/colm/index.htm, accessed October 3, 2015.

25. Wilbur Fisk Stone, *History of Colorado*, vol. 1 (Chicago: S. J. Clarke, 1918).

26. *Denver Post*, May 26, 1934, 1, 3 (quotations); May 27, 1934, 1–2; *Rocky Mountain News*, May 27, 1934, 1–4; "The Burlington Zephyr," PBS, http://www.pbs.org/wgbh/american experience/features/general-article/streamliners-burlington/, accessed March 9, 2015.

27. *Rocky Mountain News*, May 28, 1861, 2; Thomas L. Karnes, *William Gilpin, Western Nationalist* (Austin: University of Texas Press, 1970), 254–55, 264, 266 (quotations).

28. Guy Raz, "For Albright and Rice, Josef Korbel Is Tie That Binds," NPR, www.npr.com, June 28, 2006; "About Our School: History," Josef Korbel School of International Studies, University of Denver, http://www.du.edu/korbel/about/history.html, accessed June 13, 2016.

Sources

29. Dan Schultz, *Dead Run: The Murder of a Lawman and the Greatest Manhunt of the Modern American West* (New York: St. Martin's, 2013).

30. Jere True and Victoria Tupper Kirby, *Allen Tupper True: An American Artist* (San Francisco: Canyon Leap, 2009).

31. *Rocky Mountain News*, June 1, 1935, 1–6 (quotation 1); June 2, 1935, 1–4, 6, 8; June 3, 1935, 5; "1935 Kiowa Creek Flood," *Smoky Hill Express* 24: 1 (Spring 2015), 4.

June

1. Nikola Tesla, *Colorado Springs Notes: 1899–1900*, ed. Aleksandar Marinčić (Joliet, IL: BN Publishing, 2007), 132 (quotation); Inez Hunt and Wanetta W. Draper, *Lightning in His Hand: The Life Story of Nikola Tesla* (Hawthorne, CA: Omni, 1964).

2. *Congressional Globe*, 37th Congress, 2nd session, April 18, 1862, 1711; May 29, 1862, 2432; May 30, 1862, 2439; June 3, 1862, 2506; "State by State Numbers," National Park Service, Homestead National Monument of America, http://www.nps.gov/home/learn/historyculture/statenumbers.htm, accessed September 1, 2015.

3. *Chaffee County Democrat*, June 11, 1921, 3 (quotation); Guy E. Macy, "The Pueblo Flood of 1921," *Colorado Magazine* 17: 6 (November 1940), 201–11; Joanne West Dodds, *Pueblo at a Glance* (Pueblo, CO: Focal Plain, 2003).

4. Donald Worster, *A River Running West: The Life of John Wesley Powell* (New York: Oxford University Press, 2001); "The Powell Expedition," Grand Canyon Explorer, http://www.bobspixels.com/kaibab.org/powell/powexp.htm, accessed June 12, 2015 (quotation).

5. Frank Gibbard, "*Wyoming v. Colorado*: A 'Watershed' Decision," *Colorado Lawyer* 34: 3 (March 2005), 37–38.

6. *Colorado Transcript* (Golden), June 9, 1904, 2 (quotation); George G. Suggs Jr., *Colorado's War on Militant Unionism: James H. Peabody and the Western Federation of Miners* (Norman: University of Oklahoma Press, 1972).

7. *Rocky Mountain News*, June 7, 1964, 22; June 8, 1964, 5–6 (quotation); June 9, 1964, 6; June 10, 1964, 18, 20; Carl Abbott, Stephen J. Leonard, and Thomas J. Noel, *Colorado: A History of the Centennial State* (Boulder: University Press of Colorado, 2005).

8. "Decade after Hayman Fire, Questions Linger about Fire's Start," *Denver Post*, www.denverpost.com, June 3, 2012; "Colorado's Massive 2002 Hayman Fire Seared in Memories of Victims," *Denver Post*, www.denverpost.com, June 8, 2012 (quotation); "Colorado Wildfires, Major Fires from 1971–2013: Interactive Graphic," *Denver Post*, www.denverpost.com, June 7, 2014.

9. Agnes Wright Spring, "The Founding of Fort Collins, United States Military Post," *Colorado Magazine* 10: 2 (March 1933), 47–55 (quotations 49, 51).

10. Erik M. Gantt, "The Claude C. and A. Lynn Coffin Lindenmeier Collection: An Innovative Method for Analysis of Privately Held Artifact Collections and New Information on a Folsom Campsite in Northern Colorado," MA thesis, Colorado State University, Fort Collins, 2002; Jason M. LaBelle, "Lindenmeier Folsom Site," Colorado Encyclopedia, coloradoencyclopedia.colostate.edu, accessed September 29, 2015.

11. *Weekly Commonwealth* (Denver), June 15, 1864, 2 (first quotation); *Rocky Mountain News*, August 11, 1864, 2 (second quotation); Elmer R. Burkey, "The Site of the Murder of the Hungate Family by Indians in 1864," *Colorado Magazine* 12: 4 (July 1935), 139–42.

12. *Denver Post*, June 12, 1996, 1A, 19A, 21A–23A (quotation); June 13, 1996, 1AA–3AA; "Colorado Avalanche," Sports E-cyclopedia, http://www.sportsecyclopedia.com/nhl /colavs/avalanche.html, accessed September 29, 2015.

13. "National Register Digital Assets—Devils Head Lookout," National Park Service, http://focus.nps.gov/AssetDetail/NRIS/03000518, accessed November 21, 2015.

14. James E. Fell Jr., *Ores to Metals: The Rocky Mountain Smelting Industry* (Boulder: University Press of Colorado, 2009); Jerome C. Smiley, *History of Denver* (Denver: Times-Sun, 1901); *Weekly Commonwealth* (Denver), June 22, 1864, 2 (quotation).

15. Thomas J. Noel, *Sacred Stones: Colorado's Red Rocks Park and Amphitheatre* (Denver: Division of Theatres and Arenas, 2004), 59 (quotation).

16. Robert Athearn, *The Denver and Rio Grande Western Railroad* (Lincoln: University of Nebraska Press, 1977).

17. Liston E. Leyendecker, *The Griffith Family and the Founding of Georgetown* (Boulder: University Press of Colorado, 2001); Liston E. Leyendecker, Christine A. Bradley, and Duane A. Smith, *The Rise of the Silver Queen: Georgetown, Colorado, 1859–1896* (Boulder: University Press of Colorado, 2005), 25 (quotation).

18. *Rocky Mountain News*, June 19, 1960, 1, 3; *Denver Post*, June 19, 1960, 1A, 3A, 18A; Rob Mohr and Leslie Mohr Krupa, *Golf in Denver* (Charleston, SC: Arcadia, 2011); "1960 Presidential Election," the American Presidency Project, http://www.presidency.ucsb .edu/showelection.php?year=1960, accessed March 9, 2015.

19. *Dolores News*, June 27, 1885, 2; July 4, 1885, 2 (quotations); October 24, 1885, 2; *Aspen Daily Times*, June 28, 1885, 1.

20. "Chronological History of National Grasslands," United States Forest Service, http://www.fs.usda.gov/Internet/FSE_DOCUMENTS/fsm9_032448.pdf, accessed May 10, 2015; Francis Moul, *The National Grasslands: A Guide to America's Undiscovered Treasures* (Lincoln: University of Nebraska Press, 2006).

21. *Denver Post*, June 21, 1997, 1A, 14A–16A, 1AA–8AA; June 22, 1997, 1A, 6A–11A, 1AA–8AA; June 23, 1997, 1A, 5A–7A, 1AA–8AA (quotation 7AA); *Rocky Mountain News*, June 21, 1997, 1S–162; June 23, 1997, 3A, 38A.

22. Arvada Historical Society, *Waters of Gold: A History of Arvada during the Period 1850–1870* (Arvada, CO: Arvada Heritage Printers, 1973).

23. Daniel Tyler, *The Last Water Hole in the West: The Colorado–Big Thompson Project and the Northern Colorado Water Conservancy District* (Niwot: University Press of Colorado, 1992); "Colorado–Big Thompson Project," Northern Water, http://www.northern water.org/WaterProjects/C-BTProject.aspx, accessed June 24, 2015.

24. *Aspen Daily Chronicle*, June 26, 1889, 1 (quotation); *Solid Muldoon Weekly* (Ouray, CO), June 28, 1889, 2; Wilson Rockwell, *Uncompahgre Country* (Denver: Sage Books, 1965).

25. *Denver Post*, June 25, 1923, 1–5, 16; *Denver Times*, June 25, 1923, 1–4; *Rocky Mountain News*, June 26, 1923, 1–5 (quotation 1).

Sources

26. Emma Burke Conklin, *A Brief History of Logan County, Colorado* (Denver: Welch-Haffner, 1928); Roger L. Nichols and Patrick L. Halley, *Stephen Long and American Frontier Exploration* (Norman: University of Oklahoma Press, 1995), 167 (quotations).

27. Dennis J. Hutchinson, *The Man Who Once Was Whizzer White: A Portrait of Justice Byron R. White* (New York: Free Press, 1998); "Byron R. White, Longtime Justice and a Football Legend, Dies at 84," *New York Times*, www.nytimes.com, April 16, 2002; "Biography of the Honorable Neil M. Gorsuch," Supreme Court of the United States, https://www.supremecourt.gov/about/biographyGorsuch.aspx, accessed April 9, 2017.

28. F. R. Carpenter, "Establishing Management under the Taylor Grazing Act," *Rangelands* 3: 3 (June 1981), 105–15; Joseph V.H. Ross, "Managing the Public Rangelands: 50 Years since the Taylor Grazing Act," *Rangelands* 6: 4 (August 1984), 147–51.

29. *Colorado Springs Gazette*, June 29, 1975, 1B–2B; "Fannie Mae Bragg Duncan," *Colorado Springs Gazette*, obits.gazette.com, September 18, 2005 (quotation); "Colorado Experience: Fannie Mae Duncan," Rocky Mountain Public Broadcasting Service, www.rmpbs.org/coloradoexperience/culture/fannie-mae-duncan, accessed December 12, 2018.

30. G. Clell Jacobs, "The Phantom Pathfinder: Juan Maria Antonio de Rivera and His Expedition," *Utah Historical Quarterly* 60: 3 (Summer 1992), 200–223; Phil Carson, *Across the Northern Frontier: Spanish Explorations in Colorado* (Boulder: Johnson Books, 1998); Steven G. Baker, *Juan Rivera's Colorado, 1765: The First Spaniards among the Ute and Paiute Indians on the Trails to Teguayo* (Lake City, CO: Western Reflections, 2016).

July

1. "State Climate Extremes Committee (SCEC)," National Oceanic and Atmospheric Administration, www.ncdc.noaa.gov/extremes/scec/records, accessed March 11, 2015; J.L.H. Paulus, "Record Snowfall of April 14–15, 1921, at Silver Lake, Colorado," *Monthly Weather Review* 81: 2 (February 1953), 38–40; "Colorado Tornado History," KKTV 11 News, www.kktv.com, April 15, 2015; Chris Bianchi, "It's Official, Colorado Has a New Record Hottest Temperature," *Denver Post*, www.denverpost.com, October 15, 2019.

2. William C. Jones and Kenton Forrest, *Denver: A Pictorial History* (Boulder: Pruett, 1973); Stephen J. Leonard and Thomas J. Noel, *Denver: Mining Camp to Metropolis* (Niwot: University Press of Colorado, 1990); Ken Fletcher, *A Mile High and Three Feet Six Wide* (Aurora, CO: Mountain West Enterprises, 1993).

3. John L. Dyer, *The Snow-Shoe Itinerant* (Cincinnati, OH: Cranston and Snow, 1890), 296, 313 (quotations); John Ophus, "The Lake County War, 1874–75," *Colorado Magazine* 47: 2 (Spring 1970), 119–35.

4. Frank Waters, *Midas of the Rockies* (Denver: University of Denver Press, 1949).

5. Dorothy Burgess, *Dream and Deed: The Story of Katharine Lee Bates* (Norman: University of Oklahoma Press, 1952), 102 (quotation); Lynn Sherr, *America the Beautiful: The Stirring True Story behind Our Nation's Favorite Song* (New York: Perseus Books, 2001); "Our History," Colorado College, www.coloradocollege.edu/basics/welcome/history/, accessed March 15, 2016.

6. *Denver Post,* July 6, 1994, 1A, 11A; July 7, 1994, 1A, 7A, 6B (quotation); July 8, 1994, 13A; July 9, 1994, 4A; John N. Maclean, "20 Years Later, Legacy of a Deadly Colorado Wildfire Endures," *National Geographic,* news.nationalgeographic.com, July 3, 2014.

7. *Rocky Mountain News,* July 7, 1908, 1–4, 6; July 8, 1908, 1–5, 7, 10 (quotation 1); July 9, 1908, 1–3; July 10, 1908, 1–2; July 11, 1908, 1.

8. "Northeast Colorado Counties Favor More Representation Instead of Secession," *Greeley Tribune,* www.greeleytribune.com, July 8, 2013; "Colorado Election Results," Colorado Secretary of State, http://www.results.enr.clarityelections.com/CO/48370/122768/en-select-county.html, accessed November 7, 2013; "Restoring Colorado: Suspending Campaign and Thank You," Facebook, www.facebook.com, accessed July 5, 2014.

9. *Report from the Secretary of War, Communicating, in Compliance with Two Resolutions of the Senate, a Copy of Lieut. Fremont's Report of His Exploring Expedition to the Rocky Mountains,* United States Serial Set, vol. 416, 27th Congress, 3rd session, S. Doc. 243, March 3, 1843, 28 (quotations).

10. Phil Carson, *Across the Northern Frontier: Spanish Explorations in Colorado* (Boulder: Johnson Books, 1998), 52 (quotation).

11. Fred H. Werner, *The Summit Springs Battle* (Greeley, CO: Werner, 1991); Robert M. Utley, *Frontier Regulars: The United States Army and the Indian, 1866–1891* (Lincoln: University of Nebraska Press, 1973).

12. *Colorado Transcript* (Golden), July 14, 1869, 2; July 21, 1869, 1 (quotation); July 28, 1869, 1; August 25, 1869, 1; *Rocky Mountain News,* September 20, 1869, 4; Richard A. Bartlett, *Great Surveys of the American West* (Norman: University of Oklahoma Press, 1962).

13. *Carbonate Chronicle,* June 20, 1887, 8 (quotation); *Aspen Weekly Times,* July 16, 1887, 4; John J. Lipsey, *The Lives of James John Hagerman: Builder of the Colorado Midland Railway* (Denver: Golden Bell, 1968).

14. *Steamboat Pilot,* November 24, 1915, 9 (quotation); July 28, 1938, 6; August 11, 1938, 6; Steven C. Schulte, *Wayne Aspinall and the Shaping of the American West* (Boulder: University Press of Colorado, 2002); "Dinosaur," Colorado Tourism Office, http://www.colorado.com/cities-and-towns/dinosaur, accessed June 12, 2015, "Park Statistics," National Park Service, http://www.nps.gov/dino/learn/management/statistics.htm, accessed June 12, 2015.

15. Jack A. Benson, "Skiing at Camp Hale: Mountain Troops during World War II," *Western Historical Quarterly* 15: 2 (April 1984), 163–74 (quotation 165); "Camp Hale History," Metropolitan State University of Denver, https://www.msudenver.edu/camphale/camphalehistory/, accessed December 17, 2015.

16. Wilson Rockwell, *Uncompahgre Country* (Denver: Sage Books, 1965); Michael A. Amundson, *Yellowcake Towns: Uranium Mining Communities in the American West* (Boulder: University Press of Colorado, 2002).

17. *Rocky Mountain News,* July 18, 1880, 1; *Leadville Weekly Herald,* July 24, 1880, 1; July 31, 1880, 2; August 21, 1880, 4; *Saguache Chronicle,* August 6, 1880, 4; *Boulder News and Courier,* August 13, 1880, 3; August 27, 1880, 2; *Colorado Transcript* (Golden), August 25, 1880, 3; Duane Vandenbusche, *The Gunnison Country* (Gunnison, CO: B&B Printers, Gunnison, 1980); John Y. Simon (ed.), *The Papers of Ulysses S. Grant,* vol. 29: *October 1, 1878–September 30, 1880* (Carbondale: Southern Illinois University Press, 2008).

18. Karal Ann Marling (ed.), *Designing Disney's Theme Parks: The Architecture of Reassurance* (Paris: Flammarion, 1997); "Magic Mountain," Golden Landmarks Association, http://goldenlandmarks.com/magic-mountain/, accessed February 12, 2016; "Some History," North Pole, http://northpolecolorado.com/about-us/history/, accessed February 12, 2016.

19. Robert B. Houston, "On the Face of the Earth: Marking Colorado's Boundaries, 1868–1925," *Colorado History* 10 (Denver: Colorado Historical Society, 2004), 87–105; Frank Jacobs, "Colorado Is a Rectangle? Think Again," Bigthink.com, October 31, 2018 (quotation).

20. "Aurora Theater Shooting," *Denver Post*, http://www.denverpost.com/theater shooting, accessed November 28, 2015; Natasha Gardner and Patrick Doyle, "The Politics of Killing," *5280: The Denver Magazine*, www.5280.com, December 2008.

21. Wilson Rockwell, *Uncompahgre Country* (Denver: Sage Books, 1965); Robert W. Frazer, *Forts of the West* (Norman: University of Oklahoma Press, 1972); Virginia McConnell Simmons, *The Ute Indians of Utah, Colorado, and New Mexico* (Boulder: University Press of Colorado, 2000); Peter R. Decker, *"The Utes Must Go!": American Expansion and the Removal of a People* (Golden, CO: Fulcrum, 2004).

22. Beulah Historical Society, *From Mace's Hole, the Way It Was, to Beulah, the Way It Is: A Comprehensive History of Beulah, Colorado* (Pueblo, CO: Schusters' Printing, 2000).

23. *Denver Post*, July 23, 1951, 1, 3, 16; *Rocky Mountain News*, July 24, 1951, 5, 20; Rodney L. Preston, *Stetson, Pipe, and Boots: Colorado's Cattleman Governor—a Biography about Dan Thornton* (Victoria, BC: Trafford, 2006).

24. *Denver Post*, July 25, 2007, 1A, 4A (quotation); *Rocky Mountain News*, July 25, 2007, 4–6, 30, 34; Robert M. O'Neil, "Limits of Freedom: The Ward Churchill Case," *Change* 38: 5 (September–October 2006), 34–41; "Supreme Court Denies Appeal from Former University of Colorado Professor Ward Churchill," *Denver Post*, www.denverpost.com, April 1, 2013.

25. John C. Frémont, *Report of the Exploring Expedition to the Rocky Mountains in the Year 1842, and to Oregon and North California in the Years 1843–44*, United States Serial Set, vol. 467, 28th Congress, 2nd session, February 25, 1845, H. Doc. 166; Diane Brotemarkle, *Old Fort St. Vrain* (Boulder: Johnson, 2001).

26. Gordon S. Chappell, *The South Park Line: A Concise History*, Colorado Rail Annual 12 (Golden: Colorado Railroad Museum, 1974); Charles A. Page, *Tour Guide to Historic Alpine Tunnel* (Gunnison, CO: Page Books, 1978).

27. Frederick S. Allen, Ernest Andrade Jr., Mark S. Foster, Philip I. Mitterling, and H. Lee Scamehorn, *The University of Colorado, 1876–1976* (New York: Harcourt Brace Jovanovich, 1976); *Colorado Banner* (Boulder), September 6, 1877, 4 (quotation).

28. *Rocky Mountain News*, July 29, 1871, 1 (quotation); Robert Athearn, *The Denver and Rio Grande Western Railroad* (Lincoln: University of Nebraska Press, 1977).

29. Phil Carson, *Across the Northern Frontier: Spanish Explorations in Colorado* (Boulder: Johnson Books, 1998); Alfred Barnaby Thomas, *After Coronado: Spanish Exploration Northeast of New Mexico, 1696–1727* (Norman: University of Oklahoma Press, 1966 [1935]), 65 (quotations).

30. Mark Twain, *Roughing It* (New York: Penguin Books, 1985), 85, 86 (quotations); Doris Monahan, *Julesburg and Fort Sedgwick: Wicked City, Scandalous Fort* (Sterling, CO: self-published, 2009).

31. "Colorado Remembers Big Thompson Canyon Flash Flood of 1976," National Oceanic and Atmospheric Administration, http://www.noaanews.noaa.gov/stories/s688 .htm, accessed May 21, 2015; "Big Thompson Flood of 1976," *Denver Post*, www.denverpost .com, July 31, 2012; Deborah Watts, *A Flood of Memories: The Big Thompson Flood* (Laporte, CO: Legacy, 2001), 10 (quotation).

August

1. *Rocky Mountain News*, July 2, 1876, 1 (first quotation); August 2, 1876, 1; *Colorado Daily Chieftain* (Pueblo), July 4, 1876, 2 (second quotation); *Colorado Banner* (Boulder), August 3, 1876, 5 (third quotation).

2. John R. Morris, *Davis H. Waite: The Ideology of a Western Populist* (Washington, DC: University Press of America, 1982); Richard D. Lamm and Duane A. Smith, *Pioneers and Politicians: 10 Colorado Governors in Profile* (Boulder: Pruett, 1984); *Sacramento Daily Union*, August 3, 1893, 1 (quotation).

3. *Denver Post*, August 4, 1964, 3; *Rocky Mountain News*, August 5, 1964, 31; "Beloved Turnpike Dog, Shep, Moved to Broomfield Museum," *Broomfield Enterprise*, www.broom fieldenterprise.com, October 14, 2009.

4. *Boulder News and Courier*, June 13, 1879, 3 (quotation); "Lance Armstrong Helps People Remember Bill Ritter's Still Governor at Bike Race Announcement," *Westword* (Denver), www.westword.com, August 4, 2010; "Red Zinger Race in Boulder Paved the Way for Pro Cycling Challenge," *Boulder Daily Camera*, www.dailycamera.com, August 23, 2012.

5. Edward T. Divine, John A. Ryan, and John A. Lapp, *The Denver Tramway Strike of 1920* (Denver: Denver Commission of Religious Forces, 1921).

6. LeRoy R. Hafen and Frank M. Young, "The Mormon Settlement at Pueblo, Colorado, during the Mexican War," *Colorado Magazine* 9: 4 (July 1932), 121–36.

7. *Aspen Daily Times*, August 9, 1904, 1; August 14, 1904, 1; *Durango Democrat*, August 9, 1904, 1; August 21, 1904, 1.

8. *Summit County Journal*, August 7, 1936, 1 (first and second quotations), 3–4, 9; August 14, 1936, 1; *Rocky Mountain News*, July 19, 1936, 3 (third quotation); August 8, 1936, 6; August 9, 1936, 1, 7; *Denver Post*, August 9, 1936, sec. 5, 7.

9. Steven K. Madsen, *Exploring Desert Stone: John N. Macomb's 1859 Expedition to the Canyonlands of the Colorado* (Logan: Utah State University Press, 2010), 219 (quotation).

10. "Christo and Jean-Claude," http://christojeanneclaude.net/, accessed July 6, 2015; *Denver Post*, August 11, 1972, 1, 88; August 12, 1972, 1 (quotations); "Christo Pulls Plug on Controversial 'Over the River' Public Art Installation, Citing New 'Landlord' Trump," *Denver Post*, www.denverpost.com, January 25, 2017.

11. John L. Dyer, *The Snow-Shoe Itinerant* (Cincinnati, OH: Cranston and Snow, 1890), 124 (quotation); Mark Fiester, *Look for Me in Heaven: The Life of John Lewis Dyer* (Boulder: Pruett, 1980).

Sources

12. Corrine Hunt, *The Brown Palace: Denver's Grande Dame* (Denver: Brown Palace Hotel, 2003).

13. "The South Park Anniversary: The First Trey Parker–Matt Stone Interview," *Westword* (Denver), www.westword.com, August 14, 2007; James Hibberd, "How 'South Park' Was Born," *Entertainment Weekly*, http://www.ew.com/microsites/longform/southpark/, accessed November 1, 2015.

14. *Denver Post*, August 12, 1993, 1A, 7A–10A; August 13, 1993, 1A (first quotation), 19A–22A; August 14, 1993, 1A, 8A, 16A; August 15, 1993, 1A–2A, 5A–6A, 12A–15A, 19A; August 16, 1993, 1A, 6A (second quotation), 8A–9A.

15. Emma Michell, *Comanche Crossing Centennial, 1870–1970* (Strasburg: Eastern Colorado News, 1970), 11 (first quotation); *Rocky Mountain News*, August 18, 1870, 2 (second quotation).

16. *Rocky Mountain News*, August 17, 1999, 5A, 14A–17A; *Denver Post*, August 17, 1999, 1A (quotation), 8A.

17. Joanne West Dodds, *Custer County at a Glance* (Pueblo, CO: Focal Plain, 2007); *Colorado Weekly Chieftain* (Denver), February 24, 1870, 1 (quotation); November 10, 1870, 3; May 30, 1878, 1; *Rocky Mountain News*, April 5, 1870, 4; *Colorado Daily Chieftain* (Pueblo), November 13, 1872, 2.

18. "Fort St. Vrain Power Station History," FSV Folks, http://www.fsvfolks.org/FSV History_2.html, accessed March 11, 2015.

19. Frances Bollacker Keck, *Conquistadors to the 21st Century: A History of Otero and Crowley Counties, Colorado* (La Junta, CO: Otero Press, 1999); *Logan County Advocate*, September 14, 1889, 4 (first quotation); *Rocky Mountain News*, January 5, 1900, 1 (second quotation).

20. *Burlington Record*, August 18, 2005, 1A, commemorative supplement; August 25, 2005, 8C, 1D; "Kit Carson County Carousel," Kit Carson County Carousel Association, http://www.kitcarsoncountycarousel.com/, accessed July 17, 2015.

21. *Bent's Old Fort* (Denver: State Historical Society of Colorado, 1979); Stella M. Drumm, *Down the Santa Fe Trail and into New Mexico: The Diary of Susan Shelby Magoffin, 1846–1847* (Lincoln: University of Nebraska Press, 1962), 60, 61, 65 (quotation).

22. *Castle Rock Journal*, August 28, 1889, 2; *Aspen Weekly Times*, July 11, 1891, 2 (quotation); "History of Mineral Palace Park," City of Pueblo, http://www.pueblo.us/Facilities/Facility/Details/36, accessed April 15, 2015.

23. Robert C. Black III, *Island in the Rockies: The Pioneer Era of Grand County, Colorado* (Granby, CO: Country Printer, 1977).

24. "Nine Colorado Photographs by William Henry Jackson," *Colorado Quarterly* 2: 1 (Summer 1953), 25–36 (quotation 27); Donald E. English, "William H. Jackson: Western Commercial Photographer," *Colorado Heritage* 1 and 2 (1983), 60–68; Richard A. Bartlett, *Great Surveys of the American West* (Norman: University of Oklahoma Press, 1962); Thomas J. Noel and John Fielder, *Colorado 1870–2000 Revisited: The History Behind the Images* (Englewood, CO: Westcliffe, 2001).

25. *Leadville Chronicle*, August 27, 1888, 3 (quotation); María E. Montoya, *Translating Property: The Maxwell Land Grant and the Conflict over Land in the American West, 1840–1900* (Lawrence: University Press of Kansas, 2005).

26. Angelico Chavez (trans.) and Ted J. Warner (ed.), *The Domínguez-Escalante Journal: Their Expedition through Colorado, Utah, Arizona, and New Mexico in 1776* (Provo, UT: Brigham Young University Press, 1976).

27. Robert Harvey, *Amache: The Story of Japanese Interment in Colorado during World War II* (Dallas: Taylor Trade, 2004).

28. *Rocky Mountain News*, August 23, 2008, special section; *Denver Post*, August 26, 2008, 4P (first quotation); August 27, 2008, 1P–6P; August 28, 2008, 1P, 3P, 6P; August 29, 2008, 1P–9P (second quotation 2P).

29. *Denver Post*, August 30, 1965, 7; *Rocky Mountain News*, August 30, 1965, 41; "Astronaut Bio: Scott Carpenter," National Aeronautics and Space Administration, http://www.jsc.nasa.gov/Bios/htmlbios/carpenter-ms.html, accessed September 17, 2015; "CU-Boulder Alum, NASA Astronaut Scott Carpenter Dies at 88," University of Colorado News Center, www.colorado.edu, October 10, 2013 (quotation).

30. "John Swigert, Jr.," Architect of the Capitol, http://www.aoc.gov/capitol-hill/national-statuary-hall-collection/john-swigert-jr, accessed February 24, 2015; "Astronaut Bio: John. L Swigert," National Aeronautics and Space Administration, http://www.jsc.nasa.gov/Bios/htmlbios/swigert-jl.html, accessed February 26, 2015.

31. Derek R. Everett, *The Colorado State Capitol: History, Politics, Preservation* (Boulder: University Press of Colorado, 2005); Second Biennial Report of the Board of Capitol Managers, State of Colorado, 1886 (quotations).

September

1. *Rocky Mountain News*, August 28, 1927, special Lindbergh section, 1–10; August 31, 1927, 1–3; September 1, 1927, 1–5 (quotation 2), 11; September 2, 1927, 1, 9; *Denver Post*, August 31, 1927, 1, 10–11; September 1, 1927, 1–6, 32; September 2, 1972, 3.

2. Nolie Mumey, *John Williams Gunnison: The Last of the Western Explorers* (Denver: Artcraft, 1955), 42 (first quotation); *Reports of Explorations and Surveys, to Ascertain the Most Practicable and Economical Route for a Railroad from the Mississippi River to the Pacific Ocean*, vol. 1 (Washington, DC: A.O.P. Nicholson, 1855), 71 (second quotation).

3. Pekka Hämäläinen, *The Comanche Empire* (New Haven, CT: Yale University Press, 2008); Wilfred O. Martinez, *Anza and Cuerno Verde: Decisive Battle* (Colorado Springs: Old Colorado City Historical Society, 2004).

4. Jerry J. Frank, *Making Rocky Mountain National Park: The Environmental History of an American Treasure* (Lawrence: University Press of Kansas, 2013); *Wray Rattler*, September 9, 1915, 3 (quotation).

5. Duane A. Smith, *The Irrepressible David F. Day* (Lake City, CO: Western Reflections, 2010), 65, 68, 76, 85 (quotations).

6. Jack Dempsey and Barbara Piattelli Dempsey, *Dempsey* (New York: Harper and Row, 1977); Toby Smith, *Kid Blackie: Jack Dempsey's Colorado Days* (Ouray, CO: Wayfinder, 1987).

7. *Montrose Daily Press*, September 9, 1968, 1; September 10, 1968, 1, 8; September 13, 1968, 1 (quotation); "Movies Filmed in Colorado," Film in Colorado, http://www.filmincolorado.com/filmography.html, accessed May 30, 2015; "True Grit: Then and Now,"

Colorado Vibes, http://www.coloradovibes.com/2010/02/true-grit-then-and-now/, accessed May 30, 2015.

8. Franklin Rhoda, *Summits to Reach: Report on the Topography of the San Juan Country*, ed. Mike Foster (Boulder: Pruett, 1984), 11, 68 (quotations); Richard A. Bartlett, *Great Surveys of the American West* (Norman: University of Oklahoma Press, 1962).

9. Debra Faulkner, *Touching Tomorrow: The Emily Griffith Story* (Palmer Lake, CO: Filter Press, LLC, 2005), 29 (quotations).

10. "Mike the Headless Chicken," City of Fruita, www.miketheheadlesschicken.org, accessed September 17, 2013; Lauren Keating, "Here's How Mike the Chicken Lived for 18 Months without a Head," *Tech Times*, www.techtimes.com, September 30, 2014.

11. Len Ackland, *Making a Real Killing: Rocky Flats and the Nuclear West* (Albuquerque: University of New Mexico Press, 1999).

12. *Plainsman Herald* (Springfield), September 15, 1977, 1 (first quotation); September 22, 1977, 1, 17 (second quotation); September 29, 1977, 1; October 6, 1977, 1; December 15, 1977, 1; December 22, 1977, 1; "History," American Agriculture Movement, http://www.aaminc.org/history.htm, accessed May 30, 2015.

13. Charles J. Kappler (ed.), *Indian Affairs: Laws and Treaties*, vol. 1 (Washington, DC: Government Printing Office, 1904), 151–52; Virginia McConnell Simmons, *The Ute Indians of Utah, Colorado, and New Mexico* (Boulder: University Press of Colorado, 2000).

14. "Mork and Mindy," TV.com, www.tv.com/shows/mork-and-mindy, accessed March 24, 2015; "Mourners Stop by Boulder's 'Mork and Mindy' House to Remember Robin Williams," *Boulder Daily Camera*, www.dailycamera.com, August 11, 2014.

15. *Rocky Mountain News*, September 14, 1879, 3 (quotation); September 16, 1879, 5; Maxine Benson, "A Centennial Legacy," entire issue of *Colorado Magazine* 57 (1980).

16. *Denver Post*, September 16, 1949, 1 (quotation); "As Denver Coliseum Turns 60, Many Years Still Seen Ahead," *Denver Post*, www.denverpost.com, January 7, 2012; "Denver Rockets," Remember the ABA, http://www.remembertheaba.com/denver-rockets.html, accessed June 27, 2015.

17. John H. Monnett, *The Battle of Beecher Island and the Indian War of 1867–1869* (Boulder: University Press of Colorado, 1992), 5 (quotation).

18. *Solid Muldoon Weekly* (Ouray, CO), September 18, 1891, 1; Duane A. Smith, *A Time for Peace: Fort Lewis, Colorado, 1878–1891* (Boulder: University Press of Colorado, 2006).

19. *Boulder Daily Camera*, September 19, 1953, 4; George T. Simon, *Glenn Miller and His Orchestra* (New York: Da Capo, 1974), 24 (quotation).

20. *Colorado Springs Gazette*, July 21, 1877, 1 (first quotation); *Colorado Miner* (Georgetown), September 1, 1877, 2; September 8, 1877, 2; *Saguache Chronicle*, September 8, 1877, 3; *Denver Daily Times*, September 14, 1877, 1; *Silver World* (Lake City), September 22, 1877, 3; *Colorado Weekly Chieftain* (Denver), October 4, 1877, 1 (second quotation); October 11, 1877, 2; Edward Blair, *Leadville: Colorado's Magic City* (Boulder: Fred Pruett Books, 1980); Marcia T. Goldstein, "Colorado Women and the Vote," *Denver Westerners Roundup* 51: 4 (July–August 1995), 3–14.

21. "Chimney Rock to Be Named a National Monument," *Denver Post*, www.denverpost.com, September 19, 2012; "San Juan National Forest—Special Places," United States

Forest Service, http://www.fs.usda.gov/detail/sanjuan/specialplaces/?cid=stelprdb 5390324, accessed March 17, 2015; "Chimney Rock National Monument," Chimney Rock Interpretive Association, http://www.chimneyrockco.org, accessed March 17, 2015.

22. Robert Allan Nauman, *On the Wings of Modernism: The United States Air Force Academy* (Urbana: University of Illinois Press, 2004), 60, 116, 117, 135 (quotations).

23. *Montrose Enterprise*, September 23, 1909, 1 (first quotation), 4 (second quotation); September 27, 1909, 1; Shelly C. Dudley, "The First Five: A Brief Overview of the First Reclamation Projects Authorized by the Secretary of the Interior on March 14, 1903," in *The Bureau of Reclamation: History Essays from the Centennial Symposium* (Denver: US Department of the Interior, Bureau of Reclamation, 2008), 289–313.

24. Clarence G. Lasby, *Eisenhower's Heart Attack: How Ike Beat Heart Disease and Held on to the Presidency* (Lawrence: University Press of Kansas, 1997), 126 (quotation); *Denver Post*, August 16, 1999, 2B.

25. J. Michael Hogan, *Woodrow Wilson's Western Tour: Rhetoric, Public Opinion, and the League of Nations* (College Station: Texas A&M University Press, 2006), 2 (quotation).

26. Richard E. Tope, "Objective History of Grand Junction, Colorado, Part I," *Journal of the Western Slope* 10: 1 (Winter 1995), 1–69; Peter R. Decker, *"The Utes Must Go!" American Expansion and the Removal of a People* (Golden, CO: Fulcrum, 2004), 180 (quotation).

27. Fred H. Werner, *Heroic Fort Sedgwick and Julesburg: A Study in Courage* (Greeley, CO: Werner, 1987); Dallas Williams, *Fort Sedgwick, Colorado Territory: Hell Hole on the Platte* (Julesburg, CO: Fort Sedgwick Historical Society, 1993); Dee Brown, *The Galvanized Yankees* (Lincoln: University of Nebraska Press, 1986), 139 (quotation).

28. Phil Carson, *Across the Northern Frontier: Spanish Explorations in Colorado* (Boulder: Johnson Books, 1998); Alfred Barnaby Thomas, *After Coronado: Spanish Exploration Northeast of New Mexico, 1696–1727* (Norman: University of Oklahoma Press, 1966 [1935]).

29. Virginia McConnell Simmons, *The Ute Indians of Utah, Colorado, and New Mexico* (Boulder: University Press of Colorado, 2000); Robert Silbernagel, *Troubled Trails: The Meeker Affair and the Expulsion of Utes from Colorado* (Salt Lake City: University of Utah Press, 2011).

30. Isabella Bird, *A Lady's Life in the Rocky Mountains* (Norman: University of Oklahoma Press, 1960 [1879]), 58, 82, 98 (quotations).

October

1. *Denver Post*, October 1, 1991, 1A, 7A; October 2, 1991, 1A, 6A–8A (quotation 6A); Roger Alan Walton, *Colorado Gambling: A Guide* (Lakewood, CO: Colorado Times, 1991); Patricia A. Stokowski, *Riches and Regrets: Betting on Gambling in Two Colorado Mountain Towns* (Niwot: University Press of Colorado, 1996); Richard K. Young, *The Ute Indians of Colorado in the Twentieth Century* (Norman: University of Oklahoma Press, 1997).

2. Richard C. Huston, *A Silver Camp Called Creede: A Century of Mining* (Montrose, CO: Western Reflections, 2005), 34, 474 (quotations); Robert Athearn, *The Denver and Rio Grande Western Railroad* (Lincoln: University of Nebraska Press, 1977).

Sources

408

3. Steven C. Schulte, *Wayne Aspinall and the Shaping of the American West* (Boulder: University Press of Colorado, 2002), 1, 288 (quotations); "Public Law 96–375," Government Printing Office, http://www.gpo.gov/fdsys/pkg/STATUTE-94/pdf/STATUTE -94-Pg1505.pdf, accessed November 22, 2015.

4. *Denver Post*, October 4, 1982, 2B; October 5, 1982, 1A, 9A; Stephen J. Leonard and Thomas J. Noel, *Denver: Mining Camp to Metropolis* (Niwot: University Press of Colorado, 1990).

5. Mark E. Miller, *Hollow Victory: The White River Expedition of 1879 and the Battle of Milk Creek* (Niwot: University Press of Colorado, 1997).

6. LeRoy R. Hafen, "Fort Jackson and the Early Fur Trade on the South Platte," *Colorado Magazine* 5: 1 (February 1928), 9–17; "Fort Jackson," Mountain Men and Life in the Rocky Mountain West, http://www.mman.us/FortJackson.htm, accessed June 28, 2015.

7. Charles J. Kappler (ed.), *Indian Affairs: Laws and Treaties*, vol. 2 (Washington, DC: Government Printing Office, 1904), 856–59; Virginia McConnell Simmons, *The Ute Indians of Utah, Colorado, and New Mexico* (Boulder: University Press of Colorado, 2000); Charles F. Price, *Season of Terror: The Espinosas in Central Colorado, March–October 1863* (Boulder: University Press of Colorado, 2013).

8. Joan A. Lowy, *Pat Schroeder: A Woman of the House* (Albuquerque: University of New Mexico Press, 2003).

9. "George Bush: Statement on Signing the Rocky Mountain Arsenal National Wildlife Refuge Act of 1992," American Presidency Project, http://www.presidency.ucsb.edu /ws/index.php?pid=21600, accessed December 7, 2015 (first quotation); Jeffrey P. Cohen, "A Makeover for Rocky Mountain Arsenal," *Bioscience* 49: 4 (April 1999), 273–77 (second quotation 275); David Havlick, "Logics of Change for Military-to-Wildlife Conversions in the United States," *Geojournal* 69: 3 (2007), 151–64.

10. Wilson Rockwell, *Uncompahgre Country* (Denver: Sage Books, 1965); Richard L. Fetter and Suzanne C. Fetter, *Telluride: From Pick to Powder* (Caldwell, ID: Caxton, 1979); "Galloping Goose Rail Cars Reunited in Golden after 60 Years," *Denver Post*, www.denverpost.com, June 15, 2012.

11. F. H. Knowlton, "A Review of the Fossil Plants in the United States National Museum from the Florissant Lake Beds at Florissant, Colorado," *Proceedings of the United States National Museum* 51: 2151 (November 24, 1916), 241–97; Estella B. Leopold and Herbert W. Meyer, *Saved in Time: The Fight to Establish Florissant Fossil Beds National Monument, Colorado* (Albuquerque: University of New Mexico Press, 2012).

12. *Keyes v. School District No. 1, Denver, Colorado*, 413 US 189 (1973); Thomas A. Shannon, "The Denver Decision: Death Knell for *de Facto* Segregation?" *Phi Delta Kappan* 55: 1 (September 1973), 6–9; James Brooke, "Court Says Denver Can End Forced Busing," *New York Times*, www.nytimes.com, September 17, 1995.

13. *Park County Bulletin*, June 23, 1899, 2; *Durango Democrat*, August 12, 1900, 3 (first quotation); *Durango Wage Earner*, June 22, 1899, 4 (second quotation); "First Train Steams into Pagosa Springs," *Pagosa Springs Sun*, www.pagosasun.com, December 11, 2008.

14. *Denver Post*, October 14, 1992, 7B; October 15, 1992, 1B (quotations), 4B; "CDOT History," Colorado Department of Transportation, https://www.codot.gov/about/ CDOTHistory, accessed May 23, 2015.

15. Duane Vandenbusche and Rex Myers, *Marble, Colorado: City of Stone* (Denver: Golden Bell, 1970).

16. *Report of the Commissioner of the General Land Office to the Secretary of the Interior* (Washington, DC: Government Printing Office, 1907); *Aspen Weekly Times*, October 31, 1891, 2; *Aspen Daily Chronicle*, November 4, 1891, 3 (first quotation); *Aspen Daily Times*, January 18, 1892, 3 (second quotation); "White River National Forest," United States Forest Service, http://www.fs.usda.gov/main/whiteriver; accessed March 22, 2015.

17. John H. Davis, *The Guggenheims: An American Epic* (New York: William Morrow, 1978); "History," Colorado School of Mines, http://www.mines.edu/History, accessed July 25, 2015; *Colorado Transcript* (Golden), October 18, 1906, 1 (quotation).

18. Thomas J. Noel, *Colorado: A Liquid History and Tavern Guide to the Highest State* (Golden, CO: Fulcrum, 1999) (first quotation); *Denver Post*, blogs.denverpost.com/beer, July 9, 2014 (second quotation).

19. "Vail Fires Were Probably Arson, U.S. Agents Say," *New York Times*, www.nytimes. com, October 23, 1998 (quotation); "Arson on the Mountain: Vail's 1998 Arson Fires at Two Elk Were Country's Worst Eco-Terrorist Attack," *Vail Daily*, www.vaildaily.com, October 18, 2018; "A Community Battles Back: Vail Rallies around Rebuilding What Terrorists Destroyed in 1998 Fire," *Vail Daily*, www.vaildaily.com, October 20, 2018.

20. Pekka Hämäläinen, *The Comanche Empire* (New Haven, CT: Yale University Press, 2008); Joaquín Rivaya-Martínez, "San Carlos de los Jupes: une tentative avortée de sédentarisation des bárbaros dans les territoires frontaliers du nord de la Nouvelle-Espagne en 1787–1788," *Recherches amérindiennes au Québec* 41: 2–3 (2011), 29–42.

21. "William J. Clinton: Statement on Signing the Black Canyon of the Gunnison National Park and Gunnison Gorge National Conservation Area Act of 1999," American Presidency Project, http://www.presidency.ucsb.edu/ws/?pid=56778, accessed November 21, 2015; Duane Vandenbusche, *The Black Canyon of the Gunnison* (Charleston, SC: Arcadia, 2009).

22. *Denver Post*, October 22, 1976, 59 (quotation), 62; October 23, 1976, 17; "Denver Nuggets," Sports E-cyclopedia, http://www.sportsecyclopedia.com/nba/denver/nug gets.html, accessed October 8, 2015.

23. *Fort Lupton Press*, October 13, 2004, 1, 34; October 27, 2004, 1, 34; William B. Butler, *The Fur Trade in Colorado* (Lake City, CO: Western Reflections, 2012).

24. *Rocky Mountain News*, October 20, 1859, 2–3; Frank Hall, *History of the State of Colorado*, vol. 1 (Chicago: Blakely, 1889), 266 (quotation).

25. *Colorado Transcript* (Golden), October 26, 1887, 2; *Aspen Daily Times*, April 10, 1889, 1; Robert W. Frazer, *Forts of the West* (Norman: University of Oklahoma Press, 1972); Jack Stokes Ballard and the Friends of Historic Fort Logan, *Fort Logan* (Charleston, SC: Arcadia, 2011).

26. "Animas-La Plata Project—Background," United States Bureau of Reclamation, http://www.usbr.gov/uc/progact/animas/background.html, accessed June 20, 2015;

"MO92: Animas-La Plata Project Collection," Center of Southwest Studies, Fort Lewis College, https://swcenter.fortlewis.edu/finding_aids/Animas_La_Plata_Project. shtml, accessed June 20, 2015; Leslie Karp, "Whose Water Is It Anyway?: Bureaucrats, the Animas–La Plata Project, and the Colorado Utes," *Journal of the Western Slope* 9: 3 (Summer 1994), 1–22.

27. Robert W. Larson, *Shaping Educational Change: The First Century of the University of Northern Colorado at Greeley* (Boulder: Colorado Associated University Press, 1989), xi (first quotation), xiv (third quotation); James A. Michener, *Centennial* (New York: Ballantine Books, 1974), 965 (second quotation); "About the James Michener Collection," University of Northern Colorado Archives, http://library.unco.edu/archives/michener collectionabout.htm, accessed June 24, 2015.

28. Nancy Lourine Lynch, *Rattlesnake Kate: The Amazing—but True—Story of Katherine McHale Slaughterback* (Greeley, CO: City of Greeley Museums, 2006).

29. Wilbur Fisk Stone, *History of Colorado*, vol. 1 (Chicago: S. J. Clarke, 1918), 678 (quotation).

30. "The Snowmastodon Project," Denver Museum of Nature & Science, http://www .dmns.org/science/the-snowmastodon-project/, accessed January 22, 2016; "Pleistocene Treasures, at a Breakneck Pace," *New York Times*, www.nytimes.com, July 4, 2011; "Colorado Discovery Rocks the World," Denver Museum of Nature and Science, https:// coloradosprings.dmns.org/, accessed October 27, 2019 (quotation).

31. Liping Zhu, *The Road to Chinese Exclusion: The Denver Riot, 1880 Election, and the Rise of the West* (Lawrence: University Press of Kansas, 2013), 239 (quotation).

November

1. Andrew J. Field, *Mainliner Denver: The Bombing of Flight 629* (Boulder: Johnson Books, 2005), 210 (quotation).

2. *Fairplay Flume*, October 4, 1918, 3; October 11, 1918, 2; *Silverton Standard*, November 2, 1918, 4 (quotation); *Steamboat Pilot*, November 6, 1918, 2; *Haswell Herald*, November 7, 1918, 6; "The 1918 Influenza Outbreak: An Unforgettable Legacy," *Denver Post*, www. den verpost.com, May 3, 2009.

3. *Out West* (Colorado Springs), November 28, 1872, 8; Richard A. Bartlett, *Great Surveys of the American West* (Norman: University of Oklahoma Press, 1962), 203 (first quotation); *Daily Register Call* (Central City), December 6, 1872, 3 (second quotation); *Weekly Rocky Mountain News*, December 11, 1872, 1.

4. *Aspen Daily Times*, November 3, 1924, 1; David M. Chalmers, *Hooded Americanism: The History of the Ku Klux Klan* (Chicago: Quadrangle Books, 1968); Carl Abbott, Stephen J. Leonard, and Thomas J. Noel, *Colorado: A History of the Centennial State* (Boulder: University Press of Colorado, 2013), 315 (quotation).

5. *Denver Post*, November 5, 1911, magazine section, 10 (first quotation); Melanie Shellenbarger, *High Country Summers: The Early Second Homes of Colorado, 1880–1940* (Tucson: University of Arizona Press, 2012); "Mount Falcon Park History," Jefferson County, Colorado, http://jeffco.us/open-space/parks/mount-falcon-park/history/, accessed April 18, 2015 (second quotation).

6. *Klondike and Snow: The Denver Zoo's Remarkable Story of Raising Two Polar Bear Cubs* (Boulder: Roberts Rinehart), 1995; Carolyn Etter and Don Etter, *The Denver Zoo: A Centennial History* (Boulder: Roberts Rinehart, 1996); "Polar Bear Klondike Dies at Sea World," *Denver Post*, www.denverpost.com, September 14, 2013.

7. Marcia T. Goldstein, "Colorado Women and the Vote," *Denver Westerners Roundup* 51: 4 (July–August 1995), 3–14; Carl Abbott, Stephen J. Leonard, and Thomas J. Noel, *Colorado: A History of the Centennial State* (Boulder: University Press of Colorado, 2011), 275 (quotation).

8. Gary L. Roberts, *Doc Holliday: The Life and Legend* (Hoboken, NJ: John Wiley and Sons, 2006), 332, 372 (quotations).

9. Elinor Bluemel, *Florence Sabin: Colorado Woman of the Century* (Boulder: University of Colorado Press, 1959); Mary Kay Phelan, *Probing the Unknown: The Story of Dr. Florence Sabin* (New York: Thomas Y. Crowell, 1969).

10. "Jimmy Carter: Acts Approved by the President, Week Ending Friday, November 10, 1978," American Presidency Project, http://www.presidency.ucsb.edu/ws/index.php?pid=30154, accessed March 5, 2016; James D. Drake, "A Divide to Heal the Union: The Creation of the Continental Divide," *Pacific Historical Review* 84: 4 (Fall 2015), 409–47 (quotations 442); "History of the CDT," Continental Divide Trail, http://continentaldividetrail.org/history-of-the-cdt/, accessed March 5, 2016; "History of the Colorado Trail," Colorado Trail Foundation, http://www.coloradotrail.org/history.html, accessed March 5, 2016.

11. *Sugar Press* 7: 11 (November 1923), 20–21 (first and second quotations); 9: 3 (March 1925), 20; *Record-Journal of Douglas County*, November 23, 1923, 2 (third quotation); Lee Scamehorn, *High Altitude Energy: A History of Fossil Fuels in Colorado* (Boulder: University Press of Colorado, 2002).

12. *Colorado Transcript* (Golden), November 12, 1873, 3 (quotation); William Kostka, *The Pre-Prohibition History of Adolph Coors Company, 1873–1933* (Golden, CO: Adolph Coors Company, 1973); *Coors: Golden's Salute to Coors* (Golden, CO: Jeffco Publishing Company, 1998).

13. Mary Louise Sullivan, "Mother Cabrini: Missionary to Italian Immigrants," *US Catholic Historian* 6: 4 (Fall 1987), 265–79; "Mother Cabrini Shrine," http://www.mothercabrinishrine.org/, accessed February 1, 2016.

14. Brian K. Trembath, "The Untold Story Behind Colorado's Iconic State Flag," Denver Public Library, https://history.denverlibrary.org/news/story-behind-colorados-iconic-state-flag, accessed July 2, 2015 (first quotation); Andrew Carlisle Carson, *Colorado: Top of the World* (Denver: Smith-Brooks, 1912), 12 (second and third quotations).

15. Stephen Harding Hart and Archer Butler Hulbert (eds.), *The Southwestern Journals of Zebulon Pike, 1806–1807* (Albuquerque: University of New Mexico Press, 2006), 138, 144 (quotations).

16. *Aspen Democrat*, November 10, 1900, 1; *Colorado Transcript* (Golden), November 14, 1900, 7 (quotations); Stephen J. Leonard, *Lynching in Colorado, 1859–1919* (Boulder: University Press of Colorado, 2002).

Sources

17. William John May Jr., *The Great Western Sugarlands: The History of the Great Western Sugar Company and the Economic Development of the Great Plains* (New York: Garland, 1989); *Fort Collins Courier*, November 29, 1905, 9 (quotation); State Board of Immigration, *Agricultural Statistics of the State of Colorado, 1924* (Denver: Bradford-Robinson, 1925); *Record-Journal of Douglas County*, November 19, 1926, 7.

18. Vine Deloria Jr., *Custer Died for Your Sins: An Indian Manifesto* (Norman: University of Oklahoma Press, 1998), 1 (first quotation), 35 (third quotation); *Rocky Mountain News*, November 15, 2005, 6A (second quotation), 11A.

19. Thomas J. Noel, "All Hail the Denver Pacific: Denver's First Railroad," *Colorado Magazine* 50: 2 (Spring 1973), 91–116.

20. Dorothy M. Degitz, "History of the Tabor Opera House at Leadville," *Colorado Magazine* 13: 3 (May 1936), 81–89; Edward Blair, *Leadville: Colorado's Magic City* (Boulder: Fred Pruett Books, 1980).

21. Elinor McGinn, *A Wide-Awake Woman: Josephine Roche in the Age of Reform* (Denver: Colorado Historical Society, 2002); "History," Colorado Mounted Rangers, https://www.coloradoranger.org/history, accessed September 24, 2015.

22. Jerome C. Smiley, *History of Denver* (Denver: Times-Sun, 1901); Stephen J. Leonard and Thomas J. Noel, *Denver: Mining Camp to Metropolis* (Niwot: University Press of Colorado, 1990).

23. *Eagle Valley Enterprise*, August 25, 1939, 4; *Aspen Daily Times*, August 31, 1939, 7; *Denver Post*, November 17, 1939, 25; November 19, 1939, 1, 4; November 22, 1939, 3; November 23, 1939, 2 (quotation).

24. Reuel Leslie Olson, "The Colorado River Compact," PhD thesis, Harvard University, Cambridge, MA, 1926; Daniel Tyler, *Silver Fox of the Rockies: Delphus E. Carpenter and Western Water Compacts* (Norman: University of Oklahoma Press, 2003); *Citizen's Guide to Colorado's Interstate Compacts* (Denver: Colorado Foundation for Water Education, 2010).

25. Marjorie Hornbein, "The Story of Judge Ben Lindsey," *Southern California Quarterly* 55: 4 (Winter 1973), 469–82; D'Ann Campbell, "Judge Ben Lindsey and the Juvenile Court Movement," *Arizona and the West* 18: 1 (Spring 1976), 5–20; Ben B. Lindsey and Harvey J. O'Higgins, *The Beast* (Boulder: University Press of Colorado, 2009).

26. Bruce Cook, *Dalton Trumbo* (New York: Charles Scribner's Sons, 1977); Irene Middleman Thomas, "Dalton Trumbo: Grand Junction's Blacklisted Hometown Hero," *Colorado Life Magazine*, www.coloradolifemagazine.com, accessed March 6, 2016; Larry Celpair and Christopher Trumbo, *Trumbo: Blacklisted Hollywood Radical* (Lexington: University Press of Kentucky, 2015).

27. Dena S. Markoff, "The Sugar Industry in the Arkansas River Valley: National Beet Sugar Company," *Colorado Magazine* 55: 1 (Winter 1978), 69–92; Frances Bollacker Keck, *Conquistadors to the 21st Century: A History of Otero and Crowley Counties, Colorado* (La Junta, CO: Otero Press, 1999); *Denver Times*, December 31, 1899, 5 (quotation).

28. Wilbur Fisk Stone, *History of Colorado*, vol. 1 (Chicago: S. J. Clarke, 1918); MaryJoy Martin, *The Corpse on Boomerang Road: Telluride's War on Labor, 1899–1908* (Montrose, CO: Western Reflections, 2004).

29. Stan Hoig, *The Sand Creek Massacre* (Norman: University of Oklahoma Press, 1961); George E. Hyde, *Life of George Bent: Written from His Letters* (Norman: University of Oklahoma Press, 1968); Ari Kelman, *A Misplaced Massacre: Struggling over the Memory of Sand Creek* (Cambridge, MA: Harvard University Press, 2013).

30. *Denver Post*, December 1, 1994, 8B; "14 Infamous Inmates in Colorado's Supermax Prison," *Business Insider*, http://www.businessinsider.com/famous-supermax-inmates-2012-8?op=1, September 3, 2012; "Federal Prison in Colorado Marks 20th Anniversary," *Colorado Springs Gazette*, www.gazette.com, October 20, 2014.

December

1. Michael H. Levy and Patrick M. Scanlan, *Pursuit of Excellence: A History of Lowry Air Force Base, 1937–1987* (Lowry AFB, CO: Air Training Command, 1987); "SAC Bases: Lowry Air Force Base," Strategic Air Command, http://www.strategic-air-command.com/bases/Lowry_AFB.htm, accessed March 11, 2016; "Buckley Air Force Base: 460th Space Wing," http://www.buckley.af.mil/library/factsheets/factsheet.asp?id=4422, accessed March 11, 2016.

2. Session Laws of Colorado, Twenty-eighth General Assembly, 1931; *Steamboat Pilot*, May 8, 1931, 8 (quotation); "History of the Colorado State Forest," Colorado State Forest Service, http://csfs.colostate.edu/districts/colorado-state-forest/csf-history/, accessed April 12, 2015.

3. "Harms Marks 50 Years as Town of Paoli Mayor," *Holyoke Enterprise*, www.holyokeenterprise.com, December 8, 2011; "Virgil Harms' Way: 50 Years as Mayor in the 'Other' Colorado," *Los Angeles Times*, www.latimes.com, February 11, 2012 (first and fourth quotations); "50 Years in Office, Colorado's Accidental Mayor," 9News, www.9news.com, December 11, 2011 (second and third quotations).

4. "107 Bill Profile S. 1946 (2001–2002)," ProQuest, http://congressional.proquest.com, accessed June 18, 2015; Jack Nelson, "North Branch of the 'Old Spanish Trail,'" *Journal of the Western Slope* 11: 4 (Fall 1996), 1–43.

5. *Rocky Mountain News*, December 5, 1913, 1 (first quotation); William E. Wilson, "'Colorado Is Snowbound!' The Great Front Range Blizzard of 1913 (and Its 2003 Counterpart)," *Colorado Heritage* (Autumn 2003), 2–35 (second quotation 35).

6. Patricia Joy Redmond, *Trail to Disaster* (Denver: Colorado Historical Society, 1990); David Roberts, *A Newer World: Kit Carson, John C. Frémont, and the Claiming of the American West* (New York: Simon and Schuster, 2000); Charles Preuss, *Exploring with Frémont*, trans. Erwin G. Gudde and Elisabeth K. Gudde (Norman: University of Oklahoma Press, 1958), 153 (quotation).

7. *Colorado Transcript* (Golden), December 24, 1908, 6 (quotations); *Creede Candle*, June 28, 1918, 1; Bob Janiskee, "Pruning the Parks: Wheeler National Monument (NPS 1933–1950) Was a Great Idea Until Colorado Got Good Roads," *National Parks Traveler*, www.nationalparkstraveler.com, December 7, 2009.

8. *Cañon City Daily Record*, December 7, 1929, 1–6, 9; December 9, 1929, 1, 6, 8 (quotation); "The Royal Gorge," Royal Gorge Bridge and Park, http://www.rgbcc.com/, accessed September 24, 2015.

9. Derek R. Everett, *The Colorado State Capitol: History, Politics, Preservation* (Boulder: University Press of Colorado, 2005); Harry E. Kelsey Jr., *Frontier Capitalist: The Life of John Evans* (Boulder: Pruett, 1969), 121 (first quotation); *Rocky Mountain News*, December 7, 1866, 4 (second quotation); December 9, 1867, 1.

10. Adam Schrager, *The Principled Politician: The Ralph Carr Story* (Golden, CO: Fulcrum, 2008), 89, 193 (quotations).

11. Eugene H. Berwanger, "William J. Hardin: Colorado Spokesman for Racial Justice, 1863–1873," *Colorado Magazine* 52: 1 (Winter 1975), 52–65; Eugene H. Berwanger, *The Rise of the Centennial State: Colorado Territory, 1861–1876* (Urbana: University of Illinois Press, 2007).

12. Robert C. Olson, *Speck: The Life and Times of Spencer Penrose* (Lake City, CO: Western Reflections, 2008); "Colorado Luxury Resorts," the Broadmoor, http://www.broadmoor.com/five-star-hotel/, accessed October 5, 2015.

13. *Routt County Courier*, December 17, 1908, 1 (first quotation); Tom Bie, *Steamboat: Ski Town USA* (Boulder: Mountain Sports Press, 2002); David M. Primus (ed.), *Steamboat Springs: Memories of a Young Colorado Pioneer* (Lake City, CO: Western Reflections, 2008), 183 (second quotation).

14. James Earl Sherow, *Watering the Valley: Development along the High Plains Arkansas River, 1870–1950* (Lawrence: University Press of Kansas, 1990).

15. *Denver Post*, December 16, 1962, 31C; Sandra Dallas, *Vail* (Boulder: Pruett, 1969); William Philpott, *Vacationland: Tourism and Environment in the Colorado High Country* (Seattle: University of Washington Press, 2013).

16. Ernest H. Cherrington, *Anti-Saloon League Yearbook, 1921* (Westerville, OH: American Issue, 1921), 154 (quotations).

17. *Rocky Mountain News*, December 18, 2008, 4–7; William A. DeGregorio, *The Complete Book of US Presidents*, 8th ed. (Fort Lee, NJ: Barricade Books, 2013).

18. Gilbert R. Wenger, *The Story of Mesa Verde National Park* (Denver: Visual Communication Center, 1980); Duane A. Smith, *Mesa Verde National Park: Shadows of the Centuries* (Boulder: University Press of Colorado, 2002).

19. *Mancos Times-Tribune*, January 9, 1920, 1; "Yucca House National Monument," US National Park Service, www.nps.gov/yuho, accessed March 16, 2015 (quotation).

20. Junius P. Rodriguez (ed.), *The Louisiana Purchase: A Historical and Geographical Encyclopedia* (Santa Barbara, CA: ABC Clio, 2002).

21. *Denver Post*, December 22, 1979, 3; William Philpott, *Vacationland: Tourism and Environment in the Colorado High Country* (Seattle: University of Washington Press, 2013).

22. Bruce A. Woodard, *The Garden of the Gods Story* (Colorado Springs: Democrat Publishing, 1955), 6 (first quotation); *Eagle Valley Enterprise*, January 21, 1910, 3 (second quotation).

23. James F. Willard (ed.), *The Union Colony at Greeley, Colorado, 1869–1871* (Denver: W. F. Robinson, 1918), 390 (quotation).

24. Janet Lecompte, *Pueblo, Hardscrabble, Greenhorn: The Upper Arkansas, 1832–1856* (Norman: University of Oklahoma Press, 1978); Edward Broadhead, *Fort Pueblo* (Pueblo, CO: Pueblo County Historical Society, 1995), 3 (quotation).

25. William J. Convery, "Reckless Men of Both Races: The Trinidad War of 1867–1868," *Colorado History* 10 (Denver: Colorado Historical Society, 2004), 19–35; *Rocky Mountain News*, January 6, 1868, 1 (quotation).

26. Lawrence Schiller, *Perfect Murder, Perfect Town* (New York: HarperCollins, 1999); "Family Cleared in JonBenét Ramsey's Death," NBC News, www.nbcnews.com, July 9, 2008.

27. Jerome C. Smiley, *History of Denver* (Denver: Times-Sun, 1901), 850 (quotation); "Centennial Celebration, 1861–1961," Grand Lodge A.F.&A.M. of Colorado, http://www.coloradofreemasons.org/history/1961.shtml, accessed July 30, 2015.

28. Douglas R. McKay, *Asylum of the Gilded Pill: The Story of Cragmor Sanatorium* (Denver: State Historical Society of Colorado, 1983), 82 (quotation); Andrea Cordova, "History," University of Colorado–Colorado Springs, http://www.uccs.edu/about/history.html, accessed November 12, 2015.

29. Mark J. Stegmaier, *Texas, New Mexico, and the Compromise of 1850: Boundary Dispute and Sectional Crisis* (Kent, OH: Kent State University Press, 1996).

30. *Middle Park Times*, January 5, 1912, 1 (quotations); Tom Bie, *Steamboat: Ski Town USA* (Boulder: Mountain Sports Press, 2002); Abbott Fay, *A History of Skiing in Colorado* (Lake City, CO: Western Reflections, 2008).

31. John Denver and Arthur Tobier, *Take Me Home: An Autobiography* (New York: Harmony Books, 1994), 112 (quotation); "John Denver, 53, Who Sang of Natural Love and Love of Nature, Dies in a Plane Crash," *New York Times*, www.nytimes.com, October 14, 1997; "John Denver Statue Finds New Home at Red Rocks," *Aspen Times*, www.aspentimes.com, June 3, 2015.

INDEX

Index

Nevada, 88, 146, 222, 289, 343
New Castle, Colo., 206
New England, 23, 69, 202, 215, 328
New Jersey, 88, 150, 173, 289
New Mexico, 24, 40, 41, 47, 58, 60, 62, 71–72,
    75–76, 85, 86–87, 94, 104, 112, 116, 120, 123, 133,
    146, 151, 155, 168, 172, 174, 190–191, 203, 208,
    211, 220, 221, 234–235, 237, 249, 250, 260–261,
    275, 277, 283–284, 294, 300, 305, 312, 323, 331,
    343, 355, 368, 375, 380
New Orleans, La., 108, 154, 370
New York (state), 17, 64, 150, 248
New York City, 15, 61, 64, 95, 142, 163, 215, 240,
    249, 259, 264, 271, 330, 333, 349, 373, 380
Newberry, George S., 234–235
Nicaagat, 42, 271, 284–285, 293
Nicholson, Samuel D., 88
Nixon, Richard M., 13, 123, 138, 280, 299, 380
Nordenskiold, Gustaf, 368
Norlin, George, 219
North American Aerospace Defense
    Command, 43
North High School (Denver), 73
North Korea, 27–28, 89
North Park, 58, 107, 151, 354
North Platte River, 31, 47, 55, 136, 151, 167, 170,
    217, 294, 309
North Pole, 44, 211
North, Frank J., 204
Northglenn, Colo., 75
Norton, Gale, 149, 368
Norwegians, 76–77, 364, 379
Nucla, Colo., 82, 209, 250
Nuclear power, 34, 242–243
Nuclear weapons, 9, 43, 145–146, 208–209,
    268–269, 282, 295, 353
Nugent, "Mountain Jim," 286
Nunn, Lucien L., 163
Nusbaum, Jesse L., 171–172

O'Brien, Nicholas, 12–13
Obama, Barack, 56, 71, 252–253, 277, 304, 367
Ochinee, 52
Ohio, 46, 75, 89, 115, 138, 201, 237, 262, 263, 266,
    291
Oil industry, 17, 22, 131–132, 141, 175, 201, 331, 372
Oil shale, 17, 131–132, 140, 145, 292, 304
Oklahoma, 54, 103, 113, 182, 188, 204, 211, 273, 349
Olathe, Colo., 214
Old Main (Colorado State University), 48–49,
    137–138

Old Main (University of Colorado), 219
Old Spanish Trail, 65, 234–235, 355–356
Olsen, Lloyd and Clara, 267–268
Olympics, 45, 51, 142–143
Omaha, Neb., 121, 240
Onís, Luis de, 58
Ophir, Colo., 163, 184, 297
Oregon Trail, 170, 232, 330
Oregon, 71, 79, 169, 203
Orman, James B., 347
Oro City, Colo., 69, 237, 339
Osgood, John C., 118
Otero County, Colo., 59, 165, 181, 243, 245, 252,
    361
Otto, John, 152
Ouray (Ute leader), 25, 42, 63, 97, 213, 270–271,
    282, 285, 294–295
Ouray, Colo., 11, 109, 112, 114, 215, 262–263, 265,
    379
Ouray County, Colo., 214, 246, 262, 265, 297, 347
Ovid, Colo., 336–337
Owens, Bill, 169, 216, 245, 314–315
Owl Creek Pass, 265

Pacific Ocean, 14, 22, 31, 65, 77, 79, 89, 127, 155,
    185, 190, 251, 253, 330, 355, 361, 380
Packer, Alfred, 18, 25, 238
Paepcke, Walter, 51
Pagosa Junction, Colo., 300
Pagosa Springs, Colo., 234, 275, 300
Paige, Woody, 29
Paiutes, 260
Paleontology, 206, 315. *See also* Dinosaurs;
    Fossils
Palisade, Colo., 291
Palmer, Arnold, 179
Palmer, William J., 197, 198, 206, 220, 308, 362,
    372, 378
Palmer Divide, 220
Palmer Lake, Colo., 220
Panama, 150
Pando, Colo., 207
Panic of 1857, 54, 136, 182
Panic of 1873, 19, 77, 218, 270, 332
Panic of 1893, 18, 32, 41, 69, 81, 96, 107, 114, 153,
    198, 206, 228, 249, 290, 297, 336
Paoli, Colo., 354–355
Parachute, Colo., 132, 146, 250
Park County, Colo., 31, 110, 169, 237, 239, 241,
    298, 361
Parker, Colo., 137

Index

Railroads, 17, 19–20, 22, 52, 77–78, 91–92, 116, 119–120, 126–127, 147, 151, 154, 177, 205–206, 217–219, 220, 228, 232–233, 240–241, 249, 260, 297, 300, 306, 322, 330, 335, 338–339, 357–358, 363–364, 368, 375. *See also* Narrow gauge; Standard gauge; *specific rail lines*

Ralston, Lewis, 54, 182

Ralston Creek, 54, 182

Ramsey, JonBenét, 375–376

Ranching, 10, 13, 17, 30, 32–34, 41–42, 45, 49, 51–52, 96, 105, 107, 133, 147, 179, 188, 197, 242, 273, 313, 366, 372. *See also* Cattle; Sheep

Raton Pass, 40, 71, 94, 119–120, 133, 284

Raverdy, John B., 314

Reagan, Ronald, 102, 268, 295

Recreation. *See specific activities*

Red Hill Pass, 110

Red River, 39, 334

Red Rocks Park, 93, 133, 139, 175–177, 325, 381

Redstone, Colo., 118

Reeves, Dan, 29–30

Reeves, Rollin S., 211–212

Referenda, 28, 52, 149, 289

Reform Party, 133

Regional Transportation District, 196, 292

Regis University, 239, 295

Religion, 34, 46–47, 60, 71, 74, 89–90, 93, 102, 105, 110, 114, 117, 141–142, 231–232, 236–237, 239–240, 250, 278–279, 300–301, 314–315, 323, 370–372, 378. *See also specific faiths*

Remington Arms Company, 10

Republican Party, 29, 52, 53, 56, 69, 73, 76, 83, 85, 88, 101, 115, 122, 149, 157, 168, 201, 215, 216, 247, 253, 254, 262, 316, 323–324, 354, 358, 361, 362

Republican River, 159, 204

Rhoda, Franklin, 265–266

Rice, Condoleezza, 156–157

Richards, Alonzo, 211

Rico, Colo., 180, 263, 297, 322

Ridgway, Colo., 265, 297

Rifle, Colo., 17, 235

Rifle Gap, 235–236

Ringsby, Bill, 308

Rio Blanco County, Colo., 17, 132, 145–146, 292–293, 302, 331

Rio Grande, 39, 76, 84, 94, 104, 190, 203, 220, 261, 283–284, 290, 355, 367, 368, 379

Rio Grande County, Colo. *See* Del Norte, Colo.

Rio Grande Southern Railroad, 23, 297

Rio Grande, Pagosa & Northern Railroad, 300

Ritter, Bill, 14, 98, 216, 229–230, 253, 315

Rivera, Juan María Antonio de, 190–191, 368

RMS *Titanic*, 113–114

Roads, 21–22, 40, 75, 109, 116, 184, 214, 228–229, 243, 261–262, 282, 297, 359, 366. *See also specific roads*

Roaring Fork River, 50, 107

Robbins, Chandler, 60, 211

Robidoux, Antoine, 65, 97, 151, 356

Roche, Josephine A., 26–27, 340

Rockmount Ranch Wear, 73

Rocky Flats, 268–269

Rocky Ford, Colo., 14, 215, 243–244, 281, 345

Rocky Mountain Arsenal, 10, 120, 296

Rocky Mountain Fuel Company, 27, 340

Rocky Mountain National Park, 22, 91, 184, 207, 261–262, 286, 359

Rocky Mountain News, 18–20, 24, 29, 31–32, 61, 70, 74, 90, 110, 113, 121, 147–148, 159, 201, 220, 227, 240, 244, 272, 356, 30, 373, 375

Rocky Mountain Public Broadcasting Service, 34

Rocky Mountains, 11, 17, 20, 31, 33, 42, 44, 54–55, 59, 65, 80, 115, 118–120, 122, 125, 126, 136, 145, 148, 150, 174, 177, 178, 182, 186, 190, 197, 201, 202, 205, 208, 217, 219, 220, 237, 240, 268, 286, 289, 294, 301, 302, 305, 315, 342, 366, 370, 380. *See also specific mountain ranges and mountains*

Rodeo, 32–34, 41, 215, 339

Rollins Pass, 126, 177

Roman Nose, 274

Romer, Roy, 149, 157, 181, 199, 300, 349, 367

Romer v. Evans, 148–149

Roosevelt, Franklin D., 10, 27, 139, 180, 183, 187, 206, 251, 342–343, 354

Roosevelt, Theodore, 13, 16–17, 70, 89, 107, 133–134, 238, 279, 344, 358–359, 369

Roosevelt National Forest, 70, 170, 354

Rosita, Colo., 95, 115, 361

Rouse, Colo., 79–80

Routt County, Colo., 188, 302, 363–364, 380

Routt, John L., 82, 141, 197, 210, 276, 327, 339, 364

Routt National Forest, 354

Roy, Patrick, 174

Royal Gorge, 39, 119–120, 141, 186, 210, 339, 359–360

Royal Gorge Bridge, 359–360

Royal Gorge War, 106, 328, 359

Rulison, Colo., 146

Russell, William G., 54, 136, 182, 341

Russia, 24, 28, 43, 51, 112, 140, 141, 181, 243, 268, 279, 337

Index

Index